Mass Media
and
American Politics

Second Edition

Mass Media
and
American Politics

Second Edition

Doris A. Graber
University of Illinois at Chicago

A division of Congressional Quarterly Inc.
1414 22nd Street N.W., Washington, D.C. 20037

Library of Congress Cataloging in Publication Data

Graber, Doris A. (Doris Appel), 1923-
    Mass media and American politics.

    Includes bibliographies and index.
    1. Mass media—Social aspects—United States.
2. Mass media—Political aspects—United States.
I. Title.
HN90.M3G7   1984   320.973'028   84-12150
ISBN 0-87187-320-6

To

Tom, Susan, Lee, Jim, Jack—
my very special students

Preface to the Second Edition

The French saying "plus ça change, plus c'est la même chose" (the more things change, the more they remain the same) sums up what has been happening in the mass media and politics field since the first edition of this book was published in 1980. There have been changes in media institutions, changes in the interpretation of First Amendment guarantees, changes in technology, and, of course, changes in the political scene. Still, the basic features of the interrelation between mass media and American politics have remained firm, testimony to the maturity of the relationship.

It is appropriate, therefore, to retain the organization of the original book. Within this basic structure, political events have been brought up to date, and the findings of the most recent scholarship have been incorporated. Older examples have yielded to fresh accounts. A number of sections have been expanded to include, for instance, more information about public broadcasting, fresh data on the influence of lobby groups on media output, and additional facts about media-sponsored public opinion polls.

New data from my own research expand the discussion of how average people process political stories from newspapers and television. The chapter on media impact on elections presents updated information on presidential elections in 1980 and 1984. In addition, it now focuses on media coverage of congressional and mayoral contests. Besides drawing on the recent scholarship of others, I have relied on my own research for much of this added information.

The second edition of *Mass Media and American Politics* features a completely new chapter on the role played by the media as policymakers. Performed through investigative journalism and other types of direct media intervention into the political process, this increasingly common role is stirring strong public interest and considerable controversy. The new chapter also expands my analysis of several important topics, such as the interaction of the media with various governmental institutions and the link between media coverage and public opinion.

The major reasons for writing the book initially are as valid in 1984 as they were in 1980. Mass media impact on contemporary American politics remains pervasive, profound, and an essential aspect of the study of politics. The need for a college-level, up-to-date introductory text that analyzes the connection between media and politics continues. In the past, most research focused on the relationship between media and politics during elections, neglecting other types of interactions. The scope of research has broadened considerably since 1980, as the many new references in the text and in the suggested readings at the end of each chapter indicate. But research on media impact on elections still predominates. Moreover, most of the studies published in the last four years have been specialized, focusing on single segments of the total picture. Hence it remains important to explore and highlight other areas and to provide an overview of the entire field. *Mass Media and American Politics, second edition,* serves that purpose.

As in the first edition, Chapters 1, 2, and 3 examine how electronic and print media, as institutions, form part of the U.S. political system and how they affect that system and are affected by it. Chapters 4 and 5 scrutinize the impact of the mass media on individuals; various aspects of learning and opinion formation, media-induced behaviors, and the legal rights of ordinary individuals, public officials, and newspeople are examined. Chapters 6 through 10 analyze media coverage of elections; the major political institutions, such as the presidency, Congress, and the courts; natural and man-made crises; and foreign affairs. Muckraking and its effects on public policy also are described. The book concludes with a discussion of the impact of new technologies and trends in media policy.

Besides the relentless march of events, which dictated a number of changes, the new edition owes much to the many colleagues and students who have commented on the book and to the scholars whose research has provided new insights. I thank them all. Likewise, thanks are due to my research assistant, Robert Cohen, who tracked down many elusive references and data and helped me clarify ambiguities in the text. The finished product also has benefited immensely from the writing skills and careful editing of Barbara de Boinville, senior editor at CQ Press, and from the helpful suggestions of Joanne Daniels, director of CQ Press.

The time required to write a book, or to prepare a major revision, usually is taken from the category labeled "family time." When it is willingly and even cheerfully surrendered by those who hold claim to it, research and writing progress with a minimum of emotional strain. Family time donated to a book is a generous, treasured gift. I am grateful to my family for this indispensable contribution to my work and for the love and understanding that it represents.

Doris A. Graber

Preface to the First Edition

Three major concerns prompted me to write this book. First among them is my strong conviction that the mass media play a tremendously important role in contemporary politics, a role that needs to be fully and continuously explored. Just imagine what would happen if all mass media ceased to function and remained inactive for an entire year! No news about events at home and abroad. No explanations about shortages or failures of public services. No announcements of new programs and facilities. Presidents, governors, and mayors, and legislators at all levels would be slowed or immobilized by lack of information and interpretation. And you—how would you fare, relying solely on your own daily experiences and word-of-mouth? Indeed, media are vital for public and private life; the image of a modern world without them is eerie and frightening.

My second major reason for writing this book is dissatisfaction with the way in which the story of the impact of the mass media on politics is commonly treated. Most social science accounts tell merely part of the story, concentrating on the effects of the media in election campaigns. Even within this narrow compass, they usually explore only the impact of the media on attitudes and voting behavior of individual citizens. They do not often acknowledge that the media have become a central part of the campaign, determining who may or may not run, what issues will be stressed, and the political shape of future elections. More significantly, such a narrow focus on elections ignores the much larger area of politics that does not concern elections, and that, too, is crucially affected by media performance.

Finally, this book was written to fill a gap in social science teaching. Students in the social sciences, by and large, are not exposed enough to the role the media play in the political system and in the lives of politicians. Politicians themselves have long known of the importance of publicity or lack of publicity and the use of media images as bases for political action, but teachers and students have largely neglected these matters. The time therefore has come to provide a book written from a political perspective that will both stimulate and facilitate study of the mass media in their political context.

The plan of the book is simple. The first three chapters deal with the mass media as institutions in the American political system. These chapters show how the media are both molded by and reflect that system and how they affect its performance and the interplay among public and private institutions. Media organizational structures and operations, and the impact that structure and personnel have on media offerings, are explained and assessed.

The next two chapters focus on the effects of news on individuals. Chapter 4 deals with the rights that newspeople and the general public enjoy to make their views heard and to be protected from harmful publicity. Chapter 5 examines the effects of media on individual perceptions and political behavior. Much of this material on political learning is based on hitherto unpublished data from my own research combining content analysis and interview techniques. The text therefore contains numerous references to the Three Sites Project in which I collaborated with Maxwell E. McCombs, John Ben Snow Professor of Newspaper Research at Syracuse University, and David H. Weaver, Associate Professor and Director of the Bureau of Media Research, Indiana University. In 1976-77, we undertook a massive year-long study of mass media impact on political learning and perceptions of four panels of voters in three American cities.

The impact of the media in a variety of political situations is the subject of Chapters 6 through 9 of the book. The focus is on the functions media perform in elections, in presidential, congressional, and judicial politics, during man-made and natural crises and disasters, and the steadily growing part they play in the conduct of foreign policy. Chapter 10 looks at emerging policy trends and the major forces shaping them.

Although the book deals with all of the mass media, primary emphasis is on news produced by television and newspapers. I chose this emphasis so that I could explore the various topics in reasonable depth while still keeping the book modest in size. The choice is justifiable because television and newspapers are the chief information sources for people in public and private life. Late in 1979, a Roper poll showed television as a prime source of news for 67 percent of the public and newspapers as a prime source for 49 percent. Only 20 percent of the public named radio as a prime source of news, and only 5 percent named either magazines or personal conversations.

The choice of topics for the book and the manner of presentation have been strongly influenced by my students at the University of Illinois, Chicago Circle. I am grateful for their keen interest and probing questions about the political impact of the mass media that encouraged me to develop a series of courses—and now this book—to answer these questions.

So many people have helped in the creation of *Mass Media and American Politics* that I cannot mention them all. Their contributions are deeply appreciated. Special thanks are due to Jean L. Woy, political science editor at Congressional Quarterly, who worked with the manuscript beyond the call of duty to keep the presentation orderly and the length moderate. Edie N. Goldenberg and William C. Adams, the two colleagues who read the manuscript, did so with exceptional care, and I am grateful to them for a number of very constructive suggestions. I hope that they have saved me from most of the errors that manage to creep into every book. If errors remain, I assume responsibility for the gremlins who put them there. I am also indebted to Anne Spray, my research assistant, who did yeoman work in gathering data for several chapters, checking the accuracy of facts and the smoothness of form, and compiling the index. Finally, Mary Lou Jackowicz performed various editorial tasks with zest and efficiency, and Angie Garcia presided at the typewriter, thanks to the generosity of the Political Science Department at the University of Illinois, Chicago Circle.

Doris A. Graber

Contents

Contents

Media Power and Government Control

"Jimmy Carter was a media president. There is little likelihood that a one-term governor of Georgia would have been elected president without the instant celebrity that television brought him in 1976. . . . But what television gives, television can take away. . . . By reminding Americans of international humiliations, military weaknesses, and administration blunders during the Carter years, the media set the stage for the Reagan landslide." So wrote political scientists Thomas R. Dye and L. Harmon Zeigler in a vignette about the political rise and fall of Jimmy Carter, aptly titled "Live by the Tube, Die by the Tube." [1]

Jimmy Carter, the story goes, was unknown to the American public in 1974 when he began his quest for the presidency. Through shrewd campaign strategies, he managed to win a number of early primaries that were likely to attract nationwide media attention. This earned him the prized "front-runner" label that then enables a presidential candidate to garner the lion's share of media coverage. Ample opportunities for media exposure, in turn, gave Carter the chance to tell the nation that he was the answer to every American voter's prayer: a God-fearing, trustworthy, family man, unsullied by Washington politics, yet experienced in public and private life. Carter, the media told the public, was a successful former governor, an expert in science, business, and military matters, an engineer, and a prosperous peanut farmer. Although he hailed from the South, he was a fighter for civil and human rights and a close friend of the family of civil rights leader Martin Luther King, Jr.

And so the unknown southerner "Jimmy Who?" became "Jimmy Front-runner," who defeated all his Democratic rivals for the presidential nomination and went on to defeat incumbent president Gerald R. Ford by a narrow margin. Four years later, when the 1980 presidential campaign opened, President Carter's fortunes were at a low ebb. Sen. Edward M. Kennedy of Massachusetts was as much as 30 percentage points ahead of him in the polls. Then the media came to Carter's rescue again, although only temporarily. For weeks they focused on the shocking sights of 52 Americans held captive in Iran, thus stirring feelings of patriotism and national unity in much of the

1

American public. The president's approval ratings soared in public opinion polls, as is common in the wake of perils lurking abroad for Americans.

But during the final phases of the campaign, a series of media events apparently changed the public's mood of support. Most importantly, Ronald Reagan, the Republican challenger, turned out to be a superb media performer with just the right touch to engender public confidence. By contrast, Jimmy Carter appeared wooden and insincere. Consequently, Carter's charges about the dangers of a Reagan presidency fell on deaf ears, and Reagan's reassurances that he would be a kindly but firm leader who would restore old-fashioned moral values carried the day. To top it off, during the final days of the campaign, the media chose to commemorate the beginning of the hostage crisis a year earlier, a crisis that the president had been unable to solve. Reminding the nation of the humiliating episode was the final blow to Carter's reelection chances.[2]

Political Importance of Mass Media

Jimmy Carter's rise from political obscurity to the presidency and his failed bid for reelection in the aftermath of the Iranian crisis are but one example of how mass media, in combination with other political factors, can influence American politics. News stories often play a crucial part in shaping the perceptions of reality of millions of people in all walks of life, whose actions then reflect their perceptions.[3] News stories take Americans to the battlefields of the world in Central America or the Middle East. They give them ringside seats for walks on the moon or oil explorations beneath the sea. They provide the nation with shared political experiences, such as watching presidential election debates or Senate confirmation hearings on presidential appointees, which then form a basis for developing public opinions and uniting people for political actions.

The media often serve as behavior models. In the process of image creation, the media indicate which attitudes and behaviors are acceptable and even praiseworthy in a given society and which are unacceptable or outside the mainstream. Audiences can learn how to conduct themselves in ordinary social and work situations, how to cope with personal crises, and how to evaluate major social institutions like the medical profession or the police. Media stories indicate, too, what is deemed important or unimportant by America's dominant groups, what conforms to prevailing standards of justice and morality, and how various events are related to each other.[4] In the process the media present a set of cultural values that their audiences are likely to accept in whole or in part as typical for American society. The media thus serve as agents of social control that help to integrate and homogenize American society.[5]

Attention to the mass media is all pervasive among twentieth-century Americans. The average recent high school graduate has spent more time in front of a television set than in school, much of it during preschool and elementary school days. Even in school much learning of current events is based on information provided by the media. As adults, Americans spend nearly half of their leisure time watching television, listening to the radio, or reading newspapers and magazines. Averaged out over an entire week, this amounts to seven hours of exposure per day to some form of mass media news or entertainment. Television occupies three-fourths of this time. It is the primary source of news and entertainment for the average American. It is also the most trusted, despite considerable disillusionment with the quality of television programs.

On a typical evening 98 million people—nearly half the country's population—are watching television between 8:00 and 9:00 P.M. If a "special" is broadcast, as many as 75 to 80 million people may watch it simultaneously.[6] The debate between Carter and Reagan during the 1980

"YOU WANT TO KNOW HOW MUCH TV I WATCH A DAY? ON WHICH CHANNEL?"

Reprinted by permission. Tribune Media Services, Inc.

presidential campaign was watched by 120 million Americans, not to mention millions of foreign viewers.

Such vast audiences of ordinary people, as well as political elites, are a major ingredient of the power of the mass media. They are able to provide a nationwide forum for the views of the individuals and groups that they choose to cover. In psychological terms, the mass media are powerful because people believe in them and trust them. In terms of social norms, they are powerful because the American public believes that a free press should keep it informed about the wrongdoings of government.[7]

Media images are especially potent when they involve aspects of life that people experience only through the media, rather than directly in their own neighborhoods. The lives and work habits of politicians, the intrigues of criminals and the execution of crimes, big business power-plays, heart transplants, and space shuttle landings are not generally experienced first-hand. Rather, popular perceptions of these activities are shaped largely by the images portrayed in news and fictional stories in print and electronic media. For example, prime time television exaggerates the likelihood of becoming a victim of crime. Heavy viewers, therefore, fear crime more and take more protective measures than do light viewers.[8]

Much politically relevant information is conveyed through programs that are not explicitly concerned with politics. Many entertainment shows on television, for example, depict social institutions, such as the police or the schools, in ways that convey esteem or heap scorn on them. They also express social judgments about various types of people. For instance, in the past, television often depicted blacks and women as socially inferior and limited in abilities. This type of coverage conveys messages that audiences may accept at face value. They may believe that social conditions and judgments depicted on television as widely accepted are socially sanctioned and therefore ought to be maintained.

Not only are the media the chief source of nearly every American's views of the world, but they are also the fastest way to disperse information throughout the entire society. News of the assassination of President John F. Kennedy and the attempt on the life of President Reagan spread with incredible speed. In both cases better than 90 percent of the American people heard the news within 90 minutes of the event, either directly from radio or television or secondhand from other people who had received mass media messages.

Functions of the Mass Media

What major functions do the mass media perform? According to political scientist Harold Lasswell, there are three major types:

- Surveillance of the world to report ongoing events
- Interpretation of the meaning of events, and
- Socialization of individuals into their cultural settings.[9]

To these three types, a fourth should be added:

- Deliberate manipulation of the political process.

The manner in which these four functions are performed affects the lives of individuals, groups, and social organizations, as well as the course of domestic and international politics. Let us look at each of them in turn.

Surveillance

Surveillance involves two major tasks. For the political community at large, "public" surveillance throws the spotlight of publicity on selected people, organizations, and events. This publicity may make them matters of concern to politicians and to the general public, regardless of the intent of newspeople. It may determine which political demands are exposed and which are kept hidden. It also may force politicians to respond to situations on which their views would not otherwise have been aired. For individual citizens in their private capacities, "private" surveillance informs them about current events. While it may lead to political activities, its primary functions are gratification of personal needs and quieting of anxieties. The media, as Marshall McLuhan has observed, are "sense extensions" for individuals who cannot directly experience most of the events of interest to them and their communities.[10]

Public Surveillance. Because it sets the agenda for civic concern and action, public surveillance is politically significant. Newspeople determine what is "news"—which political happenings will be covered and which will be ignored. In this way they affect who and what will have a good chance to become matters for political discussion and action.[11] Without media coverage the people and events that make the news might have no influence, or reduced influence, on decisionmakers. Undesirable conditions that may be tolerated while they remain obscure may quickly become intolerable in the glare of publicity. This is why politicians, who seek to avoid publicity or to garner it for themselves and for their causes, time and structure events with media coverage in mind.

An example will illustrate the power of publicity to produce public action. On June 19, 1979, a controversial Chicago medical clinic, described by the *Chicago Tribune* as the Midwest's largest prescription mill, closed its doors for good. The reason was a series of reports published in the paper about the activities of the clinic. In the wake of revelations that the clinic was dispensing vast quantities of dangerous sedatives and other pills under the guise of treating patients for stress and weight problems, six clinic doctors quit hastily, forcing suspension of operations. Following the newspaper stories, a suit was brought by the Cook County state's attorney charging the clinic with violation of the Illinois Medical Practices Act, and the American, Illinois, and Chicago medical associations took action to ensure better protection of the public from prescription mills staffed by unethical physicians. Because the Chicago clinic had branches in Miami and Atlanta, officials at those locations, alerted by the *Tribune* reports, began comparable investigations.[12]

In the summer of 1979, many other prescription mills were operating in Chicago and throughout the nation. Had the media publicized them prominently, action might have been taken to close them too. Without public surveillance through the media, they continued to function. Of course, not all media publicity is beneficial. In many instances media stories have created misperceptions and scares that have undermined confidence in good policies, good people, and good products. The human and economic costs have been vast.[13]

Fear of publicity can be as powerful a force in shaping action as actual exposure. Politicians and business leaders are always aware of the damage an unfavorable story can do, and so they act accordingly. The effects of public surveillance may arise indirectly, as a consequence of impressions created by news stories. If media stories dwell on crime and corruption in the central city, individuals may move their homes and businesses to the suburbs, leaving the central city deserted and even less safe, and depriving it of tax revenues. Speculation that international conflicts or oil embargoes are in the offing may scare investors, producing fluctuations in domestic and international stock markets and commodity exchanges. This may have serious economic, and hence political, consequences.

The media not only bring matters to public attention; they also can doom people and events to obscurity by inattention. The media ignore matters that do not seem newsworthy by accepted journalistic criteria or that fail to catch their attention. Lack of coverage may spring from the necessity to limit publication because the information supply exceeds the media's capacity to transmit it. Newspapers have only limited amounts of space available for news; time constraints on television and radio newscasts are even more stringent. Lack of coverage also may spring from conscious attempts to suppress information for ideological or political reasons.

For many years left-liberal social critics have charged that mainstream American journalists have used their selection power to strengthen white middle-class values and suppress socialist viewpoints. They claim that these choices are made deliberately to perpetuate capitalist exploitation of the masses, in line with the ideological preferences of media owners. Critics also claim that the media have intentionally suppressed the facts about dangerous products, such as alcohol and tobacco, and about the socially harmful activities of large corporations, which may be responsible for water and air pollution or unsafe consumer goods.[14] Right-wing critics complain that the media give undue attention to the views of the enemies of the established social and political order in hopes of destroying it. Each camp can cite a long list of stories that apparently supports its contentions.[15]

Media people deny these charges from both ends of the political spectrum. They disclaim political motives in news selection and defend their choices on the basis of the general criteria of newsworthiness (treated more fully in Chapter 3). Like the social critics, they can muster a lot of evidence from news stories to support their claims. At the heart of such controversies lie two basic questions that cannot be answered conclusively. The first concerns people's motivations. How can one judge what motivates journalists to act in certain ways? And is it fair to ascribe motivations to them in the face of their denials? The second question relates to story effects. To what degree can media stories produce the goals owners and news professionals are allegedly seeking?

Besides calling attention to matters of potential public concern, the media also provide cues to the public about the degree of importance of an issue. Matters covered prominently by the media—on the front page with big headlines and pictures or as a major television or radio feature—are likely to be considered most important by media audiences. Matters buried in the back pages generally are perceived as less important.[16] However, nearly all coverage, even though it is brief and comparatively inconspicuous, lends an aura of significance to most publicized subjects.

Through the sheer fact of coverage the media also are able to confer status on individuals and organizations. They "function essentially as agencies of social legitimation—as forces, that is, which reaffirm those ultimate value standards and beliefs, which in turn uphold the social and political status quo." [17] Television made black civil rights leaders household names around the nation. Martin Luther King, Jr., and Stokely Carmichael became national figures. A political candidate whose efforts to win an election are widely publicized, a social crusader or movement whose goals become front-page news, a convicted murderer or terrorist who wins a hearing on radio or television, often become instant celebrities. Their unpublicized counterparts remain obscure and bereft of political influence.

Because the attention of the media is crucial for political success, actors on the political scene deliberately engage in behavior or create situations likely to receive media coverage. Daniel Boorstin has labeled events arranged primarily to stimulate media coverage as "pseudo-events." [18] They may range from news conferences called by public figures when there is really no news to announce to physical assaults on people and property designed to dramatize grievances.

Decisions about what to publish and thereby put on the civic agenda, as well as what to omit, are not completely up to the discretion of media personnel. Some things must be covered because of their extraordinary significance or because of high audience interest or competitive pressures. For example, news about well-known persons and major domestic or international events must be reported.[19] But once all the mandatory events are reported, there remains an extremely wide range of persons and events for which coverage is optional.

The power of the media over setting the civic agenda is a matter of concern because it is not controlled by a system of formal checks and balances like power at the government level. It is not subject to periodic review through the electoral process. If media emphases or claims are incorrect, remedies are few. Under current laws, citizens can be protected from false advertising of consumer goods through "truth in advertising" laws. But there is no way in which they can be protected from false political claims or improper news selection by media personnel without impairing the crucial rights to free speech and a free press. English media critic Jay Blumler expresses the dilemma well:

> Media power is not supposed to be shared: That's an infringement of editorial autonomy. It is not supposed to be controlled: That's censorship. It's not even supposed to be influenced: That's news management! But why should media personnel be exempt from Lord Acton's dictum that all power corrupts and absolute power corrupts absolutely? And if they are not exempt, who exactly is best fitted to guard the press guardians, as it were?[20]

Private Surveillance.   Average citizens may not think much about the broader political impact of the stories they read and the news they watch. Rather, they are interested in using the media to keep in touch with what they see as personally important. The media are their eyes and ears to the world, their means of surveillance, which tell them about economic conditions, weather and sports, jobs, fashions, social and cultural events, health and science, and the public and private lives of famous people.

Being able to stay informed makes people feel secure, whether or not they remember what they read or hear or see. Even though the news may be bad, at least they feel that there will be no unsettling surprises. News reassures them that the political system continues to operate in the face of constant crises and frequent mistakes. Reassurance is very important for people's peace of mind. It tends to keep them politically quiescent because there is no need to act if political leaders seem to be doing their jobs. In turn, this has important consequences for the stability of the political system and the ability of government to function.[21] For good or ill, it helps to maintain the political and economic status quo.

Other significant private functions that the mass media fulfill for many people are entertainment, companionship, tension relief, and a way to pass the time without physical or mental exertion. The mass media can satisfy these major personal needs more conveniently than other institutions in modern

America. Through the media, people who otherwise might be frustrated and dissatisfied can participate vicariously in current political happenings, in sports and musical events, in the lives of famous people, and in the lives of television families and communities.[22]

Interpretation

Media not only survey the events of the day and make them the focus of public and private attention, they also interpret their meanings, put them into context, and speculate about their consequences. Most incidents lend themselves to a variety of interpretations, depending on the values and experiences of the interpreter. The kind of interpretation that is chosen affects the political consequences of the report. For example, in January 1984, the Reverend Jesse Jackson, a black civil rights leader and a candidate for the Democratic presidential nomination, decided to go to Syria to seek the release of a black navy airman held captive by the Syrian government. Jackson succeeded in his mission and returned to the United States with Lt. Robert Goodman, Jr., the released flier.

Although there was great rejoicing over the safe return of Lieutenant Goodman, media interpretations varied about the motives that prompted the Jackson mission and the risks entailed for United States' policies in the Middle East. Some commentators agreed with the Reverend Jackson's claim that his motives had been primarily humanitarian and nonpolitical and that the risks were small. Others suggested that the venture was largely a dangerous political gamble through which Jackson hoped to demonstrate to blacks and whites his capabilities as a foreign affairs negotiator. Depending on which view was expressed, Jackson appeared either as a courageous, effective humanitarian or as a shrewd and self-seeking political operator, willing to risk damage to the foreign policy of his country to further his bid for the presidency. It is easy to see that these divergent interpretations entailed quite different political consequences.

Similarly, media voices varied in estimating the impact that the Syrian mission would have on Jackson's chances to win the Democratic nomination. While some commentators thought that the mission had produced major gains for Jackson that were likely to snowball as the campaign progressed, others thought that the gains, if any, would be short-lived and would accrue largely in the black community. Again, the political consequences of such estimates are considerable. A winning image gains a candidate increased publicity and attracts money and workers. A losing image does the opposite.

The type of interpretation the Jackson mission received depended on a number of circumstances. But the primary factor was the reporter's or editor's decision—made independently or in response to pressures from the community or from within the news organization—to stress a particular image and to choose available informants and facts accordingly. Such journalistic choices play a large role in determining the political consequences of various situations.

By suggesting the causes and relationships of various events, the media may shape opinions even without telling their audiences what to think or think about. For example, for many years the American public has been highly supportive of the state of Israel in its perennial battles with Arab states. However, this support began to erode in the 1980s in the wake of reports that linked Israeli government officials to the slaying of Arab civilians in Lebanon and in Arab territories under Israeli rule. The official stand of the U.S. government—as reported, and supported, by most media—continued to back Israel and its policies. But the stories that suggested improper Israeli behavior led many Americans to reconsider their pro-Israel attitudes.

The items that media personnel select to illustrate a point or to characterize a political actor need not be intrinsically important to be influential in shaping opinions and evaluations. During the 1976 presidential election campaign, for example, the media quoted extensively from an interview that candidate Jimmy Carter had granted to *Playboy* magazine. In that interview Carter confessed to having "looked on a lot of women with lust" and having "committed adultery in [his] heart." [23] Although these confessions shed little light on Carter's political capabilities, nationwide publicity raised fears that the incautious remarks might seriously damage Carter's chances for election.

Socialization

The third major mass media function mentioned by Lasswell is political socialization (discussed more fully in Chapter 5). It involves the learning of basic values and orientations that prepare individuals to fit into their cultural milieu. Originally, mass media studies did not put much stress on the socialization function because it was thought that it was primarily performed by parents of young children and by the schools. [24] Studies conducted in the 1970s finally established that the media are primary agents of political socialization. [25] The bulk of information that young people acquire about the nature of their political world comes from the mass media. It reaches them either directly through exposure to the electronic and print media or indirectly through exposure of their families, teachers, acquaintances, and peers. Mass media information presents to the young specific facts as well as general values. It teaches them which elements produce power, success, and dominance in society, and it provides them with models for behavior. [26] Young people make heavy use of such information to develop their opinions because they lack established attitudes and behavior patterns.

Public opinion polls show that most of the new orientations and opinions that adults acquire during their lifetime also are based on information supplied by the mass media. People do not necessarily adopt the precise attitudes and opinions that may be suggested by the media. Rather, mass media information provides the ingredients that people use to adjust their existing attitudes and opinions to keep pace with a changing world. The mass media must be credited, therefore, with a sizable share of continuing adult political socialization and resocialization. Examples of resocialization—the restructuring of established basic attitudes—are the shifts in sexual morality and racial attitudes that the American public has undergone since mid-century and the changing views on relations with mainland China and with the United Nations.[27]

Manipulation

During the post-Watergate era, direct manipulation of the political process by the media has become very common again, after decades of neutral reporting when most American journalists saw themselves primarily as chroniclers of information provided by others. In recent years major print and electronic media have created their own investigative units, and television shows devoted exclusively to revealing the results of investigations have become highly popular. "Sixty Minutes," the CBS weekly collection of minidocumentaries, is the foremost example and has been able to reach and maintain top audience ratings for many years.

The purpose of these modern shows, like their predecessors early in the century, is to "muckrake." The term comes from a special rake designed to collect manure. President Theodore Roosevelt was the first to apply it to journalists who conducted their own investigations into corruption and wrongdoing in hopes that governmental action would follow to clean up the "dirt" they had exposed. Muckraking today may have several different goals.[28] The journalist's purpose may be to write stories that stir public reactions and produce public demands for reform. Alternatively, the purpose may be to arouse political elites who are in a position to remedy the evils under consideration or who are in a position to spur remedies. Finally, the stories may be part of a cooperative enterprise between government officials and media personnel where the official seeks remedies for an unwholesome situation and enlists the media to publicize the story to stir up support among publics or elites. The investigations by *Washington Post* reporters that led to President Richard Nixon's resignation in the wake of the Watergate scandal were in the muckraking tradition. That story and others involving manipulation can be found in Chapter 8.

Studying Mass Media Effects

The public believes that the media have an important impact on the conduct of politics and on public thinking, and politicians behave on the basis of the same assumption. But many studies conducted by social scientists fail to show substantial impact. Why is there such a discrepancy between many social science appraisals of mass media effects and the general impression, reflected by public policies, that the mass media are extremely influential?

Three major reasons are primarily responsible. To begin with, many studies, particularly those in the 1950s and 1960s, have taken a narrow approach to media effects. Second, theories about the ways in which people use newspapers, television, radio, and other mass media have enhanced the belief in "minimal effects" because these theories suggest that people are disinclined to learn from the media. Finally, social scientists have encountered great difficulties in measuring effects because media stimuli make their impact as part of a complex combination of social stimuli.

Early Studies and Results

Focus on Vote Choices. Eager for neat, readily quantifiable research designs, American social scientists began to study the effects of the mass media primarily in one narrow area: vote change as a result of media coverage of presidential elections. Among these early studies, several are considered classics. The first was *The People's Choice* by Paul Lazarsfeld, Bernard Berelson, and Hazel Gaudet of Columbia University.[29] It reported how people made their voting choices in Erie County, Pennsylvania, in the 1940 presidential election. Sequels followed in short order. The best known are *Voting: A Study of Opinion Formation in a Presidential Campaign,* by the Columbia group of researchers, Bernard Berelson, Paul Lazarsfeld, and William McPhee;[30] *The Voter Decides,* by a group of researchers from the University of Michigan, Angus Campbell, Gerald Gurin, and Warren E. Miller;[31] and the Michigan group's *The American Voter,* by Angus Campbell, Philip E. Converse, Warren E. Miller, and Donald Stokes.[32]

The basic assumption behind the early voting studies was that media influence could be ascertained by measuring its impact on voting choices. A well-publicized campaign should change votes. If it did not, this meant that the media lacked impact. Later studies have shown that this assumption is incorrect. There may be measurable media influence even when vote choice remains stable. Besides, media effects vary, depending on the office at stake and the historical period. At the time of the early voting studies, change of vote choice was quite uncommon in presidential elections because people's choices hinged heavily on their allegiance to one of the two major parties. Predictably, only a few people changed their voting intentions as a result of media coverage. In recent years, when party allegiance has weakened substantially among many voters, the opportunities for media influence have been far greater.

Had the investigators concentrated on other settings, such as judicial or nonpartisan elections (for which few voting cues outside the media are available), they might also have discovered greater media-induced attitude change. Substantial media influence might have been discovered even in presidential elections if changes in people's trust and affection or knowledge about the candidates and the election had been explored. The early studies largely ignored these other types of media influences because they did not result in easily measurable behavior and attitude changes. Yet such changes constitute important media influences that are crucial components of a variety of political behaviors, quite aside from voting decisions.

The early voting studies focused almost exclusively on the individual citizen and failed to trace the linkages between effects on individuals and effects on the social groups to which they belong and through which they influence political events. Farm workers in California might not change their votes after hearing a candidate charge that illegal Mexican immigrants were taking jobs from American workers and depressing wage scales. But they might well use their union to testify against legislation permitting illegal immigrants to remain in the United States. They might even participate in violence against farmers who hire large numbers of alien workers. In turn, these activities might well affect U.S.-Mexican relations and harm the worldwide image of the United States. Yet the early studies of media effects totally ignored such impacts on the total political system and its component parts.

The findings that media effects were minimal were so pervasive in early research that, after an initial flurry in the 1940s and 1950s, social science research into mass media effects fell to a low ebb. Social scientists did not want to waste their time studying inconsequential effects. In the face of seemingly solid evidence of media impotence, they did not care to swim against the stream of established knowledge. Consequently, in study after study dealing with political socialization and learning, the mass media were hardly mentioned as an important factor.

Learning Theories. The early findings were all the more believable because they tied in well with *theories of persuasion*. Mass media messages presumably missed their mark because they are impersonal, directed to no one in particular. They are not tailored to the needs of specific individuals, as are the messages of parents, teachers, and friends. They do not permit immediate feedback, which then could lead to the adjustment of the message to make it more suitable for the receiver. Furthermore, there is no compulsion to listen and no need to answer. Hence it is easy to ignore the message.

Although there is a lot of truth to these claims, they fail to acknowledge the effects of the intimate personal setting that television can create. Audiences frequently interact with the television image as if it were actually present in front of them. They may look upon television commentators and actors as personal friends or enemies. Children are apt to imitate people and situations seen on television, making them a part of their direct personal experiences.

Further support for the "minimal effects" findings came from a series of so-called *cognitive consistency theories.* They are based on the notion that it is painful for average individuals to be presented with information that is incompatible with cherished beliefs. To avoid this painful experience, people expose themselves very selectively to the media. Social scientists do have evidence that people are indeed selective in their use of the media and search for information that reinforces what they already believe and know. But, as we shall discuss more fully in Chapter 5, the evidence is anything but clear-cut.

Recent Research

When research into mass media effects resumed in the wake of persistent evidence of media impact, the net was cast more broadly. Researchers began to look beyond media effects on voting to other effects during elections and in situations involving other types of political events. In this vein, researchers examined media impact on factual learning, on opinion formation, and on the satisfaction of a variety of human needs. They have also looked beyond the individual to effects on political systems and subsystems, a search that promises to be highly rewarding. But despite improvements in research designs and techniques, research into mass media effects has remained hampered by serious measurement problems.

Measuring Complex Effects.   Mass media effects are difficult to measure, both at the level of the individual and at the societal level, because they are highly complex and elusive. The most common measuring device at the individual level—self-assessment of impact elicited during a poll—is notoriously unreliable. We do not know at the present time how to measure objectively what people think and how they form their thoughts. Even if their thoughts lead to overt behavior, we cannot accurately discern their thoughts from their actions. Actions spring from a variety of motivations among which media impact may play only a small part.

Assessing mass media impact is especially difficult because people who are exposed to the mass media already possess a fund of knowledge and attitudes that they bring to bear on new information. Since we do not know precisely what this information is, nor the rules by which it is combined with incoming information, we cannot pinpoint the exact contribution that particular mass media stories have made to an individual's cognitions, feelings, and actions. To complicate matters further, the impact of the mass media varies depending on the subject matter. For instance, media impact apparently was greater on people's perceptions of civil rights policies and the conduct of the Vietnam War than on their views about energy policy.[33]

Assessments of television's role in spurring opposition to the Vietnam War illustrates the problems faced in proving media impact. A number of analysts ascribe the public's growing dissatisfaction with United States involvement in Vietnam in the late 1960s and early 1970s to media treatment of the war.[34] Television for the first time brought an ongoing war into American living rooms. In vivid color it showed the dead and wounded, blazing villages, and the faces of horrified children. Starting with the Tet offensive in 1968, which called into question optimistic reports about the impending victorious conclusion of the Vietnam War, there was a constant barrage of antiwar stories.[35] Demands to get out of the war were featured, but little attention was paid to requests to escalate the fighting. It is easy to demonstrate the thrust of coverage and to document the growth of the antiwar sentiment. It is well-nigh impossible to establish the precise contribution that media coverage made to changing the public's view by picturing the war as an unnecessary, rather than a necessary, evil.

Similarly, it is difficult to prove that sharp curtailment of media coverage of Vietnam, after United States forces had been withdrawn in 1973, prevented a turnaround in policy and public sentiment. Americans in and out of government learned very little about what happened in Vietnam and the adjacent countries in the wake of the Communist takeover. For instance, atrocity stories coming from Cambodia, which the French press published because of that country's earlier ties to Cambodia, were given very little play in the American press. But one cannot be sure that ample coverage of the atrocities in the American press would have made Americans regret the withdrawal of U.S. troops from Southeast Asia.

Unanticipated Effects. Measurement of media effects has also suffered because unanticipated effects are frequently ignored. If the anticipated effects fail to materialize, the researcher may claim that there are no effects. For example, there have been frequent mass media campaigns by public service organizations and private groups to foster concern about environmental pollution. These campaigns have shown the ill effects of pollution and the steps needed to clean up the environment. After some of these publicity campaigns, researchers have tested how much people learned about pollution and ways to reduce it. The investigations generally showed that most people learned very few facts from the campaigns.

But when the attitudes of individuals toward big business were measured, social scientists found a sizable change between pre- and postcampaign attitudes. Although most people had not learned the specific messages that the sponsors had tried to convey, they had learned that big business was responsible for much pollution. Therefore, they blamed big business and voiced resentment against it. The antipollution campaigns had a distinct effect, but not the effect that had been expected and would normally be measured in postcampaign tests.[36]

A Case Study: Britain and Appeasement. Britain's decision to appease Nazi dictator Adolf Hitler rather than to fight him prior to Germany's conquest of Czechoslovakia clearly demonstrates the difficulty of measuring the contribution that mass media publicity makes to a particular political situation. In 1936 Hitler marched into the Rhineland in violation of German treaty obligations. In 1938 he annexed Austria. Annexation of Czechoslovakia followed in 1939. Until then, major European powers, including Britain, had pursued a policy of appeasement. But after the fall of Czechoslovakia, appeasement ended and Britain belatedly pledged to fight against further German aggression.

During and after World War II, the question was frequently raised in Britain and elsewhere why the British had not opposed Hitler earlier, before he had gained strength through his early conquests. British scholar Colin Seymour-Ure has placed the brunt of the blame for the appeasement policy on the *Times* of London.[37] His views find support in the writings of British notables such as Prime Minister Anthony Eden and Lord Vansittart of the British Foreign Office, as well as well-known historians such as Martin Gilbert and A. J. P. Taylor.[38]

The *Times* did not have to persuade government leaders to adopt the appeasement position (although the newspaper's top brass were in a good position to do so because of close ties of friendship with Britain's political leaders). Most of these leaders were convinced already. Rather, the *Times*, through its advocacy of appeasement, gave a strong boost to their cause and made it extremely difficult for the opposition to organize. It also reinforced the general consensus in the country and among the leadership that appeasement was the proper policy for a nation still war-weary from World War I, which had ended only 20 years earlier.

During the late 1930s in Britain, the *Times* was considered a national institution that watched wisely and well over the interests of the nation. It was ranked as the best and most influential of all British daily papers, read by nearly every prominent person in public and private life. When the *Times* supported a policy, Britain's leaders and people took note.

The *Times* also was widely regarded abroad as the official voice of the British government, which gave its editorials extraordinary political weight. This is why British historians claim that "no single factor contributed so much" to the German annexation of Czechoslovakia as a pro-appeasement *Times* editorial in 1938 "suggesting that Czechoslovakia might be wise in her own interests to let the Sudeten-German areas go." The editorial may have assured Hitler that he could safely proceed with the conquest without British military opposition.[39] Protests against the editorial and warnings about its dangerous consequences came immediately from members of the British cabinet, the British Foreign Office, British diplomats abroad, Czech leaders, the Russian ambassador in London, and the French government. There were even rumors that the editorial had been planted by the German embassy in

London as a clever ploy to aid the cause of Germany. The warnings about the Fuehrer's next move proved correct. Hitler took Czechoslovakia.

The role of the *Times* is not as clear as it may seem, however. Other analysts of the events that preceded World War II believe that the *Times* played only a minor role. They note that even without prodding from the *Times*, appeasement was extremely popular before 1939 with Britain's political leaders, particularly Prime Minister Neville Chamberlain, and with the British public. They point to the unexpected outcome of a 1933 special election in which a pacifist Labour party candidate soundly defeated a pro-rearmament Conservative in a normally Conservative district. Furthermore, in 1935 an antimilitary lobby group, the Peace Pledge Union, was able to collect 11,500,000 votes in Britain for its Peace Ballot straw poll. Natural hatred of war was reinforced by bitter memories of the losses suffered by Britain in World War I and fears that World War II, with the rapid development of air warfare capabilities, would be infinitely more horrible for soldiers and civilians alike. Moreover, Britain was militarily unprepared for war, and assistance from France, the United States, and the Soviet Union was uncertain.

It is impossible to prove conclusively how crucial the position of the *Times* was to Britain's maintenance of an appeasement policy and to Hitler's decision to invade Czechoslovakia. It is equally impossible to prove that the *Times* played no role because British policymakers already favored appeasement. Neither will we ever know for sure whether Hitler would have ventured the invasion had he lacked the intimation that Britain would not interfere.

Inability to prove mass media impact beyond a doubt has made social scientists shy away from assessing its influence on many important political events. In fact, social scientists often go to the other extreme and deny that effects exist simply because these effects defy measurement. This is unfortunate since many effects that cannot be measured precisely can be observed in the field and studied in the laboratory.

Statistical versus Political Significance. Social scientists also have been rather rigid in interpreting the significance of media influence when it has been found. They have falsely equated statistical significance with political significance, despite the fact that media impact on small numbers of individuals can have great political consequences.

For example, during an election only 1 or 2 percent of the voters may change their voting decision because of media stories. That is a very small, statistically negligible effect. Politically, however, it may be a major effect because many important elections, including several presidential elections, have been decided by a margin of 2 percent of the voters. If 2 percent of the vote had gone to the losing candidate in the 1976 presidential race, Gerald Ford would have stayed in the White House and Jimmy Carter would have remained a peanut farmer. Two percent of the voters sounds like a small number, but it runs into thousands, and even hundreds of thousands, when translated into actual numbers.

On an even smaller scale, if a broadcast of details of a race riot attracts a few listeners to the riot site and stimulates some to participate, the situation may escalate beyond control. Similarly, the impact of a single news story may change the course of history if it induces one assassin to kill a world leader or convinces one world leader to make a strategic political decision.

Influencing Elites. Another major problem with social science research on mass media effects has been the concentration on measuring effects on ordinary individuals, rather than on political elites. This ignores that the average individual, democratic fictions to the contrary, is politically fairly unimportant. Mass media impact on a handful of political decisionmakers usually is vastly more significant than similar impact on ordinary individuals. In addition, the impact on decisionmakers is likely to be far more profound because mass media information relates more directly to their immediate concerns. They may pay close attention to stories in which the public is not interested and which it often fails to understand.

A case in point is a brief column that appeared in the *Washington Post* in the summer of 1983. In it a Carter cabinet member complained that there had been little public reaction to reports that a campaign briefing book prepared for President Carter had fallen into the hands of the Reagan campaign staff. The information in the book allegedly had been used to brief Ronald Reagan for his debate with Jimmy Carter, in violation of campaign ethics and, possibly, national security. The column caught the attention of one member of the congressional subcommittee with jurisdiction over the Ethics in Government Act. He, in turn, called it to the attention of the subcommittee chairman, Rep. Donald J. Albosta, a Michigan Democrat. The upshot was a major congressional investigation into the entire affair. While the initial story had produced no noticeable political waves—even though it had reached a worldwide audience—the second story brought results. It caught the eye of two political decisionmakers who were in a position to act.[40]

In light of what we have discussed thus far, it seems totally unrealistic to deny that the media are important in setting the stage for ongoing political developments, in shaping the views and behaviors of political elites and other selected groups, and in influencing the general public's perception of political life. As Theodore White put it hyperbolically:

> The power of the press in America is a primordial one. It sets the agenda of public discussion; and this sweeping political power is unrestrained by any law. It determines what people will talk and think about—an authority that in other nations is reserved for tyrants, priests, parties and mandarins.
>
> No major act of the American Congress, no foreign adventure, no act of diplomacy, no great social reform can succeed in the United States unless the press prepares the public mind.[41]

Even if one takes a totally negative position, arguing that the media are nothing but a conduit of information over which they have no control, one cannot deny that people throughout the world of politics consider the media important and behave accordingly. This importance—which is an effect of media coverage—is reflected in efforts by governments everywhere, in authoritarian as well as democratic regimes, to control the flow of information produced by the media lest it subvert the prevailing political system.

Government Control of Mass Media: Assumptions and Methods

Governmental attempts to control and manipulate the media are universal because governments throughout the world believe media effects are important political forces. This belief is based on the assumption that institutions that control public information can shape public knowledge and behavior and thereby determine the support or opposition of citizens and officials to the government and its politics. Through control over mass information institutions and the stories they produce, governments everywhere seek to preserve the political system as a whole as well as to regulate the media and other social institutions that depend on media publicity. Although control occurs in all societies, its extent, nature and purposes vary.

Several major reasons account for these variations. Political ideology is one of them. In countries where free expression of opinion is a paramount value and where dissent is respected, the media tend to be comparatively unrestrained. The right of the press to criticize government also flourishes when the accepted ideology grants that governments are fallible and often corrupt and that average citizens are capable of forming valuable opinions about the conduct of government. Finally, freedom of the press, even when it becomes a thorn in the side of government, is more easily tolerated where governments are well established and politically and economically secure. In Third World nations, for instance, where governments are unstable and resources limited, it may be difficult to tolerate press behavior that is apt to topple the government or retard its plans for economic development.

Nowhere are the media totally free from formal and informal governmental and social controls, even in times of peace. On the whole, authoritarian countries control more extensively and more rigidly than nonauthoritarian ones. But all systems represent specific points on a continuum of control. There are also gradations of control within nations, depending on the current regime and political setting, regional and local variations, and the nature of news. We will outline common types of control systems used in authoritarian and nonauthoritarian societies without specifying any particular country.[42]

Authoritarian control systems are of two types: those that are nonideological and simply represent a desire by the ruling classes to tightly control media output so that it does not interfere with the conduct of government and those that are based on a totalitarian ideology, such as communism. The latter type actively uses and controls the media to support ideological goals. Examples of nonideological authoritarian control can be found in states ruled by military governments, such as Chile or Ethiopia. Examples of control based on communism are found in the Soviet Union and the People's Republic of China.

There are also two types of *nonauthoritarian approaches to control,* although they are not linked to differences in political ideology. Rather, these types are linked to differences in philosophies about the role that the media ought to carve out for themselves in countries where they enjoy a great deal of freedom. The two types of nonauthoritarian approaches have been labeled "libertarian" and "social responsibility." When journalists in democratic societies subscribe to the libertarian philosophy, they feel free to report whatever they wish as long as public tastes are satisfied. By contrast, when social responsibility philosophies prevail, newspeople expect to contribute to the betterment of society, spurring media audiences to behave in socially responsible ways. Journalists in the United States and Western Europe furnish examples of both of these philosophies. Often libertarian and social responsibility journalism occur simultaneously, or they may alternate during successive historical periods.[43]

In today's world, authoritarian systems of media control prevail in the majority of countries. Authoritarian countries would like to impose such systems universally by controlling international aspects of news reporting in all countries. In sessions of the United Nations Educational, Scientific and Cultural Organization (UNESCO), they have opposed freedom of reporting about their countries even when the stories are gathered by journalists from democratic societies for their own media. The argument has been made that only news that supports the established regime should be permitted and that all newspeople should be subject to supervision by officials of the country whose laws they report. This story is told more fully in Chapter 10.

Role of Media in Authoritarian Regimes

What are the basic assumptions that underlie authoritarian and nonauthoritarian philosophies of media operation, and what types of governmental structures and practices have been invented to implement these philosophies?

Communist and other authoritarian systems operate on the assumption that the government always knows and represents the best interests of the people. Since the government is invariably well intentioned, and its policies are carefully determined, the mass media must not interfere with the operations of the government or endanger its survival. It is not appropriate for the press to criticize the basic system or its rulers, beyond pointing out minor deficiencies and suggesting adjustments in line with prevailing policies. Rather, the press must firmly support the government and its policies. However, criticism about inefficiencies or corruption of minor officials may be allowed. For instance, in 1977 and 1978 *Pravda,* the official Russian newspaper, published a series of articles on shoddy housing construction and industrial pollution on the Dnieper River. Likewise, once top leaders have been ousted from leadership, they may be criticized severely, but only in conformity with official guidelines.

In most authoritarian polities the mass media must take positions that further the goals of the government. News must accord with the prevailing ideology and confirm its accuracy. Its also must engender support for major policies, such as economic development laws or literacy campaigns. It must echo official stands about who the country's domestic and international friends and enemies are. But the media may be free to provide information or entertainment of their choice, as long as the offerings do not hurt the state or interfere with public policies.

In totalitarian societies the role of the media is more stringently defined. The likely political and social effects of a story, rather than its general significance, novelty, or audience appeal, determine what will be published and what will be buried in silence. For instance, Soviet media report comparatively few stories about accidents, disasters, and crimes because these matters are believed to be devoid of value in teaching citizens proper conduct. Events reflecting favorably on politics in capitalist countries are usually ignored because they would undermine the official images presented of the non-Communist world.

Newspeople are encouraged to publish socially useful information that will strengthen the people's allegiance to the Communist system. According to Lenin, the press must be a propagandist, agitator, and organizer for the revolutionary aims of Communist societies. It must be closely integrated with other instruments of state power, serving the public by publishing stories that will unify people around the approved ideas of life and politics.

Even entertainment programs must serve political purposes. Thus music and drama performances, and even cartoon shorts in movie theaters, must carry appropriate social messages or have historical significance. Many kinds of Western music, modernistic art, and sexually explicit theater are banned, particularly if performances and exhibits will reach large audiences. For entertainment that is deemed to have social merit, funding is available even if the audience is small. The government supports such entertainment financially because it serves the important public purpose of shaping people's minds in support of the system.

Role of Media in Nonauthoritarian Regimes

The basic assumptions underlying mass media control in democratic countries contrast sharply with those of authoritarian societies. In democracies, governments are viewed as fallible servants of the people. They are deemed to be potentially corrupt, stupid, or abusive of citizens. Consequently, they must be constantly watched and criticized if they misbehave.

The media are regarded as objective reporters of good and evil who scrutinize the passing scene on behalf of a public that can and must appraise the performance of its officials. Journalists serve as the watchdog fourth branch of government, which monitors excesses and misbehavior of the executive, legislative, and judicial branches. Through playing an adversary role, journalists provide the feedback that democratic systems need to remain on course. If, as the result of their scrutiny, governments fall and public officials are ousted, this is as it should be.

Broadly stated, this is the *theory* behind the role of media in democratic societies. The *practice* is less clear-cut. In the United States, for example, neither newspeople nor government officials are completely at ease with the media's watchdog role. The media usually support the political system and rarely question its fundamental tenets. They limit their criticism to what they perceive as perversions of fundamental social and political values or noteworthy examples of corruption and waste. Their links to the existing power structures are strong because they depend heavily on the high and mighty as sources of news. Newspeople may even share information with government agencies, such as the FBI and CIA. At times, reporters in a democratic society withhold important news at the request of the government to spare it or particular officials from embarrassment or interference. This happened in the United States, for instance, when the *New York Times* withheld news about the forthcoming Bay of Pigs invasion of Cuba in 1961.[44] Government officials, in an effort to keep their images untarnished by media attacks, may use rewards and punishments to keep the media watchdog in line. These tactics are described more fully in Chapter 7.

The chief obligation of the mass media in free societies is to provide information and entertainment to the general public. According to the libertarian philosophy, anything that happens which is interesting or involves important people or events may become news. Following appropriate verification, news should be reported quickly, accurately, and objectively, without any attempt to convey a particular point of view. Matters with the widest audience appeal should be stressed, even if that means sex and violence stories and entertainment rather than serious information. The fact that this emphasis also serves the market orientation of the media is an extra benefit.

Although audiences may learn important things from the media, teaching is not the media's chief task. Nor is it their task to question the truth or accuracy or merits of the information supplied to them by their sources. Rather, interpretation is left to the news audience, which must decide what to believe and what to question.

In contrast to libertarians, adherents to social responsibility tenets believe that news and entertainment presented by the mass media should reflect social consciousness. Media personnel should be participants in the political process, not merely reporters of the passing scene. As guardians of the public welfare, they should foster political action when necessary. If reporters think, for instance, that pollution or racial segregation are prevalent social evils, they should cover these stories in depth and make them news, even when nothing new has happened. Likewise, undesirable viewpoints and questionable accusations should be denied exposure, however sensational they may be. If reporters believe that government is hiding information under the cloak of national security, they should try to discover the facts and publicize them.

Comparison of the type of journalism advocated by social responsibility journalists with the type of journalism advocated by totalitarian journalists reveals philosophical resemblances. Adherents of both approaches advocate using the media to support the basic ideals of their societies and to shape people into more perfect social beings. They are convinced that their goals are good and would not be achieved in a media system dominated by the whims of media owners or audiences.

But the similarities should not be exaggerated. Social advocacy in nonauthoritarian systems lacks the fervor, clout, and single-mindedness it has in systems where media control is monopolized by the government. It rarely speaks with a single, uncontested voice throughout the entire society. Nevertheless, social responsibility journalism frightens and antagonizes many news professionals and news audiences. If one agrees that the media should be used to influence social thought and behavior for "good" purposes, it becomes difficult to determine which purposes deserve to be included in that category. Critics of social responsibility journalism point out that journalists do not have a public mandate to act as arbiters of social values and policies in a society without a single vision of truth and goodness. Newspeople lack the legitimacy that in a democracy comes only from being elected by the public or appointed by elected officials.

Whatever the merits or faults of these arguments may be, at the present time social responsibility journalism is popular with a sizable proportion of the news profession.[45] Pulitzer prizes and other honors go to journalists who have successfully exposed questionable practices in the interest of social improvement. The most prominent "villains" targeted for exposure are usually big government and big business.[46]

Control Methods: Authoritarian Regimes

Four types of controls are widely used: *legal, normative, structural,* and *economic.*[47] Accordingly, there are laws everywhere to prevent serious press misbehavior; there are also social norms that journalists dare not defy. The way the media are structurally organized and operated shapes their product, and they are also affected by the nature of their economic support. The combination of methods by which governments control the media varies and so do the major objectives of control.

In authoritarian societies, the major objective of control is to restrict access to mass communications to voices friendly to the regime and to ensure that news stories remain supportive of most government policies. By contrast, nonauthoritarian regimes seek to avoid publicity that endangers national defense capabilities or violates widely held social norms. There is little formal attempt to deny foes of the regime access to the media.

In many authoritarian societies control over media content is established by limiting entry into the media business. For example, the government may grant newspaper franchises only to carefully selected people who support the government fully in all its endeavors. Often such franchises bestow monopoly control, and people who lack them cannot enter the newspaper business. Control through franchising media entrepreneurs is quite common for electronic media, even in democratic countries, because of the limited availability of television and radio channels. But in democratic countries it is less frequently used to shut out political opponents. Nor is it applied to newspapers. In the United States, for instance, anyone who has sufficient money may start a newspaper or newsletter. No permits are required.

Other methods used primarily by authoritarian countries to control publications are subsidies to favorite publishers or favoritism in the allocation of tightly controlled paper stocks for printing newspapers and magazines. Newspaper publishers whose activities displease the government may find themselves out of business because they cannot obtain paper. These types of economic controls may be imposed quite openly through formal rationing and subsidy schemes, or they may be imposed informally. The government may merely inform a disliked publisher that paper stocks are insufficient to supply that particular enterprise.

Media also may be controlled through manipulating access to news. For instance, the government may release information only to favored publications, putting less favored ones effectively out of business. While such practices are common in authoritarian societies, they occasionally happen on a smaller scale in more open societies as well. Angered by press coverage of his presidency, President Nixon at one point barred *Washington Post* reporters from his press plane.[48]

In addition to controlling entry into the news business through franchises and access to news, authoritarian governments often limit *what* may be published. This may be done routinely or only at times of political upheaval. In some countries nothing may be printed or broadcast until it has been approved by the government censor, who may suppress any story that the government deems objectionable. At times, deletions are made after papers or magazines have already been prepared for printing or printed. This leaves tantalizing white spaces or missing pages. Television and radio scripts are often written or edited directly by government officials and must be broadcast without editorial changes.

Authoritarian societies frequently use treason and sedition laws to control media output. Treason and sedition are usually defined broadly in these countries so that anything that is critical of the government is branded as treasonable or seditious. People judged guilty of these crimes may be severely punished. The punishment may be removal from the media business, prison sentences, or even death. These are extremely strong deterrents to publishing stories that attack the government.

Because of the strong deterrent effect, instances of disobedience are rare. Most publishers in totalitarian societies avoid difficulties with the official censor and with treason and sedition laws by refraining from using material that is likely to be objectionable. Government censorship then becomes replaced largely by self-censorship, making the job of the official censor much easier.

When authoritarian regimes are totalitarian, media control is simplified because the government owns and operates all mass media and fully controls their programs. Additionally, totalitarian countries frequently block out all unapproved communications from abroad. This includes jamming of foreign broadcasts and prohibition on the importation of foreign printed materials. The strictness with which these controls are applied waxes and wanes, depending on the country's relations with other powers. But even during friendly interludes, totalitarian regimes rigidly control any information from abroad that might undermine their political system. They view such censorship as an intellectual quarantine that must be imposed to keep evil influences from undermining a beneficial political system.

Control Methods: Nonauthoritarian Regimes

In democratic societies, official control of the content of mass media is deemed largely unnecessary. Entry to the mass media business is open to people representing a wide spectrum of political views. In the United States, the First Amendment to the Constitution, which provides that "Congress shall make no law . . . abridging the freedom of speech, or of the press," has given the media an exceptionally strong basis for resisting government controls. But the courts have ruled that the protection is not absolute and must give way on occasion to social rights that the courts deem superior.

Competition among papers, magazines, and television and radio stations will presumably generate a variety of viewpoints. If some media attack the government, other media will support it. Positive and negative as well as right and wrong information will somehow balance out. The underlying, intriguing but questionable assumption is that the audience will be able to extract the truth from these conflicting reports. Unfortunately, average citizens generally do not have time to expose themselves to a wide array of different media. When confronted with clashing opinions, they find it difficult to determine their merits. Anyone who has listened to the promises and claims made by contending politicians knows how difficult it is to evaluate them. Confusion and resigned disinterest, rather than enlightenment, are the likely outcomes.

Even in societies with basically open communication systems, some controls, such as laws and court decisions and informal social pressures, guard against excesses by the media. In the United States, the courts have generally ruled that these controls may be enforced only after the bounds of proper publication have been exceeded. Courts have been very loathe to impose "prior restraint" by granting injunctions that would stop publication of information on the grounds that it would cause irreparable harm. But informal social and political pressures and the fear of indictments after publication have restrained presentation of potentially dangerous stories.

Controls in nonauthoritarian societies generally fall into four categories: (1) guarding state survival through treason and sedition laws, (2) shielding sensitive governmental proceedings, (3) protecting individual reputations and privacy, and (4) safeguarding the prevailing moral standards of the community. All societies have treason and sedition laws that prohibit publication of information which must be kept secret to protect the country against foreign and domestic enemies who endanger its national survival. The big problem is to determine the point at which secrecy is so essential that freedom to publish must give way. In democratic societies, media and the government are in perennial disagreement about the exact location of this point. Governments lean toward protection; the media lean toward disclosure.

There is little argument that treason and sedition are beyond the boundaries of unrestricted publication, even in an open society. More controversial are curbs on publication of government secrets—so-called "classified information." Governments try to establish controls over the publication of material that may be harmful to themselves or to individuals. For instance, confidential reports about the performance of government agencies, records of bidding on public jobs, and conversations during closed meetings are generally shielded from publicity. Finally, most governments also have laws protecting the reputations of individuals or groups and laws against obscenity. All of these controls on publication are discussed more fully in Chapter 4.

Defining the limits of government restraint on information raises difficult questions for democratic societies. Does any degree of official censorship open the way for the destruction of free expresssion? What guidelines are available to determine how far censorship should go? What types of material, if any, can harm children? Or adults? Should expressed prejudice be prohibited on the ground that it damages the self-image of minorities? The answers are controversial and problematic.

In addition to formal control of potentially "dangerous" news in authoritarian and nonauthoritarian societies, many informal restraints exist as well. As we shall see in Chapter 7, all governmental units, and often many of their subdivisions, have their own information control systems by which they determine what news to release, how to present it, and what news to cover up.

The limitations on the freedom of publication that are encountered even in nonauthoritarian societies raise questions about the actual freedom enjoyed by the media, compared with their counterparts in authoritarian societies. Is there really a difference, for example, in the independence of televison networks in France and in the Soviet Union, since the state operates the system in both countries? The answer is a resounding "yes." The degree of restraint varies so sharply that the systems are fundamentally different. In authoritarian societies the media are essentially an arm of government whose main purpose is to support the regime in power. In nonauthoritarian societies the media are usually free to oppose the regime, to weaken it, and even topple it. While they rarely carry their power to the latter extreme, the potential exists. It is this potential that makes the media in nonauthoritarian societies a genuine restraint on governmental abuses of power and a potent shaper of governmental action.

Summary

The mass media are an important influence on politics because they regularly and rapidly present politically crucial information to huge audiences. These audiences include political elites and decisionmakers, as well as large numbers of average citizens whose political activities, however sporadic, are shaped by information from the mass media.

The mass media are more than passive transmission agents for available information. Decisions made by media personnel determine what information becomes available to media audiences and what remains unavailable. By putting stories into perspective and interpreting them, media personnel assign meaning to the information and indicate the values by which it ought to be judged. News shaping is unavoidable because space is limited and because facts do not speak for themselves. Hence the media have the power to control much of the raw material needed by political elites and the general public for thinking about the political world and planning political action. At times, newspeople even generate political action directly through their own investigations or indirectly through their capacity to stimulate pseudo-events.

Although many social scientists have remained somewhat skeptical about claims of large-scale media impact on politics, governments everywhere are keenly aware of the political importance of the media. Governments therefore have developed philosophies about the political role to be played by the media in their societies and about the proper ways to control the impact of the media on government activities. These philosophies have been implemented by constitutional and legal rules as well as by a host of informal arrangements. In this chapter we have briefly described how the basic philosophies, constitutional arrangements, and legal provisions differ in authoritarian and nonauthoritarian regimes.

Notes

1. Thomas R. Dye and L. Harmon Zeigler, *American Politics in the Media Age* (Monterey, Calif.: Brooks/Cole, 1983), pp. 20-23; the title comes from an article by David Halberstam in *Parade* magazine, January 11, 1981.
2. For an assessment of media influence in 1976 and 1980, see Michael J. Robinson, "The Media in 1980: Was the Message the Message?" in *The American Elections of 1980,* ed. Austin Ranney (Washington, D.C.: American Enterprise Institute for Public Policy Research, 1981).
3. For a compact overview of the literature on mass media effects, particularly television, see George Comstock, "The Impact of Television on American Institutions," *Journal of Communication* 28 (Spring 1978): 12-28.
4. The clues that mass media stories supply to the culture of their societies are discussed by George Gerbner, "Toward 'Cultural Indicators': the Analysis of Mass Mediated Public Message Systems," in *The Analysis of Communication Content,* ed. George Gerbner, Ole R. Holsti, Klaus Krippendorff, William J. Paisley, Philip J. Stone (New York: John Wiley, 1969), pp. 123-132.
5. John M. Phelan, *Mediaworld: Programming the Public* (New York: Seabury Press, 1977).
6. A good source for media statistics is Christopher H. Sterling and Timothy R. Haight, eds., *The Mass Media: Aspen Institute Guide to Communication Industry Trends* (New York: Praeger, 1982).
7. These figures are averages based on Roper Organization Surveys. People's media exposure patterns differ, depending on age, social background, education, ethnic origins, and similar characteristics. These variations are discussed in Chapter 5. For politicians, close attention is a professional requirement. Michael Gurevitch and Jay G. Blumler, "Linkages between the Mass Media and Politics: A Model for the Analysis of Political Communications Systems," in *Mass Communication and Society,* ed. James Curran, Michael Gurevitch, and Janet Woolacott (Beverly Hills, Calif.: Sage, 1979), p. 274.
8. George Gerbner, Larry Gross, Michael Morgan, and Nancy Signorielli, "Charting the Mainstream: Television's Contributions to Political Orientation," *Journal of Communication* 32 (1982): 106-107.
9. Lasswell discusses the three functions in Harold D. Lasswell, "The Structure and Function of Communication in Society," in *Mass Communications,* ed. Wilbur Schramm (Urbana: University of Illinois Press, 1969), p. 103.
10. Marshall McLuhan, *Understanding Media: The Extensions of Man* (New York: McGraw-Hill, 1965).
11. Chapter 3 gives a more detailed definition of "news." Evidence that the media set the agenda for national issues is presented in Donald L. Shaw and Maxwell

McCombs, *The Emergence of American Political Issues: The Agenda-Setting Function of the Press* (St. Paul: West Publishing, 1977) and sources cited there. Wenmouth Williams, Jr., and David C. Larsen, "Agenda-Setting in an Off-Election Year," *Journalism Quarterly* 54 (Winter 1977): 744-749 reviews agenda-setting for local issues as well as the differential role played by various types of media in setting civic and personal agendas.

12. William Gaines and Eileen Ogintz, " 'Prescription Mill' Closes as Heat's Put on Pill Centers," *Chicago Tribune,* June 20, 1979.

13. Colin Seymour-Ure, *The Political Impact of Mass Media* (London: Constable, 1974), p. 21, outlines the various types of media influences.

14. Examples of such criticism can be found in Herbert Schiller, *Mass Communication and American Empire* (New York: Augustus Kelley, 1971) and Robert Cirino, *Power to Persuade: Mass Media and the News* (New York: Bantam, 1974).

15. An example of a conservative Washington-based media analysis group is Accuracy in Media (AIM). It publishes periodic reports of its media investigations.

16. Maxwell E. McCombs and John B. Mauro, "Predicting Newspaper Readership from Content Characteristics," *Journalism Quarterly* 54 (Spring 1977): 3-7.

17. Jay G. Blumler, "Purposes of Mass Communications Research: A Transatlantic Perspective," *Journalism Quarterly* 55 (Summer 1978): 22.

18. Daniel Boorstin, *The Image: A Guide to Pseudo-Events* (New York: Atheneum, 1971).

19. Criteria of what constitutes "news" are discussed fully by Bernard Roshco, *Newsmaking* (Chicago: University of Chicago Press, 1975), Chapter 3.

20. Blumler, "Purposes of Mass Communications Research," p. 228.

21. The results of reassuring publicity are discussed by Murray Edelman, *The Symbolic Uses of Politics* (Urbana: University of Illinois Press, 1964), pp. 38-43.

22. George Comstock, Steven Chaffee, Natan Katzman, Maxwell McCombs, and Donald Roberts, *Television and Human Behavior* (New York: Columbia University Press, 1978), pp. 423-451.

23. Robert Scheer, "Interview: Jimmy Carter," *Playboy* (November 1976): 63-86.

24. Earlier writings include David Easton and Jack Dennis, *Children in the Political System: Origins of Political Legitimacy* (New York: McGraw Hill, 1969); Fred I. Greenstein, *Children and Politics* (New Haven: Yale University Press, 1965); Richard Dawson and Kenneth Prewitt, *Political Socialization* (Boston: Little, Brown, 1969); and Robert D. Hess and Judith Torney, *The Development of Political Attitudes in Children* (Chicago: Aldine, 1967).

25. Examples include Sidney Kraus and Dennis Davis, *The Effects of Mass Communication on Political Behavior* (University Park, Pa.: Pennsylvania State University Press, 1976); Gary O. Coldevin, "Internationalism and Mass Communications," *Journalism Quarterly* 49 (Summer 1972): 365-368; Neil Hollander, "Adolescents and the War: The Sources of Socialization," *Journalism Quarterly* 48 (Autumn 1971): 472-479; and Steven H. Chaffee, H. L. Scott Ward, and Leonard Tipton, "Mass Communication and Political Socialization," *Journalism Quarterly* 47 (Winter 1970): 647-659.

26. In *Mediaworld: Programming the Public,* Phelan contends that the mass media have replaced more traditional social groups as the source of behavior models and demonstrator of the ideals of society.

27. Evidence that the public links attitude changes to mass media information comes from successive Roper polls and the author's Three Sites Project reported more fully in Doris A. Graber, *Processing the News: How People Tame the Information Tide* (New York: Longman, 1984).

28. Fay Lomax Cook, Tom R. Tyler, Edward G. Goetz, Margaret T. Gordon, David Protess, Donna R. Leff, and Harvey L. Molotch, "Media and Agenda Setting: Effects on the Public, Interest Group Leaders, Policy Makers, and Policy," *Public Opinion Quarterly* 47 (1983): 16-35.
29. Paul Lazarsfeld, Bernard Berelson, and Hazel Gaudet, *The People's Choice* (New York: Columbia University Press, 1944).
30. Bernard Berelson, Paul Lazarsfeld, and William McPhee, *Voting: A Study of Opinion Formation in a Presidential Campaign* (Chicago: University of Chicago Press, 1954).
31. Angus Campbell, Gerald Gurin, and Warren E. Miller, *The Voter Decides* (Evanston, Ill.: Row, Peterson, 1954).
32. Angus Campbell, Philip E. Converse, Warren E. Miller, and Donald Stokes, *The American Voter* (New York: Wiley, 1960).
33. Edmund B. Lambeth, "Perceived Influence of the Press on Energy Policy Making," *Journalism Quarterly* 55 (Spring 1978): 11-18.
34. David Halberstam, *The Powers That Be* (New York: Knopf, 1979), pp. 483-515. See also Michael Arlen, *Living-Room War* (New York: Viking, 1969).
35. Peter Braestrup, *Big Story* (New York: Doubleday Anchor, 1978).
36. "Public Opinion and Public Policy: Reciprocal Influences" (Roundtable at the annual meeting of the Midwest Political Science Association, Chicago, Ill., 1979).
37. The analysis that follows is based on his account in *The Political Impact of Mass Media*, pp. 67-98.
38. Martin Gilbert, *The Roots of Appeasement* (London: Weidenfeld & Nicholson, 1966) and A. J. P. Taylor, *The Origins of the Second World War* (London: Hamish Hamilton, 1961).
39. Seymour-Ure, *The Political Impact of Mass Media*, p. 79.
40. *New York Times*, July 13, 1983.
41. Theodore White, *The Making of the President, 1972* (New York: Bantam, 1973), p. 327.
42. Fred Siebert, Theodore Peterson, and Wilbur Schramm, *Four Theories of the Press* (Urbana: University of Illinois Press, 1963).
43. For a brief account of media history in the United States, see Bernard Roshco, *Newsmaking* (Chicago: University of Chicago Press, 1975), pp. 23-57.
44. James Aronson, *The Press and the Cold War* (Indianapolis: Bobbs-Merrill, 1970), pp. 165-169.
45. A study of North American journalists in the early 1970s showed that only 35 percent believed in neutral reporting. See John Johnstone, Edward Slawski, and William Bowman, *The Newspeople* (Urbana: University of Illinois Press, 1976), pp. 117-123. This figure has been shrinking.
46. See, for example, Bernard Rubin, *Media, Politics, Democracy* (New York: Oxford University Press, 1977) and Erik Barnouw, *The Sponsor: Notes on a Modern Potentate* (New York: Oxford University Press, 1978).
47. Gurevitch and Blumler, "Linkages between the Mass Media and Politics," p. 283.
48. This and many similar incidents are reported in William E. Porter, *Assault on the Media: The Nixon Years* (Ann Arbor: University of Michigan Press, 1976).

Readings

Abel, Elie, ed. *What's News: The Media in American Society.* San Francisco: Institute for Contemporary Studies, 1981.

Edelstein, Alex. *Comparative Communication Research.* Beverly Hills: Sage, 1982.

Graber, Doris A., ed. *Media Power in Politics.* Washington, D.C.: CQ Press, 1984.

Nimmo, Dan, and James E. Combs. *Mediated Political Realities.* New York: Longman, 1983.

Paletz, David L., and Robert M. Entman. *Media Power Politics.* New York: The Free Press, 1981.

Ranney, Austin. *Channels of Power: The Impact of Television on American Politics.* New York: Basic Books, 1983.

Tuchman, Gaye. *Making News: A Study in the Construction of Reality.* New York: Free Press, 1978.

Ownership, Regulation, and Guidance of Media 2

On November 15, 1971, Clay T. Whitehead, director of President Richard Nixon's White House Office of Telecommunications Policy, suggested that public broadcasting be reorganized to give local stations more power. "We stand to gain substantially from an increase in the relative power of local stations," he wrote to the president, who had asked for the reorganization. "They are generally less liberal and more concerned with education than with controversial national affairs. Further, a decentralized system would have far less influence and be far less attractive to social activists." [1] Why was President Nixon eager to reorganize public broadcasting? Why did Whitehead propose to move control from a national corporation to local stations?

We might also ask why Rep. Morris K. Udall on December 14, 1978, told delegates to a conference on media concentration: "I firmly believe we have seen the emergence of media giants with such potential for economic abuse and without redeeming social benefit that the time has come to say, 'Enough. There has to be a limit to gigantism.' " [2]

And why did media critic William Small state flatly, "The control of the news product ... is spread across many people. ... The multiplicity of this responsibility is the greatest protection for the public"? [3]

At the root of these questions lies concern about the immense power available to those who are in charge of supplying the information that reaches political elites and the general public. President Nixon knew that the Corporation for Public Broadcasting, which controlled access to public television, was opposed to his political philosophy and the aims of his administration. This is why he resented its members, why he wanted to remove them and put control into more docile hands. Representative Udall warned that "monopolization of our mass media" will put control of the public information supply into the hands of a few giant business enterprises that could wield it to their own advantage. William Small repeats the traditional American remedy for large and menacing concentrations of power—checks and balances and diversification of control.

33

Concern about control of the media has been a central issue in American politics since colonial days. It has become particularly important in the twentieth century because new technological developments and forms of business concentration have raised major public policy issues. In this chapter we will explore some of these issues and the evidence put forth to support different points of view about what the best public policies are. The pros and cons of public and private control will be weighed, along with arguments for and against big business influence in the media industry. We will also assess the impact of internal and external pressures on the industry, including those arising from the nature of its personnel and from citizen lobby groups. The public policy issues involved in media control are so complex, so intertwined with political predispositions and preferences, that no approach stands out as clearly "best." It therefore is no wonder that attempts to legislate have produced clashes of views, litigation, and little agreement on what the laws should be.

Public, Semipublic, and Private Control and Ownership

Control and ownership of the media takes a number of forms, each of which affects the nature of media output. We have already discussed the authoritarian pattern of total government control and its effects. As we have seen, some government control and ownership of media, particularly radio and television, is common in nonauthoritarian countries as well. But control over content is much looser, and penalties for violations are much lighter.

Public Control

In the United States, outright government ownership and control over media has been comparatively limited. However, it is growing as more and more local governments become involved in owning cable television systems or operating channels on privately owned systems. The federal government is most heavily involved in broadcasting. Abroad, it controls broadcasts to American military posts and owns various types of foreign propaganda outlets. Some of the programs put out by propaganda agencies such as the Voice of America are barred from the domestic airwaves because members of Congress have been reluctant to expose American audiences to deliberate propaganda.

Nearly half of the total available radio frequency space belongs to the federal government, which uses it for radio services supplied by the executive branch. Consequently, a substantial proportion of broadcast space—ranging from 50 percent in the pre-Carter years to 25 percent currently—is outside the control of ordinary regulatory agencies. Another 40 percent of the space is shared between the government and private interests, leaving only 35 percent for the exclusive use of the private sector.[4] Altogether, foreign and domestic federal broadcasts equal the volume of commercial broadcasts produced in the United States.

Semipublic Control

Another control pattern involves media operation by semipublic institutions. The American public broadcasting system is one example. It represents a mixture of public financing and programming, and private operation of radio and television stations. The public broadcasting system was created through the Public Broadcasting Act of 1967 to support educational or public service television stations whose programs do not generally attract large audiences. These stations usually cannot find enough commercial sponsors to pay for their shows.

Roughly one-fourth of American television stations are involved in the public broadcasting system. In 1983 the system encompassed 286 noncommercial television stations and 280 noncommercial FM radio stations linked together as National Public Radio (NPR).[5] The administrative arrangements for the public broadcast system, regulated now under the Public Telecommunications Act of 1978, have been complex. A Corporation for Public Broadcasting (CPB), staffed by political appointees, has handled the general administration, but it has been deliberately kept separate from the programming side of the operation to insulate public broadcasting from political pressures. These arrangements have not been totally successful. Rather than telling public television stations what specific programs they should feature, the corporation has guided programming by paying for some types of programs and refusing to pay for others. This has constituted effective pursestring control by government. A separate Public Broadcasting Service (PBS) has produced television programs. In the field of radio, NPR was created both to produce and distribute programs. Since cost considerations made it impossible to include all noncommercial radio stations, only the largest, best organized ones were included. Roughly 20 percent qualified and are eligible for CPB funding grants and participation in NPR programs.[6]

Because the division of labor in television between program production and distribution did not work out well, the Carter administration, and the *Carnegie Commission Report on the Future of Public Broadcasting*, proposed major organizational changes. These involved splitting the Corporation for Public Broadcasting into separate management and program development units and transforming the Public Broadcasting Service into a triple network, offering three simultaneous program options: continuation of current offerings, regional and local programs, and instructional services. These recommendations were too far-reaching to win approval readily and therefore have not been implemented. They were intended to eliminate barriers to innovative programming, particularly for news and public affairs, and to increase barriers to politically inspired meddling by government.

Private foundations, which are usually backed by big business enterprises and large corporations, have also put money into the public broadcasting system. This has given them, like government, influence over programming. In recent years nearly half of all prime time programs distributed by public broadcasting have involved corporate financing. To further ease the financial woes of public television, the Federal Communications Commission during the Reagan years permitted some public broadcasting stations to accept a limited amount of advertising. The general public also has had an impact on the system through donations and community advisory boards attached to public television. Nevertheless, inadequate financing remains a problem.

Because public television represents a decentralized bevy of local stations, the nature and quality of programming varies widely. Public television is distinguished primarily by an emphasis on experimental programs, cultural offerings like classical music and ballet, academic lectures and documentaries, selected sports broadcasts, and minority-oriented shows. Although public broadcasting has provided a sophisticated alternative to commercial programs, its appeal to the general public—aside from its children's programs—has been small. On an average day or evening only 7 percent of the television audience tunes in to public television or public radio.[7] Even minority groups, for whom a number of public broadcast programs are presumably tailored, prefer the entertainment provided by commercial stations. Because of the limited appeal of public broadcasting and pressures to reduce public expenditures ($145 million in federal funds were allocated for CPB for 1984), there have been demands to disband the system completely and reallocate its frequencies to commercial channels. Some of its programs might then be shown on commercial stations with federal subsidies.[8]

Supporters of the system contend that audience size should not be a criterion in judging its merits. Rather, the system should be viewed as a provider of needed special services that are neglected by commercial television precisely because they lack mass appeal or are commercially unattractive. For instance, a third of public television's programming time has been directed to child audiences. Public broadcasting has also pioneered innovations that have then spread to commercial broadcasting. It played a leading role in developing the system of captions for the hearing-impaired. Public radio and public television also were among the first to move to satellite distribution systems that made it possible to deliver multiple national program services to communities.[9]

Since its inception, and particularly since public funding has increased beyond the minute initial amounts, the public broadcasting system has been subject to considerable political pressures. As mentioned, President Nixon tried to pressure the Public Broadcasting Service to alter its programming. To make the system more responsive to government wishes, some control over local programming was shifted from Washington personnel to the more pliable local managers. As expected, this change led to more traditional programming. Such attempts are evidence that dependence on public funds, even when these funds constitute only one-quarter to one-third of total funding, may mean subservience to government control, despite barriers to direct government influence.

The ultimate fate of public broadcasting currently appears in doubt. As one communication expert has noted, "It is likely that legislative and regulatory provisions regarding public broadcasting will continue to be influenced more substantially by the struggles among much larger political and economic forces than by the most careful analysis of the needs of the enterprise. There is considerable conflict among these external agendas, and to various degrees they all detract from a discussion of how the long-term broader public interest might be realized through public broadcasting." [10]

Private Control

We have considered public ownership of the mass media as well as semipublic control, as exemplified by the Corporation for Public Broadcasting and National Public Radio. Finally, there are many arrangements in which control is essentially in private hands, even though it is exercised subject to the laws and regulations of different governmental agencies. Private control arrangements, discussed in detail in the section on patterns of private ownership later in this chapter, range from individual ownership, where one person owns a newspaper or radio or television station, to ownership by huge corporate conglomerates.

Forms of Control: Pros and Cons

One reason for concern about media control and ownership is expressed in the old adage, "He who pays the piper calls the tune." If the "wrong" social forces assume control of media output, they acquire power to shape politics and public opinion. If you fear government and its policies, you are likely to disapprove of direct operation of the media by government. You will be leery about extensive government regulation of privately operated media. But if you are afraid of the business ethics of private individuals and corporations, you would not want media control in private hands or directly influenced by large corporate enterprises.

Public policy issues raised by the debate over the merits of public versus private ownership of television illustrate the pros and cons. When television is owned and operated by government, programming tends to reflect governmental policies closely, even in democratic countries. Control by government is apt to be single-minded and political, judging from most government-controlled systems throughout the world. France, Israel, and Sweden furnish examples. However, Britain's experiences with operating radio and television through the British Broadcasting Corporation (BBC) show that governments can, if they wish, set up systems where programming is reasonably free from direct political interference.

Big business control over television, if divided among various large corporations, is likely to bring more conflicting interests into play than is true for government control. For instance, a conglomerate heavily involved in export industries will not share the views on tariffs of a conglomerate interested primarily in domestic manufacturing. Even within conglomerates, the interests of various components may clash, thus moderating the stands of the general management and lessening the chances that specific business interests will dominate programming.

Although there is more chance for a spirited debate about appropriate policies in the business setting than in government, the pressures springing from profit considerations are well-nigh irresistible under business control. Media offerings must be structured so that they yield financial returns to the owners of media enterprises. Governments are free from such pressures because they can use tax money to finance whatever programs they deem to be in the public interest. They must consider intragovernment power struggles, but they do not need to concern themselves with the size of their audiences. Private owners do because their income depends on small fees from audiences or on large fees from advertisers and other sponsors. The latter want to attract large numbers of viewers, particularly those in the 18- to 49-year age group who hold the bulk of purchasing power. Mass appeal, rather than any social or cultural concerns, becomes the primary goal.

Given the pros and cons of government and business control, which is the better system? The answer depends on one's assessment of the motivations of the public and private sectors and one's beliefs about the proper role of the media. Today, when distrust of government is high and people view "Big Media" as a counterfoil to "Big Government," private control is the option preferred by most Americans. In terms of programming, the choice of this option means that the bulk of television fare will be geared to simple, emotion-laden programming that attracts large, diverse audiences. It also means shying away from controversial or troublesome issues that may antagonize and deplete media audiences and subsequently diminish advertising revenues.

Although such programming draws the wrath of many people, particularly intellectual elites, one can argue that their disdain constitutes intellectual snobbery. Who is to say that the mass public's tastes are inferior to those of elites? The argument that people would choose educational programs over fluffy entertainment, if they had the chance, also can be refuted easily. Proof is plentiful that the mass public does indeed prefer light entertainment to more serious programs.[11] In print news, for example, magazines featuring sex or violence far outsell journals that treat political and social issues seriously. In fact, scholarly political journals frequently require subsidies to remain in print. Movies featuring sex or violence attract huge crowds willing to pay heavily in time and money to be exposed to heinous crimes and explicit sex. The most popular pay television channels show what is euphemistically called "adult entertainment," while channels devoted to highbrow culture languish and perish.

Related to the concerns about domination of the media by government or private business interests is the fear of undue concentration of power. Diversity of ownership presumably encourages the expression of a great variety of views, which, to many Americans, is the essence of democracy. There must be a wide open marketplace into which ideas and opinions flow freely. But there is no agreement on how diverse ownership must be to ensure this adequate flow of information and the opportunity for freedom of expression. The American public appears to be more concerned about the concentration of media ownership in comparatively few hands than about control of media by private enterprise. Social reformers, on the other hand, are more concerned about business control, claiming that it caters to the lowest levels of taste.

Patterns of Private Ownership

The facts about media control patterns are relatively simple to explain, but there is much disagreement about their consequences. The overarching feature of media control in the United States is that it is predominantly in private hands. This may mean small or big business interests, labor groups, religious or ethnic organizations, or any other type of interest represented in American society.

Business Configurations

The general trend in America toward business combinations is strongly evident in the media business. Of course, there are *independents,* individuals or corporations that run a single media enterprise and nothing else. The small-town publisher who owns one newspaper or radio or television station is an example. However, their numbers are declining, except for the tiniest enterprises.

Multiple owners have become increasingly common. These are individuals or corporations who own media of the same type—several radio stations, several newspapers, or several television stations. Since in the entire United States there are fewer than 2,000 daily newspapers, fewer than 5,000 AM and 4,000 FM radio stations, and fewer than 900 commercial VHF television stations, one might question whether a chain of 20 or 30 of these media ought to be controlled by a single owner.[12] However, this has been the trend.

Even more common than the trend toward multiple owners has been the trend toward *cross-media ownership,* ownership by an individual or corporation of a combination of several media, such as newspapers *and* television stations or newspaper *and* radio stations. This ownership pattern is of most concern when one owner controls a variety of media in the same location. For instance, the same person might own a town's newspaper and television and radio station. One owner would then effectively control all information sources.

A fourth pattern encompasses *conglomerates,* individuals or corporations who own media enterprises along with other types of businesses. Radio Corporation of America (RCA) is an example. Figure 2-1 illustrates the diversity of RCA's interests. Those who are wary about the public-mindedness of large corporations fear that their business interests may color their news policies. If, for instance, there is a soundly based demand to reduce the defense establishment, or to oppose construction of a missile system, the management of a conglomerate such as RCA, which holds many defense contracts, may not examine these questions open-mindedly.

In major urban centers most media are owned by individuals or corporations who fall into the multiple-owner, cross-media, and conglomerate classifications. In Chicago, for instance, this holds true for all major papers and television and radio outlets. The *Chicago Sun-Times* is owned by News America, which also owns a variety of other media in the United States and abroad. The *Chicago Tribune* is owned by the Tribune Company, which owns more than 61 different kinds of companies inside and outside the media field.[13] The major television stations are owned by the national television networks and the Tribune conglomerate.

Similarly, the major radio stations are owned by ABC, CBS, and NBC, the Tribune, Westinghouse, and other conglomerates. The radio stations that remain under single ownership are mostly very small with comparatively weak signals. Nationwide, only 14 percent of all VHF and 32 percent of all UHF radio stations in the 100 largest markets remain under control by independents. For television stations in the 100 largest markets, the figure is 21 percent.[14]

The number of media outlets controlled by individuals or corporations varies widely. In 1982, Cox Broadcasting Corporation owned 12 radio stations, 6 television stations, and 57 cable systems; the New York Times Company owned 30 newspapers, 2 radio stations, 3 television stations, 1 cable outlet, and 12 other types of communication enterprises. The Tribune Company had 8 newspapers, 6 radio stations, 3 television stations, and 1 cable outlet.[15] But one cannot judge the sweep of control exercised by any group merely by looking at the number of its outlets. Three additional factors need to be considered: *market size, competition within the market,* and *prestige of each media institution.*

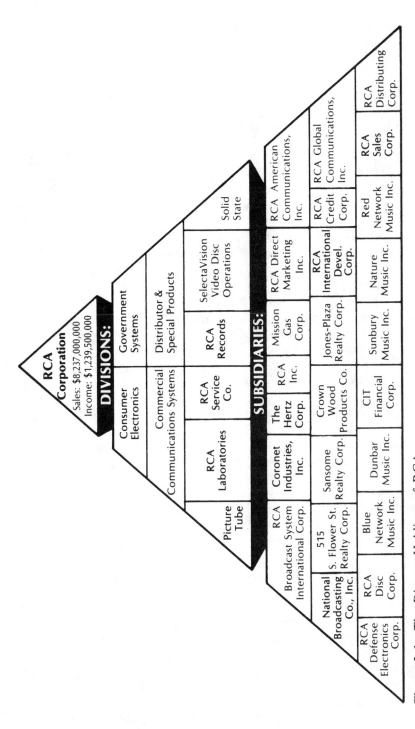

Figure 2-1 The Diverse Holdings of RCA

SOURCE: Standard and Poor, corporation records January 1984, and Dun and Bradstreet, *America's Corporate Families*, 1983.

Market Size

For purposes of assessing mass media performance and regulating electronic media, the country is generally divided into "markets" rather than states or regions. A market is the area in which a particular station or paper attracts a substantial audience. For instance, each television station has a signal that can be clearly received by people living within a certain radius of that station. All of the people within that radius who can receive the signal are considered to be within the market. This means that they can be expected to respond to advertising for products and services provided by program sponsors.

Altogether, there are 400 newspaper markets in the country and 270 broadcast markets. Their size varies widely. In major metropolitan areas such as New York, Chicago, or Los Angeles, a market with a 50-mile radius may have a population of several million people. The same radius for a station in Wyoming might cover more range animals than people.

The Federal Communications Commission, the federal government's watchdog over media enterprises, has taken market size into consideration only partially in its regulations designed to prevent concentration of ownership and ensure that people throughout America are exposed to a wide variety of media voices. These regulations stipulate top limits for the *numbers* of stations that can be under the same ownership.[16] Additional restrictions are imposed on multiple and cross-media ownership within the same market. But there are no limits on the size of audiences that may be within the reach of a particular media owner. If the owner's allowable share of stations would be able to reach every single household in the nation, current FCC rules would not bar such a vast reach.

On July 26, 1984, the FCC limited owners to 12 AM radio stations, 12 FM radio stations, and 12 television stations, any number of which can be very high frequency.[17] This means that in the electronic field, it is possible for an owner to be in 36 different markets, each reaching the homes of millions of people. At present, four out of every five television stations in the 100 most densely populated markets, which serve nearly 90 percent of the nation's households, belong to multiple-owner groups.

For newspapers, there are no limits to the numbers of markets that may be entered. Consequently, newspaper chains can expand at will, up to the limits allowed by antitrust and antimonopoly laws. More than 65 percent of America's daily papers, boasting 73 percent of total circulation, are now controlled by national and regional chains. There are more than 150 such chains, but the majority control fewer than 10 papers. However, the 26 groups (17 percent) that own 10 or more papers control 55 percent of all chain-owned papers. In terms of circulation, Gannett was the leader in 1981 with 3,563,000 papers per day, each reaching several readers. In 1982, it also became the first chain to launch a national daily paper, *USA Today*, which was expected to reach a two million circulation figure within five years. Second in line, behind Gannett, was Knight-Ridder (3,493,000 daily circulation), followed by Newhouse (3,167,000), the Tribune Company (2,854,000), Dow Jones (2,339,000), and the Times Mirror Company (2,316,000).[18] In terms of numbers of papers under its control, Gannett also was first, with 81 papers. Knight-Ridder was fourth with 33 papers, Newhouse eighth with 28 papers, Dow Jones ninth with 21 papers, and the Tribune Company and the Times Mirror Company both trailed with 8 papers.

The 10 largest chains accounted for slightly over one-third of the total daily newspaper circulation in the United States. This means that one-third of the papers read in the United States on any given day transmit news screened by personnel from only 10 large business enterprises. The proportion of circulation controlled by chain-owned papers has been growing over the decades, but not by leaps and bounds. While individual papers within chains generally enjoy editorial page autonomy, they tend to be more uniform in political endorsements than independently owned papers.[19]

Influence is even more concentrated for television. Instead of 10 companies controlling one-third of the market, three huge conglomerate-owned networks—NBC, CBS, and ABC—dominate 38 percent of the television households in the nation. Each network owns five television stations with a combined audience of roughly 47 million households.[20] In addition, the parent companies—RCA, the Columbia Broadcasting System, and the American Broadcasting Company—own other media enterprises such as recording companies, publishing houses, movie theaters, and radio and television equipment and supply companies, as well as such unrelated ventures as real estate firms, car rental companies, food supply houses, and home furnishing manufacturers.[21]

The networks specialize in the production of television and radio programs. Unlike other owners of large numbers of radio and television stations, they are not directly under FCC control because production of programs is not deemed part of the regulated broadcasting business.[22] However, the broadcast stations that each network owns are within the regulatory reach of the FCC, as are the "affiliates"—stations that regularly subscribe to the programs produced by a network.

The 15 network-owned television stations are in the largest media markets. This means New York, Chicago, and Los Angeles for all three networks, supplemented variously by Philadelphia; Washington, D.C.; St. Louis; Detroit; and San Francisco. In addition to controlling programming for its five wholly owned stations, each network also supplies approximately 65 percent of the programming for its affiliates. Even nonaffiliated stations make extensive use of network programs following their initial runs. Because the vast majority of commercial stations are network affiliated (roughly 550 affiliates to 90 independents), most televised information reaching American households is subject to choices and decisions made by network personnel. In addition, networks also control radio outlets domestically as well as radio and television stations abroad. To keep these figures in proper perspective, one must keep in mind that the three networks compete vigorously with each other for public favor and that they do not dominate programming completely for affiliates.

The capstone to the picture of narrowly held control over information outlets is supplied by the wire service companies. A huge share of the news stories appearing in nearly every paper in the country, and featured on television or radio news, comes from the wires of the Associated Press (AP) and United Press International (UPI). The roots of these two organizations go back to 1848, when six New York newspapers formed a cooperative association to share the cost of collecting foreign news. Out of this initial effort grew large organizations that employ reporters scattered throughout the world to collect and report news. News stories and bulletins are then transmitted electronically to subscriber papers and radio and television stations. Ninety-nine percent of news sources in the United States that disseminate news daily are served by either AP, UPI, or both. A handful of other wire services, such as those operated by the *New York Times,* the *Los Angeles Times,* and the *Chicago Tribune,* serve their own papers, along with a more limited clientele of subscribers.

News stories and bulletins supplied by the wire services are either used verbatim or rewritten by their clients. Depending on the resources available to a particular news organization for gathering and writing its own news, the proportion of wire service stories used directly or in rewritten form may vary from less than 10 percent to 80 percent or more of all stories. For many newspapers, a look at the mix of stories carried by wire services on any particular day will accurately foretell the mix of stories carried by the paper.[23] Wire service stories tend to predominate for foreign news and even for national news for smaller papers and stations that cannot afford their own correspondents. This means that a large share of news production in the United States is dominated by two giant news producing companies. However, none of the situations of limited competition that we have discussed involves monopoly controls. Even in one-newspaper towns, there is usually some intermedia competition.

Intramarket Competition

To preserve competition within each market, FCC rules now prohibit multiple and cross-media ownership within the same market. However, this rule does not affect most radio and television combinations existing prior to 1970 or newspaper and broadcast media combinations existing before 1975.

To reduce dominance by the networks, the FCC also mandates that in markets with more than three television or radio broadcast stations at least one of every three stations must be reserved for owners who are not affiliated with any network.

Despite efforts to increase intramarket competition, limited competition (oligopoly) conditions prevail in the majority of markets. Electronic media are generally owned in pairs, limiting the total number of media owners in the community. Intramarket newspaper competition has also become rare. Ninety-eight percent of all American cities have only one daily newspaper.[24] Newspaper competition continues in the largest cities, but their populations constitute less than one-third of the total U.S. population. The birth of a number of suburban dailies in a few major cities has not substantially altered the situation.[25] In addition to a monopoly over local print news, paper owners frequently own a local television or radio station as well. However, the FCC has forced newspapers to relinquish broadcast properties whenever the combination enjoyed a total monopoly within the market.

Prestige Leadership

Another reason for homogeneity in news supply is the general agreement among journalists about the nature of "news" and the elements of good reporting. There are widely accepted standards of professionalism in journalism, just as there are in law or medicine or engineering. As part of this system of norms, certain members and products are widely accepted as models whose influence reaches far beyond their own organization. Critics call this the "jackal syndrome" or "pack journalism." [26] In the political news field, the *New York Times* is the lion whom the jackals follow. In television, Dan Rather or Tom Brokaw are models for the profession. Other news professionals watch what information these sources present, how they present it, and what interpretations they give to it, and they often adjust their presentations accordingly.[27]

Small Business versus Big Business Control

The steady trend toward consolidation in the media industry has left control of information to an increasingly limited number of organizations. Because concentration has not increased sufficiently in most cases to infringe antitrust and antimonopoly laws, these laws have been of little help in halting or reversing concentration.[28] As pointed out in Chapter 3, economic factors are largely responsible for consolidation. Worldwide news gathering and production of television programs are very expensive. Only large, well-financed organizations, which are able to spread the costs over many customers, can provide the type of lavish programming to which the American public has become accustomed.[29]

Even when there is no infringement of antitrust and antimonopoly laws, is it sound public policy to allow the rapid pace of consolidation of media enterprises to continue? Is there a danger that centralized control, besides bringing undesirable uniformity, also will lead to neglect of local needs? [30] Because local governments in the United States are responsible for many vital functions, such as education, health care, land use, and policing, there is a need for local media to cover these services.

The evidence does not support the fear that local coverage has been increasingly neglected. Neither does it support claims that the media giants routinely suppress diversity among the news outlets under their control, squelch antibusiness news, and stress antilabor, pro-Republican, and jingoistic stories. Many important stories are not published, including some that would be poor publicity for big business, but there is no hard evidence that the choices that must be made to cope with an oversupply of news are predominantly dictated by a conservative political orientation.[31] In fact, many prominently featured broadcasts, movies, and magazine and newspaper articles in recent years have carried stories critical of conservative policies in general and of the business community in particular.

The charge that media owners pressure media personnel into supporting the existing political system also is not borne out. American journalists in large organizations, like their colleagues in small, independently owned enterprises, are interested in appealing to their audiences and therefore reflect the values of mainstream American society, regardless of their personal political orientations. All of this does not prove that probusiness bias is nonexistent in the media, but it raises some doubts about its nature and extent.[32]

What about the argument that small, individually owned enterprises would produce better programming, more suited to local needs? One way to test this assertion is to compare the amount of news and other public service programs offered by various types of television stations. Such a comparison shows that, by and large, news and public service programming has been more plentiful on stations owned by big business and by conglomerates than on individually owned stations.[33] Network stations do best of all. Similarly, radio stations and newspapers that have the best public service coverage, as judged by professional journalists, generally are controlled by large business enterprises or are part of a large network.

The contention that individually owned, small enterprises provide poorer public service than their larger, group-owned cousins is subject to some reservations. The measures of public service programming used by the FCC and most media studies are primarily quantitative. They gauge how much broadcasting time is spent on certain kinds of programs, but they do not analyze the quality of the programming. So it is possible that small stations make up in quality what they lack in quantity. However, it is quite plausible that big business control actually does mean qualitatively superior programs. Larger enterprises are able to absorb the losses that are often incurred in the production of documentaries and public service programs. They have more talent and money available to spend on research, investigations, and costly entertainment shows. For example, in the fall of 1983, ABC could present a lengthy documentary on the dangers of nuclear warfare, limiting commercial interruptions, even though it meant losing money. High costs explain why more than 80 percent of television programs produced in the United States in 1981, a fairly typical year, failed to recapture their initial investment.[34]

In 1981, it cost at least $10 million to produce a typical feature film; the average cost of a single episode of "Hill Street Blues" was $865,000. In 1983, NBC News spent $1 million to cover a week-long papal trip to Poland, and ABC spent slightly less. CBS, able to budget only $600,000, could not give live coverage to the Pope's arrival in Poland and, unlike its rival networks, had no special reports about the visit. Television production costs rise by roughly 8 percent annually.

In short, some of the arguments made against big business control of media are exaggerated. So are some of the arguments in favor of control by small enterprises. When FCC rules have forced small stations to spend some of their time on non-network programs, the results generally have been poor. Unable to afford costly original programs produced locally, these stations have filled their non-network hours with cheap canned movies or syndicated quiz or talent shows. The arguments concerning the respective merits of big and small media enterprises cannot be settled definitively until more thorough comparisons of the quality of programs have been made. In the meantime, it is important to recognize that present policies designed to reduce media concentration and encourage local programming rest on questionable assumptions and have failed to meet their objectives.

Curbs on Private Control of the Media

FCC Regulations

Even though control over media offerings is largely in private hands in the United States, the federal government regulates some aspects of media management. The chief control agency is the FCC, a bipartisan body appointed by the president with Senate approval. It was a 7-member body until the summer of 1984, when cost considerations reduced its size to 5 commissioners. In theory, the commission is an independent regulatory body. In practice, congressional purse strings, public and industry pressures, and presidential control over appointment of new members, including naming the chairman, have gravely curtailed its freedom of operation. The commission's independence is also weakened because its rulings can be appealed to the courts and have been overturned on a number of occasions. These often conflicting political pressures from outside the agency, as well as internal political pressures, influence the policy-making process at the FCC. As Erwin G. Krasnow, Lawrence D. Longley and Herbert A. Terry observe in *The Politics of Broadcast Regulation:*

> The broadcast policy-making system is usually modest in its goals, flexible in policy choices, sensitive to feedback, and prone to dealing with immediate problems through steps and options that are only incrementally different from existing policies. . . . A consequence of these characteristics is a reactive rather than an innovative system—sluggish to respond to change in its environment, particularly to technological change that probably will be very rapid in the next decade or so. Clearly there are problems with this kind of policy-making system.[35]

Given the vagueness of its mandate under the Communications Act of 1934—to "serve the public interest, convenience, and necessity"—the FCC has found it difficult to identify the objectives that should guide regulations. It has had to determine what social, economic, and technical goals the industry should achieve. It also has had to deal with conflicts over the adoption of various technologies and with the philosophical issue of regulation versus deregulation. On balance, the FCC's record of setting goals and enforcing its rules has earned it the reputation of being a benign and ineffective watchdog over the public interest at best, and an industry-kept, pressure group dominated lapdog at worst.

The FCC's primary area of responsibility is control over the electronic media. The print media are essentially uncontrolled except for antitrust and monopoly laws that have been used by the Justice Department to curtail print media monopolies. However, economically weak newspapers have been permitted to combine their business and production facilities, free from these restraints, as long as their news and editorial operations remain separate. It remains uncertain to what degree, if any, print media will be subject to electronic media controls when they use electronic transmission means. Teletext is one example; satellite transmission of newspaper copy is another.

FCC control takes four forms: (1) rules limiting the number of stations owned or controlled by a single organization, (2) examination of the goals and performance of stations as part of periodic licensing, (3) rules mandating public service and local interest programs, and (4) rules to guarantee fair treatment to individuals and to protect their rights. While none of these rules deal directly with content, all of them increase the chances that content will be diverse and of civic importance.

Rules Limiting Station Ownership.   As explained earlier, to prevent high concentrations of media ownership and ensure diversity of information sources, the FCC limits the number of stations that television and radio owners may control. It does not limit the number of households that may be within the range of any one group of owners. Consequently, while most media chains reach only a small percentage of the nation's homes, 13 of the largest groups each command an audience in excess of 5 million households, with three to six people each.[36] This gives each owner a chance to dominate the radio or TV information supply of up to 30 million people, nearly one-sixth of the nation.

Since 1970, the FCC has also had a one-to-a-customer rule that prohibits any party from acquiring more than one AM and FM radio station or more than one television station in the same market. This rule now also includes cable systems. The rule has led to greater dispersion of station ownership, but it has not required the breakup of existing groups that violate the one-to-a-customer rule. Similar rules restrict newspaper-television, newspaper-radio, or newspaper-cable combinations. About one-third of all groups with television interests still have newspaper properties. Many of these were combined at the urging of the FCC, which thought at one time that this type of arrangement would lead to better news services. In anticipation of rules forcing the divestiture of properties in the same market, several owners have arranged swaps of properties. For instance, late in 1977 the *Washington Post* and *Detroit News* arranged to exchange television stations so that the *Post* would own a Detroit station and the *News* a Washington station.

Station owners are very eager to retain their licenses because station ownership is usually enormously profitable. In 1980, the average television station was four times more profitable than the average *Fortune* 500 company, and the average network-owned station was six times more profitable.[37] Moreover, no investment is initially required to get a license from the government. The steep costs of acquisition enter the picture only when a station is later resold. In 1983, a Houston television station was sold for $342 million and a Los Angeles television station went for $245 million. Stations in top markets yield millions of dollars in advertising revenues and profits. For instance, Standard and Poor corporation records showed that in 1982, ABC's revenues were $2,341,860,000. Revenues were $2,160,378,000 for CBS and $1,787,429,000 for NBC. Licenses of profitable stations can be sold for a high price since the demand exceeds supply. Many buyers represent chains that are eager to enlarge their reach so that they can guarantee an audience of many million households to their advertisers.

The FCC rarely uses its major power—refusal of license renewal at the end of five years for television and seven years for radio—to lessen ownership concentration. When it did so in 1969, it sent shock waves through the media industry. The case involved a Boston television station, WHDH-TV, which was owned by a local newspaper company that also operated two local radio stations and held a controlling interest in a cable television company. Even though the station had performed well, the FCC awarded the license to a competitor, Boston Broadcasting Inc., controlled by a citizens' group. It was the first time that a license had been granted to a competing applicant on grounds involving the media concentration issue. Sen. John O. Pastore, then chairman of the Senate Communications Subcommittee, expressed fear that license withdrawal might henceforth be used capriciously for political reasons. His efforts finally led to new FCC rules that nearly guarantee license renewal to stations that perform their job satisfactorily.

In the past, the FCC has rarely used its power to encourage new communications media to stimulate increased competition and diversity. It initially discouraged innovations, such as FM broadcasting, VHF and UHF telecasting, and cable television. This attitude has changed in recent years and the commission now encourages new entrants into the marketplace. It has, for instance, fostered direct satellite broadcasting, pay television, and low-power television stations for small markets.

Licensing as Performance Control. What does satisfactory performance entail? Television and radio must "serve the public interest, convenience, and necessity," but beyond requiring broadcasters to ascertain the community needs and interests by talking with community leaders, there are no guides for interpreting these rules. Even this requirement was dropped in June 1984. This leaves the media and the FCC great leeway in determining programming. In applying the rules, the FCC has looked at the mix of programs, the proportion of public service offerings, and the inclusion of programs geared to selected groups. It has not scrutinized the subject matter of broadcasts in detail.

This hands-off attitude has applied both to materials included in programs as well as excluded materials. For instance, the FCC declined a viewer's request to order stations to provide information about Russian and Chinese political and military activities in North Korea. The viewer had argued that the American public needed this information to put reports about U.S. military activities in Southeast Asia into perspective. Similarly, despite concerted public lobbying, the FCC would not order the networks to delay programming unsuitable for children until late evening and reserve the early evening broadcast hours for "family" programs. However, the FCC let it be known that it would not prevent the industry from instituting such a plan on its own. The industry did so for a while, but has now abandoned the effort.

Through its licensing of new outlets, the FCC has tried to ensure that new licensees will meet the information needs of socioeconomic groups different from those already served by existing stations in a given area. When there are several qualified applicants for new broadcasting stations, the FCC is authorized to use a lottery to make the award. But the lottery must be weighted in favor of women, minorities, labor unions, and community organizations that are deemed to be underrepresented in the ownership of telecommunications facilities.[38] Once a license has been granted, the owners hold it for good and may even sell it with little government intervention. For stations that fulfill the requirements of public service broadcasting, do not engage in discriminatory or fraudulent practices, and receive few or no complaints about poor programming, renewal has become automatic.

Since the 1970s, numerous civic groups have entered renewal hearings to protest the type of programming offered or omitted by a particular station. As a result of such pressures, the FCC has reluctantly withdrawn licenses from a few stations over the years. These withdrawals have made broadcasters more careful than in the past to avoid practices that might arouse public opposition.

Compared with regulatory agencies in other countries, even in Western Europe, Canada, and Australia, the FCC controls with a very light hand. It could, if it wished, define what constitutes "programming in the public interest." [39] It could be more rigorous about enforcing its rulings and verifying station performance records at license renewal time. The threat of license withdrawal for rule violations could be used as a much more powerful deterrent to misbehavior and a much stronger lever to guide programming. Part of the problem is that the FCC staff, which numbers around 2,000 people, is much too small to cope with all the duties assigned to the agency. In fact, it is chronically behind schedule, even for routine matters such as its annual reports.

Public Service and Local Programming. The FCC stipulated the minimum time that ought to be devoted to public service programs. Under the 5-5-10 rule, which the FCC shed in 1984, 5 percent of programming should be for local affairs, 5 percent for news and public affairs, and 10 percent for nonentertainment programs. Beyond checking a television station's log to ascertain that it recorded the minimum amount of public service programming (the requirement had already been dropped for commercial radio broadcasts), the FCC did not examine programs labeled "public service." Most stations' logs exceeded the stipulated amount. [40]

To ensure that stations leave some time for programs of interest to local communities, the FCC also requires that one prime time hour between 7 and 11 P.M. be set aside for non-network programs. However, the "Prime Time Access Rule" permits stations to fill all or part of the local programming slot with network news or public affairs programs, documentaries, or children's shows. The intent of the rule thus can be readily circumvented as long as the program choice was made by the local station. Obviously, the rule has not worked very well to promote genuinely local programming. As discussed earlier, most stations find it too costly to produce original programs. When programs are produced cooperatively by a group of stations, as in a recent venture called "PM Magazine," they must meet the needs of every member of the group. The strictly local focus suffers accordingly. [41]

Fair Treatment Rules. The FCC has also made rules about access to the airways for candidates for political office and for people who have been the subject of media attacks. These types of controls are discussed in Chapter 4.

The Decontrol Debate

The difference in treatment between the unregulated print media and the regulated electronic media has become a highly controversial issue in recent years. The argument that broadcast restrictions are justified because access to the airwaves is limited has been contested.[42] In light of new technical developments, such as cable television and communications satellites, the number of broadcasts that can reach the average American has been vastly expanded. Whereas competition has been rising among broadcasters, it has been falling among daily newspapers. The average American is generally limited to one local newspaper. The high cost of starting a paper (and a finite advertising pool) discourage would-be competitors. Some contend, therefore, that television and radio are far more competitive than the unregulated newspaper business, and so, the argument goes, should be freed of all controls.

This type of argument has been quite prominent in the debates surrounding efforts to revise the Communications Act of 1934. In 1978, House Communications Subcommittee Chairman Lionel Van Deerlin of California came up with a plan to remove nearly all the controls under which radio and television stations now operate. Under this plan, FCC rules to ensure fair treatment would be eased so that marketplace competition, rather than government rules, would be the chief regulatory mechanism. Stations would still be expected to provide news, public affairs programs, and locally produced programs throughout the broadcast day, but without specific performance rules.

The potential use of licensing as a tool to force broadcasters to conform to government policies also was to be restricted under the proposed legislation. Cable television was to be completely free from licensing controls at the federal level. Radio licenses were to be granted indefinitely, subject to revocation only for violation of law. Television licenses were to vest indefinitely after 10 years, following two initial five-year licensing terms. New licenses were to be awarded by lottery with a top limit of five radio and five television stations for any group or individual owner and a prohibition against owning more than one of each type of station per market.

Licensees were to pay fees based on the value of advertising accounts in the station's market. This income was intended to support public television, subsidize minority ownership of stations, provide rural telecommunications development, and defray the costs of telecommunications regulations. Public broadcast stations, whose programs would be federally financed, were to be prohibited from accepting any private funding, thus freeing them from all commercial pressures.

Opponents of extensive deregulation argued that the age of electronic plenty was still a far-off vision. It would be many years before cable services became available to the majority of Americans, they contended. Direct broadcast satellites were still in their infancy, as were ample numbers of low power television stations, multipoint distribution systems, and proliferation of video cassettes and discs. More channels available for broadcasting did not automatically mean more diversity, deregulation opponents claimed. It was quite possible that most channels would use the traditional sources of programs for filling air time, as was already happening in cable systems where cable operators drew heavily on materials produced by other broadcasters.[43] Finally, it was argued that the impact of television on public life in America was so profound that the public interest required continued controls.

Foes of the 1978 Van Deerlin plan consolidated their forces behind another bill, introduced by Democratic senator Ernest F. Hollings of South Carolina. Under this bill, radio was to be deregulated, but most of the restrictions then imposed on television were to remain in force. Like the earlier Van Deerlin proposal, the Hollings bill suggested a fee for radio and television licenses for use of the broadcast spectrum.

Vigorously opposed by industry lobbies, public interest groups, and representatives of public television, the 1978 proposals and various subsequent, scaled-down revisions failed. Even though full-scale attempts to rewrite the Communications Act of 1934 are doomed to rough legislative sailing, the trends toward deregulation that they represent have been strong enough to find expression in the rules and regulations issued by the FCC. For instance, radio has been deregulated so that stations can now choose their own programming formats and are no longer required to include a specified proportion of public service programs.[44] Cable television also has been freed from most of the rules imposed by the FCC at an earlier time. And rules barring network acquisition of cable stations have been relaxed.

Control by Industry Associations and Advertiser Pressures

Several other forms of mass media control need to be considered briefly. Among these are *industry lobbies*. Radio and television interests, especially the networks and their affiliated stations, are active lobbyists. Most belong to the National Association of Broadcasters (NAB), a powerful lobby in Washington despite the fact that its members have diverse and often clashing interests. NAB has a membership of nearly 5,500 radio and television stations and a staff of more than 100 people. The networks have additional lobbying agents in Washington. They are in continuous contact with the FCC and are particularly concerned about any efforts made to curb the freedom networks now enjoy in programming.

Besides the NAB, there are a number of other trade associations and publications, such as *Broadcasting* magazine, whose staffs engage in lobbying, often at cross-purposes to each other. For newspapers, the American Newspaper Publishers Association (ANPA) is one of the most prominent. These organizations try to influence appointments to the FCC and guide public policies that affect new technologies that may threaten established systems or practices. For instance, the network lobbies for many years tried to stifle cable television and to acquire control over domestic satellites.

To forestall regulation by outside bodies, the industry also has developed mechanisms for self-control. The NAB has had a radio code since 1929 and a television code since 1952 that set forth rules on program content and form. Both codes have been modernized periodically. The industry-wide codes have now been superseded by individual codes in major broadcast enterprises and codes adopted by the Council of Better Business Bureaus.

The impact of industry-wide codes has always been limited. NAB codes, for example, applied only to NAB member stations that chose to subscribe to them. In 1977, a typical year, 25 percent of all TV stations were not NAB members and nearly one-half of the members did not subscribe to the codes.[45] Penalties for code violations were minimal. The worst penalty was withdrawal of a station's right to list itself as a subscriber to the code. Therefore, the code exerted only a limited amount of moral pressure on the industry. It did serve to blunt demands by pressure groups for government intervention to set and enforce standards.

Somewhat stronger pressures on program content arose in the 1970s from advertisers who actually withdrew their commercials from programs they considered to be obscene or excessively violent. Sears Roebuck was one of the earliest and largest advertisers to do so. Other companies, such as Procter and Gamble, the top television advertiser in the nation, retained consultants to seek out acceptable programs for their advertisements and avoid unacceptable ones. In the wake of such pressures from advertisers, the number of programs featuring violence, particularly during prime time hours, dropped temporarily.

There is deep concern, however, that advertisers, spurred by pressure groups, could become unofficial censors. Unofficial censorship led to the anti-Communist black lists in the 1950s, which resulted in dismissals of performers suspected of having left-wing orientations. In recent years, advertising censorship continues to be extremely influential. General Motors' sponsorship of an Eastertime program on the life of Jesus was cancelled because evangelical groups objected, and there were crippling withdrawals of advertising from a CBS documentary on gun control, opposed by the gun control lobby, and from a series of interviews featuring ex-president Nixon, which aroused the ire of Nixon foes. In 1981, a threat that sponsors of shows featuring sex scenes, profanity, and gratuitous violence would be boycotted was potent enough to affect sponsorship patterns.

Citizen Lobby Control

Various citizen lobbies have also tried to influence broadcasting. Citizen efforts to affect the quality of broadcasting began in earnest in 1966 when the Office of Communication of the United Church of Christ, a public interest lobby, was allowed by the FCC to challenge the renewal of a TV license for a Jackson, Mississippi, station, WLBT-TV, on the grounds that the station had discriminated against black viewers.[46] Blacks then constituted 45 percent of the Jackson population. The challenge failed, but it was the beginning of efforts by many other citizen groups to use growing knowledge about pressure tactics to challenge license renewals.

A major victory was finally won in 1975 when the FCC refused to renew licenses of eight educational television stations in Alabama and failed to grant a construction permit for a ninth station because citizen groups had charged racial discrimination in employment at these stations. There also had been complaints that programs that dealt with affairs of the black community had been unduly excluded.[47] Since then, numerous stations have yielded to citizen pressure for increased minority employment and programming. Yielding to

" ... AND IF ANY STATION SHOWS PROGRAMS NOT APPROVED OF BY THE PTA, THIS SET WILL AUTOMATICALLY SELF-DESTRUCT! "

Reprinted, courtesy of the *Chicago Tribune*

demands or forestalling them seemed easier than facing protracted legal action, regardless of the outcome.

One of the most influential citizen lobby groups was the National Citizens' Committee for Broadcasting (NCCB), headed by former FCC commissioner Nicholas Johnson. A colorful, articulate individual, Johnson became widely known for his sharp attacks on the shallowness of broadcasting and the weakness of government control. His organization, besides watching and criticizing national media policy, also aided local groups in media surveillance activities. The National Citizens' Committee for Broadcasting has now been absorbed into the broadcast media monitoring group of the Ralph Nader consumer protection organization. Other prominent national citizens' lobby groups include Accuracy in Media (AIM), a well-financed conservative media-monitoring organization; the Coalition for Better Television (CBTV), representing fundamentalist religious groups; Action for Children's Television (ACT); the National Black Media Coalition (NBMC); and the National Latino Media Coalition (NLMC).

Despite the substantial impact of such groups on FCC rule making and licensing procedures, the 1980s saw a decline in citizens' lobby efforts at the national level.[48] One reason was the difficulty of sustaining citizen interest over long periods of time; another was lack of financial support and loss of leadership. The broadcast lobby defeated efforts to obtain public funding, and foundation support dried up. Many groups were also discouraged by the fact that substantial victories won in the lower courts were often reversed at higher levels. Some of the energies of citizen groups have been redirected into lobbying at the local level to ensure that the emerging cable system serves the interests of various publics.

In addition to the more than 60 organizations concerned exclusively with media reform, other organizations, such as the Parent Teacher Association, National Organization for Women, and the American Medical Association, have lobbied on a variety of media issues. These include concern about coverage, stereotyping, access to the media and to media employment and ownership, advertising on children's programs, and enforcement of existing program regulations. The groups' tactics include monitoring media content, publicizing their findings, and directly pressuring broadcasters, advertisers, media audiences, and government control agencies. Protest by PTA members led to advertiser pressures, which helped to reduce the number of violent programs shown in the early evening hours. Legal activities range from challenges of license renewals to damage suits for the harmful effects of media content.[49]

It is difficult to assess the precise influence of these organizations, either individually or collectively, because many of their goals overlap with each other and with other forces that affect media policy. It seems defensible to argue, nonetheless, that the causes for which they have worked have prospered over the years and that part of the credit belongs to them. It also seems fair to say that these groups, if they remain active, have a long road to travel before they can match the clout and resources enjoyed by the broadcast lobby and by public officials involved in media control.[50]

Control by Media Personnel

Thus far we have discussed the influence that government, media owners, associations, and audiences have over media output. We now turn to the influence of the people who actually produce the news and entertainment programs: reporters, writers, editors, and producers. They control the specific stories that become news. As William Small puts it: "This is the rubbing point, the actual confrontation with what is happening. It is also the point of greatest influence." [51] What determines their choices and thus shapes the flow of news and entertainment?

We will employ three approaches to answer this question. First, there is *personality theory,* which explains newspeople's professional behavior in terms of personality and social background factors. A second approach is *organization theory.* Because newspeople operate within news production organizations, this approach seeks to explain their behavior by examining organizational pressures and goals. Lastly, one can seek clues to the influence of media personnel in *role theory.* Depending on the professional role conceptions that media personnel adopt, the products will vary. For instance, journalists who take a libertarian approach to the news will behave differently from those who take a social responsibility approach.

Background and Personality Factors. Factors known to influence occupational performance include social background qualities (which may be shared by large groups of people of similar backgrounds) and traits that are idiosyncratic to particular individuals. Examples of background factors are level of education, race, and sex. Their impact on professional orientations is often a matter of heated scientific and political controversy. Idiosyncratic factors, which include artistic tastes, emotional outlook, and intellectual interests, explain why newspeople who come from similar backgrounds will nonetheless choose one story over another or will give a different emphasis to the same news story or entertainment plot. Personality factors and organizational logic intertwine, with the latter setting the broad boundaries of what is acceptable news.

What are some of the personality and background factors that influence the substance and shape of news? To answer this question we shall present data collected by G. Cleveland Wilhoit, David H. Weaver, and Richard G. Gray for their study *The American Journalist.*[52] Other studies support these findings, which are based on telephone interviews with 1,001 randomly selected newspeople in the United States.[53] The sample was divided into two groups—one comprised of journalists working in "prominent" news organizations such as the major networks, big city newspapers, and wire service organizations; the other included newspeople from small towns and relatively little-known news enterprises. The sample was further divided into supervisory (42 percent) and nonsupervisory (58 percent) personnel.

Wilhoit, Weaver, and Gray found that the social profile of newspeople closely resembled the profile of professionals in the United States. Ninety-five percent were white, 66 percent were male, 60 percent were Protestants, and 74 percent had graduated from college. Sixty percent had taken some college-level journalism courses. The vast majority (93 percent) had been brought up in a church and claimed to derive their journalistic ethics from their upbringing (72 percent) or from their job environment (88 percent).

In 1982, the year of the survey, 5 percent of the executives in the prominent media were black, as Table 2-1 indicates. At the staff level, blacks constituted 3 percent. In the less prominent organizations, 2 percent of the executives and 4 percent of the staffers were black. Most of them worked for organizations serving the black community. The ratios for Hispanics were even worse. At a time when blacks, Hispanics, and Asian-Americans constituted nearly 14 percent of the population, they owned less than 1 percent of radio and television stations. This was true despite federal efforts to bring ownership more in line with the demographic composition of the country on the assumption that a heterogeneous country is best served by media reflecting this diversity in their owners and staffs. If it is true that demographically distinct groups are uniquely qualified to assess their own needs, racial, ethnic, and cultural underrepresentation is undesirable.

Likewise, if balanced presentation of information requires that media organizations have women staffers in proportion to their numbers, the media do not measure up, even though conditions have vastly improved in recent years. In the prominent organizations, women made up 28 percent of the executives and 23 percent of the staff. In the nonprominent media, 28 percent of the executives and 41 percent of the staffers were women. Newspeople are also generally younger, more urbanized, and have greater job mobility than the general population.

What effect do demographic characteristics have on the news product? The evidence does not allow us to make definite claims. It also may be debatable whether media organizations need to be a microcosm of the larger society. Nevertheless, there appear to be certain connections between the product and the demographic characteristics of the personnel. For example, most general media emphasize established white middle-class groups and values and neglect minorities and poor people and their concerns. They also stress urban rather than rural affairs and supply a heavy dose of primarily

Table 2-1 Selected Characteristics of Journalists

Characteristics	Prominent Organizations		Nonprominent Organizations	
	Executives (N=58)	Staffers (N=78)	Executives (N=413)	Staffers (N=450)
Female	28%	23%	28%	41%
Black	5	3	2	4
College graduate	64	56	50	58
Democrats	33	51	38	40
Republicans	9	4	22	20
Independents	58	44	38	39
Other	—	1	2	1
Left orientation*	31	33	22	25
Middle roaders	57	55	57	59
Right orientation	12	12	21	17

* Designations are self-identifications and include people claiming the orientation or claiming to lean toward it.

SOURCE: G. Cleveland Wilhoit, David H. Weaver, and Richard G. Gray, *The American Journalist* (Bloomington: Indiana University Press, 1985).

male-dominated sports. These patterns suggest that news output reflects reporters' backgrounds and interests.[54] An alternative explanation is that the patterns cater to the tastes of the kinds of audiences that advertisers find most attractive.

Like other professionals, newspeople have far more formal education than the general population. In the group working for prominent organizations, 64 percent of the executives and 56 percent of the staffers were college graduates, as were 50 percent of the executives and 58 percent of the staffers in the less prominent organizations. Newspeople without college degrees usually had received no professional training as journalists and so were less likely to have been exposed to social responsibility attitudes so prevalent on American college campuses. When asked about their professional goals, they were more likely to stress neutral reporting of facts, rather than interpretation and social advocacy. In fact, education appears to be the single most important factor among background characteristics that affect newspeople's general philosophy of reporting. People with more schooling are likely to be more liberal and more social-responsibility oriented.[55]

Only a very small percentage of the working press in prominent news organizations were Republicans. Among executives, 33 percent were Democrats, 58 percent were Independents, and 9 percent were Republicans. Among the staffers, 51 percent were Democrats, 44 percent were Independents, and 4 percent were Republicans. The rest had other affiliations. Comparable figures for the general population were 44 percent Democrats, 30 percent Indepen-

dents, and 24 percent Republicans.[56] The large numbers who called themselves "Independents" were more likely to lean in a Democratic than a
Republican direction.

These data on party affiliation show that owners of prominent media hire
Democrats and liberal Independents to operate their media properties although they themselves usually share the Republican leanings of the big
business community.[57] The political orientations of the personnel frequently
are reflected in the overall tone of the prominent media. Economic and social
liberalism prevails, as does a preference for an internationalist foreign policy,
caution about military intervention, and some suspicion about the ethics of
established large institutions, particularly Big Business and Big Government.
However, in deference to the greater conservatism of media audiences,
reporters claim that they restrain their liberalism somewhat.[58] Media personnel also take meticulous care to treat the major parties fairly in election
campaign coverage. Such evenhandedness may spring from anticipation of
scrutiny and criticism on that score. Media bias has rarely been investigated in
other subject areas. Hence we do not fully know in which topic areas it may be
a problem.[59]

Among the nonprominent media, the patterns of party affiliation and
political leanings were different and far more representative of political
patterns throughout the United States. Among the executives, 38 percent were
Democrats, 22 percent were Republicans, and 38 percent were Independents.
Among the staffers, 40 percent were Democrats, 40 percent were Independents, and 20 percent were Republicans. This distribution, with its substantially larger share of Republicans, mirrors rural, small-town politics in many
sections of the country. A circular effect seems to be at work: people in small
towns perpetuate their more conservative outlook because their media, taking
their cues from the audience, are comparatively conservative. However, the
strength of Republican influence is less than appears on the surface because
the majority of Independents lean toward the Democrats.

When newspeople were asked about their general political orientations,
23 percent claimed to be left or left-leaning and 19 percent right or right-leaning. Fifty-nine percent saw themselves as middle-of-the-road. Obviously, these
political orientations are muted by organizational pressures. In fact, by
newspeople's evaluation, 30 percent of the media for which they are working
are right or right-leaning, only 12 percent are left or left-leaning, and 57
percent are characterized as middle-of-the-road.[60]

Journalists as a group, like the general public as a whole, apparently have
become more conservative in recent decades. However, these trends are less
noticeable among the leaders of the profession, judging from surveys of media
elites at the *New York Times,* the *Washington Post,* the *Wall Street Journal,*
Time, Newsweek, U.S. News & World Report, the three major networks, and
public television. These media elites, who have a disproportionately large

influence on political elites, remain liberals with cosmopolitan, antibourgeois orientations. Fifty-four percent see themselves as left-of-center, compared with 19 percent who lean to the right. In their judgment, seven out of every eight of their colleagues lean to the left.[61]

On the idiosyncratic level, a person who enters the journalism profession, compared with personnel in other business enterprises, is generally more idealistic and more humanistic and prefers nonroutine work.[62] Social psychologists have discovered that such people tend to be on the left end of the political spectrum, with a sense of mission about reforming the injustices of society. They are opposed to regimentation and fiercely protective of their personal and professional independence.

Reporters' unique life experiences are also important in shaping their views of the world. It matters what personal contacts they are able to make. Washington-based reporters, for instance, may be able to use friendships with well-connected government officials to get important scoops. But, as a result of close personal ties with these officials, they may become captives of their sources' perspectives on the world.

Organizational Factors. The influence of colleagues and setting are important elements for the news fraternity. Every news organization has its own internal power structure, which develops from the interaction of owners, producers, publishers, managing editors, editors, advertisers, news sources, reporters, audiences, and government authorities. In most news organizations today, this power structure tends to be slightly left of middle America and predominantly supportive of the basic tenets of the current political and social system.

When asked how much their editors try to influence their reports and how frequently they are prevented from reporting stories they want to report, three out of four newspeople indicate that explicit directives are rare. However, when top executives do exercise control, it usually involves politically crucial matters. More than half of the reporters concede that higher-ups select story assignments for them, and two-thirds say they are required to submit their stories to editorial scrutiny.[63] Thus the crucial phases of initiation of stories and final acceptance are subject to organizational controls. Although editorial censorship is rare, the possibility exists and serves to tether reporters to organizational norms.

Organizational pressures begin to operate even before the job starts. Most people join news organizations and remain with them only if they share the organization's basic philosophy. To win approval, professional recognition, and advancement, reporters learn very fast which types of stories are acceptable and which are likely to be squelched. They behave accordingly. This is particularly true if morale is high within the organization and if, as is generally the case, newspeople feel that their organization is producing a good product (85 percent do).

Relationships with colleagues in the organization are particularly important within the larger, more prominent news enterprises, where newspeople
receive their main social and professional support from their peers, rather than
from the community at large. The opposite holds true in smaller towns, where
newspeople often interact quite freely with the local power structure and
receive its support.

Which news media do people within the profession consider to be leaders
in their field? A 1971 survey asked newspeople to name the news organizations
that were "the fairest," "most reliable," and "most relied on" by *them*.[64]
Answers to these questions were quite parallel, with high scorers holding
nearly identical ranks in each of the three categories. As Table 2-2 shows, the
New York Times ranked highest when the answers were combined. Among
the top 10, it captured 28 percent of the votes. The *New York Times* was followed by the Associated Press with 19 percent of the votes, the United Press
with 13 percent, the *Washington Post* with 10 percent, the *Wall Street
Journal* with 9 percent, and the *Los Angeles Times* with 5 percent. *Newsweek*
also scored 5 percent and the *Christian Science Monitor* and *Time* magazine
tied at 4 percent. Only one television system, CBS News, appeared among the
top 10 with 3 percent of the votes. Given the brevity and sketchiness of
televised news, it is not surprising that most news professionals prize print
sources more. Ten years later, the ratings had changed little.[65]

All of these highly rated, influential news organizations give ample
coverage to news and usually shy away from sensational treatment. Most of
them have headquarters along the northeastern seaboard. This distribution
supports the frequently heard claim that American journalism is intellectually
dominated by the Eastern press, which accounts for roughly 8 percent of the
news profession. These are the "generative" media that produce the news that
"derivative" media distribute. These are the media staffed by elite journalists
whose social perspectives are left-liberal in contrast to the views characterized
as "middle America." [66] The heavy reliance by newspeople throughout the
country on these Eastern "elite" news sources is one reason why patterns of
American news coverage are broadly similar. Regardless of regional and local
differences that shape social and political views, Americans share most of
their news. This provides a basis for nationwide public opinions that bear, to a
marked degree, the imprint of the pace-setter media.

Despite the substantial evidence of media influence on the public's views,
most newspeople refuse to take responsibility for the impact springing from
their choice of news stories. The self-appointed watchdogs of government and
other social institutions who insist routinely and appropriately that government
and business must take responsibility for the intended and unintended
consequences of their actions, refuse to do the same. Instead, journalists
commonly argue that journalism is a craft, and not a profession, in which the
craftsmen are little more than conveyors of bits of information created by
others for which these others are solely responsible.

Table 2-2 Percentage of Newsmen Voting News Organization "Fairest,"
"Most Reliable," "Most Relied On"*

Organization	Rank	Percent of Vote
New York Times	1	28
Associated Press	2	19
United Press International	3	13
Washington Post	4	10
Wall Street Journal	5	9
Los Angeles Times	6	5
Newsweek	7	5
Christian Science Monitor	8	4
Time	9	4
CBS News	10	3

* Based on votes of 1,349 newspeople.

SOURCE: John Johnstone, Edward Slawski, and William Bowman, *The Newspeople* (Urbana, Ill.: University of Illinois Press, 1976), p. 244.

Role Models. While editors and reporters take many cues about story importance and interpretation from the Eastern elite media, they shape their basic news policies according to their own views about the role that media should play in society. We have already considered the effects of the social responsibility role compared with libertarian stances. News products also vary depending on whether newspeople see themselves largely as objective observers who must present facts and diverse views voiced by others or as interpreters who must supply meanings and evaluations. In the United States and Britain, journalists value the role of "objective" reporter highly. Explicit expressions of reporters' opinions are kept out of news stories and relegated to editorial and feature pages. In France and Germany, by contrast, all news tends to be editorialized.[67]

Obviously, role choices shape news and so are politically significant. They also often lead to conflict among newspeople. This was graphically demonstrated in 1978 when the Australian publisher Rupert Murdoch bought several American publications, including the *New York Post,* the *Village Voice,* the *New West* magazine, and the *New York* magazine. The staffs of these organizations brought suit to stop the sale because they were unhappy about the role model Murdoch had adopted for his other publications—one designed primarily to entertain and shock the public. The courts declined to interfere on the grounds that the choice of a role model is an editorial function.[68] A number of key staff people then resigned, unwilling to work for a publication following a role model they disliked.

Readers who live in the large cities or subscribe to out-of-town papers often can select the types of papers they want. They may choose role models represented by, for example, the *Wall Street Journal,* which tailors its news to the tastes of business people, or the *New York Times,* which emphasizes broad general coverage. Most people, however, cannot pick and choose so easily. They are limited to a single print source and a few radio and television stations, and therefore to the role models represented by these sources.

Summary

In this chapter we have examined the most common types of ownership and control of the media. The national government owns and controls a vast overseas radio and television operation. It exercises partial control over a far-flung system of public television and radio broadcasting that provides an alternative to commercial programming.

For the average American, these government-controlled systems are peripheral, compared with privately owned print and electronic media enterprises. The major political problem in the private sector is concentration of ownership of media and concentrated control over news and entertainment programs. With much of the media output produced and controlled by large business conglomerates, and with limited newspaper competition in most cities, there has been great concern that the American public is ill served. Comparatively few, potentially biased, minds control the news and entertainment supply that shapes public perceptions of political issues.

We have looked into the structure of the media business and into government regulations designed to avert the potential dangers of concentration. We also have tried to evaluate the impact of the existing system on the form and slant of news and entertainment. The limited evidence available suggests that many prevailing views about the interrelation between media structures and functions are wrong. Further research is needed to provide a sounder basis for public policies intended to regulate the media in the public interest.

Going beyond ownership patterns, we have traced other major influences that shape media operations and products. These include the activities of industry lobby groups and citizens' lobbies. They also include the roles played by members of the media establishment. Because media output is influenced by the people who collect information and produce stories, by the organizations that shape their approaches to their tasks, and by the conceptions of media roles that prevail among them, we have examined these facets of the control picture. They show some clearly discernible patterns and trends that are reflected in media products. Still, given the diversity of influences that are brought into play when news and entertainment are produced, we as yet lack the techniques to assess the precise impact that each of these influences has on media content in general, or even on a particular story. In the next chapter we will focus more closely on the actual news production process for additional clues to the mystery of the mix of influences shaping the news.

Notes

1. *New York Times,* February 24, 1979.
2. *New York Times,* December 15, 1978.
3. William Small, *To Kill a Messenger* (New York: Hastings House, 1970) p. 280.
4. Erwin G. Krasnow, Lawrence D. Longley, and Herbert A. Terry, *The Politics of Broadcast Regulation,* 3d ed. (New York: St. Martin's Press, 1982), pp. 23, 74.
5. Standard and Poor, *Industry Surveys,* October 1983; *Congressional Quarterly Weekly Report,* November 26, 1983; Benjamin M. Compaine, Christopher H. Sterling, Thomas Guback, and J. Kendrick Noble, Jr., *Who Owns the Media: Concentration and Ownership in the Mass Communications Industry,* 2d ed. (White Plains, New York: Knowledge Industry Publications, 1982), p. 342.
6. Compaine et al., *Who Owns the Media,* p. 342.
7. The composition of this audience is analyzed in George Comstock, Steven Chaffee, Natan Katzman, Maxwell McCombs, and Donald Roberts, *Television and Human Behavior* (New York: Columbia University Press, 1978), pp. 116-121. Also see Ronald E. Frank and Marshall G. Greenberg, *Audiences for Public Television* (Beverly Hills, Calif.: Sage, 1982).
8. For example, see Bruce M. Owen, *Economics and Freedom of Expression: Media Structure and the First Amendment* (Cambridge, Mass.: Ballinger, 1975).
9. Willard D. Rowland, Jr., "The Federal Regulatory and Policymaking Process," *Journal of Communication* 30 (Summer 1980): 141. Education-based audience differences are discussed in W. Russell Neuman, "Television and American Culture: The Mass Medium and the Pluralist Audience," *Public Opinion Quarterly* 46 (Winter 1982): 478-481.
10. Rowland, "The Federal Regulatory and Policymaking Process," p. 149.
11. A typical rating of the top 20 shows, reported on January 26, 1984, showed 17 light entertainment presentations. The remaining 3 programs were a sports event, the Superbowl, which rated number one; "60 Minutes," the popular investigative journalism series that shares many qualities with popular detective shows; and a popular music awards presentation.
12. Compaine et al., *Who Owns the Media,* pp. 305-306.
13. Besides media holdings, Tribune enterprises encompass the fields of energy, mining, trucking, paper, finance, and a major league baseball team. Dun and Bradstreet, *America's Corporate Families,* 1983.
14. Herbert H. Howard, "An Update on TV Ownership Patterns" *Journalism Quarterly* 60 (Fall 1983): 395-400.
15. Christopher H. Sterling and Timothy R. Haight, *The Mass Media: Aspen Institute Guide to Communication Industry Trends* (New York: Praeger, 1978), pp. 65-70; Dun and Bradstreet, *America's Corporate Families,* 1983.
16. The structure and operations of the FCC are discussed more fully on pp. 47-52.
17. AM (Amplitude Modulation) stations and VHF (Very High Frequency) stations reach the largest audiences. The newer FM (Frequency Modulation) and UHF (Ultra High Frequency) stations use different parts of the airwaves and reach fewer people. Their signals cannot be received by radio and television sets designed only for AM and VHF reception.

18. Compaine et al., *Who Owns the Media*, pp. 39-41.
19. Daniel B. Wackman, Donald M. Gillmor, Cecilie Gaziano, and Everette E. Dennis, "Chain Newspaper Autonomy as Reflected in Presidential Campaign Endorsements," *Journalism Quarterly* 52 (Fall 1975): 411-420.
20. Compaine et al., *Who Owns the Media*, p. 329.
21. ABC interests include motion pictures, advertising, insurance, marketing, and tourism. For CBS, it is production and sale of musical instruments, toys, warehousing, consulting, packaging, and audio-video products. RCA deals in financing, insurance, home furnishings, electronics, foods, and realty.
22. They are subject to operational regulations, however. For instance, one network may not operate a second network covering the same market. The amount of programming that may be produced is also limited.
23. Maxwell E. McCombs and Donald L. Shaw, "Structuring the 'Unseen Environment,'" *Journal of Communication* (Spring 1976): 18-22.
24. Compaine et al., *Who Owns the Media*, pp. 36-37.
25. In 1983, there were 90 professional, business, and special service dailies, 27 foreign language dailies, and 7,497 less-than-daily frequency newspapers in the United States. *IMS '83 Ayer Directory of Publications* (Fort Washington, Pa.: 1983).
26. J. Herbert Altschull, "The Journalist and Instant History: An Example of the Jackal Syndrome," *Journalism Quarterly* 50 (Autumn 1973): 389-396.
27. For example, see J. Herbert Altschull, "Krushchev and the Berlin 'Ultimatum': The Jackal Syndrome and the Cold War," *Journalism Quarterly* 54 (Fall 1977): 545-551.
28. David C. Coulson, "Antitrust Law and the Media: Making the Newspapers Safe for Democracy," *Journalism Quarterly* 57 (Spring 1980): 79-85; Ben H. Bagdikian, "Conglomeration, Concentration, and the Media," *Journal of Communication* 30 (Spring 1980): 59-64; James N. Rosse, "The Decline of Direct Newspaper Competition," *Journal of Communication* 30 (Spring 1980): 65-71.
29. A brief comparison of media systems throughout the world is presented in Jeremy Tunstall, *The Media Are American: Anglo-American Media in the World* (New York: Columbia University Press, 1977). Also see Michael Rice with James A. Cooney, eds., *Reporting U.S.-European Relations: Four Nations, Four Newspapers* (New York: Pergamon, 1982).
30. These issues are discussed at length in Richard Bunce, *Television in the Corporate Interest* (New York: Praeger, 1976); Martin H. Seiden, *Who Controls the Mass Media? Popular Myths and Economic Realities* (New York: Basic Books, 1975); and Walter S. Baer et al., *Concentration of Mass Media Ownership: Assessing the State of Current Knowledge* (Santa Monica, Calif.: Rand Corp., 1974).
31. For a contrary view, see Erik Barnouw, *The Sponsor: Notes on a Modern Potentate* (New York: Oxford University Press, 1978).
32. A scientific appraisal of the effects of owners on media output is presented in Frank Wolf, *Television Programming for News and Public Affairs: A Quantitative Analysis of Networks and Stations* (New York: Praeger, 1972).
33. Michael O. Wirth and James A. Wollert, "Public Interest Program Performance of Multimedia-Owned TV Stations," *Journalism Quarterly* 53 (Summer 1976): 223-230.
34. Don R. Le Duc, "Deregulation and the Dream of Diversity," *Journal of Communication* 32 (Autumn 1982): 174.
35. Krasnow, Longley, and Terry, *The Politics of Broadcast Regulation*, p. 284.
36. Compaine et al., *Who Owns the Media*, p. 329.
37. Ibid., computed from pp. 33 and 397.
38. Krasnow, Longley, and Terry, *The Politics of Broadcast Regulation*, p. 93.

39. Ibid., p. 18.
40. Several contradictory bills have been introduced in Congress to deal with news and public service programming requirements. See *Congressional Quarterly Weekly Report,* January 21, 1984, pp. 93-94.
41. Nancy R. Csaplar, "Local Television: The Limits of Prime-Time Access," *Journal of Communication* 33 (Spring 1983): 124-131.
42. See Owen, *Economics and Freedom of Expression.*
43. Because the practice is so widespread, a Copyright Royalty Tribunal has been set up to administer payments made by cable systems to the owners of the various programs used by cable. Le Duc, "Deregulation and the Dream of Diversity," p. 171.
44. Krasnow, Longley, and Terry, *The Politics of Broadcast Regulation,* p. 23.
45. Joel Persky, "Self Regulation of Broadcasting—Does It Exist?" *Journal of Communication* 27 (Spring 1977): 200-210.
46. *Office of Communication of the United Church of Christ v. FCC,* 359 F. 2d, 994, D.C. Cir., 1966.
47. Krasnow, Longley, and Terry, *The Politics of Broadcast Regulation,* pp. 54-62.
48. Ibid., pp. 56-57.
49. These activities are summarized in Anne W. Branscomb and Maria Savage, "The Broadcast Reform Movement at the Crossroads," *Journal of Communication* 28 (Autumn 1978): 25-34.
50. Forrest P. Chisman, "Public Interest and FCC Policy Making," *Journal of Communication* 27 (Winter 1977): 77-84.
51. Small, *To Kill a Messenger,* p. 280.
52. G. Cleveland Wilhoit, David H. Weaver, and Richard G. Gray, *The American Journalist* (Bloomington: Indiana University Press, 1985.
53. See, for example, the study by S. Robert Lichter and Stanley Rothman, "Media and Business Elites," *Public Opinion* 4 (November 1981): 42-60.
54. Herbert J. Gans, *Deciding What's News: A Study of CBS Evening News, NBC Nightly News, Newsweek and Time* (New York: Pantheon Books, 1979), pp. 39-69, 116-145, 182-213.
55. John Johnstone, Edward J. Slawski, and William T. Bowman, "The Professional Values of American Newsmen,"*Public Opinion Quarterly* 36 (Winter 1972-1973): 522-540.
56. Center for Political Studies, University of Michigan, 1982.
57. For a comparison of the values of media and business elites, see Stanley Rothman and S. Robert Lichter, "Media and Business Elites: Two Classes in Conflict," *The Public Interest* 69 (1982): 111-125.
58. Gans, *Deciding What's News,* pp. 39-69, 182-213.
59. C. Richard Hofstetter, *Bias in the News: Network Television Coverage of the 1972 Election Campaign* (Columbus: Ohio State University Press, 1976), pp. 187-207.
60. Richard G. Gray and G. Cleveland Wilhoit, "Portrait of the U.S. Journalist, 1982-83" (Paper presented at the ASNE convention, Denver, Colorado, 1983), p. 4 Appendix.
61. Lichter and Rothman, *Public Opinion,* pp. 42-60; also Rothman and Lichter, *Public Interest,* p. 43.
62. John Hohenberg, *The Professional Journalist,* 4th ed. (New York: Holt, Rinehart & Winston, 1978) and Idowu Sobowale, "The Social-Psychological Predictors of Commitment to Journalism" (Paper presented at the Midwest Association for Public Opinion Research, Chicago, Illinois, 1978).
63. John Johnstone, Edward Slawski, and William Bowman, *The Newspeople* (Urbana, Ill.: University of Illinois Press, 1976), p. 86. Twenty percent of the

journalists in the Wilhoit, Weaver, and Gray study believe in neutral reporting. However, 49 percent subscribe to both neutral and participant philosophies. These philosophies thus do not appear to be mutually exclusive.

64. Johnstone, Slawski, and Bowman, *The Newspeople,* p. 224.
65. Wilhoit, Weaver, and Gray, *The American Journalist.*
66. Thomas E. Patterson and Ronald P. Abeles, "Mass Communications Research and the 1976 Presidential Election," *Items* 2 (June 1975): 13-18.
67. See, for example, Rice and Cooney, *Reporting U.S.-European Relations.*
68. Charles Whelton, "Getting Bought: Notes from the Overground," *Village Voice,* May 2 1977, p. 51.

Readings

Arnoff, Craig E., ed. *Business and the Media.* Santa Monica, Calif.: Goodyear Publishing, 1979.

Ettema, James S., and D. Charles Whitney, eds. *Individuals in Mass Media Organizations: Creativity and Constraint.* Beverly Hills, Calif.: Sage, 1982.

Krasnow, Erwin G., Lawrence D. Longley, and Herbert A. Terry, *The Politics of Broadcast Regulation.* 3d ed. New York: St. Martin's 1982.

Mosco, Vincent. *Broadcasting in the United States: Innovative Challenge and Organizational Control.* Norwood, N.J.: Ablex, 1979.

Tunstall, Jeremy. *The Media Are America: Anglo-American Media in the World.* New York: Columbia University Press, 1977.

Wilhoit, G. Cleveland, David H. Weaver, and Richard G. Gray, *The American Journalist.* Bloomington: Indiana University Press, 1985.

Wright, John W., ed. *The Commercial Connection: Advertising and the American Mass Media.* New York: Dell Publishing Co., 1979.

Newsmaking and News Reporting   3

On a cold January afternoon during the 1984 presidential campaign, eight major Democratic contenders gathered for a debate at Dartmouth College. The three-hour confrontation was intended to be a test of the intellectual and political strength of each candidate so that Americans would know which man provided the best alternative to incumbent president Ronald Reagan. People in 10 million American households watched the debate, evidence of substantial public interest in the showdown. The wide-ranging debate covered foreign policy in Lebanon and Central America, the nuclear freeze issue and the role of conventional arms, economic issues such as inflation, unemployment, and poverty, and social policies affecting education and health care. Here is how the *Chicago Tribune* highlighted this significant story on its front page the next day:

> Walter Mondale and John Glenn engaged in a short but spirited shouting match Sunday, perhaps to the benefit of one of the other Democratic presidential candidates sharing the stage with them.
>
> Near the end of the year's first debate among all eight Democratic contenders, Glenn started the fireworks by calling Mondale's economic policies "vague gobbledygook of nothing." Glenn said he was "disgusted and tired of all the vague promises" Mondale had made.
>
> By the time Glenn finished claiming that Mondale's proposals would add billions of dollars to the federal budget and that the former vice president was indiscriminate with his campaign promises, Mondale was on his feet, waving his arms and saying, "Point of personal privilege, Mr. Chairman."
>
> Mondale claimed that Glenn was using "voodoo numbers" in his attack and defended his policies, while Glenn, off to his right, muttered that Mondale was using "third-grade arithmetic."
>
> When the candidates finished, former Florida Gov. Reubin Askew said, "You're both right." After the laughter died down, Askew explained, "They're both right in what they had to say about each other." [1]

The exchange between candidates Glenn and Mondale became the *Tribune's* major theme, although it had taken up only a tiny fraction of the three-hour debate, which had been polite and calm. A very brief résumé of the important topics aired in the debate was relegated to back pages in the paper.

Emphasis on trivial aspects of the news, at the expense of more substantive subject matter, is characteristic of televised news as well. Ron Powers, a Pulitzer-Prize-winning television critic, has charged that much of television news is nothing more than show business that does not deserve to be called "journalism." The consequences of this show business approach to news, Powers believes, are ominous.[2] When "news" programs are dominated by trivial chatter to gratify "the audience's surface whims, not supplying its deeper informational needs ..., an insidious hoax is being perpetrated on American viewers.... The hoax is made more insidious by the fact that very few TV news-watchers are aware of what information is *left out* of a newscast in order to make room for the audience-building gimmicks." [3]

What should be news? What can be news? What is news? How do newspeople decide what to publicize? Of all the new developments each day that may be relevant to the lives and interests of audiences, which are *the news* that is likely to be published? Which are likely to be ignored? In the first two chapters we have discussed some of the important factors that have a bearing on these questions. In this chapter we will describe the newsmaking process in detail and suggest the effects it has on the product brought forth by the mass media and the consequences it spells for politics.

Models of the Newsmaking Process

Four models of the newsmaking process have been proposed and debated among scholars: *the mirror model, the professional model, the organizational model,* and the *political model.* Each represents a judgment of what the major forces behind newsmaking are or ought to be, and each has profound consequences for the nature of news and its political impact.

Proponents of the mirror model contend that news is and should be a reflection of reality. Newspeople observe the world around them and report what they see as accurately and objectively as possible. "We don't make the news, we merely report it," proponents of this view claim. The implication is that newspeople are nothing more than a conduit for information produced by others. They reflect whatever comes to their attention; they do not shape it in any way.

Critics of the mirror model charge that this conception of newsmaking is unrealistic. In a vast world in which millions of significant events take place daily, it is impossible for the media to merely reflect events. Choices must be made about the general categories and specific stories to be included. Stories that are chosen inevitably loom larger than life, reshaping the picture that the real world presents. Stories that are omitted leave unrealistic gaps. Even films and photographs distort reality. A small group of demonstrators looks like an invading army when cameras zoom in on them.

In the professional model, newsmaking is viewed as an endeavor of highly skilled professionals who put together an interesting collage of events selected for importance, attractiveness to media audiences, and balance among the various elements of the news offering. For economic reasons, audience appeal is the most important consideration. This, in a sense, makes the audience the ultimate judge of which stories may pass through the gates of editorial scrutiny to publication and which will be refused passage. In a word, media audiences are "gatekeepers." What they accept, thrives. What they reject, languishes or dies.[4]

The organizational model is based on organization theory. Its proponents contend that news selection emerges from the pressures inherent in organizational processes and goals. Pressures springing from interpersonal relations and professional norms within the news organization are important, as are constraints arising from technical news production processes, cost-benefit considerations, profit orientations, and legal regulations such as the Federal Communication Commission's fairness rules.

Finally, the political model rests on the assumption that news everywhere is a product of the ideological biases of individual newspeople, as well as of the pressures of the political environment in which the news organization operates. When the prevailing political environment is capitalist democracy modified by social welfare orientations, as is true in the United States, this ideological base sets the tone for the world view implicit in most fact and fiction stories. Supporters of the prevailing system are pictured as good guys, opponents as bad guys. High-status people and institutions are covered by the media; those outside the dominant system or in low-visibility positions are generally ignored.

None of these models, by itself, can explain the newsmaking process, but rather the process reflects all of them in varying degrees. Because the influences that shape newsmaking are themselves variable, one needs to examine individual newsmaking situations carefully if one wants to account for the factors at work. Organizational pressures, for instance, vary depending on the interactions of people within the organization. Audience tastes change or are differently interpreted. Perceptions of "facts" differ, depending on reporters' dispositions. Moreover, the precise mix of factors that explains newsmaking in any particular instance depends to a large degree on chance factors and on the current demands of a particular news medium.

The Gatekeepers

The gatekeeping operation through which news is selected ordinarily involves relatively few people. They include wire service and other reporters who initially make story choices, editors who assign the stories and accept or reject what is submitted, disc jockeys at radio stations who present five-minute news breaks, and television program executives. On the average newspaper or news weekly, fewer than 25 people are involved. On the three major networks, the combined editorial personnel responsible for choosing news number fewer than 50 people.

As Malcolm Warner has described it for a single network, "*three* men constitute the 'power elite' of the television news policy." A vice president in charge of news lays down the ground rules for general news policy. An executive producer selects news and determines the sequence and length of stories and the amount of film and word coverage to be given to them. The number three person is an associate executive producer who shares the executive producer's workload. Besides these three, news decisions usually involve a Washington bureau chief, a news editor who keeps up with the progress of various stories and edits films and reports, an assignment editor who apportions staff and camera crews to various locations, and one or more writers who provide copy that they or another newscaster will present on the air. In addition, there is usually a copy editor who funnels wire service copy and stories from leading papers and newscasts to the newsroom personnel, reporters who initially collect the stories, and one or more newscasters/commentators who write and rewrite their own copy, or simply read it, and who decide which stories need verbal commentary or merely a raised or lowered eyebrow.[5] Most network personnel are totally unknown to the public, although not to publicity seekers who vie for their attention.[6]

These few people, particularly those who make news choices for nation-wide audiences, have a tremendous amount of political power at their disposal. In public opinion polls that rank the influence of various American institutions on public life, the news media routinely rank high among the top 10. Television personalities such as Walter Cronkite and Dan Rather, along with *Washington Post* publisher Katharine Graham, are listed regularly in the top rank of influential national figures.[7] As we saw in Chapter 1, recent studies have amply demonstrated that news stories influence what issues ordinary people as well as political elites will think about. Of course, media gatekeepers are not entirely free in their story choices. Coverage of certain stories, such as wars, assassinations, and airline hijackings, is almost mandatory. But others can be included or omitted at will; roughly 40 percent of nightly network news is unique to a particular network.[8]

Another important aspect of news selection springs from the fact that newspeople select the sources through whose eyes the public views the world. For example, a study of stories dealing with the controversy about the consequences of marijuana use and the need for laws to protect public health and safety revealed that the views of top scientists specializing in marijuana studies were rarely aired. Reporters gave widest publicity instead to the views of "celebrity" authorities in tangentially related fields and to administrative officials in government agencies such as the National Institute of Mental

Health, the Food and Drug Administration, and the Department of Health and Human Services. The outcome was portrayal of the issue almost exclusively from the perspective of health administrators with scant attention to the views of science specialists. The groups most likely to call press conferences or otherwise interact with reporters thus dominate science news, depriving the public of knowledge about the views of experts.[9] Reporters' choices of sources also have led to one-sided presentations in stories about genetic engineering (recombinant DNA) research, the swine-flu vaccination program, and the development of an artificial heart.[10] Unfortunately, once certain sources have gained recognition as "experts" through media publicity, newspeople tend to use them over and over again, neglecting other, less publicized sources.

A few, highly respected national newscasters also may become extraordinarily influential. By singling out news events for positive or negative commentary, they may sway public and official opinions. When John Chancellor, or Tom Brokaw, or Dan Rather declares that income tax cuts will benefit the rich, or that an American military presence in the Middle East will risk war, popular support for these policies may plunge. A sixty-second verbal barrage on the evening news or a few embarrassing questions can destroy programs, politicians, and the reputations of major organizations. Political leaders fear this media power, but usually they are unable to blunt it or repair the damage. For instance, President Reagan accomplished little when he telephoned anchorman Dan Rather in the middle of a CBS evening news broadcast to ask him to clarify his characterization of the administration's plans for arms sales to Taiwan as a "reversal of policy."[11] Reagan was worried about the possibly destructive impact of Rather's remarks on U.S. relations with China.

Because Americans like to view their media as effective guardians of the public interest, the positive consequences of news story choices are usually greatly emphasized. But negative or questionable consequences are common as well and should not be overlooked. Peter Braestrup, chief of the *Washington Post's* Saigon bureau during the Vietnam War, claims that unwise story choices and interpretations about the conduct of the war misled the public and government officials. After an exhaustive study of news reports and commentary about the 1968 Tet offensive of the North Vietnamese, Braestrup concluded that poor story selections led to policies that changed the course of the war. Walter Cronkite and other commentators had used available information to piece together a picture of defeat for the South Vietnamese and American forces when the information really indicated a defeat for the North Vietnamese. These erroneous interpretations heightened existing antiwar pressures. They contributed to the collapse of public support for the war, produced a speed-up of troop withdrawal, and encouraged President Lyndon B. Johnson's decision to abandon a second-term race.[12] Opinions may differ about the wisdom of the end result, but the great weight that is sometimes given to misleading media interpretations is indisputable.

General Factors in News Selection

What becomes news depends, in part, on the background, training, personality, and professional socialization of news personnel. In the United States this means, by and large, upwardly mobile, well-educated white males whose political views are liberal and who subscribe in ever larger proportions to the tenets of social responsibility journalism (discussed in Chapter 2). It does not generally mean women and minorities, although their numbers have been rising in the wake of affirmative action policies. It most certainly does not mean people who routinely beat the drums for established political leaders or their policies. While most journalists support basic American values, they are a cantankerous breed, forever looking for ways to challenge the wisdom and behavior of the high and mighty political elites.

News personnel operate within the broad political context of their societies in general and their circulation communities in particular. Most of them have internalized these contexts so that they become their frames of reference. After comparing newspaper versions of the same story in different papers, George Gerbner, dean of the Annenberg School of Communications, noted that there is "no fundamentally non-ideological, apolitical, non-partisan news gathering and reporting system." [13] If a reporter's political context demands favorable images of racial minorities, news and entertainment will reflect this outlook most of the time. If adverse criticism of minorities is officially mandated, the same stories used elsewhere to praise minorities will be used to defame them. [14]

News selection also hinges on the intraorganizational norms and professional role conceptions of newspeople. Pressures of internal and external competition influence them as well. Within each news organization, reporters and editors compete for time and space and prominence of position for their stories. News organizations also compete with each other for audience attention, for advertisers, and, in the case of the networks, for affiliates. If one station or network has a very popular program, others often will copy the format and try to place an equally attractive program into a competing time slot to capture its competitor's audiences and advertisers. Likewise, papers may feel compelled to carry stories that they might otherwise ignore, simply because another medium available in the same market has carried the same story. Story choices made by the *Washington Post, New York Times,* or *Christian Science Monitor* become models to be followed.

Political pressures also leave their mark. Media personnel depend on political leaders for much of their information and are therefore subject to

"Good news. The 'Times' has upgraded us from a 'junta' to a 'military government.'"

Drawing by Joe Mirachi; © 1984 The New Yorker Magazine, Inc.

manipulation by these sources. Vulnerability springs from intensive, frequent contacts and the desire to keep relationships cordial. For instance, when journalists were asked about their relationship with Gov. Nelson Rockefeller of New York they agreed that he "co-opted the press in varying degrees and thus avoided ... critical detachment or impassionate analysis." Newspeople admittedly were under his spell because "Rockefeller made himself and state political news interesting to reporters and their editors and then to the public. Not only did he skillfully work to make news ... but he orchestrated it superbly and, whenever he could, tried to accommodate the professional necessities of newswriters." [15] The ability to use the media to political advantage without antagonizing newspeople is the mark of the astute politician. Reporters can rarely resist such pressures for fear of alienating powerful and important news sources.

Economic pressures are even more potent than political pressures in molding news and entertainment. Newspapers and magazines need sufficient income to cover their production costs. Except for publications that are subsidized by individual or group sponsors, they must raise this income from subscription rates, from advertisers, or from a combination of these sources.

Most costs for television and radio programming are covered solely by advertising income. Media offerings must therefore appeal to large numbers of potential customers for the products that advertisers sell. This means that programs and stories must be directed either to general audiences in the prime consumption middle years or to selected special audiences who are key targets for particular advertiser appeals. For instance, toothpaste, laundry detergent, and breakfast cereals are best marketed to the huge nationwide audiences who watch the regular nighttime situation comedies or detective stories, but personal home computers, fancy foreign sports cars, or raft trips down the Amazon are most likely to find customers among a select few. Advertisers for these products are attracted to limited circulation journals such as *National Geographic* or *Psychology Today* or to specialized television documentaries.

Because the bulk of programming is directed to the general public, television and radio must maintain a smooth flow of appealing programs throughout the prime evening hours. Paul Klein, audience research executive at NBC, contends that people watch television as such, rather than specific programs. As long as they are satisfied through "Least-Objectionable Programming" (L.O.P.), they will remain with the station. In fact, viewers select fewer than half of the shows they watch in advance.[16] But if boring or controversial programs come on, a sizeable part of the audience will defect to another station and remain tuned to it for the rest of the evening. Such considerations deter producers from mixing serious audience-losing programs with light entertainment in prime time.

The need to keep audiences watching a particular station even affects the format of news and public service programs. Newscasters are selected for their physical attractiveness. Informal banter is encouraged, and nearly every newscast contains some fascinating bits of trivia or a touching, yet inconsequential, human interest story. Media people occasionally underestimate the tastes of the public for serious presentations, as shown by the popularity of programs such as "A Woman Called Golda," a documentary portraying the life of the Israeli prime minister; "The Winds of War," a dramatization of a novel about World War II; and by the massive attention given to presidential news conferences and addresses. But these are the exceptions rather than the rule. H. L. Mencken was probably right when he said that "nobody ever went broke by underestimating the public's taste." As one station manager reminded his staff somewhat condescendingly:

> Remember that the vast majority of our viewers hold blue-collar jobs. The vast majority of our viewers never went to college. The vast majority of our viewers have never been on an airplane. The vast majority of our viewers have never seen a copy of the *New York Times.* The vast majority of our viewers do not read the same books and magazines that you read . . . in fact, many of them never read anything. . . .[17]

When we say that what is publishable news is a decision that hinges on shared attitudes of newspeople and their audiences, and on the nature of their social and political settings, we are saying that there is no magical quality that makes something "news." What is publishable in one setting for one medium is not necessarily appropriate for another. Newsworthiness of individual stories will vary from country to country, audience to audience, and time to time. Thus in 1903, when Orville and Wilbur Wright invited the press to Kitty Hawk, North Carolina, to cover their attempts to fly an airplane, not a single reporter came. Only seven American newspapers considered the first controlled and sustained flight newsworthy enough to print stories about it, and only two papers gave the feat front-page play. Seventy-six years later, aviation fascinated the public. Flocks of reporters came to see a lone pilot, using human foot power, pedal across the English Channel in a light-weight aircraft called the *Gossamer Albatross*. The story received worldwide press and television coverage.

Criteria for Choosing Specific News Stories

In addition to deciding what, in general, is publishable news, gatekeepers must choose particular news items to include in their mix of offerings. The motto of the *New York Times*, "All the News That's Fit to Print," is an impossible myth; there is far more publishable news available to the paper than it can possibly use. Gatekeepers also must decide how they want to cover each item. For instance, at the height of the Vietnam War, ABC cameramen were ordered to concentrate on bloody battle scenes. This led to a story emphasis on the military. Later on the focus shifted to internal corruption in Vietnam, black-marketeering, political opposition, and the treatment of ex-Viet Cong— a change that prepared the home front for withdrawal of American troops.[18]

The criteria newspeople use in story selection relate to audience appeal rather than to the political significance of the story, its educational value, its broad social purposes, or the newspeople's own political views. This emphasis, and the economic necessities that mandate it, needs to be kept in mind when the totality of media output is evaluated. It explains why the amount and kind of coverage of important issues are not commensurate with their significance in the real world at the time of publication. For instance, a single heinous crime may focus attention on crime stories and lead to an upswing in their number and prominence. This may give the appearance of a crime wave at a time when crime rates actually may be going down. A crystallizing event, such as the surgeon general's report on smoking and health, may call attention to a longstanding problem that has not changed in substance. By the same token, an important event that has received a lot of coverage in the past may be dropped from peak attention because the audience is getting bored, even though the significance of the story may be increasing.[19] A 10-year comparison of media stories with statistics on escalation of the Vietnam War, crime rates, and urban riots revealed that the peak year for riots was 1968; the peak

Table 3-1   Comparative Frequency of Mention of Selected Index Crimes by Chicago Police Official Records and by *Chicago Tribune,* 1976

	Police Crime Mention		Tribune Crime Mention	
	N	*Percent*	*N*	*Percent*
Murder	820	0.2	689	26.2
Rape	1,172	0.4	88	3.4
Robbery	17,489	5.7	283	10.8
Assault	11,001	3.6	152	5.8
Burglary	38,369	12.4	56	2.1
Theft	111,008	36.0	90	3.4
Auto theft	32,421	10.5	19	0.7
Total	212,270	68.8	1,377	52.4

NOTE: *Chicago Tribune* coverage dates start and end one week later than police crime report dates. Police dates are January 8, 1976, to January 5, 1977. *Tribune* data include crimes outside the Chicago area and therefore are not strictly comparable to Chicago police data. All differences between police and media data are significant at the .01 level, using chi square.

SOURCE: Doris A. Graber, *Crime News and the Public* (New York: Praeger, 1980), p. 40.

year for riot stories was 1967. In 1967, the ratio of riots to riot stories was 4 to 1; in 1968, it was 12 to 1. With riots no longer anything "special," the ratio went to 16 to 1 in 1969 and 65 to 1 in 1970.[20] As shown in Table 3-1, the discrepancy between the frequency of a newsworthy event and its coverage is especially well-illustrated by crime news reporting.

Five criteria are used most often for choosing news stories. First, stories must have a *high impact* on readers or listeners. A major earthquake in China would receive less coverage than a minor tremor in California because of its lesser impact on American news audiences. People want to read about things relevant to their own lives. Stories about health hazards, consumer fraud, or a sick youngster's lost dog make more of an impact on people than unfamiliar happenings with which they cannot identify.

The second element of newsworthiness is natural or man-made *violence, conflict, disaster,* or *scandal.* Wars, murders, strikes, earthquakes, accidents, or sex scandals involving prominent people—these are the kinds of things that excite audiences. In fact, inexpensive mass newspapers became viable business ventures in the United States only when the publishers of the *New York Sun* discovered in 1833 that papers filled with breezy crime and sex stories far outsold their more staid competitors. Mass sales permitted sharp price reductions and allowed the "penny-press" to be born.

People also remember violent behavior better than nonviolent fare. For instance, in 1978 the most widely followed and remembered news event in the United States was the murder of 900 members of an American religious sect in Guyana. Ninety-eight percent of the respondents to a Gallup poll knew of the event—a number matched only by those who remembered the attack on

Pearl Harbor in 1941 and those who recalled the dropping of atomic bombs on Hiroshima and Nagasaki in 1945.

A third element in newsworthiness is *familiarity*. News is attractive if it pertains to well-known people or involves familiar situations of concern to many. The public's keen interest in celebrities is demonstrated by the amazing amount of detail that people can retain about the powerful and famous. More than a decade after the assassination of President John F. Kennedy in 1963, most Americans still remember details of the funeral ceremony, as well as where they were when they heard the news. The sense of personal grief and loss lingered, bridging the gap between the average person's private and public worlds. People value the feeling of personal intimacy that comes from knowing details of a famous person's life.[21]

The fourth element in newsworthiness, particularly important for newspapers and local television, is that an event must be *close to home*. This heavy preference for local news rests on the assumption that people are most interested in what happens near them. Local media continue to exist because local events are their exclusive province, free from competition by national television and national print media. In fact, roughly 75 percent of the space in local media is used for local stories.[22] Because national television news must concentrate on matters of interest to viewers throughout the entire country, it cannot depict events close to everyone's home. But because the public receives so much news from Washington and a few major metropolitan areas, these cities and their newsmakers have become familiar to the nation. This, in a sense, makes them "local" events in what media analyst Marshall McLuhan has called the "global village" created by television.

Lastly, news should be *timely* and *novel*. It must be something that has just occurred and is out of the ordinary, either in the sense that it does not happen all the time, like the regular departure of airplanes or the daily opening of grocery stores, or in the sense that it is not part of the lives of ordinary persons.

Among these five basic criteria, *conflict, proximity,* and *timeliness* are most important, judging from a survey of television and newspaper editors who were given 64 fictitious stories by a team of researchers and then asked which they would use and their reasons for using them.[23] Conspicuously absent from their choice criteria was the story's overall significance. Significance does play a part, however, when a major event is involved, such as the outcome of a national election, the death of a well-known leader, or a calamitous natural disaster. Nevertheless, most stories are selected primarily to satisfy the five criteria mentioned earlier.

Gathering the News

Once newspeople agree on what is publishable news, they know where this news is most likely to happen and where to place reporters to gather it.

This has led to the "beat" system. News organizations establish regular listening posts, or beats, in those places where events of interest to the public are most likely to occur. In the United States, the public presumably wants to know about the affairs of major political and social leaders and institutions, about changes in the economy and scientific developments, and about disruptive societal occurrences, such as international wars, domestic strife, or crimes against individuals.

To report such events, news organizations have established beats at the centers of government, where they cover political executives, legislative bodies, court systems, and international organizations. Places where deviant behavior is most apt to be reported, such as police stations and hospitals, are monitored. Fluctuations in economic trends are recorded at stock and commodity markets and at institutions designed to check the pulse of the nation's business. Some beats are functionally defined, such as the "health" or "education" beat. Reporters assigned to them generally cover a wider array of institutions on a less regular schedule than is true of the more usual beats. Stories emanating from the traditional beats at the national level, such as the White House, Congress, the Pentagon, and the Justice Department, have an excellent chance of publication, either because of their intrinsic significance or because reporters stationed there have filed stories that have cost money and effort to produce. In the *New York Times* or *Washington Post,* for instance, stories from regularly covered beats outnumber other stories two to one and capture the bulk of front-page headlines.[24]

All major media tend to monitor the same places. Consequently, news patterns are stable and uniform throughout the country. As Table 3-2 documents, the media are "rivals in conformity."[25] The table is based on daily content analysis of three Chicago newspapers and five nightly news telecasts, two of them local to Chicago. It shows the proportionate frequency of mention of various news topics and presents striking evidence that the same kinds of stories and story types—*although not necessarily identical stories*—are reported by newspapers, local television, and national television. The same holds true for other media appealing to similar clienteles in other cities throughout the country.[26] Predictably, the greatest variations in individual stories occur when local news is covered. Media that feature a lot of stories from their localities therefore will show substantial variations in content in the categories that encompass such stories.

News, as media scholar Leon Sigal has put it, is always "the standardized exceptional."[27] Each day's or week's news is like a familiar play with slight changes in the scenes and dialogue and with frequent replacements in the casts of minor actors, although not major ones. News is exceptional in the sense that it does not portray ordinary events, like eating breakfast or washing clothes or taking the bus to work. It is standardized in the sense that it deals with the same types of topics in familiar ways and produces standardized patterns of news and entertainment throughout the country. Repeated coverage of the same familiar scenes conveys to the public the feeling that all is going according to expectations and that, even when the news is bad, there is little to worry about. It has all happened before and people have managed to cope.

News organizations, including the giants in the business, cannot afford to have full teams of reporters and camera crews dispersed across the country. They generally station teams in only half a dozen cities. Locations are chosen for the availability of good resources in terms of equipment, support staff, and news personnel. They are not selected with an eye to covering all parts of the nation equally well or to providing diverse settings.

Table 3-3 shows the percentage of network news time that was devoted to various regions of the United States, not including Washington, D.C., in broadcasts monitored from 1973 to 1975. The table also contains the percentage of the population that lived in these states in 1970, and an "Attention Index" showing the discrepancy between percentage of total population and percentage of total news about the region. One or two states in each region received the bulk of coverage while the rest were ignored. For instance, 72 percent of the Northeast news time went to New York. Ninety percent of Pacific region time went to California. For the coverage-poor states, only one or two state stories, often trivial ones, were reported. For some, there was no coverage at all, denying their news and their problems a national audience.

Ninety percent of picture coverage comes from the cities in which camera crews are regularly stationed. Besides Washington, where fully 50 percent of all news originates, these generally include New York, Cleveland, Boston, Chicago, and Los Angeles.[28] Of course, special events will be covered anywhere in the country. Every network reported the 1984 Republican presidential nominating convention in Dallas and routinely followed President Reagan's visits to Camp David in the Maryland mountains or to his ranch in California. A sensational murder trial in a small community such as Aspen, Colorado, attracted teams of reporters, as did the crash of a large meteorite in the Alaskan wilds. But these are exceptional happenings. Events in remote sites are more likely to be covered if they are scheduled in advance so that plans can be made to have media crews available.

To a certain extent, prior planning is desirable for more accessible events as well. Time is needed to allocate camera crews, move them into position, and process and edit pictures. The necessity of planning ahead leads to an emphasis on the predictable, such as formal visits by dignitaries, legislative hearings, or executive press conferences. The news output reflects this preference for formally scheduled events. The development of portable camera equipment producing videotapes that can be broadcast with little further processing has eased this problem, however. Today "spot news" can be filmed and broadcast rapidly. This is only one example of the profound impact of technological developments on the content of the news.

Table 3-2 Frequency of Mention of Various Topics in the *Chicago Tribune, Chicago Sun-Times, Daily News*, CBS and NBC Local News, ABC, CBS, NBC National News (in percentages)*

	Chicago Tribune N=33,200	Chicago Sun-Times N=581	Daily News N=506	CBS local N=7,597	NBC local N=12,274	ABC national N=7,962	CBS national N=8,193	NBC national N=7,667
Government/Politics								
Presidency	2.7	0.9	1.8	2.3	1.9	4.5	4.2	4.2
Congress	2.5	4.1	3.0	1.7	1.2	3.7	4.4	4.1
Bureaucracy	1.9	1.9	1.6	1.9	2.0	4.9	4.5	4.4
Foreign affairs	9.8	9.8	10.3	4.6	5.2	16.5	17.1	15.0
Domestic policy	12.6	13.1	13.8	5.6	4.5	6.6	7.6	7.4
Elections	7.6	10.0	11.5	6.8	6.2	15.7	15.2	15.2
State government	1.8	1.4	0.8	2.7	2.2	0.6	0.9	0.8
City government	1.9	0.3	1.2	4.3	3.2	0.7	0.5	0.5
Miscellaneous	0.6	0.7	0.0	0.9	1.0	0.7	0.6	0.4
	41.4	42.2	44.0	30.9	27.4	53.9	55.0	52.0
Crime & Justice								
Police/security	4.7	7.2	7.7	3.3	3.1	1.5	1.6	1.5
Judiciary	5.7	5.0	4.0	4.6	4.7	3.6	3.4	3.7
Corruption/terrorism	4.0	5.7	5.5	4.0	3.3	3.1	3.3	3.1
Individual crime	7.5	10.2	9.5	7.8	8.5	4.1	4.0	4.6
	21.9	28.1	26.7	19.7	19.6	12.3	12.3	12.9

Economic/Social Issues

State of economy	2.4	2.1	2.4	1.1	1.0	1.7	1.7	1.9
Business/labor	5.9	6.4	4.9	6.6	10.2	7.8	6.8	6.8
Minorities/women	2.7	2.9	3.8	2.1	2.0	2.7	2.9	2.4
Environment/ transportation	3.2	4.1	1.8	9.1	9.1	3.5	4.0	4.0
Disaster/accident	2.2	1.9	2.4	3.8	5.0	3.2	2.8	3.3
Health/medicine	2.5	2.4	1.6	3.3	4.6	2.1	2.8	3.2
Education/media/ religion	4.4	2.2	2.8	4.0	4.0	2.8	3.0	2.5
Leadership style	1.2	1.5	1.4	0.2	0.2	0.8	0.7	0.6
Miscellaneous	1.7	0.7	0.6	1.3	1.2	1.8	1.4	1.5
	26.2	24.2	21.7	31.5	37.3	26.4	25.1	26.2

*Human Interest/Hobbies***

General human interest	2.9	1.9	3.4	6.0	6.8	1.8	1.8	2.3
Celebrities	3.6	1.4	2.0	2.2	2.1	1.4	1.5	1.7
Political gossip	1.6	0.5	1.2	1.4	1.4	1.4	1.1	1.4
Sports/entertainment	2.6	1.7	1.4	8.3	5.3	2.9	2.1	3.4
	10.7	5.5	8.0	17.9	15.6	7.5	6.5	8.8

* *Sun-Times* and *Daily News* data are based on sample coding of one constructed week for each paper. NBC local news is based on full hour broadcast, others on half hour. National news data are based on nine months of coding, April-December 1976.
** When stories of this type appeared in special sections (for example, People, Leisure, Food, etc.) they were not coded individually. Rather, the entire section was counted as one story. This depresses the Human Interest/Hobbies story count.

Table 3-3 Network News Time Devoted to Regions of the United States*

Region	% of news time	% of population	Attention index**
Midwest	18.5	25	−6.5
Northeast	24.5	21	+3.5
South	12.2	12	+0.2
Southwest	5.8	10	−4.2
Pacific	21.4	13	+8.4
Middle Atlantic	4.8	7	−2.2
New England	6.5	6	+0.5
Mountain	3.1	4	−0.9
Plains	3.2	2	+1.2
Total	100	100	
Total news time (in minutes)	2,301		

* Excludes Washington, D.C., news and stories not limited to a particular location.
** This index shows the discrepancy between percentage of total population and percentage of total news devoted to the region.

SOURCE: Reprinted from "Geographic Bias in National TV News" by Joseph R. Dominick in *Journal of Communication* 27 (Fall 1977): p. 96. © 1977 by Annenberg School of Communications.

News Production Constraints

Many of the factors that affect news story selection spring from the requirement that news be processed rapidly and published as quickly as possible. Time pressures explain why the press reports so many pseudo-events—events created for easy reporting by the media or for the media. In television news, pseudo-events constitute almost 70 percent of all stories.[29] For example, politicians frequently plan pictorially attractive happenings, like bridge dedications or county fair visits, at just the right time and place to accommodate newspaper or broadcast deadlines. When newspeople need a quick story about a revolution in Central America or ways to cope with youth gang activities, they arrange interviews with familiar leaders, whose remarks, knowledgeable or not, then instantly become *the* Central America or *the* youth gang problem story.

Once stories reach print and electronic media news offices, selections must be made extremely rapidly. Ben Bagdikian, a former *Washington Post* editor who studied gatekeeping at eight newspapers, found that stories usually are sifted and chosen on the spot. They are not assembled and carefully examined for their overall policy effects. Here is how Bagdikian described the scene in a typical newspaper office:

The news editor arrives at 6 A.M. to find an overnight accumulation of fifty thousand words, most of it regional and national news from the wire services, some of it from the paper's reporters in outlying bureaus, who transmitted it by teletype the night before.

In addition to making decisions on incoming wire stories, this particular news editor makes decisions on local stories handed him by the city editor and the state editor. He also is handed the output of two wire-photo machines that during the day produce ninety-six photographs from which he selects sixteen.[30]

In the course of the day, the news editor chooses additional items for publication by scanning wire service as well as locally originated news. The editor examines about 110,000 words of wire news daily , equivalent to the size of an average book, and 5,000 words of news from the local staff. The editor also must select photographs, consult with city editors about story assignments, and decide what to place on page one in light of the changing news scene.

Bagdikian reports that the typical newspaper gatekeeper was able to scan and discard stories in one to two seconds. His study of the reasons stories are rejected revealed that only 2.5 percent were turned down because the editor did not care for the substance of the story or objected to its ideological slant. Twenty-six percent were rejected because of lack of space. The remaining 71.5 percent were rejected because they were judged to lack some or all of the elements of newsworthiness discussed earlier.

Rejection rates varied for different types of stories. Overall, 89 percent of all wire service news was rejected. So were 93 percent of all human interest stories, 92 percent of crime news, 74 percent of farm news, and 69 percent of science news. Even though much of the human interest information was rejected, it still constituted the largest single news category—23 percent of total news. By contrast, science news took 5 percent of total space and farm stories 6 percent.[31]

Bagdikian reports that for stories that were accepted, fast gatekeepers could skim through the entire story and even make minor changes in only four seconds. The average reading time was six seconds. At such speeds, judgments are almost instantaneous, with no time for reflection or weighing of alternatives among the total batch of news available for the day. Stories are judged more by how they balance previously selected stories than by their intrinsic importance. If the gatekeeper has ideological preferences, these are served instinctively, if at all, rather than deliberately.

Because the flood tide of information continues throughout the day, the gatekeeper accepts very few stories in the early hours of each shift. Closer to the deadline, when news has to go to press, the pace of story selection quickens. When the deadline arrives, a news story must be extraordinarily important to replace stories that have already been accepted or are already in press. Ordinarily, stories left over at the end of the day will not be used on the next day because by then they will be old, and newer stories will have replaced them. This means that a late-breaking story, unless it is very unusual or significant, has little chance for publication. What becomes news thus depends heavily on *when* it happens. West Coast afternoon stories are frequent casualties because they are generally too late to be incorporated into the network evening news, which is run on an East Coast schedule.

Public relations managers know the deadlines of important publications, such as the *New York Times, Wall Street Journal, Time, Newsweek,* and the network television news. They time events and news releases so that stories arrive in gatekeepers' offices precisely when needed. Thus the news production process, although it has its own irresistible momentum, is not immune to conscious control. News for which a minimum of publicity is desired is announced just past the deadlines, preferably on weekends, when few newscasts are scheduled. For instance, the Nixon administration fired the special Watergate prosecutor on the weekend in what became known as the "Saturday night massacre." In that case, the hope that the timing would minimize publicity was only partially fulfilled.

Publications with less frequent deadlines, such as weekly news magazines, have a lot more time to decide what to publish. News magazine staffs also have more resources than most daily papers to dig out background information and present stories in a context that helps readers to evaluate them. These magazines are therefore ideal for people who want quick, interpretive news that concentrates on a limited number of events.

Televison news staffs have even less time than newspapers for investigating most stories that they are reporting and far less time to provide background and interpretation for the news they present. When background or investigative stories do appear on television, they frequently originate in the print media. However, there are a number of highly popular investigative and interpretive television programs, such as CBS's "Sixty Minutes." Besides inadequate time for *preparing* stories, radio and television news also have the problem of insufficient time for *presenting* them. The average news story takes about a minute. Thus, it is not surprising that it is little more than an announcement that an event has taken place. Complex stories may have to be scratched entirely if they cannot be condensed into a brief enough format.

Print media have space problems as well, but they are less severe than time constraints faced by electronic media. The average newspaper reserves 55 percent of its space for advertising. Out of its 45 percent "newshole," generally 27 percent goes for straight news stories, the remainder for features of various types. Some papers reserve a standardized amount of space for news; others expand or contract the newshole depending on the flow of news and advertising. But whether the paper is a slim eight-page version or five to ten times that size, there is rarely enough space to cover stories as fully as reporters and editors would like.[32]

Besides the need to condense a news story into a brief capsule, television reporters also want stories with visual appeal. Unfortunately, what is visually appealing may not be important. For instance, during political campaigns, motorcades, rallies, hecklers, and cheering crowds make good pictures. Candidates delivering speeches are visually dull by comparison. Television cameras therefore concentrate on the colorful scenes rather than on the speechmaker. If these happenings are flashed on the screen in competition with the speech, they often distract from what the candidate is saying. Events that make dull pictures may have to be omitted.

Because picture production is expensive for television as well as print, picture stories selected early are likely to be kept even if more important stories break later. Financial considerations, as well as personnel reasons, also favor information originated by the staff. News organizations prefer stories by people already on their payroll to wire service stories by unknown reporters or stories from outside sources for which additional fees must be paid. News executives also have personal relationships with their own staffs and do not want to disappoint them by rejecting their stories.

Effects of Gatekeeping

The gatekeeping influences that we have been discussing give a distinctive character to the American news product considered as a whole. There are many exceptions, of course, when one looks at individual news outlets or at individual programs or specific news and feature stories. There are also noticeable differences in emphasis as one moves from the conservative rural press, to more moderate papers in small and middle-size towns, to the liberal press in major metropolitan centers. For instance, a study of the women's page/lifestyle section of a representative sample of American daily newspapers showed that serious political news constituted 20 percent of the coverage of such news in rural papers and nearly double that amount in papers in metropolitan areas.[33] Despite these variations, several attributes of American news stand out. We shall discuss them under four headings: *people in the news, actions in the news, general characteristics of the news,* and *support for the establishment.*[34]

People in the News

The gatekeeping process winnows the group of newsworthy people down to a very small cadre of familiar and unfamiliar figures. Herbert Gans's study of news magazines and network television news showed that familiar people appear in three out of every four news stories. Most are political figures. Fewer than 50 politicians are in the news regularly. The list is headed by the incumbent president. Other people receive coverage primarily for unusual or important activities, but incumbent presidents are covered regardless of what they do. News about presidential candidates ranks next. In presidential election years, it often outnumbers stories about the president.

A third well-covered group consists of major federal officials, such as political leaders in the House and Senate, the heads of major congressional committees, and cabinet members in active departments. In the post-Watergate period, major White House staff members have joined the circle. The Supreme Court is in the news only intermittently, generally when important decisions are announced. Agency heads rarely make the news except when they announce new policies or feud with the president. Finally, some people are regularly in the news regardless of what their current political status may be, merely because their names are household words. Members of the Kennedy clan are a prime example.

Below the federal level, the activities of governors and mayors from the larger states and cities are newsworthy if they involve major public policy issues or if the incumbent is unusual because of race, sex, or prior newsworthy activities. Notorious individuals also receive frequent news attention if their deeds have involved well-known people. Presidential assassins, mass murderers, or members of extremist political groups, such as the Palestine Liberation Organization (PLO), fall into this category. Ample coverage also goes to targets of congressional investigations and defendants in political trials, such as the Watergate defendants or key figures in the Koreagate scandal, in which several legislators were accused of trading their influence in return for money and favors from the South Korean government.

Many powerful people are rarely covered in the news. Among the excluded are economic leaders (such as the heads of large corporations), financiers, and leaders of organized business (such as the National Association of Manufacturers or the U.S. Chamber of Commerce). A few colorful labor leaders, such as George Meany and James Hoffa, have been news figures, but this was probably due more to their personalities than to their jobs. Important military leaders also remain obscure except on rare occasions when they are involved in major military operations. Political party leaders surface during elections but remain in the shadows at other times. Political protest leaders, such as civil rights figures or the heads of minority parties, or consumer activists, such as Ralph Nader, come and go from the news scene, depending on the amount of visible conflict they are able to produce. The same holds true for the heads of voluntary associations, such as antiabortion groups or church leaders.

Most ordinary people never make the news because their activities must be unusual to come to the attention of newspeople. Ordinary people have their best chance for publicity if they protest or riot or strike, particularly against the government. The next best chance goes to victims of disasters, personal tragedy, and crime, and to the actors who brought about their plight. The grisly nature of crimes, disasters, or other human tragedies, rather than the identity of the people involved, determines their newsworthiness. Ordinary people also make the news if their life styles or social activities become highly unusual or if their behavior diverges greatly from the norm for persons of their age, sex, and status. Finally, ordinary people make the news in large numbers as nameless members of groups whose statistical profile is reported or whose opinions have been tapped through polls or elections.

Action in the News

Few types of activities are likely candidates for news coverage. The list is headed by conflicts and disagreements among government officials, particularly friction between the president and Congress. Many of these conflicts concern economic policies. Other types of conflict action that are routinely reported include violent and nonviolent protest (much of it about government activities), crime, scandals and investigations, and impending or actual disasters. When the nation is involved in war, a large number of war stories are reported.

Stories about government policies also provide frequent story material. These generally deal with policymaking rather than policy operation. Government personnel changes, including campaigns for office, are another news focus. Finally, two aspects of normal social change receive substantial coverage from time to time: major national ceremonies, like inaugurations or moon landings, and important social, cultural or technological developments, like the participation of women in the space exploration program or advances in the fight against cancer.

General Characteristics of the News

The criteria for newsworthiness and the constraints on news production that we have described also contribute in a general way to the shape of American news and to its impact, regardless of the particular subject under discussion. Three features stand out. American news tends to stress novel occurrences and entertaining events, familiar people and situations, and lastly, conflict and violence. As a result, social problems are often neglected.

Novelty and Entertainment. The demand for stories that are new and exciting often means that sensational and novel occurrences drown out news of more lasting significance. For instance, eight times as much space and time is devoted to sports news as it is to news about local community problems such as school finance or housing.[35] High drama certainly drowned out other news of importance in March 1977, when the media focused on the terrorist activities of a Moslem sect in Washington, D.C. A remarkable presidential press conference occurring at the same time was practically ignored. In this conference President Jimmy Carter proposed a $1.5 billion youth employment bill, a Youth Conservation Corps, a new approach to peace in the Middle East, new procedures for the withdrawal of American troops from South Korea, and a new atomic weapons agreement with the Soviet Union. As James Reston commented in the *New York Times,* "It is hard to remember any time since the last World War when an American President made so much news in a press conference or anywhere else . . . but nobody could hear him for the noise and the headlines about the terrorists."[36] Similarly, in 1984, blow-by-blow accounts of the release of an American navy lieutenant from captivity in Syria all but obliterated news about Sen. Walter F. Mondale's official entry into the presidential contest. A foreign policy speech by him was also ignored.

The emphasis on entertainment also leads to stress on trivial aspects of serious stories. Complex issues are presented as simple human interest dramas. Inflation is likely to become a story about Jane Brown, typical American housewife, who is forced to pay high prices in the supermarket, or John Doe, working class homeowner, who is struggling to pay his mortgage. Such personalized stories do not explain the larger issues involved in inflation. But, judging from attention patterns, they are far more likely to be noticed than learned discussions by economic experts.

The search for novelty and entertainment also produces news that focuses on the present and ignores the past and future. The here and now is what counts. This leads to news that tends to be fragmented and discontinuous. It is aired as it is received, so that the background needed to place a story into its context is often missing. Clarifications are usually buried in the back pages. On television, snippets of news may be presented together to drive home an easily understandable theme, such as "Washington is in a mess" or "the inner city is decaying." The theme may come through, but the individual news item is blurred.

Fragmentation makes it difficult for audiences to piece together a coherent narrative of events. More background and interpretation would help, but it would also increase the chance for subjective interpretation by news commentators. A few papers, such as the *Christian Science Monitor,* do cover fewer stories in more detail. People who carefully read *Monitor* stories acquire a better background for understanding social issues, but they miss out on other news for which there is no space. They may also get skewed information if newspeople misinterpret the significance of complex events.

Familiarity and Similarity. The demand for stories that involve familiar people and events close to home also has a number of consequences for the shape of the news. One of these is the circular nature of such coverage;

familiar people and situations are covered minutely, which makes them even more familiar and therefore even more worthy of publicity. The reverse is also true. During the 1976 presidential election campaign, Sens. Hubert H. Humphrey and Edward M. Kennedy, who were frequently in the news, became candidates in many people's minds even though they never entered the race officially. Sen. Lloyd Bentsen and Fred Harris, official entrants, received less media attention and remained unfamiliar. They were forced to abandon the quest.

Familiar people may become objects of prying curiosity. The details of their private lives may take up an inordinately large amount of time and space in the mass media. This happened when Mayor Richard Daley of Chicago died in 1976. The media provided a minute-by-minute account of his last moments. The public was kept informed about his blood pressure, the emergency medical procedures being performed, and the manner in which his family was told about his death. For several days, much of the news in the Chicago area was taken up by these minutiae, to the exclusion of more salient stories. The important story, obscured initially, was that the mayor's death had launched a major power struggle for control of Chicago's politics.

Another significant consequence of the criteria of newsworthiness is that American news is very parochial compared with news in other countries. This neglect of news about foreign people and cultures leaves Americans deficient in their understanding of international affairs, a subject explored more fully in Chapter 10. Again, the pattern is circular. For instance, if events in Afghanistan are rarely covered, stories about Afghanistan will require a lot more background to make sense to Americans. This may take more time and space than the media are willing to give to any story, except during a crisis. Therefore, foreign coverage in American media is usually about people to whom Americans feel culturally close and whose policies are somewhat familiar, like the English, the Canadians, and people of Northern European countries. Foreign news concentrates on situations that are easy to report, which often means violent events like revolutions, major disasters, and the like. This type of coverage conveys the impression that most foreign countries are always in serious disarray.

Conflict and Violence. The heavy news emphasis on conflict and bad news, most prevalent in big city media, has three major consequences. The first and perhaps most far-reaching consequence is the dangerous distortion of reality that emphasis on negative news events may create. This is particularly true with crime coverage. Media stories rarely mention that many neighborhoods are relatively free of crime. Instead they convey the impression to many people that the whole city, and particularly inner city areas, are dangerous jungles. This impression may become a self-fulfilling prophecy. In the wake of crime publicity many people avoid the inner city. They even shun comparatively safe neighborhoods after a single, highly publicized crime. The empty streets then make crime more likely.

Studies of people's perceptions of the incidence of crime and the actual chances that they will be attacked indicate that their fears are geared to media realities. In the world of television drama, the average character has a 30 to 64 percent chance of being involved in violence; in the real world, the average person's chances of becoming a crime victim is a small fraction of that number.[37] Similarly, heavy media emphasis on air crashes and scant coverage of automobile accidents have left the public with distorted notions of the relative dangers of these modes of transportation.

A second result of the emphasis on news involving conflict is the perception of many people that violence is an acceptable way to settle disputes. Some argue that by bringing conflict into the open, media may promote its resolution, but clearly they may also make it worse.[38] This often happens when media dramatize a conflict by highlighting its more sensational aspects and oversimplifying it, picturing it as a confrontation between two clearly defined sides. It is the hawks against the doves in war, the victors or losers in a legislative battle, the Communists versus anti-Communists in a struggle abroad. Even when a situation is not actually confrontational, the media may present it as a battle and call it a clash or a feud or a fight. Yet divergent viewpoints expressed by parties, or unions, or members of a legislature may not mean that they are locked in battle.

Average people, when presented with clashing claims, often feel confused and find it extremely difficult to determine where the truth lies. They have neither the facts nor the time to explore the issues. They are also left with the disquieting sense that conflict and turmoil reign nearly everywhere. This impression is likely to affect people's feeling toward society in general. They may contract "videomalaise," characterized by lack of trust, cynicism, and fear.[39] Many social scientists believe that such feelings undermine support for government, destroy faith in leaders, produce political apathy, and generally sap the vigor of the democratic process.

Finally, the popularity of violence stories has encouraged groups who seek media coverage to behave violently or sensationally to enhance their chances for publicity. One example comes from a lengthy strike by a union of Chicano workers against a Texas furniture company. During the first year, the nonviolent strike received very little publicity. To attract media coverage the leaders decided to stage noisy marches to the Capitol on the first and second anniversaries of the strike. Moderate language in appeals to the company and city authorities were replaced by fighting words. City councilors were called "rednecks" and challenged to stop the union's marches. These inflammatory accusations created a confrontation, brought city police to the scene, and heightened tensions. Celebrities, including Sens. Edmund Muskie of Maine and Birch Bayh of Indiana and farm labor leader Cesar Chavez, were invited to enter the fray. These maneuvers broke the year-long dearth of media coverage. No longer peaceful, the strike finally received ample publicity. In turn, this created sufficient pressure to bring about a settlement.[40]

A taste for conflict is not the same as a taste for controversy, however. Fear of offending members of the mass audience, wire service subscribers, or affiliated station managers often keeps stories dealing with controversial subjects like abortion or corruption in the church out of the media, especially network television. If those stories are reported, the treatment is ordinarily bland, carefully hedged, and rarely provocative. In fact, the world that television presents to the viewer generally lags behind the real world in its recognition of controversial social changes. The civil rights struggle, women's fight for equality, and changing sexual mores all were widespread in real life long before they became common on the television screen or received serious attention in the print media. Newspapers can afford to be more daring than television because normally there is no other daily paper in the same market. Moreover, the nature of the medium makes it easier for the audience to ignore stories they find offensive or distasteful.

Neglect of Social Problems. Despite the ascendancy of social responsibility journalism, the constraints of news production still force the media to neglect major ongoing social problems, such as alcoholism, drug addiction, environmental pollution, or care of the elderly and disabled. The pattern changes when a dramatic event takes place, such as a rash of deaths in nursing homes or a big welfare fraud case. If a reporter investigates and finds that six elderly people starved to death because of neglect, the spotlighted incident may then lead to a series of reports on food in retirement homes. The shocking deaths provide the element of novelty. After that novelty has worn off, interest dims and media attention flags, even if the problem remains unsolved.

Another reason why social problems are neglected is that most media staffs are inadequately trained to cover them. Proper appraisal of the administration of nursing homes or prisons or pollution control programs requires technical knowledge. Specialized reporters with expertise in areas such as urban affairs, science, or finance are available, as yet, only in the larger news organizations. Morever, a science reporter can hardly be expected to be an expert in all fields of science. Nor can a reporter skilled in urban problems be expected simultaneously to master the intricacies of a major city's budget, its transportation system, and its services to juveniles. Because most news organizations throughout the country lack the trained staffs needed to discuss major social problems constructively, politicians and all kinds of "experts" can easily challenge the merits of unpalatable media stories.

Then, too, judging from media use patterns, most of the public is not very interested in social problems or the hazards of alcohol and tobacco use. For those who are interested and might be in a position to combat such problems, lack of adequate media coverage makes it more difficult to rouse public support and become newsworthy in the process.

Support for the Establishment

The gatekeeping process also yields news that basically supports current political and social institutions in America. Although the media regularly expose the misbehavior and inefficiencies of government officials, for the most part they display a favorable attitude toward the established power structure and its methods of operation. Misconduct and poor policies are treated as deviations from the norms prescribed by the American political system. American political symbols and rituals, such as the presidency, the courts and elections, and patriotic celebrations, are treated with a high degree of respect, which lends legitimacy to them. By contrast, news stories cast a negative light on anti-establishment behavior, such as inflammatory speeches by militants or looting during a riot. Obscenity and profanity in public places usually are edited out of news events.

Generalized support for the establishment and the status quo is not unique to the media, of course.[41] Most institutions within any particular political system go along with it if they wish to prosper. People on their staffs have been socialized to believe in the merits of their political structures. Moreover, financial concerns make it essential for the media to cater to advertisers and audiences who firmly support the American political system. Staff members whose personal ideologies differ usually conform with established norms to avoid conflict with their bosses, advertisers, or affiliated stations, which may refuse to carry offensive programs.[42] People desperately want to believe that their government is competent, honest, and working hard to solve the nation's major problems. They do not welcome exposés that call into question their comfortable sense of security. Media support for the establishment thus helps to maintain respect for it and perpetuate it.

Establishment support is further strengthened by media reliance on government information and press releases. In the United States the bulk of news, particularly news pertaining to activities beyond the local community, comes from officials and agencies of the government.[43] Official viewpoints are likely to be particularly dominant when reporters must preserve access to their special beats, like the Pentagon or Justice Department, or when story production requires government assistance in collecting or gaining access to data. For instance, when military personnel are needed to transport correspondents to war zones, or when film producers want demonstrations of moon-flight research, the resulting stories are apt to support official views.[44]

Government officials and agencies are also used routinely to verify information. Reporters generally equate official position and rank of sources with accuracy. The higher the official level and rank the better. The assumption that government sources, such as police departments, or Department of Agriculture spokesmen, or presidential press aides, are reliable is, of course, debatable, especially since the particular thrust given to a story may put agencies into a good or bad light. Many private groups have complained that nearly exclusive reliance on government sources deprives them of the chance to publicize their own, more accurate versions of stories and that it results in one-sided reporting, tilted toward support of the establishment.

An interesting illustration of establishment support is provided by a study of media coverage of the Durham, North Carolina, city council. A team of researchers at Duke University observed city council sessions and then examined the newspaper reports about them. The sessions had been rather disorderly with little work done for much of the time. Council members had been seen "dozing off to sleep just as a vote is being taken on a crucial issue" and one was observed "smacking with abandon on a large wad of gum" while the intricacies of a public housing dispute are discussed." The mayor had cracked a number of jokes about the issues under consideration. The audience had screamed and had booed council proposals. Finally, toward the end of the lengthy session when everybody was tired, a few resolutions were passed.[45]

The published reports of the sessions conveyed an entirely different impression. No mention was made of the unprofessional behavior. Council members' meaningful remarks were quoted, not their often pointless or facetious quips. Members were described respectfully, each designated by official title. The stories made it appear that the city council sat down at the appointed time, immediately began its business, and completed it promptly and efficiently without interruptions by the audience. This impression was conveyed by indicating the precise time the sessions were called to order, outlining the agenda topics, quoting a few of the arguments made during the debates, and then reporting the final decisions. Decisionmaking appeared to be a careful, deliberate, logical process, with the likely consequences of these decisions fully explored. Of course, nothing could have been further from the truth.

The type of reporting practiced in Durham is quite typical of reports of meetings in other places. Most Americans knew little about the conduct of meetings during the Nixon administration until the unexpurgated Watergate tapes provided a realistic inside view. People in public life frequently behave in ways that do not meet the highest standards of decorum and honesty. But newspeople normally wink at this type of behavior, at least while the actors are in high office. For instance, the romantic relationship between a Mafia-linked showgirl, Judith Campbell Exner, and President John F. Kennedy did not surface until the mid-1970s. Such protective conventions have been relaxed somewhat in the post-Watergate era, but public annoyance over unsavory revelations keeps them infrequent. Ironically, people are curious about the sordid details in the lives of the famous while at the same time wanting their leaders to be above reproach.

Although newspeople commonly overlook personal misconduct and scandals, they often draw the line when matters of official conduct become involved. For instance, the sex scandal surrounding Rep. Wilbur Mills, a powerful and highly respected member of Congress, was publicized when Mills became embroiled in a public incident involving police action. In earlier years even that might have brought only casual mention. Two members of Congress received extensive media coverage when they admitted to sexual liaisons with congressional pages. The involvement of juveniles employed by Congress made an otherwise private affair into a public concern. The more usual practice, however, is to give public officials an aura of dignity and professionalism and to underplay their peccadillos.

Failure to disclose private and public misbehavior by government officials, as well as sugarcoating of political reality, are both detrimental and beneficial to the public interest. It is detrimental if politicians neglect public business or behave irresponsibly in official matters. Such stories should be told. The fear of publicity might have salutary effects and voters might be put on guard. There are, however, situations in which covering up official misconduct may be helpful if negative publicity about public officials seems disproportionately harmful. For instance, disclosure of John F. Kennedy's indiscretions might have undermined his effectiveness as president.

Appraising the Newsmaking Process

Do newspeople do a good job in selecting the types of news and entertainment categories to be covered? Do they allot appropriate amounts of time and space to each of these categories? Do they fill them with good individual stories? The answers depend on the standards that the critic is applying. If one contends that news can and should be a *mirror of society* faithfully reproducing a miniature version of life, the newsmaking process leaves much to be desired. With its emphasis on the exceptional rather than the ordinary, its focus on a limited number of regular beats to the exclusion of other sources of news, and its preference for conflict and bad news, it pictures a world that is far from reality.[46] Reality becomes further distorted because the process of shaping news events into interesting, cohesive stories often gives these events totally new meanings and significance. This is why critics claim that the news creates reality rather than reports it.[47]

If one adopts the classical albeit debatable American notion that the media should be the eyes and ears of intelligent and aware citizens who are interested primarily in news of major *social* and *political significance* to their community and country, one will again find fault with the gatekeeping process. Obviously, much space and time are given to trivia, and many significant developments are ignored or reported so briefly that their meaning is lost. Often the human interest appeal of a story is emphasized over its substance or true import.

To find fault is easy; to suggest widely acceptable remedies is far more difficult. Few critics would agree on a list of significant events that failed to receive the amount and kind of coverage they deserved. What is and is not significant, as well as gradations and ranks in significance, depend on the observer's world view and political orientation. Much of the published criticism of the media consists of polemical works that take the media to task for omitting the author's areas of special concern. But what is one person's intellectual meat is another's poison. Conservatives would like to see more stories about the misdeeds of America's enemies and about waste and abuse in social service programs. Liberals complain that the media legitimize big business and the military and neglect social reforms and radical perspectives. Frequently, there is the additional charge that political bias dictates the choices made about inclusion and exclusion of media fare and about story focus and tone. These charges have been particularly common when the media have featured controversial public policy issues such as the dangers of atomic energy generation or the merits of a new weapons system, or when political campaigns or demonstrations were covered.

A number of content analyses of such events definitely refute the charges of political bias, if bias is defined as deliberately lopsided coverage or intentional slanting of news. These analyses show instead that most newspeople try to cover a balanced array of issues in a neutral manner and do include contrasting viewpoints.[48] Most studies of bias have involved situations, such as elections, in which bias charges could be anticipated. Media personnel may therefore have taken exceptional care to treat the situation evenhandedly. But even in more general realms, such as the coverage of American business enterprises, evenhandedness is more in evidence than one might expect from the frequent charges of both pro- and antibusiness bias in the media. A team of investigators sampled more than 2,000 households nationwide to analyze the public's perceptions of bias in business news coverage. It discovered that 61 percent of the respondents considered business news biased. But half thought the bias was probusiness while the other half thought it was antibusiness.[49]

When coverage is imbalanced, as happens often, the reasons generally spring from the newsmaking process itself rather than from politically or ideologically motivated slanting. For instance, candidate Ronald Reagan received more coverage of his campaign activities during the 1980 primaries than Rep. Philip Crane, a candidate who campaigned far more vigorously. Reagan was a familiar, newsworthy figure, and Crane was not. Events happening in Chicago are reported more fully nationwide than similar events in Denver because the networks have a permanently leased wire from Chicago to New York but not from Denver to New York. The New Hampshire presidential primary receives disproportionately ample coverage because it happens to be the first one.

Inevitably, the stories that are publicized represent a small, unsystematic sample of the news of the day. In this sense every issue of a newspaper or every television newscast is a "biased sample" of current events. Published stories often generate follow-up coverage, heightening the bias effect. Attempts to be evenhanded may lead to similar coverage for events of dissimilar importance, thereby introducing bias.

In addition to evaluating news as a mirror of society or as a reflection of socially and politically significant events, one can evaluate it from the standpoint of *audience preference.* By and large the media gatekeepers appear to be doing well by that standard. A 1983 study showed that on a scale of 0 to 100, Americans rated the appeal of television shows at 73. More than 90 percent of all shows received ratings of 50 or above.[50] People like the products of the mass media industry well enough to consume them on a scale unheard of in the past. Three out of every four adults say they read newspapers regularly; nearly all homes have radio and television and use them extensively. In the average household the radio is turned on for three hours a day and television for seven. Millions of viewers, by their own free choice, have switched from other pretelevision age sources of diversion to watching shows condemned as "trash" by social critics and often even by the viewers themselves. These same people ignore shows and newspaper stories with the critics' seal of approval.

If one views the media simultaneously from all three perspectives, one can say that they have developed, overall, a balanced approach. Most newspapers and broadcast enterprises try to mirror at least a portion of the world. Most of the larger news organizations also see it as their function to present some serious political and social information and analysis. At the same time, most cater to the audience's appetite for easily digested entertainment and diversion. The end product cannot fully satisfy everyone.

Summary

What is *news* depends on what a particular society deems socially significant and/or personally satisfying to media audiences. The prevailing political and social ideology therefore determines what type of information will be gathered and the range of meanings that will be given to it. News collection is structured through the beat system to produce the desired information.

Beyond the larger framework, which is rooted in America's current political ideology, overt political considerations rarely play a major part in news selection. Instead, the profit motive and technical constraints of news production become paramount selection criteria. These criteria impose more stringent constraints on television than on print media because television deals with larger, more heterogeneous audiences and requires pictures to match word stories. Television—unlike newspapers, which rarely have competition in the local market—must compete for attention with several other electronic outlets.

The end products of these various constraints on newsmaking are news media that generally support the American political system, but emphasize its shortcomings and conflicts because journalists see themselves as watchdogs of public honesty and because conflict is exciting. News is geared primarily to attract and entertain rather than to educate the audience about politically significant events. The pressures to report news rapidly while it is happening often lead to presentation of disjointed fragments and disparate commentary. This leaves the audience with the impossible task of weaving the fragments into a meaningful tapestry of interrelated events.

If judged in terms of the information needs of the ideal citizen in the ideal democracy, the end product of the gatekeeping process is inadequate. This is especially true of television, which provides little more than a headline service for news and which mirrors the world like the curved mirrors at the county fair. Reality is there, but badly out of shape and proportion.

But if one concedes, as I do, that most of us only faintly resemble the ideal citizen and that most look to the media for entertainment rather than for enlightenment, a different appraisal suggests itself. By and large, American mass media serve the general public about as well as that public wants to be served in practice rather than in theory. Entertainment is interspersed with a smattering of serious information. Breadth of coverage is preferred over narrow depth. In times of acute crisis, as we shall see in Chapter 9, the media can and do follow a different pattern. Serious news displaces entertainment, and the broad sweep of events turns into a narrow, in-depth focus on the crisis. Short of acute crisis, superficiality prevails most of the time.

Notes

1. Jon Margolis and Lea Donosky, "Mondale, Glenn Set Off Fireworks During Debate," *Chicago Tribune,* January 16, 1984; see also Howell Raines, "Debate Among Democrats Draws Sharpest Exchanges of Campaign," *New York Times,* January 16, 1984.
2. Ron Powers, *The Newscasters* (New York: St. Martin's Press, 1977), p. 1.
3. Ibid., p. 234.
4. Popularity of specific newspaper stories or television programs is assessed through audience surveys. These are done most systematically for television, where major rating services such as A. C. Nielsen and the American Research Bureau (ARB) use viewer diaries and electronic devices to monitor the shows being watched. Advertising rates are based on audience size for particular radio and television shows. A 1 percent increase in audience size can mean as much as $15 million additional advertising income. For newspapers, rates are based on paid circulation, which is monitored by an independent agency, the Audit Bureau of Circulations.

Audiences are rarely asked if they would prefer different programs to existing fare. Qualitative appraisals, which are not currently used, are under consideration.

5. Malcolm Warner, "Decision-Making in Network News," in *Media Sociology,* ed. Jeremy Tunstall (Urbana: University of Illinois Press, 1970), pp. 158-167. See also David L. Altheide, *Creating Reality: How TV News Distorts Events* (Beverly Hills, Calif.: Sage 1976).
6. The share of the networks in television gatekeeping has increased steadily. In 1957, the networks produced roughly 41 percent of evening programming. This increased to 96 percent by 1968. Tracy A. Westen, "Barriers to Creativity," *Journal of Communication* 28 (Spring 1978): 38.
7. "11th Annual Survey: Who Runs America," *U.S. News & World Report,* May 14, 1984.
8. James Lemert, "Content Duplication by Networks in Competing Evening Newscasts," *Journalism Quarterly* 51 (Summer 1974): 238-244; Joseph R. Dominick, "Business Coverage in Network Newscasts," *Journalism Quarterly* 58 (Spring 1981): 179-185; see also Norman R. Luttbeg, "News Consensus: Do U.S. Newspapers Mirror Society's Happenings?" *Journalism Quarterly* 60 (Autumn 1983): 484-488, 578.
9. R. Gordon Shepherd, "Selectivity of Sources: Reporting the Marijuana Controversy," *Journal of Communication* 31 (Spring 1981): 129-137.
10. Nancy Pfund and Laura Hofstadter, "Biomedical Innovation and the Press," *Journal of Communication* 31 (Spring 1981): 138-154.
11. Barbara Matusow, *The Evening Stars: The Rise of the Network News Anchors* (Boston: Houghton Mifflin, 1983).
12. Peter Braestrup, *Big Story* (Garden City, N.Y.: Anchor Books, 1978).
13. George Gerbner, "Ideological Perspective and Political Tendencies in News Reporting," *Journalism Quarterly* 41 (August 1964): 495-508.
14. The social systems framework for mass communications analysis is sketched out in James S. Ettema, "The Organizational Context of Creativity," in *Individuals in Mass Media Organizations: Creativity and Constraint,* ed. James S. Ettema and D. Charles Whitney (Beverly Hills, Calif.: Sage, 1982), pp. 91-106.
15. David Morgan, *The Capitol Press Corps: Newsmen and the Governing of New York State* (Westport, Conn.: Greenwood Press, 1978), pp. 44-47.
16. Powers, *The Newscasters,* p. 30.
17. Quoted in Ibid., p. 79. The evidence on whether or not editors and reporters assess their audiences' tastes properly is mixed. Ralph K. Martin, Garrett J. O'Keefe, and Oguz B. Nayman, in "Opinion Agreement and Accuracy Between Editors and Their Readers," *Journalism Quarterly* 49 (Autumn 1972): 460-468, say they do. Leo Bogart, in "Changing News Interests and the Mass Media," *Public Opinion Quarterly* 23 (Winter 1968-69): 560-574, holds to the contrary.
18. Edward Jay Epstein, *News from Nowhere* (New York: Vintage Books, 1974), pp. 17-18.
19. G. Ray Funkhouser, "Trends in Media Coverage of the Issues of the '60's," *Journalism Quarterly* 50 (Fall 1973): 533-538.
20. Ibid.
21. Somewhat similar feelings are harbored even toward the casts of soap operas. People whose lives are confined largely to their homes often adopt soap opera people as part of their family. They avidly follow the trials and tribulations of these people and may even try to model themselves after them.
22. A study of 149 small and large newspapers reports the following news space allocations: local, 75 percent; sports, 6 percent; national, 4 percent; women's, 4 percent; international, 3 percent; editorial, 3 percent; state, 3 percent; financial, 2

percent. The measurements refer to space in column inches of total newshole. Dan Drew and G. Cleveland Wilhoit, "Newshole Allocation Policies of American Daily Newspapers," *Journalism Quarterly* 53 (Fall 1976): 434-440.

23. Robert W. Clyde and James K. Buckalew, "Inter-Media Standardization: A Q-Analysis of News Editors," *Journalism Quarterly* 46 (Summer 1969): 349-351.
24. Leon V. Sigal, *Reporters and Officials: The Organization and Politics of Newsmaking* (Lexington, Mass.: D. C. Heath, 1973), pp. 119-130.
25. The phrase is from Stanley K. Bigman, "Rivals in Conformity: A Study of Two Competing Dailies," *Journalism Quarterly* 25 (Autumn 1948): 127-131.
26. Joseph S. Fowler and Stuart W. Showalter, "Evening Network News Selection: A Confirmation of News Judgment," *Journalism Quarterly* 51 (Winter 1974): 712-715; for a discussion of variations in individual stories, see Luttbeg, "News Consensus," pp. 484-488.
27. Sigal, *Reporters and Officials,* p. 66.
28. Joseph R. Dominick, "Geographic Bias in National TV News," *Journal of Communication* 27 (Fall 1977): 94-99.
29. Robert Rutherford Smith, "Mythic Elements in Television News," *Journal of Communication* 29 (Winter 1979): 75-82.
30. Ben Bagdikian, *The Information Machines* (New York: Harper & Row, 1971), pp. 99-100.
31. David M. White, "The Gatekeeper," *Journalism Quarterly* 27 (Fall 1950): 383-390, replicated by Paul B. Snider, "Mr. Gates Revisited," *Journalism Quarterly* 43 (Autumn 1967): 419-427. See also James D. Harless, "Mail Call," *Journalism Quarterly* 51 (Spring 1974): 87-90.
32. Drew and Wilhoit, "Newshole Allocation Policies," pp. 434-440.
33. Harriet Engel Gross and Sharyne Merritt, "Effect of Social/Organizational Context on Gatekeeping in Lifestyle Pages," *Journalism Quarterly* 58 (Autumn 1981): 420-427.
34. The first two headings have been adapted from Herbert Gans's study of news magazine and network television news. Herbert J. Gans, *Deciding What's News: A Study of CBS Evening News, NBC Nightly News, Newsweek & Time* (New York: Pantheon Books, 1979), pp. 8-31. See also Gaye Tuchman, *Making News: A Study in the Construction of Reality* (New York: Free Press, 1978).
35. Sandra William Ernst, "Baseball or Brickbats: A Content Analysis of Community Development," *Journalism Quarterly* 49 (Spring 1972): 86-90.
36. *New York Times,* May 11, 1977.
37. George Gerbner, Larry Gross, Michael Morgan, and Nancy Signorielli, "Charting the Mainstream: Television's Contributions to Political Orientations," *Journal of Communication* 32 (Spring 1982): 106-107. Small-town newspapers are more apt to highlight the positive, telling what is good rather than what is bad, because conflict is less tolerable in social systems where most of the leaders constantly rub elbows.
38. For evidence that media watchdog functions increase as differentiation and pluralism increase in a social system, see Clarice N. Olien, George A. Donohue, and Phillip J. Tichenor, "The Community Editor's Power and the Reporting of Conflict," *Journalism Quarterly* 45 (Summer 1968): 243-252. See also Bruce Cole, "Trends in Science and Conflict Coverage in Four Metropolitan Newspapers," *Journalism Quarterly* 52 (Fall 1973): 465-474.
39. The term is Michael J. Robinson's in "American Political Legitimacy in an Era of Electronic Journalism: Reflections on the Evening News," in *Television as a Social Force: New Approaches to TV Criticism,* ed. Richard Adler (New York: Praeger, 1975), pp. 97-139.

40. Stephen E. Rada, "Manipulating the Media: A Case Study of a Chicano Strike in Texas," *Journalism Quarterly* 54 (Spring 1977): 109-113.
41. A strong attack on status-quo support is contained in Herbert J. Schiller, *The Mind Managers* (Boston: Beacon Press, 1973). See also Claus Mueller, *The Politics of Communication* (London: Oxford University Press, 1973).
42. Social forces are "more important than reporters' personalities in shaping the news" according to Warren Breed in "Social Controls in the Newsroom," *Social Forces* 33 (1955): 326-335. Reporters think otherwise. See Ruth C. Flegel and Steven H. Chaffee, "Influence of Editors, Readers, and Personal Opinions on Reporters," *Journalism Quarterly* 48 (Winter 1971): 645-651.
43. Sigal, *Reporters and Officials,* pp. 119-130.
44. A comparison of war movies made with and without Pentagon aid showed that aided movies depicted the military in a more favorable light. Russell E. Shain, "Effects of Pentagon Influence on War Movies, 1948-70," *Public Opinion Quarterly* 38 (Fall 1972): 641-647.
45. David L. Paletz, Peggy Reichert, and B. McIntire, "How the Media Support Local Government Authority," *Public Opinion Quarterly* 35 (Spring 1971): 80-92; quotation appears on pp. 83-84.
46. George Comstock and Robin Cobbey, "Watching the Watchdogs: Trends and Problems in Monitoring Network News," in *Television Network News: Issues in Content Research,* ed. William Adams and Fay Schreibman (Washington, D.C.: George Washington University, 1978), pp. 47-63.
47. For a fuller exploration of this issue, see Altheide, *Creating Reality;* Gaye Tuchman, *Making News;* or Mark Fishman, *Manufacturing the News* (Austin: University of Texas Press, 1980).
48. Comstock and Cobbey, "Watching the Watchdogs," pp. 53-55.
49. Robert A. Peterson, George Kozmetsky, and Isabella C. M. Cunningham, "Perceptions of Media Bias Towards Business," *Journalism Quarterly* 59 (Fall 1982): 461-464.
50. Ron Aldridge, "New TV Rating System Stresses Quality Viewing," *Chicago Tribune,* April 25, 1983.

Readings

Altheide, David L. *Creating Reality: How TV News Distorts Events.* Beverly Hills, Calif.: Sage, 1976.
Brendon, Piers. *The Life and Death of the Press Barons.* New York: Atheneum, 1983.
Goodfield, June. *Reflections on Science and the Media.* Washington, D.C.: American Association for the Advancement of Science, 1981.
Matusow, Barbara, *The Evening Stars: The Rise of the Network News Anchors.* Boston: Houghton Mifflin, 1983.
Roshco, Bernard. *Newsmaking.* Chicago: University of Chicago Press, 1975.
Schiller, Dan. *Objectivity and the News: The Public and the Rise of Commercial Journalism.* Philadelphia: University of Pennsylvania Press, 1981.
Sigal, Leon V. *Reporters and Officials: The Organization and Politics of Newsmaking.* Lexington, Mass.: D. C. Heath, 1973.

Press Freedom and the Law

If prisoners confess to a visiting reporter that they have raped fellow prisoners should the reporter be forced to reveal their identity? If a prominent army general becomes the subject of a documentary that allegedly libels him must the media reveal how they compiled the story? Should journalists be allowed to destroy a citizen's privacy by disclosing his personal life simply because he has become involved in a well-publicized event?

The answers vary depending on whether a journalist or an average citizen outside the media ranks is polled. Most journalists agree that the press must be kept as free as possible to publish what it wishes and to shield the identity of the sources who provide sensitive information. The courts, especially at higher levels, generally agree. But the public increasingly feels otherwise. In 1983 the Libel Defense Resource Center reported that the media lose 9 out of 10 libel cases heard by juries of ordinary citizens. Moreover, the monetary penalties assessed against the media at lower judicial levels have increased sharply in recent years. Despite these indications of public dissatisfaction, the media victory score remains high, close to 80 percent, when libel cases dismissed before trial and those reversed on appeal are considered.[1]

The conflict between juries representing average citizens on the one side and media personnel and high level judges on the other reflects perplexing dilemmas faced by democratic societies. How can freedom of the press to report all news be reconciled with protection of society from the dangers of unrestrained publicity? How can the right to compel needed testimony be squared with the media's need to protect news sources?

We shall begin to answer those questions by probing the problems that arise when a free press claims the exclusive right to decide what to publish and what to omit. This right often clashes with demands by citizen groups for newspaper space and air time to publicize social and political causes. Next we shall look at the problems faced by the press in gaining unrestrained access to information that it needs as raw material for news when government claims the right to conceal this information. Finally, we shall examine barriers to publication imposed to safeguard private and public interests.

The First Amendment is the constitutional basis for most of the laws and court decisions about the right of access to the press and freedom to gather news and publish it. The amendment guarantees that "Congress shall make no law . . . abridging the freedom of speech or of the press." This makes the news business the only private industry in America that is expressly protected by the Constitution. However, the dimensions of this protection have remained in flux since the amendment was ratified in 1791.

The Founding Fathers granted this special protection to the press because they believed that the right to collect and disseminate information and opinions is the bedrock of a free society. If restraints are needed to protect society from harmful information, they must come through the deterrent effects of punishment *after publication,* not through "prior restraint." Publication can be prevented only if it "will surely result in direct, immediate, and irreparable damage to our nation or its people." [2] The belief in the political importance of a free press has stood the test of time and still remains a cornerstone of American democracy. Therefore, anything that affects the interpretation or the scope of this basic right is a matter of major political significance.

Access to the Media

The notion of government "by the people" would seem to imply that the people have a right to make their voices heard. Ralph Nader's consumer protection movement or Howard Jarvis's tax revolt could never have gathered widespread support throughout the country without mass media publicity. What would have happened if the media had refused to tell these stories? Did Nader and Jarvis have a right to publicity for their views and for their organizing activities?

The answer is "No." In the absence of such a right, it is very difficult for most people, other than journalists or major public figures, to gain access to the media. In his book entitled *Freedom of the Press for Whom? The Right of Access to the Mass Media,* Jerome Barron, a lawyer interested in civil liberties, accused the media of fighting for broad rights of free expression for themselves while denying these same rights to the public.[3] Media personnel decide what stories are publicized and whose views are presented. This leaves many who want to proclaim their views without a suitable public forum.

Barron argued that the First Amendment right to publish freely should be open to all individuals and groups, not only to news professionals. If individuals have a special cause or feel that some of the situations depicted by the mass media are not presented accurately, or that certain information is omitted, they should have an opportunity to use the mass media to state their views. Without this right, they may be doomed to political ineffectiveness.

Print Media Access

What rights of access to the mass media do individuals in private and public life have? To answer this question accurately a distinction must be made between the print media and the electronic media. American courts have usually held that the freedom of the print media to determine what they will or will not print, and whose views they will or will not present, is nearly absolute. As long as the media stay clear of deliberate libel and slander and do not publish top secret information, they may make publishing decisions unhampered by legal restraints.

The freedom of the press to publish or suppress information is delineated in the case of *Miami Herald Publishing Company v. Tornillo,* decided in 1974.[4] The case involved the constitutionality of a Florida statute that provided a right of reply to persons running for public office who had been personally attacked by a newspaper. Under this law, a candidate who was attacked on the editorial page had the right to reply on the editorial page in a format similar to that used by the accuser. If the attack appeared in the news pages, the candidate had the right to equal space, type, and position there. The law had been passed to deal with the problem of personal attacks published very late in a campaign, giving candidates little time for a rebuttal. The consequence might be loss of the election.

The case arose in 1972 when Patrick Tornillo, Jr., leader of the Dade County Teachers Union, was running for the Florida State Legislature. Just before the primary, the *Miami Herald* published two editorials objecting to Tornillo's election because he had led a recent teachers' strike. Tornillo demanded that the paper print his replies to the editorials. The paper refused. After Tornillo lost the primary decisively, he brought suit against the paper.

The case went through the Florida court system, with lower court rulings overturned at higher stages. Finally, in 1974 it reached the U.S. Supreme Court, which ruled unanimously that newspapers can print or refuse to print anything they like. Editors have an unlimited right to decide what goes in or what stays out of the paper. No one, including a candidate whose reputation has been damaged, has the right to demand space in a newspaper. Therefore the Florida statute granting a right to reply was unconstitutional. The decision reaffirmed what had been the thrust of the law all along. Private citizens may *request* that a story or response to a personal attack be printed and that request may be granted, but they have no right to *demand* publication.[5]

Electronic Media Access

The rules have been different for the electronic media, based on the view that limited spectrum space makes them semimonopolies. Unlike the print media business, which is open to anyone, entry into the electronic media business requires a license from the government. License holders are subject to government regulations, including rules ensuring that the license holders do not prevent public access to the airways in situations where access may be especially crucial.

The public's access rights fall under three categories: *the equal time provision, the fairness doctrine,* and *the right of rebuttal.* These access rights are based on Section 315 of the Communications Act of 1934 and its amendments and interpretations. The equal time provision requires that broadcasters who permit a candidate for political office to campaign on their stations must give equal opportunities to all other candidates for the same office. Under the fairness doctrine, broadcasters who air controversial issues of public importance must provide reasonable opportunities for the presentation of conflicting viewpoints. The right of rebuttal requires that an attack on the honesty, character, or integrity of an identified person or group entitles the target of the attack to a reply. The broadcaster must notify the targets about the offending broadcast and must supply a transcript or summary. Thereafter, a reasonable opportunity to respond must be provided. All of the regulations that mandate public access are subject to one very important implicit condition: the rights arise only *after* the station has broadcast the information in question.

The Right to Equal Time. Under the equal time rule, a station need not allow candidates for political office to broadcast. But if it gives or sells time to one candidate for a specific office, it must give equal time to all of the candidates for the same office. Even if there are 15 candidates for the same office, and most of them have few backers, they all have a right to equal time. By the same token, whenever the station denies time to all candidates for the same office, none of them has a right to demand access under the campaign coverage provisions of Section 315. The rules do not apply to regular news stories in which reporters describe what various candidates are doing and saying.

Stations faced with the all-or-none alternative of the equal time rule for candidates often opt for "none," particularly for state and local offices. This avoids the problem of cluttering their programs with numerous campaign broadcasts that would be of little interest to their listeners and costly to the station in lost advertising revenues. It also keeps many viable candidates off the air who might otherwise have gained exposure.

To make lengthy debates among mainline candidates for major offices possible, without running afoul of the equal time provisions, Congress suspended these provisions in 1960 to permit the Kennedy-Nixon debates. A different tactic was used in 1976 and 1980 to facilitate the Carter-Ford and Carter-Reagan debates. The Federal Communications Commission (FCC) ruled that it would be permissible to circumvent the equal time rule by staging the debates as public meetings, which were then covered by the news media like regular news and were not subject to the equal time rule.

Billing the 1976 and 1980 presidential debates as public meetings arranged by the League of Women Voters and covered by the press like any newsworthy event was obviously a subterfuge that strained the intent of the law. Several minor party candidates, eager to be included in the debates, sued in 1976 on the ground that this circumvention of equal time provisions was an illegal ruse. But the courts ruled against them. Finally, in November 1983, the FCC reversed its previous position by declaring that radio and television broadcasters were free to stage political debates at all political levels among candidates of their own choosing. The sole remaining restriction is that broadcasters must not "favor or disfavor" any particular candidate. Candidates who feel that they have been unfairly shut out may appeal to the commission.[6] Given the inclination of the courts to make political debates feasible when many candidates crowd the field, it is likely that the 1983 ruling will withstand judicial challenges.

The curbs on political dialogue engendered by the equal time rule have led to widespread dissatisfaction with Section 315. Many observers believe that the rule has done more political harm than good. It has blocked important messages by current and prospective public officials from reaching the public. For instance, when President Gerald R. Ford set forth his farm policy in a speech to the Future Farmers of America in 1976, the networks shied away from full-length coverage because it might involve them in an equal time allotment for the Democratic candidate. Normally, they would have broadcast a presidential speech outlining major policy proposals. Critics are also unhappy about public sanction of subterfuges to evade the rule and about piecemeal legalized exceptions.

The Right to Fair Treatment.   The fairness doctrine has a broader reach than the equal time provision because it is not limited to candidates for political office. Under the fairness doctrine, reasonable time must be given for the expression of opposing views if a highly controversial public issue is discussed. What constitutes such an issue is a matter to be ultimately decided by the courts.

Like the equal time provision, the fairness doctrine has given rise to a number of problems. Most importantly, it impoverishes public debate by suppressing controversy. The media frequently shy away from programs dealing with controversial public issues so as to avoid demands to air opposing views in place of regular revenue-producing programs.

When controversial programs have been aired, it has been difficult to decide who has the right to reply. For instance, when President Richard Nixon justified America's incursion into Cambodia during the Vietnam War, three groups immediately demanded time to broadcast counterarguments. One was a group of Democratic senators; another was the Democratic National Committee. The third was a group of business executives organized to oppose the war. The three groups differed in their assessment of the errors committed by the president, and none was willing to yield to any of the others.

The media finally gave air time to the Democratic National Committee, which was to speak for the opposition. Members of the Republican National Committee then claimed that the Democratic National Committee had used its time for political propaganda unrelated to the Cambodian invasion. Therefore they asked for time to counter the views expressed by the Democrats. The whole affair became almost ridiculous. The courts settled the problem of choosing among opponents by ruling that no group has the right to expound its particular brand of opposition. Rather, it is up to the media to decide which opposing group will be heard.

This decision gives the media a great deal of control over the types of opposition views that will be aired. If media personnel favor certain views they can select representatives of those views. Furthermore, the most prominent groups who wish to be heard are the most likely to be selected. For instance, if a group of senators and prestigious business people is competing with members of a student organization to speak for the opposition, it is unlikely that the students will be selected as spokespersons. Groups who hold unconventional views or are on the extreme right or left of the political spectrum are also unlikely choices. This sharply reduces their chances for challenging the existing power structure. It is one of many ways in which media practices perpetuate the established social order.

The media can avoid the problem of air time for opposing views entirely by including opposing views on controversial issues in their regular news programs. For instance, when Democratic party officials demanded air time in 1982 to rebut Republican television commercials that supported President Reagan's economic policies, the networks declined. The FCC upheld their position, ruling that opposition to Reagonomics had been fully aired in regular newscasts. Generally, such media contentions have been sustained by the FCC and the courts if they are supported by reasonably good evidence. The courts have also ruled against an automatic right to oppose statements made during presidential news conferences, as long as the media air contrary views in news analyses immediately after such conferences.

The media thus retain a substantial degree of control over the array of viewpoints that receive a hearing. However, the pressures and litigation that they have faced have made them more receptive to featuring opposing views voluntarily, particularly after major messages and news conferences presented by chief executives. Hence it has become traditional to allow spokespersons for the opposition to offer rebuttals after presidential, gubernatorial, and mayoral messages covering major policy issues. The temper of the times has thus curbed editorial freedom, even though legal rights remain unchanged.

Is there a right of reply to contentious statements made in business commercials? Must the media make such time available, and must it be free of charge? The oil industry, conservationists, and the drug industry, among other groups, have used commercials to carry controversial messages regarding public policies. Commercial firms and public interest groups have asked for time to respond. Media restrictions have varied, and the law is very unclear about the right of reply. The courts have spoken with forked tongues.

The landmark case, *Banzhaf v. Federal Communications Commission,* seemed to indicate in 1969 that there was a right to reply. It concerned television advertisements for cigarettes, before such commercials were banned from television. John W. Banzhaf III, a young Manhattan lawyer and antismoking activist, accused the cigarette companies of promoting the glamour of cigarette smoking without advertising its dangers. He demanded the right to present views opposed to smoking, a life and death public health issue. The networks countered that opposition to smoking had been adequately presented by commercials and publications from various health organizations concerned with cancer and heart and lung disease. The Supreme Court sided with Banzhaf. It held that smoking involved such an extraordinarily important health issue that, contrary to usual rules, broadcasters must balance cigarette commercials with antismoking spots.[7] But the 1969 decision did not supply a yardstick to determine which issues are exceptional enough to warrant time for countercommercials. The case has turned out to be the exception rather than the rule. All subsequent claims for countercommercial time have been refused.

The Right of Rebuttal.   The final access issue to be discussed is the right of rebuttal for a personal attack, which arises when individuals are assailed on radio or television in a way that damages their reputation. The controlling case in this area of communication law is *Red Lion Broadcasting Co. v. Federal Communications Commission,* decided in 1969. It set up a rather broad scope for the right of reply.[8] The *Red Lion* case arose because a book by Fred J. Cook, a very liberal newsman, about Barry Goldwater, a conservative senator, was attacked by the Reverend Billy James Hargis on a program conducted and paid for by the ultraconservative Christian Crusade. Fred Cook asked for broadcast time, free of charge, to reply. The station was willing to sell him reply time, but it refused to grant it free of charge. It could not be responsible for the content of all programs for which various groups had bought television time, it argued. If the station were forced to grant free rebuttal time for statements on such broadcasts, it would be impossible in the future to sell time to private broadcasters who might air controversial right- or left-wing views.

In the *Red Lion* case, to the delight of proponents of ready public access to the airwaves, the courts sided with the plaintiff. Cook was granted the right of rebuttal, free of charge, on the grounds that maligned individuals deserve a right to reply and that the public has a right to hear opposing views. It proved to be a hollow victory for supporters of free access, however, because it led to sharp curtailment of air time for controversial broadcasts.

The *Red Lion* case is one of many examples of political manipulation of the regulatory process. Cook's protest had been paid for and orchestrated by the Democratic National Committee as part of an effort to generate an avalanche of demands for rebuttals to conservative radio and television programs. The hope was that stations would then cancel these programs to avoid the costs of free rebuttal time.[9] This did, indeed, happen. By 1975, the Christian Crusade had been dropped by 300 of its 350 stations. Since 1969, the courts have retreated somewhat from their broad support for the right of rebuttal because of its chilling effects on broadcasting controversial subjects. The flood of rebuttal requests also mired the FCC in a morass of claims and counterclaims that it could not process with its limited resources.

Reform Proposals. To halt the deleterious effects on programming and the flood of FCC proceedings, strong demands have been voiced by members of Congress and many broadcasters and communication scholars to do away with all the access provisions linked to Section 315—equal time, fairness, and right of rebuttal. The pleaders contend that there is no longer any reason to consider electronic media as semimonopolies, in contrast to presumably competitive print media. In fact, print media in the age of one-newspaper towns face less competition than electronic media, with their competing networks and competition among multiple radio and television outlets. Besides, the distinction between print and electronic media is becoming increasingly blurred since newspapers can now transmit news and editorials through electronic channels for reception on television screens. For this reason the electronic media should be just as free as the print media to make publishing decisions. The quality and fairness of programming decisions, and their success in presenting a wide array of viewpoints on controversial issues, should be judged from a long-range perspective, at license renewal time, rather than case by case. Renewal of a station's license should hinge on adequate performance over the entire five-year period. Such proposals, proponents claim, would encourage stations to air controversies while still providing a balance of views over a period of time.[10]

Opponents of reform point to the airing of many controversial programs, despite Section 315. They warn that removal of access protections will leave the public at the not-so-tender mercies of media gatekeepers. As Jerome Barron has plaintively lamented, "The myth says that if the press is kept 'free,' liberty of discussion is assured. But, in how few hands is left the exercise of 'freedom'!"[11] A case for continued regulation can also be made on the grounds that the vast influence of the electronic media on public perceptions requires safeguards stronger than ordinary market forces. If audience rights are paramount, as the *Red Lion* case affirms, shouldn't the audience be protected from media unfairness and misjudgment?[12]

Problems of the Status Quo

Apart from the right to reply to a personal attack, to request time to express opposing views when controversial matters of public interest are aired, and the right of rival candidates to equal broadcast time, there are no access rights for individuals. Short of getting into the media business, there is no way to bring messages to public attention through mass media if the media are unwilling. A federal court in Birmingham, Alabama, ruled in 1981 that public television enjoys complete editorial freedom as well. A group of citizens had sued the Alabama Education Television Network because it cancelled the film "Death of a Princess" in response to protests by Saudi Arabia's royal family and threats of economic boycott. The citizens had charged unfair denial of their right of access to information and claimed that the cancellation constituted political censorship. The court disagreed.[13]

The major television networks have also been very restrictive in displaying public information programs originating from professionals outside their own organization. An example was a series on Cuban leader Fidel Castro, produced by former press secretaries for President John F. Kennedy and Senator George McGovern. Although they had excellent original film of substantial public interest, the networks refused to buy it except for a 30-second news spot. The networks relented only after a follow-up interview by a network reporter had been added. Another restraint on information dissemination springs from a growing practice of major news organizations of negotiating contracts guaranteeing exclusive broadcast rights. Once such a contract has been made, all news outlets, aside from the contract holder, are precluded from covering the event.[14]

People in public office who want access to the mass media to explain their views face problems quite similar to those of private individuals. Although the media are likely to be more sympathetic to their requests, there are many occasions when coverage is denied. For instance, Gov. Dan Walker of Illinois (1972-1976) repeatedly asked the media in his state to broadcast his speeches dealing with important public policies, such as appropriations for educational programs. The broadcast media refused his requests, saying that they had amply covered his policies in regular news broadcasts. They did not want to give him air time because it might force them to allot time for opposing views. When the governor challenged their right to deny air time in court, the judge supported the broadcasters. Not even a governor, the court ruled, has the right to demand air time to explain his policies to the public.

Prior to the Nixon presidency (1969-1974), presidential requests for air time were routinely granted. This is no longer the case. Several speeches by Presidents Nixon and Ford were not broadcast at all because the media considered them partisan political statements. Others were carried by only a limited number of stations, forcing the president to compete against regular entertainment broadcasts. This reduced the president's audience sharply. On still other occasions, broadcasts of presidential speeches have been deferred until late evening, denying the president access to prime time audiences. During the Carter and Reagan presidencies, such problems were largely avoided by tailoring presidential requests for media time to the needs of the media. In particular, schedule conflicts with major sports events were avoided.

The question of access rights to the airwaves also has been raised in connection with population groups whose concerns are different from those of the general public. Several public interest groups have objected to the lack of programs for young children and have asked for increases, even though such programming would be of little interest to the majority of listeners and viewers. The FCC has concurred that children constitute an important special audience whose needs for distinctive programming must be met. Stations have been reluctant to add children's programs because revenues from them are comparatively low, particularly since the FCC, as a result of lobby pressures, has reduced the amount of advertising permitted on children's programs from 12 to 9 minutes per hour. This rule is intended to diminish the temptations faced by immature viewers from the seduction of advertising.

Other audiences whose right of access to special programs has been recognized sporadically include blacks, Hispanics, and lovers of classical music. Occasional rulings have forced the electronic media to set aside time for broadcasts geared to such groups whose needs might be ignored if the forces of the economic marketplace were allowed full rein. The FCC has further protected the interests of these groups by giving preference in license applications to stations whose output is likely to serve neglected clienteles. But in light of the growing numbers of television and radio outlets, making access easier for everyone, such governmental protection of special interest groups is declining. In 1981 the U.S. Supreme Court freed the FCC from any obligation to weigh the effects of alternative program formats on various population groups when making licensing decisions. The Court's ruling arose from a series of cases in which radio stations had changed their format, for instance, from all news to all music.[15]

Other Approaches to Media Access

Attempts to gain access to the mass media through independently produced programs, individual requests for air time, and FCC rulings that support the interest of minority audiences have been only moderately successful. Other routes to access are even less satisfactory. Letters to the editor are an example. Due to lack of space, most papers publish only very few letters. The *New York Times,* for instance, receives more than 60,000 letters a year and publishes 4 to 5 percent of them, limiting length strictly. Even with these stringent controls, space devoted to letters equals space for editorials in the *Times*. Editors select the letters to be published, using a variety of criteria that discriminate against those from average people. Letters that are unusual or are sent by someone well-known are most likely to be printed.

Another avenue to access is the use of paid advertisements. A number of labor unions, business enterprises, lobby groups, and even foreign governments have placed advertisements in newspapers and on the air to present their side of disputes and public policy issues. This route is usually open to those who can afford the steep purchase price, which may run into thousands of dollars for full-page advertisements and national broadcast exposure. However, print and electronic media have occasionally refused to print advertisements or sell air time. In the 1970s, power companies were unable to buy air time to tell their version of the energy crisis, even when they offered to pay for rebuttal time that might be demanded by opponents.

Access to air time was also denied in 1975 to the Republican National Committee, which wanted to buy three half-hour slots on national television to explain the party's philosophy and goals to the public. The courts upheld the networks' right to refuse to sell time as long as they applied the policy evenhandedly for all similar organizations. The courts have also upheld the right of newspapers to refuse to sell advertising space as long as refusal is not used to discriminate against particular groups. However, the newspaper decisions have not been as clear-cut as the television decisions. In some instances, courts have ordered papers to accept controversial advertising as long as advertising space for miscellaneous announcements was for sale.

Most people who would like to publicize their views cannot afford the high cost of advertising. This was the problem for Peter Kiger, a young draft resister who wanted to publicize his reasons for opposition to the draft in 1969.[16] Because he earned less than $50 a week, the cost of newspaper and television advertising was way beyond his means. In 1969, the cost of a full-page ad in the *New York Times* was $7,200. One minute on a television news broadcast ranged from $1,500 to $3,000. Kiger and a friend hit upon the strategy of notifying the media where and when they would publicly burn their draft cards. Sure enough, nearly three dozen radio, television, and newspaper reporters came at the appointed time. The ensuing free publicity reached well over 2 million people. But the story ended unhappily for the protesters. Officials from the Justice Department, who had learned about the burning, set legal proceedings in motion that led to Kiger's conviction in 1970 for illegal draft card burning. While sympathetic to his plea that the illegal act was his only chance for media coverage, the judge did not consider it to be an adequate defense.[17]

The rise of lobby groups eager to ensure broad access rights to people with minority viewpoints, and the FCC's sympathy with their pleas, have made broadcasters more sensitive to pressures for access by political activists. But even if radio or television station management is willing to grant access to such people, especially when they have engaged in newsworthy activities, there still is the problem of insufficient time to air every claimant's views on the electronic media. Despite the multiplication of television and radio channels in the wake of technological advancements, there will never be enough channels—or even newspaper pages—to publicize all important views to large audiences. Nor do concerned citizens have the time or capacity to listen to all significant views and put them into proper perspectives. In fact, the capacity to broadcast and publicize already far exceeds the audience's capacity to listen and assimilate. Studies of cable system users have shown that regardless of the number of channels available and the important stories that they may feature, the average viewer rarely taps more than six.

Access to Information

Special Access for the Media?

The right to publish without restraint means little if information cannot be obtained. This raises the question of whether the media do and should have a special right of access to places where they wish to gather information. Supreme Court decisions have denied the existence of special access rights. In *Zemel v. Rusk,* for instance, a citizen sued to claim his right to a passport to visit Cuba and learn about conditions there. The Court upheld the State Department's ban on Cuban travel and ruled that neither ordinary citizens nor media personnel have a right to gather information. In the Court's words: "The right to speak and publish does not carry with it the unrestrained right to gather information." [18] Similarly, in *Branzburg v. Hayes,* a case involving a newsman's right to refuse testimony before a grand jury because he wanted to protect his sources, the Court said, "It has generally been held that the First Amendment does not guarantee the press a constitutional right of special access to information not available to the public generally." [19] The press had argued that its status as the fourth branch of government, surveying the political scene for the public, entitled it to special rights of access.

The decisions denying such rights exclude journalists from access to many politically crucial events and thus deprive the public of important, albeit sensitive, information. Closed White House and Camp David meetings provide many examples. Other events that are often barred to the media are pretrial hearings and grand jury proceedings, which determine the sufficiency of evidence of wrongdoing to justify indictments. Because grand jury proceedings frequently involve high political stakes, news about them has repeatedly been leaked to newspeople by participants. The press also has no right to attend conferences of the Supreme Court where it would learn why the justices had decided to hear certain cases and refused to hear others. Media people may be barred from attending sessions of legislative bodies closed to the general public. Such sessions ordinarily deal with secret information that may require protection or with matters that might prove embarrassing to legislators.

Newspeople have no right to be admitted to sites of crimes and disasters when the general public is excluded. Nor do they have the right to visit prisons and interview and film inmates, even for the purpose of investigating prison conditions and rumors of brutality. In many cases where access has been denied, the Supreme Court has stressed that reporters could get the information they needed without special access privileges.[20] This may indicate that the Court is willing to grant access in situations where information about prison conditions is totally lacking.

Many of the decisions in the early 1970s regarding access to information were highly controversial, as shown by 5 to 4 divisions in the Supreme Court in cases such as *Branzburg v. Hayes, Pell v. Procunier,* and *Saxbe v. Washington Post Co.*[21] This clash of views among the justices has made media access rights a very fluid and exciting area of legal development. A great deal of pressure has also been exerted on Congress to pass legislation that would clear up some of the uncertainties. Advocates of broadened access rights have been especially vocal.

By custom, although not by law, newspeople often receive preferred treatment in gaining entry to public events. Press passes ensure media access to the best observation points for affairs like inaugurations of chief executives, space shuttle landings, or political conventions. In many instances the media are admitted while the general public is kept out. Examples are accident and crime locations. But access is purely at the discretion of the public authorities in charge.

In wartime, military officials often do not want news personnel in certain combat zones. They keep them out by denying transportation to these areas or, as happened in Grenada in 1983, by keeping invasion plans secret. A secret invasion of the tiny Caribbean island of Grenada by American forces was launched early on October 25. Initial news accounts of the invasion were vague and often contradictory because the administration banned the press from Grenada. The closest reporters could get was the island of Barbados, some 150 miles away. Two days after the invasion, 15 reporters were allowed to visit Grenada for a few hours, under strict military supervision. On subsequent days two larger groups followed. Press restrictions remained in force for a full week, ending on October 31, 1983.

Government spokesmen argued that the ban was necessary to ensure secrecy for the initial assault and to protect the safety of the journalists. Journalists disagreed on both scores. The Grenada news blackout clearly exemplifies denial of access to news without any legal recourse. Such tactics can effectively shut newspeople out of reporting crucial political events, like military maneuvers, conferences in inaccessible places, briefings in airplanes, or inspections in underground mines.

Access to Government Documents

General Rules. Government documents are another extremely important source of political information to which access is frequently obstructed. The Freedom of Information Act, signed by President Lyndon B. Johnson on July 4, 1966, and amended in 1974 to make the act more enforceable, ostensibly opened many governmental files to the news media and the general public.[22] Burdensome application requirements, however, have limited the use of the act by news personnel. Nonetheless its use has led to important revelations concerning the My Lai massacre in Vietnam, CIA involvement in political affairs in Chile and Cuba, unsafe nuclear reactors, contaminated drinking water, and ineffective drugs. Most reporters, however, have been content to cover more readily available current news rather than digging into government files to unearth past happenings.

Repeated attempts, particularly by the Reagan administration, to narrow the scope of the act, have been defeated. In part, these have been efforts to reduce the high cost to the government of responding to requests, most of them from businesses seeking commercially useful information. The Defense Department alone receives more than 60,000 Freedom of Information requests annually. Other cutbacks have been attempted to shield the more sensitive operations of government from public scrutiny.

Despite the Freedom of Information Act, many types of public documents remain unavailable to reporters. When journalism professor Elsie Hebert examined federal and state access policies in 1974, she was able to get data from only 38 states and the federal government.[23] Ironically, the remaining 12 states declined to provide data about their freedom of information policies. Hebert's study disclosed wide variations. Some states are more liberal than the national government under the Freedom of Information Act in giving out information; others lag far behind. Most state laws provide for access to "public records." But the states define "public records" differently. The narrow common law definition has been broadened piecemeal, state by state. Laws obviously constitute a public record. But are citizens entitled to inspect the minutes of the meetings that preceded passage of a law, or tapes of the proceedings, or exhibits that a legislative committee considered before passing the law? In many states the term "public record" does not encompass any information about the genesis of laws and regulations.

Applicants for information often must demonstrate a special need for a particular set of data. A journalist or private citizen cannot go into a record center and say, "I would like to examine all your records on public health matters." Exactly what is wanted must be specified, which is difficult to do without knowing what is available. How much interest and the kinds of interest that must be demonstrated, and the degree of precision of information requests, are determined by administrators.

A widely used rule of thumb about access to information is that disclosure must be in the public interest and must not do excessive harm.

Access should be denied if the harm caused by opening records is greater than the possible benefit. Accordingly, if a reporter requested the records of welfare clients for a story on welfare cheating, this request would probably be denied because it is embarrassing to many people to have others know that they need public assistance. Because there are no precise guidelines for determining what is in the public interest and what degree of harm is excessive, the judgments of public officials who control documents are supreme. In many states, legislatures are unwilling to leave access policies to the discretion of administrative officials. Therefore, they list the kinds of records that may or may not be disclosed. But that approach is unsatisfactory because legislatures cannot possibly foresee all types of records that may be kept. Release of records may then be stopped simply because they are not specifically mentioned in the legislation.

Certain types of documents are routinely barred from disclosure. While the reasons are usually sound, closed access may not be in the public's best interest. For example, examination questions and answers for various tests given by government agencies are usually placed beyond public scrutiny. If questions and answers to civil service examinations were published, the value of these examinations might be totally destroyed. On the other hand, if the fairness and appropriateness of examination questions for public jobs are in doubt, public scrutiny of questions and answers might be beneficial. Favoritism in grading exams of the protégés of the powerful is a widely practiced tactic that also is difficult to expose without access to graded exams. A scandal in Chicago about the real estate broker exam grades of Mayor Richard Daley's sons is a graphic case. It came to public attention, as do many closed records, through a series of "leaks" by disgruntled public employees.

Other data frequently kept from the reach of media personnel are records that could give advantage to business competitors, such as bids for work to be performed for the government. In most states the law requires competitive bidding and mandates that contracts, with some exceptions, go to the lowest bidder. Because corruption is common in awarding government contracts, reporters often are very interested in what has been bid or what promises have been made in return for contract awards. Without access to the records, investigative reporting of suspected fraud or corruption is impossible. On the other hand, secrecy is warranted because publicizing the details of a bid would unfairly allow another firm to underbid by a few dollars and thus get the contract. The cloak of secrecy conceals untold corruption.

Clearly, some restraints on access are essential for the protection of individuals as well as the public. At the same time, restraints make betrayals of the public trust easier for potential offenders. Finding the right balance between protection of individuals and protection of the interests of the public through media access is an extremely difficult and controversial task.

Historical and National Security Documents. Another area of limited access concerns the records that major public officials keep of their administration. Generally, these records are unavailable to the media and the general public until 30 years after the death of the public official. The 30-year limit was selected to ensure that most people whose private and public lives were entangled with that of the official would be dead by that time and spared possible embarrassment. Exceptions to the 30-year rule arise when official papers are classified as public rather than private. Because the distinction between personal and public papers is not clear, exceptions frequently are contested in court. Former president Richard Nixon sued unsuccessfully to recover control of many of his records that had been released to the media.

The closure of the private records of public officials is part of the privacy protection afforded to all individuals, but it serves a public purpose as well. For uninhibited discussion in policymaking, assurance of confidentiality is essential. Without it, people will posture for an audience rather than freely address themselves to the substance of the issues that are under consideration. The danger of inhibiting free discussion also explains why deliberations prior to legislation or court decisions are generally closed to public scrutiny.

Documents concerning matters of national security usually cannot be published. Examples are information about prospective negotiations or sensitive past negotiations. News about specific new weapons adopted by the United States, or stories indicating that security warning devices are not operating properly, may also be restricted. In some cases, however, such information is available in open files and can be pieced together into a coherent story. Government efforts to stop the publication of this kind of story have been unsuccessful in recent years, except when prohibitions about publication were a matter of law. In 1982, for instance, it became a crime to publish the name of a covert intelligence agent, even when the name was taken from public documents.

In the absence of laws, the story is different. Consider this 1979 case. The government was able to obtain an injunction to prohibit a Wisconsin magazine, *The Progressive,* from publishing an article, culled from open documents, describing how a hydrogen bomb can be made. The injunction delayed publication for six months—an unusual instance of prior restraint. The injunction was lifted when the government decided to drop the case after other publications had printed a letter disclosing most of the same information that the magazine article had contained. The government's chances of ultimately sustaining the injunction in the U.S. Supreme Court had appeared to be slim.

Of course, most instances of security censorship never reach the lawsuit stage, leaving an enormous number of documents outside the public domain. Federal officials estimated in 1982 that up to one million documents are labeled as "classified" annually. Another 16 million are placed beyond easy access because they contain information taken from previously classified documents. To these staggering statistics at the federal level one must add massive numbers of documents withheld by state and local officials.[24]

The main problem with security censorship lies in the determination of what information is truly sensitive and must be protected and what information should remain available to media personnel and the public. The media and, to a lesser degree, Congress as well have been trying to expand the range of information that is made available for publication. The president and executive agencies, charged with protecting national security, have bent over backward to protect information that might compromise security.

The most graphic illustration of this perennial battle is the *Pentagon Papers* case. Daniel Ellsberg, a former aide to the National Security Council, the president's top security policy planning agency, testified in court that he had become disillusioned about United States military activities in Vietnam. He claimed that foreign policy information in a study commissioned by the Defense Department about America's gradual entrapment in the Vietnam War had been improperly classified as top secret. Its release, he thought, would turn people against the war. He copied the information surreptitiously and gave it to prominent newspapers for publication. Because the war was still in progress, the executive branch considered this a criminal breach of security and sued Ellsberg and the media that printed the information. In *New York Times Co. v. U.S.,* the U.S. Supreme Court absolved the media, ruling that the government had been overly cautious in classifying the information as top secret.[25] In the Court's view, publication did not harm the country. The case brought against Ellsberg for leaking the information was also dismissed because evidence had been collected through illegal means.

The Supreme Court decision did not end the public controversy. Analysts still disagree about whether the disclosures from the *Pentagon Papers* damaged the foreign interests of the United States. Those who concur with the Court point out that much of the information released had already been available. Dissenters counter that the information had never been compiled in a single document and had not yet been published in prominent sources such as the *New York Times* and *Washington Post.*

Prior to the Nixon years, if a government agency decided that certain information needed to be kept from the media, the courts usually went along with the decision. This has obviously changed. Many people still believe that the decisions to disclose or withhold security-related information from the media and the public should be made by the elected legislative and executive branches rather than by the nonelected courts. They contend that the agencies that routinely deal with military and foreign policy security information are infinitely better qualified to assess matters of public security than judges whose training is narrowly legal. Wise decisionmaking about disclosure of information involving national security issues is particularly difficult because the clamor of the media to obtain certain information in the "public interest" and the government's contention that it requires protection are often both self-serving. The public interest may be simply the reporters' interest in furthering their careers, or the publishers' interest in making money, or the government's interest in shielding itself from embarrassment.

At times, security issues are resolved through informal cooperation between the government and the media or through self-censorship. For instance, during the Iranian hostage crisis, six American hostages were sheltered in the Canadian embassy in Teheran for several weeks. Prominent news organizations, such as NBC, CBS, *Time, Newsweek,* and the *New York Times,* were privy to this information. Following requests from the White House and State Department, they decided to withhold the news to protect the hostages, even though it meant foregoing an excellent story. The story surfaced early in 1980, after the six hostages had been smuggled out of Iran.[26] Similarly, media have refrained from providing the public with details in a number of kidnapping incidents when news stories could have jeopardized delicate negotiations between kidnappers and the would-be rescuers of the victims.

Executive Privilege.　The doctrine of executive privilege is deeply intertwined with the question of the limits of secrecy. Chief executives have the right to conceal information that they consider sensitive. This right extends to all of their personal communications to their staffs about public matters. In the past, the courts usually have upheld executive privilege, but decisions since the Nixon years suggest that the privilege may be whittled down in the future.

Silence by various government departments and agencies also sharply restricts political news available to the media. Undisclosed information frequently concerns failures, incidents of malfeasance, malfunctions, or governmental waste. Agencies guard this type of news zealously because disclosure might harm the agency or its key personnel. Chief executives at all levels of government often have issued directives restraining top officials from talking freely to journalists. Although not usually enforceable, these directives reduce the flow of information nevertheless. In March 1983, President Reagan issued a directive providing for lie-detector tests to check compliance with disclosure rules. However, the directive was later rescinded in the face of public uproar.

Except for the ever-present opportunity to get information through leaks, reporters find it difficult to penetrate the walls of silence erected by publicity-shy agencies. It is far easier to rely on press handouts or publicity releases supplied by the agency, or on secondary reports from agency personnel. This handout information reflects the sources' sense of what is and is not news rather than the reporters' own news judgments.[27]

Private Industry Documents

While the problem of government secrecy as a restraint on information collection is formidable, it is small compared with the problem of access to news stories covering the private sector of society. Many enterprises, whose operations affect the lives of millions of Americans as much or more than most government agencies, shroud their operations in secrecy. If General Motors or International Telephone and Telegraph or General Mills wants to exclude reporters from access to information about their business practices, they may do so with impunity. So may drug companies, repair shops, or housing contractors.

The Freedom of Information Act does not cover unpublished records of private business, except for the reports made to the government about sales or inventory figures or customer lists. As noted earlier, many of these reports are withheld from the public on the grounds that business cannot thrive if its operational data are made available to its competitors.[28] Moreover, the chances that withheld information will be disclosed through leaks are infinitely less in business than in government.

Individual Rights vs. the Public's Right to Know

Thus far we have been mainly concerned with barriers to the free flow of information imposed by the mass media to protect editorial freedom or by government or industry to shield potentially sensitive information. We now will discuss barriers to circulation of information imposed by individuals or on behalf of individuals for the purpose of protecting rights such as the right to privacy, the right to an unprejudiced trial, the right to gather information freely, and the right to a good reputation.

Privacy Protection

How much may the media publish about the private affairs of people in public and private life without infringing on the constitutionally protected right of privacy? How much is excluded from public scrutiny because of privacy rights? The answers depend on the status of the people involved. Private individuals enjoy broad protections from publicity; people who have become public figures because their lives are of interest to the public or because they are public officials do not.

In general, state and federal courts have been fairly lenient in permitting the media to cover details about the personal affairs of people whose lives have become matters of public interest. The right to publish has been upheld more often than the right to privacy. This trend is epitomized by a 1975 Georgia case about a young woman who had been raped and murdered. To protect its privacy, the family wanted to keep her name out of stories discussing the crime. The news media did not honor the family's request and published gruesome details of the crime, naming the victim. The family sued for invasion of privacy, claiming that there was absolutely no need to disclose the name and that Georgia law prohibited the release of the names of rape victims. The U.S. Supreme Court disagreed and overturned the Georgia law. It held that crime was a matter of public record, making the facts surrounding it of public interest and publishable, despite protests by victims and their families.[29]

Circumstances may turn private individuals into public figures. This happened to Oliver Sipple, a young man in a crowd of people watching President Gerald R. Ford. Sipple prevented an assassination attempt on the president by grabbing the would-be assassin's gun. Newspeople who interviewed him checked his background and discovered that he was part of San Francisco's homosexual community. Although this had nothing to do with his impromptu action in protecting the president, it was publicized. The disclosure caused Sipple great personal difficulties. He brought suit for invasion of privacy, but the courts denied his claim, saying that he had become an "involuntary public figure" by seizing the gun and had thus forfeited his right to privacy.

Individuals may also lose their right to privacy when they grant interviews to reporters. Once the interview is given, reporters are free to round the story out with observations that were not part of the interview. They are also free to publish those facts that were told to them in confidence. If reporters, without malice, misrepresent some of the facts, this, too, is tolerated. The rationale is that the public is entitled to a full story, if it gets any story at all, and that reporting should not be unduly inhibited by fears of privacy invasion suits.

Many privacy invasion cases involve unauthorized photographs of people in public life. Jacqueline Kennedy Onassis, the widow of President Kennedy, went to court to sue one particularly obnoxious photographer for taking photographs of her private life. Even though she was no longer the first lady, she remained a public figure, the court ruled, and therefore pictures could be taken and printed without her consent. The court, however, ordered the photographer to stop harassing her.[30]

To strengthen privacy protection, the courts in recent years have permitted subjects of unsolicited investigative reports to use trespass laws to stop the media. An example is the trespassing judgment won by the fashionable Le Mistral Restaurant against CBS in 1976 after reporters had entered the premises and filmed a story showing violations of New York's health code.[31]

Fair Trial and the Gag Rule

The broad scope of disclosure permitted about most people in public life should be contrasted with the limited scope of disclosure that the courts permit in their own bailiwick in criminal cases. The right of accused persons to be protected against publicity that might influence judge and jury and harm their case has been zealously guarded by the judiciary. This has been true even though scientific evidence demonstrating that media publicity actually influences the parties to a trial is scant and somewhat contradictory.[32]

The stern posture of the courts in censoring pretrial publicity is weakening, however. In 1983, two U.S. Supreme Court justices refused to block a nationwide television broadcast about a sensational murder case scheduled for trial three weeks later. The trial involved seven white New Orleans policemen accused of the revenge slaying of four black men suspected of participation in the murder of a white police officer. The trial had been moved from New Orleans to Dallas because of prejudicial publicity in New Orleans. Similarly, a federal court refused in 1983 to prevent television stations from showing tapes of a cocaine transaction incriminating John DeLorean, a well-known automobile maker and jet-set celebrity. DeLorean's attorneys had argued that the pretrial publicity would make it impossible to impanel an impartial jury. In another case the courts ruled that incriminating tapes used in a corruption trial of several members of Congress could be publicly shown, even though several defendants had not been tried as yet, and the convicted defendants were appealing the case.[33]

The question of the permissible scope of media coverage of court cases was brought to wide public attention by two murder cases, *Shepherd v. Florida* in 1951 and *Sheppard v. Maxwell* in 1966.[34] In these cases the U.S. Supreme Court held that the defendants, convicted of murder, had not had a fair trial because of widespread media publicity. As Justices Robert H. Jackson and Felix Frankfurter put it in *Shepherd v. Florida*, "the trial was but a legal gesture to register a verdict already dictated by the press and the public opinion (it) generated." The convictions therefore were overturned.

Judges have the right to prohibit the mass media from covering some or all of a court case before and during a trial, even when the public is allowed to attend courtroom sessions. No evidence need be brought that publication of the information covered by the "gag" order would impede a fair trial. Gag orders may extend even to judges' rulings that tell the media to refrain from covering a case. Thus, the fact of judicial suppression of information may itself be hidden.

Gag orders interfere with the media's ability to report on the fairness of judicial proceedings. They also run counter to the general reluctance of American courts to condone "prior censorship." Nonetheless, the courts have upheld gag laws as a necessary protection for accused persons.

Numerous reporters have gone to jail and paid fines rather than obey gag rules because they felt that the courts were overly protective of the rights of criminal suspects and insufficiently concerned with the public's right to know. A 1976 decision, *Nebraska Press Association v. Stuart,* upholds, to a certain degree, the reporters' views.[35] In that case the Supreme Court reversed a gag order that had been in effect for several months concerning coverage of a murder trial. The Court declared that careless reporting which interferes with the rights of defendants should be forestalled by judicial maneuvers other than gag laws. For instance, trials can be moved to different jurisdictions if there has been excessive publicity locally. Suits also can be brought against media enterprises or individual reporters who have acted irresponsibly. Irresponsible or illegal reporting might consist of publicizing testimony from closed sessions of the courts, taking unauthorized pictures, or bribing court personnel to leak trial testimony.

The policy on gag laws is still unclear, however. Some lower courts have refused to comply with Supreme Court directives or have evaded the spirit of decisions. For example, in a number of instances in recent years judges, instead of gagging the press, have placed gags on all the principals in a case, including the plaintiffs and defendants, their lawyers, and the jury, prohibiting them from talking about the case, particularly to members of the press. In an increasing number of cases, judges have barred access to information by closing courtrooms to all observers during pretrial proceedings as well as trials.

The Supreme Court during the 1980s began to strike down a number of these restrictions. In *Richmond Newspapers v. Virginia,* the Court ruled that the public and the press had an almost absolute right to attend criminal trials.[36] In the same vein, the justices declared in 1984 that neither newspeople nor the public may be barred from observing jury selection, except in unusual circumstances.[37] These recent decisions suggest that at least the Supreme Court is moving closer to the notion that the public's access to judicial proceedings is part of the First Amendment rights guaranteed by the Constitution.

Shield Laws

Digging into the affairs of public officials and other prominent citizens or exposing the activities of criminal or dissident groups often requires winning the confidence of informants with promises to conceal their identity. Newspeople are hampered in their prepublication research if a court or legislative body has the right to know the identity of their sources, to examine undisclosed bits of information, and to issue subpoenas for them. If reporters disclose such information, they break their word. Their sources are likely to dry up, whether they are public officials who have leaked confidential information, underworld informers, crime victims, or political dissidents.

Shield laws that protect reporters against inquiries have become particularly urgent whenever law enforcement agencies find it difficult to penetrate dissident and deviant groups. At such times these agencies are tempted to use subpoenas to compel testimony from journalists, making them unwitting

'ONE MORE TIME—ARE YOU READY TO REVEAL YOUR NEWS SOURCES?'

Oliphant. © 1984 Universal Press Syndicate.
Reprinted with permission. All rights reserved.

agents of the government. Shield laws are also needed to protect the physical safety of sources who disclose the activities of organized criminals or terrorists.

Generally speaking, the U.S. Supreme Court has held that, in the absence of shield laws, newspeople, like ordinary citizens, do not have the right to protect their sources in the face of a subpoena. They have no special right to be warned about a court-approved search of their premises to uncover evidence that might reveal their sources and the information provided by them.[38] Nor may they shield records or editorial deliberations from judicial scrutiny if these records are needed to prove deliberate libel. However, if the needed information is available from unshielded sources, the judges have often excused journalists from disclosure.[39]

Recognizing the ill effects of these common law-based compulsory disclosure rules on investigative reporting of crime and corruption, more than half of the states have passed shield laws to protect reporters from forced testimony. Shield laws give journalists most of the rights enjoyed by lawyers, doctors, and clergy to shield their sources' identity and information. Shield laws also may bar searches of news offices to discover leads to criminal activity. The Privacy Protection Act of 1980 prohibits government authorities at all levels from conducting surprise searches of newsrooms, except in a few, clearly specified situations.[40]

Shield laws usually do not ensure absolute protection. For example, when the right of reporters to withhold the names of their sources clashes with the right of other individuals to conduct a lawsuit involving serious matters (such as gathering evidence for a murder or conspiracy trial or a libel suit), state shield laws and common law protections must yield. In 1978, *New York Times* reporter Myron Farber was fined and jailed for 38 days for disobeying a court order to provide information to a murder defendant. Farber's story about a series of deaths in a New Jersey hospital had led to the trial of the physician charged with murdering the patients. In 1983, the Maryland Supreme Court ruled that Loretta Tofani, a *Washington Post* reporter, must testify about prisoners in a suburban jail who had told her about committing rape and being rape victims. The reporter's articles had won a Pulitzer Prize.[41] Likewise, CBS News was required to give Gen. William Westmoreland the text of its in-house investigation of a 1982 television documentary that had allegedly libeled the general. The documentary on the Vietnam War had charged Westmoreland with falsifying enemy troop figures. In his libel suit, Westmoreland contended that producers of the documentary had deliberately omitted information that exonerated him. The U.S. District Court in New York City rejected the network's contention that its in-house report was protected by First Amendment free-press guarantees; the network had referred in court to findings contained in the report.[42]

Some journalists have recommended a federal shield law to protect all newspeople throughout the country. Others, fearing that such a law would provide conditional shielding only, prefer to do without shield laws of any kind. They contend that the First Amendment constitutes an absolute shield. These differences of opinion have taken steam out of the pressure for a federal shield law.[43] Members of the judiciary also deny that shield laws are needed, but for different reasons. In the words of Justice Byron R. White, "From the beginning of our country, the press has operated without constitutional protection for press informants and the press has flourished." Hence, absence of shield laws has "not been a serious obstacle to either the development or retention of confidential news sources by the press." [44]

The power of congressional committees to compel testimony is equal to the power of the courts, raising similar shielding questions. A prominent 1976 case involved CBS reporter Daniel Schorr, who had received secret information about the proceedings of a congressional committee investigating CIA activities. He refused to tell the committee the name of the source who had leaked the information. Although the committee had the power to cite Schorr for contempt of Congress and punish him accordingly, it chose not to do so. Insiders saw this decision as evidence of the general trend in the post-Watergate era to permit shielding when it eases investigative reporting of government misconduct.[45]

Libel Laws

The trend toward facilitating investigative reporting predates the Watergate era, which brought nationwide attention and approval for the role of reporters in ferreting out crime even in the presidential office. Pre-Watergate changes in libel law are in point. Libel suits, even when they were lost in court, always had a dampening effect on reporting. That changed substantially for cases involving public officials with the decision in *New York Times v. Sullivan* in 1964.[46] In that case an action for libel was brought by the police chief of Montgomery, Alabama, in the wake of charges of mishandling of civil rights demonstrations published in an advertisement in the *Times*. The U.S. Supreme Court absolved the newspaper, ruling that a public official must be able to show that a story containing libelous information was published "with knowledge that it was false or with reckless disregard of whether it was false or not." [47] Courts since 1964 have been lenient in construing what is reckless behavior in story verification procedures because they know that media must publish quickly if a story is to have news value.

The "Sullivan rule" has made it very difficult for public officials to bring suit for libelous statements made about them. Malicious intent and extraordinary carelessness are hard to prove, even when journalists are required to open their files to the attacked official and to report the rationale for printing the attack. By the same token, the Sullivan rule has made it much easier for media to publish adverse information about public officials, true or false, without the need for extensive checking of the accuracy of the information prior to its publication.

A number of cases have tested the range of the Sullivan rule. *Time Inc. v. Hill,* a privacy invasion case, extended the rule beyond people in public office to people whose experiences have made them public figures.[48] In that case the Court ruled that a crime victim could not sue for libel, even though *Time* magazine published fictionalized information from a play about the crime that portrayed the victim in a false light. In 1974, the Court adopted a more restrictive view of a "public figure." In *Gertz v. Robert Welch* it held that a prominent lawyer, whose name had been widely reported in the news, was not a public figure and could therefore sue for libel.[49] The Court indicated that a person who had not deliberately sought publicity would be deemed a public figure only in exceptional circumstances. What these circumstances are remains unclear.[50]

The battle between freedom of the press and the right of individuals to be protected from harmful publicity is full of confusing developments. In sum, the courts have pulled back from the position that made individual rights, except the right to a fair trial, largely subordinate. They have done so by distinguishing the rights of private individuals from those of public figures and by construing the category of "public figures" more narrowly. This leaves private individuals with substantial rights to bar the media from publishing potentially libelous or embarrassing facts, so long as those facts are not a matter of public record.

By and large, laws and court decisions protecting private individuals have not greatly benefited people in public life. The principle that full publicity for the activities of public officials and institutions is essential has been reaffirmed repeatedly. The Supreme Court, albeit by a sharply divided vote, has even encouraged appellate courts to scrutinize the facts in libel cases to prevent undue constraints on the media in cases involving the Sullivan rule.[51] The best protection for public figures from unscrupulous exposure by the media are the informal and formal codes of ethics (discussed in Chapter 2) by which most journalists abide most of the time. The increasing number of suits by public figures against media people have also become a damper on careless reporting because these suits are costly in time and money, even when the media are exonerated. By 1983, the investigative television show "60 Minutes" had successfully defended itself in 150 libel actions, but the costs were staggering. Financially weaker programs could not have paid them; neither could they have risked multimillion dollar judgments against them, should they lose a libel suit.

Other Restrictions on Publication

As discussed in Chapter 1, all governments prohibit the publication of certain information on the grounds that the public interest would be harmed. The United States is no exception. The areas where censorship is most prevalent are national security connected with external dangers, national security connected with internal dangers, and obscenity. In each category there is general agreement that certain types of information should not be publicized. In the case of obscenity, concern is especially grave when television programs are involved because the medium reaches vast child audiences. There is very little agreement, however, about where the line ought to be drawn between permitted and prohibited types of material.

It has been even more difficult to reach agreement in specific cases on whether or not security censorship was in the public interest. We have already discussed the controversy surrounding the release of the Pentagon Papers as well as the government's efforts to prohibit publication of a magazine article detailing, on the basis of available but dispersed information, how a hydrogen bomb might be manufactured. Additional foreign policy examples will be presented in Chapter 10.

News concerning internal security matters primarily involves investigations of allegedly subversive groups and reports on civil disturbances. Several relevant cases are discussed in Chapter 9. Such news also involves media portrayal of asocial behavior that might lead to imitation. Various attempts to limit the portrayal of crime and violence, either in general or on programs to which children have access, are examples. They are discussed in Chapter 5.

Closely related to restraints on the depiction of crime and violence are restraints on publication of obscene materials and broadcasts of offensive language and pictures. It is feared that such broadcasts may corrupt members of the audience, particularly children, and lead to imitative behavior. Although the 1970 report of the President's Commission on Obscenity and Pornography casts doubt on the claim that such broadcasts are socially dangerous, many foes of obscenity and "dirty" words remain unconvinced.

In addition, proponents of obscenity restraints argue that publication of obscene materials, particularly in visual form, offends community standards and should therefore be prohibited by law. This argument rests on the notion that the public, as represented generally by self-selected spokesmen, should have the right to prohibit the dissemination of material that offends the sense of propriety of many citizens. Despite the popularity of pornography, as shown by the millions of citizens who go to pornographic movies and stage shows and who read pornographic magazines, laws in many places bar free access to such information. The U.S. Supreme Court has repeatedly upheld such restrictions.

Another example of protective censorship is the ban on cigarette advertising on radio and television, in effect since 1971. It is designed to protect susceptible individuals from being lured into smoking by seductive advertisements. Pressures for additional areas of protective censorship have been considerable and range from pleas to stop liquor and sugared cereal advertisements to requests to bar information dealing with abortion or drug addiction. Legislatures and courts have rejected most of them. But the future is unclear. Some of these matters have become election issues. If candidates have committed themselves to censoring abortion or drug information, for example, they may be compelled to follow through on their promises by working for appropriate laws after election.

So-called "hate" broadcasts also remain a grey area in broadcast law. Contrary to the expressed public policy of the nation, many small stations or individual programs routinely attack racial, ethnic, and religious groups. Like broadcasts with obscene language, these attacks violate the sense of propriety of many citizens. Nevertheless, the FCC has been reluctant to withhold licenses from the offending parties because genuine freedom of expression includes "freedom for the thought we hate," as Supreme Court Justice Oliver Wendell Holmes said long ago.

The case of KTTL-FM, a small country music station in Dodge City, Kansas, illustrates the dilemma. The station has attacked blacks, Asians, Roman Catholics, Jews, public officials, the courts, and the Internal Revenue

Service. It has suggested hanging public officials, "cleansing the earth" of "black beasts," and preparing militarily for an impending racial Armageddon. But despite protests to the FCC from Kansas lawmakers and members of the public, license revocation is unlikely so long as no actual violence can be linked to the broadcasts.[52]

Summary

In a democratic society citizens have the right and civic duty to inform themselves and to express their views publicly. The press, as the eyes and ears of the public, shares these rights and must be protected against restraints that could interfere with its ability to gather information and disseminate it freely. In this chapter we have seen how these important basic principles have been modified to meet the realities of political life in the United States. Despite legislation such as the Freedom of Information Act of 1966, a great deal of information about governmental activities remains shrouded from the public's eyes. Either it has been classified as secret for security reasons, or it belongs to a broad list of information categories that are closed to the public because their release could embarrass individuals or lead to undesirable business practices. The public and press also are excluded from many official meetings if the participants so desire. Executive sessions of legislatures, grand jury sessions, or pretrial proceedings in the courts are examples.

Nearly all of these exclusions have been challenged in the courts because they constitute restrictions on the right of access to information. The courts have ruled that most of them are compatible with constitutional guarantees of free speech and press. They also have ruled, for the most part, that news professionals enjoy neither greater rights of access to information than does the general public, nor, in the absence of shield laws, greater freedom to protect their access to information by refusal to disclose their sources.

The right to publish information is also limited. Here the public is most seriously restricted because newspeople claim the exclusive right to determine what to publicize and what to omit. The power of print media to refuse a forum to most citizens is nearly absolute, aside from social pressures mandating that stories of widely recognized public concern be published. Under current rules and regulations, the electronic media must grant equal access to the air to political candidates for the same office, to people who hold opposing views on a controversial issue that has been advocated in a broadcast, and to people whose reputations have been attacked in broadcasts. But concerted efforts to abolish these rules are likely to succeed because the rules discourage broadcasters from airing controversial information.

Even when access to a media forum is ensured, the right to publish is not absolute. Public policy considerations, such as the need to safeguard external and internal security and the need to protect the moral standards of the community, have led to news suppression. The scope of permissible censorship has been the subject of countless inconclusive debates and conflicting court decisions.

The right to publish also conflicts on many occasions with the rights of individuals to enjoy their privacy, to be protected from disclosure of damaging information, true or false, and to be safeguarded from publicity that might interfere with a fair trial. The courts have been the main forum for weighing these conflicting claims, and the scales have tipped erratically from case to case. Two trends stand out from the haze of legal battles: *the right to a fair trial generally wins out over the freedom to publish* and *private individuals enjoy far greater protection from publicity than do people in public life.* Shifting definitions of what turns a private person into a public person have blurred this distinction, however.

When we look at the massive restraints on the rights of access to information, the rights of access to publication channels, and the right to publish information freely, we may feel deep concern about freedom of information. Is there cause for worry? Taking a bright view, one can point out, as Justice Byron White did in the 1972 *Branzburg* case, that "the press has flourished. The existing constitutional rules have not been a serious obstacle" stopping the press from investigating wrongdoing.[53] The press as watchdog may be chilled by legal restraints, but it is not frozen into inaction. From the perspective of champions of First Amendment rights, that may be small comfort so long as many current political and judicial trends point toward greater restraints and greater public tolerance for restraints, especially when national security is involved.

Notes

1. Joseph R. Tybor, "The Press Faces the Court—and the Public," *Chicago Tribune,* June 19, 1983.
2. Justice Potter Stewart in *New York Times Co. v. U.S.,* 403 U.S. 713 (1971).
3. Jerome Barron, *Freedom of the Press for Whom: The Right of Access to the Mass Media* (Bloomington, Ind.: Indiana University Press, 1973).
4. 418 U.S. 241 (1974).
5. For a full discussion of the case, see Fred W. Friendly, *The Good Guys, the Bad Guys and the First Amendment: Free Speech vs. Fairness in Broadcasting* (New York: Random House, 1977), pp. 192-198.
6. Phil Gailey, "F.C.C. Lets Broadcasters Hold Political Debates," *New York Times,* November 9, 1983.
7. *Banzhaf v. Federal Communications Commission,* 405 F.2d 1082 (D.C. Cir. 1968); certiorari denied, 396 U.S. 842 (1969).
8. 395 U.S. 367 (1961).
9. Friendly, *The Good Guys,* pp. 32-42.
10. Ibid., pp. 199-236.
11. Barron, *Freedom of the Press for Whom,* p. 5.
12. For a discussion of these issues, see Jerome S. Silber, "Broadcast Regulation and

the First Amendment," *Journalism Monographs*, no. 70 (Lexington, Ky.: Association for Education in Journalism, November 1980); court cases testing the First Amendment rights of cable television broadcasters are analyzed in Peter Kerr, "Cable TV Pressing Free-Speech Issue," *New York Times*, April 5, 1984.
13. Jonathan Friendly, "U.S. Court Extends Editorial Rights to Public TV," *New York Times*, October 28, 1981.
14. Paula J. Lobo, "First Amendment Implications of Exclusive Broadcast Contracts," *Journalism Quarterly* 60 (Spring 1983): 41-47.
15. *FCC v. WNCN Listeners Guild*, 450 U.S. 582 (1981).
16. Barron, *Freedom of the Press for Whom*, pp. 117-121.
17. *U.S. v. Kiger*, 421 F.2d 1396 (2d Cir. 1970); cert. denied, 398 U.S. 904 (1970).
18. *Zemel v. Rusk*, 381 U.S. 1 (1965). See also Louis A. Day, "Broadcaster Liability for Access Denial," *Journalism Quarterly* 60 (Summer 1983): 246-261.
19. *Branzburg v. Hayes*, 408 U.S. 665 (1972); quotation appears on p. 684.
20. See, for instance, *Pell v. Procunier*, 417 U.S. 817 (1974); *Saxbe v. Washington Post Co.*, 417 U.S. 843 (1974); and *Houchins v. KQED, Inc.*, 438 U.S. 1 (1978).
21. These and related cases are discussed more fully in John J. Watkins, "Newsgathering and the First Amendment," *Journalism Quarterly* 53 (Autumn 1976): 406-416. Citations in notes 14 and 16.
22. The act was an amendment to the 1946 Administrative Procedure Act—5 U.S.C.A. 1002 (1946)—which provided that official records should be open to people who could demonstrate a "need to know" except for "information held confidential for good cause found" (Sec. 22). The 1966 amendment stated that disclosure should be the general rule, rather than the exception, with the burden on government to justify the withholding of a document, if challenged in court (5 U.S.C.A. Sec. 552 and Supp. 1, Feb. 1975). Several attempts to narrow the act's scope substantially have been defeated, but minor amendments passed in the early 1980s.
23. Elsie Hebert, "How Accessible Are the Records in Government Records Centers?" *Journalism Quarterly* 52 (Spring 1975): 23-29.
24. Robert Pear, "Information Curb Assailed by Panel," *New York Times*, August 9, 1982.
25. 403 U.S. 713 (1971).
26. Deirdre Carmody, "Some News Groups Knew of 6 in Hiding," *New York Times*, January 31, 1980.
27. For comparative views of government secrecy, see Itzhak Galnoor, ed., *Government Secrecy in Democracies* (New York: Harper & Row, 1977).
28. Richard B. Kielbowicz, "The Freedom of Information Act and Government's Corporate Information Files," *Journalism Quarterly* 55 (Autumn 1978): 481-486.
29. *Cox Broadcasting Corp. v. Cohn*, 420 U.S. 469 (1975).
30. *Gallella v. Onassis*, 487 F.2d 986 (1973).
31. *Le Mistral Inc. v. Columbia Broadcasting System*, 402 N.Y.S. 2d 815 (1978).
32. Interestingly, the courts maintain the fiction that judges can command jurors to strike improper information presented in court from their memory. Presumably, judges are unable to do the same for media information that jury members might have received outside the court room. The issue is examined in Judith M. Buddenbaum, David H. Weaver, Ralph L. Holsinger, and Charlene J. Brown, "Pretrial Publicity and Juries: A Review of Research," Research Report No. 11, School of Journalism, Indiana University, Bloomington, Ind., March 1981.
33. See, for example, *U.S. v. Alexandro*, 675 F.2d 34, (1982); *U.S. v. Jannotti*, 673 F.2d 578 (1982); *U.S. v. Myers*, 692 F.2d 823, 837 (1982); *U.S. v. Williams*, 33 Criminal Law Reporter, 2122 (1983); *U.S. v. Kelly*, 33 Criminal Law Reporter, 2153 (1983).
34. 341 U.S. 50 (1951); 384 U.S. 333 (1966).

35. 427 U.S. 539 (1976).
36. 448 U.S. 555 (1980).
37. Glen Elsasser, "High Court Curbs Secret Jury Selection," *Chicago Tribune,* January 19, 1984. The controversy arose because the Riverside County, California, Superior Court closed jury selection in a rape-murder case. The Press-Enterprise Company of Riverside sued to gain access to the court proceeding and to the relevant transcripts.
38. *Zurcher v. The Stanford Daily,* 436 U.S. 547 (1978).
39. *Anthony Herbert v. Barry Lando and the Columbia Broadcasting System Inc.,* 441 U.S. 153 (1979).
40. The impact of the law is discussed in Tony Atwater, "Newsroom Searches: Is 'Probable Cause' Still in Effect Despite New Law?" *Journalism Quarterly* 60 (Spring 1983): 4-9.
41. *Tofani v. State of Maryland,* 297 Md. 165 (1983).
42. Jonathan Friendly, "CBS Is Told to Give Westmoreland Internal Study on Vietnam Report," *New York Times,* April 22, 1983; see also "Westmoreland/CBS Controversy," *Historic Documents of 1983* (Washington, D.C.: Congressional Quarterly, 1984), pp. 401-412.
43. Jonathan Friendly, "Prosecutors Increase Efforts to Make Press Name Sources," *New York Times,* November 26, 1983.
44. *Branzburg v. Hayes,* Id. at 699.
45. However, Schorr lost his job with CBS as a result of the incident. By suspending Schorr, the network discouraged this kind of coverage, even though Schorr's right to shield his sources was not challenged.
46. 376 U.S. 254 (1964).
47. Id. at 279-280.
48. 385 U.S. 374 (1967).
49. 418 U.S. 323 (1974).
50. *Time Inc. v. Firestone,* 424 U.S. 448 (1976); *Hutchinson v. Proxmire,* 443 U.S. 111 (1979) and *Wolston v. Reader's Digest,* 443 U.S. 157 (1979).
51. Linda Greenhouse, "High Court Calls for Special Care in Libel Appeals," *New York Times,* April 30, 1984. The case is *Bose Corp. v. Consumers Union,* no. 82-1246.
52. Wayne King, "Kansans Protest Broadcasts of Hate," *New York Times,* May 13, 1983.
53. *Branzburg v. Hayes,* Id. at 699.

Readings

Chamberlin, Bill F., and Charlene J. Brown, eds. *The First Amendment Reconsidered.* New York: Longman, 1982.
Drechsel, Robert E. *News Making in the Trial Courts.* New York: Longman, 1983.
Foley, John, Robert C. Lobdell, and Robert Trounson, eds. *The Media and the Law.* Los Angeles: Times Mirror Press, 1977.
Grey, David L. *The Supreme Court and the News Media.* Evanston, Ill.: Northwestern University Press, 1968.
O'Brien, David M. *The Public's Right to Know: The Supreme Court and the First Amendment.* New York: Praeger, 1981.
Pember, Don R. *Mass Media Law.* Dubuque, Iowa: William C. Brown, 1981.
Schmidt, Benno C., Jr. *Freedom of the Press vs. Public Access.* New York: Praeger, 1976.

Media Impact on Individual Attitudes and Behavior 5

In the prime time evening hours of September 10, 1974, NBC broadcast a television drama called "Born Innocent," a story about a teen-aged girl who was sexually abused by fellow inmates in a children's reformatory. Three days later, four youngsters playing on a secluded San Francisco beach imitated the crime. The parents of the nine-year-old victim sued NBC, charging that the telecast inspired the crime. The courts rejected the principle of media liability but did not rule on whether television is "a school for violence and a college for crime," as the plaintiffs had claimed. More recently, the movie "The Deer-Hunter" was repeatedly shown on television. It contains a Russian-roulette scene in which a character points a nearly empty gun to his head, pulls the trigger, and dies. At least 34 people are known to have died in reenactments of that scene after watching one of these broadcasts.

In November 1983, ABC widely advertised its forthcoming Sunday-night movie "The Day After," which depicted how Kansas City, Kansas, might fare in a nuclear attack. The prospect of exposing millions of Americans to scenes of nuclear horror greatly concerned the Reagan White House because of the potential political as well as psychological aftereffects of the film. A nuclear freeze movement, designed to change the government's defense policies, was already gaining ground. Antinuclear groups hailed the film as a godsend that would help them recruit members and raise money. Copies of the film were rushed to Western Europe in hopes that the sight of destruction would fan resistance to the installation there of new U.S. missiles. To blunt the anticipated effects of the movie, Secretary of State George Shultz agreed to comment on it immediately following the broadcast. Other cabinet members were mobilized for speaking engagements. The administration also distributed an 18-page résumé of President Reagan's positions on peace, arms reduction, and nuclear deterrence to forestall public reactions that might harm administration policies.

These examples dramatize the many puzzling questions so often asked about the impact of mass media on children and adults. Does violence in television fiction and news programs cause violence in real life? How much do people learn from the media, and what do they learn? Are people's attitudes and values influenced by what they read and see? What political effects spring from the interaction of Americans with the mass media, which paint a picture of the world around them?

In this chapter we will examine such questions, beginning with the influence the media have on general attitudes toward society and politics. We will deal first with the assimilation of attitudes as an unintended byproduct of media exposure. By and large, newspeople do not try to teach attitudes and values, nor do people try to learn them. Rather, "incidental" learning of the basic world view of society springs from exposure to individual, dramatic events or from the incremental impact of the total information flow over prolonged periods of time.

In later sections of the chapter, more deliberate attempts to teach and to learn will be considered. The ways in which various types of people choose the media to which they will pay attention and the sorts of things they learn or fail to learn will be examined. Finally, we will seek some tentative answers to the question posed at the start: to what degree does exposure to the mass media influence behavior in politically significant ways?

Differential Effects of Print and Broadcast News

As we have done before, we will talk about mass media effects in general, rather than about the separate effects of television, radio, newspapers, or magazines. There are several reasons. Most importantly, researchers have found it very difficult to separate the effects of various types of media. Nearly every individual in America today is exposed to combinations of all the media, either directly or indirectly through contacts with people who have been exposed. We may know that Americans in space suits have walked on the moon; we may view this as a scientific miracle that raised the sagging prestige of the United States abroad and at home; and we may feel pride about the venture and yet some unease about its high price tag. But do all of these thoughts and feelings or only part of them come from television, newspapers, or conversations with others? It is well-nigh impossible to disentangle such strands of information.[1]

Demographic differences among media users make it difficult to determine to what extent print and electronic media produce dissimilar effects. The finding that heavy newspaper users tend to be better informed than abstainers cannot be explained solely in terms of the qualitative differences between print and electronic media. One must also consider that, compared with television buffs, print media users are more likely to seek out current information because they generally enjoy higher socioeconomic status and better formal education. Their status in life provides above-average incentives for learning.

Attitudes toward the media matter as well. Print media are viewed by most people as sources of information, while electronic media are viewed as sources of entertainment. These attitudinal differences, rather than the nature of each medium, may explain the distinct effects.[2]

Among various types of media, television is the most unique. It appears to be a more potent stimulus than print sources for stirring emotions and creating vivid mental pictures. Again, exceptions are numerous and research is fragmentary. It also may be more difficult to learn from television than from other media because visual messages do not spell out their meanings as explicitly as verbal messages. Viewers may be forced to develop their own generalizations and abstractions from pictures with insufficient verbal guidance and interpretation. Studies of comprehension of television news show that most viewers have difficulty understanding and explaining what they have seen. In one study, viewers who were asked to relate the main points of specific stories failed to do so for up to 72 percent of the stories. Miscomprehension rates for individual stories ranged from 16 to 93 percent.[3]

Television's greatest political impact, compared with that of other media, is derived from its ability to reach millions of people simultaneously with the same images. Major broadcasts enter nearly every home in the nation instantaneously and simultaneously. Print media could never attain such a reach and the power that flows from it. Moreover, 23 million American adults are functionally illiterate and therefore are almost entirely beyond print media reach.[4] What the poorly educated now learn about politics from television may be fragmentary and hazy, but it represents a quantum leap over their previous exposure and learning.

In short, the research on the differential effects of various types of media reveals that different types present stimuli that vary substantially in nature and content. It would be surprising, therefore, if their impact were identical, even when they deal with the same subjects. At present, research cannot provide adequate answers about the precise effects of stimulus variations and about the processes by which individuals mesh a variety of media stimuli. Therefore, we shall assess the end product—the combined impact of all print and electronic media stimuli.

The Role of Media in Political Socialization

Before considering the role that mass media information plays in shaping our attitudes toward society, we need to assess the political importance of these attitudes. Political socialization—the learning, accepting, and approving of customs and rules, structures, and environmental factors governing political life—is important because it affects the quality of interaction between citizens and their government. Political systems do not operate smoothly without the support of most of their citizens, who must be willing to abide by laws, rules, and regulations and to render services, such as paying taxes or serving in the military forces.

Support is most readily obtained if citizens are convinced of the legitimacy and capability of their government and if they feel strong emotional ties to it. If political socialization fails to instill such attitudes, policies and laws of all types, such as energy conservation legislation, anti-inflation measures, or traffic regulations, may become unenforceable. Refusal to pay taxes may force sharp curtailment of governmental activities. If citizens hold government in contempt or regard it as illegitimate, political apathy, civil disobedience, revolution, or civil war may result.

In societies where the government relies on popular participation through elections and through continuous surveillance of governmental activities, political socialization must equip citizens with sufficient knowledge to partici-pate effectively. If it fails to do this, elections, at best, become a sham where people go through the motions of making a choice without understanding what this choice means. At worst, elections become a mockery in which clever politicians manipulate an ignorant electorate. Likewise, surveillance of govern-mental activities is impossible if people lack a grasp of the nature of government and public policies.

Childhood Socialization

Since political socialization starts in childhood, it is first conveyed by parents and other people in the small child's environment. From their families, children usually learn basic attitudes toward authority, property, decisionmaking, and veneration for political symbols. When children enter the more formal school setting, teaching about political values becomes quite systematic. At this point, too, children learn new factual information about their political and social world.

The people who teach children rely heavily on mass media for much of the information and values that they transmit. Hence children receive a great deal of media-based information indirectly from the very beginning of their development. Children's direct contacts with the media are equally abundant. In the United States, millions of babies watch television. In the winter, youngsters between 2 and 11 years of age spend an average of 31 hours a week in front of the television set—more time than in school. Between the ages of 12 and 17, this drops to 24 hours.[5] Eighty percent of the programs children see are intended for adults and thus differ from the child's limited personal experiences. If children can understand the message, its impact is likely to be great since, lacking experience, they are apt to take it at face value.

Research has convincingly demonstrated the strong impact that the mass media have on children's political socialization. When high school students are asked for the sources of information on which they base their attitudes about subjects such as economic or race problems, or war and patriotism, they mention the mass media far more often than they mention their families, friends, teachers, or personal experiences.[6] Comparisons of youngsters who use the media heavily with those who are light users confirm that school-age children gain substantial information from the media and that this influences their attitudes toward society. Heavy mass media users, particularly those who read newspapers, know most about current political events and show most interest in them.[7] They also show greater understanding and support for basic American values, such as the importance of free speech and the right to equal and fair treatment.[8]

Finding that mass media substantially influence socialization runs counter to earlier findings from socialization studies, which designated parents and teachers as the chief socializers. Several reasons account for the change. The first is the increasing pervasiveness of television, which makes it easy for even the youngest children to be in touch with mass media images. This pervasiveness dates back only to the early 1960s. The first official network television broadcasts in the United States took place in 1940, but widespread television viewing did not occur for several decades.

The second reason involves deficiencies in measurement. Much of the early research discounted all media influence unless it came through direct contact between the child and the media, outside the classroom setting. Learning directly from media in the classroom setting and indirect influence through media exposure of parents and teachers were ignored. These exclusions sharply reduced findings of media effects.

Finally, research designs have become more sophisticated. In the early studies, children were asked to make their own general appraisal of learning sources. A typical question might be: "From whom do you learn the most, your parents, your school, or newspapers and television?" The questions used in recent studies have been more specific. For instance, Gary Coldevin, a Canadian researcher, asked high school students in Canada and the United States what they knew about particular subjects, such as immigration policy, government in general, or education policy. Then he asked them to state arguments for and against certain policy positions. Only after the students had written down their ideas were they asked for the chief sources for their facts and, separately, about the chief sources affecting how they evaluated these issues. In nearly every case, the mass media were the chief sources of information and evaluations for U.S. as well as Canadian students. However, the media were slightly less important, and parents and schools slightly more important, as sources of evaluations than as information sources.[9]

What children learn from the mass media and how they evaluate it depends heavily on their stage of mental development. According to Jean Piaget, children between 2 and 7 years of age are keenly aware of the objects they see and hear.[10] But they do not independently perceive the connections among various phenomena or draw general conclusions from specific instances. Many of the lessons presumably taught by media stories therefore elude young children. Complex reasoning skills are fully developed only at the teen-age level. Children's interests in certain types of stories also change sharply with age, as do their attention and information-retention spans.[11] Given these variations, valid research of mass media impact on children means focusing on narrow age spans. Such research has been comparatively rare.

We do know that children are likely to be highly supportive of the political system during their early years, when they learn basic facts about prominent political figures.[12] The president and the policeman are next to father and God. By their teen-age years, youngsters have often become quite disillusioned about authority figures. This skepticism diminishes as education is completed and the young adult enters the work force. What role the media play in this transformation is unclear. It is also unclear to what extent children and adolescents imitate behavior depicted by media stories, how long they remember stories, and how long the effects of exposure last.

Adult Socialization

The pattern of heavy media exposure continues from childhood to adulthood. The average American adult spends nearly three hours a day watching television, two hours listening to radio, twenty minutes reading a newspaper, and ten minutes reading a magazine. Time spent with the mass media has jumped by 40 percent since the advent of television, mostly at the expense of other leisure time activities.[13] However, this redistribution of time has stabilized now, and there have even been occasional declines in television viewing.[14] On the average day 80 percent of all Americans are reached by television and newspapers. On a typical evening the television audience is close to 100 million people, nearly half the entire population.

This massive exposure contributes to the lifelong process of political socialization and learning. The mass media form "the mainstream of the common symbolic environment that cultivates the most widely shared conceptions of reality. We live in terms of the stories we tell—stories about what things exist, stories about how things work, and stories about what to do. . . . Increasingly, media-cultivated facts and values become standards by which we judge." [15] Once basic orientations toward the political system have been formed, attitudes usually stabilize, and later learning largely supplements and refines earlier notions. Established attitudes filter subsequent experiences. Major personal or societal upheavals may lead to more or less complete resocialization and revised political ideas. Short of drastic changes, the need to cope with information about new events and gradually shifting cultural orientations also forces the average person into continuous learning and gradual readjustments. But the basic value structure generally remains intact, even when attitudes are modified.[16]

Much of what the average person learns about political norms, rules, values, and events, and about the way people cope with these political happenings, comes of necessity from the mass media. Those with the widest exposure to political news in the mass media generally are most aware of political issues and have more opinions about these issues. Personal experiences are severely limited compared with the range of experiences that come to us directly or indirectly through the media.

Most media content is not explicitly political. It is nonetheless full of implicit messages about the social order and political activities. These messages convey information that leads to formation of politically significant attitudes. In fact, seemingly nonpolitical stories are the most widely used sources for political information. Surveys show that only one-half to two-thirds of the adult public regularly consumes explicit political news. Half of the population does not watch television news at all.[17] Only a very small proportion of the television news audience pays any serious attention to news broadcasts.

People's opinions, feelings, and evaluations about the political system may spring from their own processing of facts supplied by the media; from attitudes, opinions, and feelings explicitly expressed by the media; or from a combination of the two. It is important to distinguish between learning of facts and learning of opinions. The media play a very large role in conveying information and a much smaller role in conveying attitudes and opinions.[18] Many people who use the media for information, and as a point of departure for formulating their own appraisals, reject attitudes and evaluations that are supplied explicitly or implicitly by media stories.

A widely publicized incident on September 1, 1983, demonstrates the distinction between fact and opinion learning. A Soviet jet fighter's heat-seeking missile downed a South Korean passenger plane after it strayed over Soviet territory on a flight from New York to Seoul. Two hundred sixty-nine people died. These were the undisputed facts. The U.S. Congress denounced the shooting, calling it a "cold-blooded barbarous attack" and "one of the most infamous and reprehensible acts in history." From the Soviet perspective it was nothing of the kind. Soviet officials claimed that the plane—which they said resembled an American electronic reconnaissance plane—had been on a spy mission and had ignored warnings by intercepting military aircraft. They alleged that the United States was exploiting the tragedy as a propaganda spectacle to whip up anti-Soviet sentiments throughout the world. Apprized of the air disaster by media stories, U.S. citizens could side with congressional opinion or official Soviet views, or they could form their own, distinctive opinions.

Generally, people are prone to accept newspeople's views in those areas where personal experience and guidance from social contacts are lacking. When audiences have direct or vicarious experiences to guide them, and particularly when they have already formed firm opinions grounded in their value structures, they are far less likely to be swayed by the media. In practice, this means that the least informed and least interested are most likely to reflect the viewpoints expressed in the media, particularly television. Parroting of viewpoints espoused by political commentators explains why politically uninterested people often hold quite sophisticated opinions if they have been extensively exposed to news stories.[19]

Although we can and do form opinions independently, on many issues, particularly those concerning local problems, complete independence is impossible.[20] Rarely have we enough information and understanding to form our own views about the many complex national and international issues that succeed one another with bewildering rapidity. This puts us at the mercy of the media, not only for information, but also for interpretation. Even when we think that we are forming our own opinions about familiar issues, we may be depending on the media more than we realize. If the media fail to supply adequate information, our opinions rest on an unsound foundation.

The 1976 presidential debates between President Gerald R. Ford and Jimmy Carter provide an excellent example of the effectiveness of media opinion guidance, even in comparatively simple evaluations. A telephone survey conducted immediately after the second debate showed that viewers, by a 9 percent margin, judged the president to be the debate winner. But later, after a statement by Ford about Eastern Europe had been strongly attacked by the media, thus implying that Carter had handled himself better during the debate, viewers changed their initial evaluation. Within 24 hours, Carter's lead over Ford had risen to 42 percentage points.[21] A number of interviewees commented that they had originally judged Ford to be the winner, but felt that they must have been wrong because the media judged otherwise.

Many graphic examples of the persuasive power of the media come from advertising research, which has documented how messages can affect consumers' perceptions of unfamiliar products and activities and thus change their behavior. Broadcasting may even lead to major changes in religious beliefs. Radio and television crusades to convert people to various Christian faiths attract more than 13 million Americans each week, and thousands phone program hosts to announce their conversion or financial support.

Media's persuasiveness does not mean that exposure is tantamount to learning and change of mind. Far from it! Most media stories are promptly forgotten. Stories that become part of an individual's fund of knowledge tend to reinforce existing beliefs and feelings. Acquisition of new knowledge or changes in attitude are the exception rather than the rule. Still, they occur often enough to be highly significant.

Differences in Media Use and Socialization

Inasmuch as various groups within the population differ in their cultural environment, economic interests, and psychological make-up, it is not surprising that their media preferences differ as well. We will outline some of these differences and assess the effects that they are apt to have on political socialization. The picture is extremely complex. For example, if we look at racial differences, we cannot simply talk about characteristic media exposure and impact patterns for nonwhites and whites. We must also specify sex, age, education, income, region, and city size. Additional variations come from commonly ignored factors such as life style and social setting, family size, personality characteristics, and social and job pressures. Of course, the mere fact that individuals belong to a certain demographic category or social group does not mean that they necessarily share the media exposure characteristics of that category or group. For many individuals, group ties may be weak, with little impact on behavior. Group influence may also be weakened for people who are subject to conflicting group pressures. For instance, college students whose peer groups revel in left-wing literature may also be exposed by their families to conservative media fare. Thus, predicting their media exposure and impact patterns from these different group affiliations would be hazardous.

Race

Within the American cultural context, blacks and whites diverge in political knowledge and attitudes. Although we lack firm proof, available evidence suggests that different media exposure patterns are a partial explanation.[22] Most importantly, blacks pay considerably less attention to newspapers than whites. Fifty-nine percent read a daily newspaper, compared with 72 percent for whites. While whites show no sex differences in newspaper reading, blacks do. Black women, despite high rates of employment outside the home, trail black men by six percentage points in readership. In general, employed women show higher readership rates than women working at home. Unemployed blacks are half as likely as unemployed whites to read a daily newspaper. Since newspapers are the medium that supplies the most ample amounts of standard political news, more black than white citizens lack this information. In turn, this makes blacks less likely to share the political images and judgments of their white fellow citizens.

Blacks rely less on the mass media for political information than is true for whites. For example, only 22 percent of blacks polled in a low-income Los Angeles neighborhood said that they relied on print media for most of their political information, and only 23 percent said that they relied on radio or television. Many named instead interpersonal sources such as their families or public agencies. By comparison, 40 percent of the whites mentioned print media as major sources of political news, and 43 percent mentioned radio and television. Hispanics found print and electronic media even less useful for keeping themselves politically informed than did blacks. Only 12 percent of the Hispanics said that they got most of their political information from newspapers, and only 5 percent called radio or television their most important sources. Such alienation from the community's major political communications sources may hamper the political integration of Hispanics and blacks into the majority culture.[23]

Compared with whites, nonwhites also choose different papers and stations as their preferred news sources. This happens most often when media oriented to their racial group are available. Minority groups who primarily use ethnically oriented media are apt to live in different communication and socialization environments than people in the majority culture. Substantial differences among racial groups in attitudes toward governmental bodies, and in trust in government and feelings of political efficacy, lend credence to the belief that diverse media images, combined with different life experiences, produce distinct socialization patterns.

Blacks and whites also extract different information from the same media. Blacks are more apt than whites to believe that factual as well as fictional stories presented by the media are true to life. Therefore, the images that many blacks form about life styles or societal patterns are more likely to mirror the distortions found in media presentations.[24] A study of the diffusion of information about six assassinations showed that each racial group dwelled heavily on news that dealt with its own race. While all blacks and whites had heard about the deaths of Martin Luther King, Jr., and John and Robert Kennedy, a substantially larger number of blacks (10 to 24 percent more) knew about the assassinations of black leaders Medgar Evers and Malcolm X. Similarly, many more whites than blacks knew about the death of white Nazi leader George Lincoln Rockwell.[25]

There are many possible explanations for variations in media use and socialization patterns. Despite the successes of the civil rights movement, most blacks in the 1970s and 1980s belonged to different social groups than did whites, and they had life settings quite unlike those of the white middle class to whose tastes most media catered. The social status of many older blacks also kept them alienated from the northern urban culture in which they found themselves, often after a childhood spent in the rural South. Understandably, they were less interested in news that focused heavily on city life and politics. Higher proportions of blacks, compared with whites, fell into youthful age brackets where readership is generally lower. Fewer blacks than whites drive to work; hence radio news listening is lower among blacks. For the many blacks whose schooling has been poor, deficient reading skills make newspaper reading unattractive. Television is an appealing alternative. Accordingly, blacks on an average watch about 15 percent more television than whites.[26]

Some researchers have questioned whether the apparent differences between blacks and whites are based on race-linked cultural differences or spring instead from the fact that the black population is more frequently poor and educationally deprived. Bradley Greenberg and Brenda Dervin, for instance, contend that within the subculture of poverty, blacks and whites use the media in similar ways.[27] Accordingly, they believe that it is more accurate to talk about differences in media habits and socialization on the basis of economic and educational stratification. Other scholars argue that race and its cultural consequences are indeed important factors in media exposure and impact. Leo Bogart, for example, found racial differences in media use patterns regardless of socioeconomic status.[28] The unresolved issues thus revolve around the *causes* of subcultural differences rather than their existence. If differences are linked to race, they may be permanent. If they are linked to socioeconomic status, they may change with rising incomes, education, and occupational status.

Age, Sex, Socioeconomic Status, and Location

Sex, age, income, education, and region and city size, in addition to race, help explain differences in newspaper reading, radio listening, and television viewing. For instance, men and women differ sharply in daytime television viewing; age has a bearing on newspaper reading; southerners listen to substantially less radio than do northerners. Program preferences vary as well. Women over 50 are the heaviest viewers of television news, followed by men over 50. Twelve- to 17-year-olds are last on the trail in news watching. Men far exceed women in following sports coverage, while women spend substantially more time on television drama.

Differences in media use patterns are particularly pronounced between income levels. People of higher income, who usually are better educated than poorer people, use print media more and television less than the rest of the population. The same pattern holds for their children at all age levels. For instance, 79 percent of college graduates interviewed in one 1979 study said that they read a newspaper "yesterday," compared with 73 percent of high school graduates and 57 percent of people lacking a high school diploma.[29] The story is reversed for television viewing. College students were watching 19.8 hours of television per week, compared with 23.3 hours for high school graduates and 25.9 hours for those without a high school diploma.[30]

Upper income people also are more prone to use a variety of media. Among the upper economic groups 57 percent are multimedia users compared with 27 percent in the lower economic groups.[31] Thus, the well-to-do potentially have much more information and a greater variety of information available to them. This helps them to maintain and increase their influence and power in American society.

In part, the poor pay less attention to print media because these media carry less information of interest to them. In fact, lack of interest in politics and disillusionment with government actions are the chief reasons given for failure to read newspapers. The urban poor need consumer information on prices, goods, and services more than coverage of new business regulations or city politics. Yet the print media rarely supply adequate consumer information. While print media are largely unattractive to the poor, television and radio programs appeal to them because they carry a great deal of light entertainment. Such programs allow the poor to escape from the grim reality that surrounds their lives.

Unifying Forces

The notion of vastly different communications environments for various population groups should not be carried too far, however. The bulk of media entertainment and information is similar throughout the country and is shared by all types of media audiences. The same network television programs are broadcast on the East Coast and the West Coast, in big cities and small towns. Differences among individual networks are slight. Hence television comes close to being a single, nationwide source of news and commentary. Radio is more diverse, but even many radio news programs are little more than national wire service reports. Insofar as newspaper stories are based on wire service information, they, too, are fairly uniform everywhere.

In Chapter 3 we saw that news media cover basically the same categories of stories in the same proportions. There are variations in specific stories, of course. Newspapers on the West Coast are more likely to devote their foreign affairs coverage to Asian affairs than newspapers on the East Coast, which concentrate more on Europe and the Middle East. Tabloids, such as the *New York Daily News,* put more stress on sensational crime and sex stories than does the staid *New York Times.* Nevertheless, news sources everywhere provide a large common core of information and interpretation that imbues their audiences with a shared structure of basic values and information.

Choosing Media Stories

Uses and Gratifications Theories

General patterns of media use do not tell us why people pay attention to specific stories, but a number of theories have been formulated to help explain how and why such individual choices are made. Currently, one of the most widely accepted of these theories is the "uses and gratifications" approach. Put most simply, proponents of this approach contend that individuals ignore personally irrelevant messages and pay attention to the kinds of things they need and the kinds of things that they find gratifying, provided the expense in time and effort seems reasonable.[32]

Uses and gratifications may be behavioral, emotional, or intellectual.[33] For instance, people pay attention to stories that help them in making political decisions, such as voting or participating in protest demonstrations. They also use the media to gain a sense of security and social adequacy; media stories help people to know what is happening in their political environment and to take part in discussions with friends and coworkers. They feel gratified if the media reinforce what they already know and believe. Finally, the media are used to while away time, to participate vicariously in exciting ventures, and to reduce loneliness.

Table 5-1, based on interviews with 6,564 adults in 10 small cities throughout the United States, indicates the 25 newspaper content areas that are read most widely. People were asked to rate 30 to 35 common newspaper topics on a scale of 1 to 5. A score of 1 denoted that the topic was always ignored; a score of 5 denoted that it was always read whenever it appeared. Presumably, the topics earning the highest scores supply the broadest array of gratifications.

Special subcultural needs may lead to significant variations in attention patterns. For instance, a Jewish person may be particularly attentive to news from the Middle East and other places that concern Israel. A person of Polish ancestry may look for news that affects the Polish community. If a woman favors increased job opportunities for women, she is apt to notice stories about women's expanding presence in the business world.

What people actually select depends very much on life style and the context in which information exposure occurs. What is useful and gratifying in one setting may be less so in another. When people change their life styles, such as moving from daytime to nighttime work or trading a desk for a travel job, media patterns may change drastically. The changes are needed to bring about closer accord with people encountered in the new environment.[34]

Life style also determines the time available for media use and hence the quantity of news that can be selected. In early adulthood, when people begin their careers, or when they are raising children, the demands of home and job may leave little time for attention to the media. The cost of newspaper and magazine subscriptions may be prohibitive on a tight budget. Conversely, older people whose home and job duties have become lighter, and whose financial obligations are decreasing, frequently have much more time for reading or watching television. Life style also determines what media are readily available. People may expose themselves to media that are of little

Table 5-1   Rankings of Top 25 Content Categories and Average Ratings Across 10 Markets

Rank	Rating
1 Natural disasters and tragedies	3.93
2 Stories and columns on the national economy (prices, unemployment, inflation)	3.87
3 News of the local economy	3.82
4 Column on local people and events	3.72
5 Stories about national politics and the president	3.72
6 Service information (TV listings, weather, movie listings, etc.)	3.71
7 News of international leaders and events	3.70
8 Stories on energy, conservation, and the environment	3.67
9 Stories on things to see and do in the area	3.66
10 Good Samaritan stories (people helping people)	3.60
11 Humorous stories and features	3.56
12 Accident and crime news	3.52
13 Health and medical advice	3.42
14 How fast the community is growing	3.33
15 Editorials and letters to the editor	3.32
16 Schools and education	3.31
17 City council and local politicians	3.30
18 News about the governor and state legislature	3.27
19 Consumer stories and advice	3.27
20 Stories about human psychology (the way we think and act)	3.22
21 Nature and outdoors stories	3.19
22 How-to advice on such things as crafts, auto and home repairs	3.19
23 News of record (births, deaths, weddings, etc.)	3.10
24 Space and exploration	3.10
25 Science and technology	3.08

NOTE: Ratings are based on a 1 to 5 scale. A rating of 1 means never read; a rating of 5 means always read.

SOURCE: Judee K. Burgoon, Michael Burgoon, and Miriam Wilkinson, "Dimensions of Content Readership in 10 Newspaper Markets," *Journalism Quarterly* 60 (Spring 1983): 79. Reprinted by permission.

interest to them when this is convenient or socially appropriate. Table 5-2 shows the kinds of reasons people give when asked why they paid attention or failed to pay attention to particular news stories.

Selective Exposure Theories

While people pick up what is personally useful and gratifying, they ignore many other bits of information, regardless of their political and social significance. Most of these omissions are random. People simply fail to notice certain information or have no time or inclination to pursue it, even when it comes to their attention. But systematic omissions occur as well. According to various cognitive balance theories, people avoid information that disturbs their peace of mind, runs counter to their political and social tastes, or conflicts with information, attitudes, and feelings they already hold. Social scientists explain this type of selective exposure by pointing out that people are uncomfortable when they are exposed to ideas that differ from their own or that question the validity of their ideas. To avoid such discomforts, people select information that is congruent with their existing beliefs.

Because people differ in what they select, selectivity leads to diversification of socializing influences and lays the groundwork for differential attitudes toward politics. It also reduces the already slim chances that an individual's cognitions, attitudes, and feelings will be altered once they have become established. This then helps to explain the considerable stability we see in basic orientations such as party allegiance, conservatism or liberalism, and isolationism or interventionism in foreign affairs.

Over the years scholars have repeatedly examined the various selective exposure phenomena and have modified their earlier theories in accordance with more complete research findings. They now believe that selective exposure occurs to a lesser extent than was thought initially. Many people find it too bothersome to select new sources carefully, particularly when using electronic media. For instance, when television news carries stories that are objectionable to a viewer, there is no easy way to screen out the undesired stories and still watch the rest of the broadcast.

Some folks are actually curious about discrepant information or pride themselves on being open-minded and receptive to all points of view. For instance, Democrats may want to hear what Republicans are saying if for no other reason than to find out how the opposition is stating its case. They may also want to determine what counterarguments need to be formulated. Many people even enjoy news that contradicts their own ideas. At worst, exposure to discrepant information is not as universally painful as previously thought. It

Table 5-2 Reasons for Attention or Inattention to News Stories

Reasons for Attention*	Percent	Reasons for Inattention**	Percent
Personal relevance	26	Missed	47
Emotional appeal	20	No interest	28
Societal importance	19	Too remote	10
Interesting story	15	Too busy	6
Job relevance	12	Doubt media	3
Chance reasons	1	Too complex	3
Miscellaneous	7	Redundant/boring	2
		Doubt story	1

* N = 453 stories
** N = 1,493 stories

SOURCE: From *Processing the News: How People Tame the Information Tide* by Doris A. Graber. Copyright © 1984 by Longman Inc. Reprinted by permission of Longman Inc., New York.

can be ignored, overlooked, or distorted. The source can be discredited and the message disbelieved.[35]

Much of the evidence for markedly selective exposure has come from settings in which available media supported the preferences of the audience. No choice was necessary; selection was "de facto" rather than deliberate. For example, unionized workers, whose friends and associates are also highly involved with unions, are likely to encounter a lot of pro-union information at home and at work. They do not have to make a special effort to seek out pro-union information or reject anti-union opinions. In fact, anti-union information may be unavailable. Genuine rather than de facto selective exposure appears to be most prevalent for those relatively few people who recognize dissonance and find it painful. Therefore they avoid it through selectivity or resolve it by reconsidering already established attitudes and opinions.

Agenda-setting Theories

If selections of news items were entirely determined by individual uses and gratifications, news selection patterns would show infinite variations. But this is not the case. The similarities in the environment of the average American and social pressures impose a common structure on news selection patterns. We have already mentioned similarity in news supply, springing from gatekeeping practices, as a powerful unifying force. Media also tell people in fairly uniform fashion which individual issues and activities are most significant and deserve to be ranked highly on the public's agenda of concerns.[36] Importance is indicated through cues such as banner headlines or front-page placement in newspapers, or first story placement on television. Frequent and ample coverage also implies significance.

Many of us readily adopt the media's agenda of importance. We look at the front page of the newspaper and expect to find the most important stories there. We may watch the opening minutes of a telecast eagerly and then allow our attention to slacken. Consequently, agenda-setting by the media leads to uniformities in exposure as well as in significance ratings of news items. When the media make events seem important, politicians are likely to comment about them and to take action. This enhances widespread belief in the importance of these events and ensures even more public attention.

Numerous studies confirm the agenda-setting influence of the media.[37] For instance, in a 1976 study, several thousand responses over a year by small panels of voters revealed quite similar judgments about the salience of many current issues to their personal lives. The list of issues mentioned by the panelists, located in communities of varying sizes in the Midwest and Northeast, corresponded to cues in their news sources. It reflected the issues about which they talked most and to which they claimed to pay most attention in the media.[38] However, agenda-setting varied in potency. The audience followed media guidance, but not slavishly.

From comparisons of media agendas with public opinion polls and reports about political and social conditions, we know that media guidance is most important for new issues that have not been widely discussed and for issues beyond the realm of personal experience.[39] Prominent media coverage does ensure that an issue will be noticed, but it does not guarantee that the audience will assign it the same relative rank of importance that media play has indicated. Likewise, information that is useful or gratifying to the audience will be noted, even if it is on the back pages, receives minuscule headlines, or is briefly reported at the tail end of a newscast.[40]

Table 5-3 demonstrates that the concerns and priorities that a panel of voters expressed in 1976 and the problems emphasized by the media in that year were close but not identical. Under the heading "Personal Agenda," the table notes issues that the respondents designated as "most important" when asked: "Of the various problems and issues now facing the United States, which is most important to you personally?" Table 5-3 also shows that the issues people talked about the most (Talk Agenda) and deemed the most important to the community (Public Agenda) largely reflect news media patterns. To capture the differences attributable to demographic characteristics, the table is divided according to age and sex. For instance, 16 percent of the older women, compared with 8 percent of the younger ones, said that foreign affairs were personally important to them. Seven percent of the older women, compared with 5 percent of the younger ones, discussed foreign affairs often. But none of the older women, and only 1 percent of the younger women, thought that people in their community considered foreign affairs to be an important problem. The need for raw material for conversation with friends and associates is a particularly strong force toward selecting stories of common appeal.

Learning Processes

Media-Audience Interaction

Thus far we have discussed news selection processes, noting the forces that make for diversity and for uniformity. We now need to examine briefly what happens after the news has been selected. According to communication research, the early models that depicted a straight stimulus-response relationship were incorrect. There is no "hypodermic effect": information presented by the media is not transferred unaltered into the minds of the audience. Rather, media and audience interact; the images conveyed by the media stimulate perceptions in audience members that reflect each individual's perceptual state at the time the message was received. Recent research

Table 5-3   Personal, Talk, and Public Issue Agendas (in Percentages)*

Issue	*Personal Agenda*				*Talk Agenda*				*Public Agenda*			
	Women		Men		Women		Men		Women		Men	
	O**	Y	Y	O	O	Y	Y	O	O	Y	Y	O
Social services, crime control	15%	16%	10%	14%	17%	21%	10%	15%	10%	11%	9%	12%
Foreign affairs, defense	16	8	4	15	7	5	7	11	0	1	1	1
Economy: taxes, jobs, prices	55	65	56	55	43	53	49	40	70	74	71	69
Life styles, race issues	3	7	5	4	2	8	5	2	5	7	5	1
Resource con- servation	3	4	8	3	2	1	6	2	2	0	3	1
Feelings about politics	1	0	13	6	2	1	5	6	1	0	1	0
Current polit- ical affairs	3	0	2	1	7	2	11	5	5	2	5	7
Miscellaneous, D.K., N/A.	4	0	2	2	20	10	8	20	6	5	6	8

* N = 2,342 replies.
** O stands for older women and men (over age 40).
   Y stands for younger women and men (age 40 and under).

SOURCE: Doris A. Graber, "Agenda-Setting: Are There Women's Perspectives?" in *Women and the News,* ed. Laurily Keir Epstein (New York: Hastings House, 1978), p. 18. Tables 5-3 through 5-5 reprinted by permission of Hastings House, Publishers, from *Women and the News,* © 1978 by Laurily Keir Epstein.

indicates that, from childhood on, people develop ideas about how the world operates and feelings about various aspects of these operations. Cognitive psychologists refer to these mental configurations by various names, including "schemas" and "scripts." [41] Items of news are selected, interpreted, and integrated in accordance with a number of culturally influenced reasoning rules.[42] For instance, in Marxist oriented societies, most political events are viewed as results of economic forces. Hence Marxist observers interpreted racial rioting in the United States in the late 1960s as proletarian uprisings, whereas most Americans viewed them as protests against racial injustice and its consequences.

In the United States much subcultural diversity is maintained despite the matrix of basic uniformity created by the shared dominant culture. The fact that most political schemas developed by average Americans come from the mass media rather than from direct experiences is also a homogenizing influence. Coherence springs, too, from the human effort to organize perceptions into internally consistent images that are meaningful from the perceiver's perspective.[43] As journalist Walter Lippmann explained more than 60 years ago:

For the most part we do not first see, and then define, we define first and then see. In the great blooming, buzzing confusion of the outer world, we pick out what our culture has already defined for us, and we tend to perceive that which we have picked out in the form stereotyped for us by our culture.[44]

Because individuals pick up information that is related to things they already know and for which they have developed appropriate schemas, numerous "knowledge-gap" studies show that political elites and other well-informed people tend to absorb a great deal more mass media information than people who are poorly informed.[45] It is not functionally advantageous for the poorly informed to acquire knowledge that appears to them to be irrelevant. This explains why information-poor population groups, although they spend a lot of time with the mass media, generally extract far less political information than do more politically sophisticated audiences. The upshot is that the knowledge gap between the privileged and underprivileged widens during the course of a lifetime. Those with the least political knowledge are likely to remain politically impotent. Moreover, the knowledge gap between the privileged and underprivileged makes mutual understanding more difficult. Improved public education, which might shrink the gap, remains a distant goal.

Transient Influences

Many transitory factors impinge on news processing. Our frame of mind may be accepting or rejecting. Our attention may be focused totally on the media source or partly diverted. Up to half of the television audience eats dinner, washes dishes, reads, or talks on the phone while watching television. Examination time at school, illness in the family, or the year-end rush at work may eat up the time normally devoted to media.

The other people present when news is received or discussed are also significant. For instance, if one watches or talks about a presidential inauguration with friends who are making fun of the way the president talks and acts, the occasion loses solemnity and becomes banal. If one watches or talks about the event with a group who admire the president, one comes away feeling inspired. We cannot predict the effect of media messages without knowing the group context in which exposure or conversation took place.[46]

How a person interacts with information also depends on the format of that information. If news reports are conflicting in fact or opinion, if they are overly long or overly short, if they are repetitious, dull, or offensive, their effect is apt to be diminished. The total communications matrix also affects the influence of its parts. Print news impact may be blunted by prior television and radio presentations that have removed the edge of novelty.

Source credibility and appeal are other significant factors in news processing. Once President Richard Nixon had lost his credibility and respect in the wake of Watergate disclosures, any statement he made was suspect for most Americans. His manner and bearing were more closely watched for clues to his general state of mind. Partisanship, too, may play an important role in source appraisal. It may cast a rosy glow over fellow partisans and a pall over the opposition.

Perceptual and Image Factors

When people receive new information they combine it with existing beliefs. But does the new reshape the old or the old reshape the new in the final images? Research on the impact of media information on images of political candidates supplies some answers. Images are largely *perceiver-determined* for those aspects for which the audience already has developed complex schemas. For instance, people assume that Democratic presidential candidates will pursue policies typically associated with Democrats. They read or view the news in that vein, picking up bits of information that fit, and rejecting, ignoring, or reinterpreting those that do not fit. The same is likely to hold true for information about big business or big labor, the Arab world, or the Soviet Union.

Information about aspects of events or people that are not widely known or stereotyped leads to *stimulus-determined* images. What the media present then largely determines what is perceived. Candidates' personalities, assessments of their capabilities, and appraisals of the people with whom they surround themselves, for example, usually are stimulus-determined, except when a candidate is already well known.[47] Likewise, when the media describe present-day China, when they cast doubt on the safety of nuclear energy production, or when they discuss the merits of a new wage insurance plan, they create images that are likely to dominate people's schemas.

The general rule that media are most influential in areas where the audience knows least does not apply to specialized publications. Professional journals, for instance, often have a strong impact on their readers' images of professional matters. This happens because of the high credibility of the sources, which makes audiences for these publications subordinate their own expert views to those of the experts whose views they read.

Learning Effects: Knowledge and Attitudes

Measurement Problems

What kinds of politically relevant knowledge, attitudes, feelings, and actions spring from people's contacts with the media? The answer is difficult because the precise impact of particular stories is nearly impossible to measure in most circumstances, given the limitations of currently available measuring instruments. Some of these problems were discussed in Chapter 1 in which we pointed to the difficulty of isolating media influence when it is one of many factors in a complex environment.[48] For instance, the rising levels of cynicism about the U.S. government that occurred following the disclosure of the Watergate scandal in the Nixon administration cannot be directly and solely attributed to the disclosure stories. It is possible that cynicism was produced primarily by the experience of paying higher prices in the grocery store, facing fuel shortages at the gas station, or living through a public transit strike. Until we can trace an individual's mental processes, and isolate the components that interact and combine to form mental images and reactions to these images, we cannot fully assess the impact of media on knowledge and attitudes.

Our inability to trace mental processes also keeps us from understanding just what is learned from media. Research up to now has focused on very small facets of learning of specific facts about political candidates or about a limited number of public policies. Even within such narrow areas, testing has been severely limited, zeroing in on learning the substance of explicit messages rather than on assessing total knowledge gains. For instance, election coverage of a presidential candidate teaches more than facts about the candidate. It may also inform the audience about the role played by White House correspondents in campaign coverage and about living conditions in other cities. Because researchers usually ask only about learning campaign information, such ancillary learning, however important it may be, is overlooked. Much learning may even be subconscious. People may be unaware that they have learned something new and therefore fail to retrieve it when asked what they have learned.

At times, information can be recalled only after the passage of time. For example, in one experiment soldiers saw information films of armies in other countries. The soldiers were asked questions immediately after the viewing and then again six weeks later. Some things that were not recalled in the initial interviews surfaced in the later ones. It is not known how frequently such "sleeper effects" occur and how much learning remains unmeasured as a consequence.

Although many assumptions about learning that seem intuitively correct remain untested, we continue to judge media practices as if these assumptions were true. The assumption that people deduce important social lessons from specific stories presented by the media is one example. We believe that adults as well as children often model their behavior after the behavior of characters they encounter in the media. We assume that unfavorable stereotypes will hurt the self-esteem of the groups so characterized, and so we urge newspeople to present these groups in a better light. News reports and dramatic shows presumably teach people how lawyers or policemen or hospitals conduct their business. We assume that impressionable people who watch these shows, and like what they see, will be motivated to aspire to these professions. Conversely, we worry that distortions in the portrayal of these roles may mislead inexperienced people who regard them as accurate.

But while we assume these effects, and while there is every reason to believe that many are quite common, most of them remain unmeasured. An important exception is the Cultural Indicators project conducted since the mid-1960s at the University of Pennsylvania's Annenberg School of Communications. Using "cultivation analysis," the investigators study trends in network television dramatic content and the conceptions of social reality produced in viewers. Findings from this project confirm that heavy viewers of television drama (more than four hours daily) see the world as television paints it and react to that world rather than to reality more than do light viewers of the same demographic background and similar circumstances. For instance, heavy viewers, exposed to large doses of crime in television drama, believe that the dangers of becoming a crime victim are far greater than they actually are.[49] They fear crime more and are more distrustful and suspicious than light television viewers are. They also are generally more pessimistic and tend to gravitate toward the middle-of-the-road "mainstream" politics depicted on television.

As is true of most research on mass media effects, findings from the Cultural Indicators project have been challenged on the grounds that factors other than mass media exposure account for the results. Psychological factors, as well as the characteristics attributed to heavy viewers, may produce heavy viewing. Questions have also been raised about technical aspects of the Cultural Indicators project. Such scientific controversies indicate that mass media effects research needs a lot more refinement before the findings can be considered definitive.

Another neglected research sphere concerns forgetfulness. Much that is learned from the media is evanescent. When Iran is engulfed by revolution or Philadelphia rocked by a patronage scandal, the salient names and facts are on many lips. But after the crisis has passed, this knowledge evaporates rapidly. How rapidly seems to depend on a number of factors. Most importantly, we know that people vary in their ability to store and retrieve information. There is also some evidence that after three months of total silence, most ordinary stories have been forgotten, even by people with good memories. If stories are periodically revived with follow-ups or with closely related stories, memory becomes deepened and prolonged. It also is well established that a small number of crucial incidents are so deeply etched into human memory that they become permanent. The Great Depression, World War II, and the assassination of President John F. Kennedy are examples.[50]

Factual Learning

Given these limitations on initial learning and on remembering, what can we say about the extent of political learning from the mass media? The data that follow come from the 1976 research project mentioned earlier in which the information supply and political learning of four small panels of adults living in Evanston, Illinois; Indianapolis, Indiana; and Lebanon, New Hampshire, were monitored intensively throughout an entire year.[51] The investigators found that the panelists in the "Three Sites" Project became aware of a large number of the topics featured by the media, but the mix of topics varied from person to person. Four broad topic areas were mentioned by nearly every panel member as receiving "a lot of coverage" in 1976: the economy in general, government spending, busing for school desegregation, and national defense. Unemployment, corruption in government, and the drop in the prestige of the United States received nearly as much mention. Sixteen other topics were recalled by a somewhat smaller majority of the panel members as receiving a lot of media attention, including such diverse issues as the Middle East, alcohol and drug addiction, abortion, and dirty campaign tactics. This is an impressive array of politically important topics to be remembered by an average mass media audience.

By and large, however, people do not seem to gain much specific knowledge from the media. They recognize details if they are mentioned to them, but fail to recall them without such assistance. For instance, the panelists in the Three Sites Project were asked at the height of the 1976 presidential campaign what they knew about the positions taken by presidential candidates Gerald R. Ford and Jimmy Carter on the issues of inflation and unemployment—issues of personal importance to the panelists and discussed by them with friends and associates. Most of the panelists planned to vote for one of the candidates. Yet as Table 5-4 indicates, specific knowledge about the issue positions was abysmally small. Half of the answers were "don't know's." Specific information about each policy was contained in less than 10 percent of the answers on unemployment and less than 5 percent of the answers on inflation. Women, especially those 40 years of age and under, recalled much less information than the men.

More generally, when people were tested on their recall of prominent news stories to which they had been exposed several weeks earlier, men, on the average, recalled specific details for only 14 percent of the stories. For women, the figure was even lower: 5 percent. Table 5-5 tells the story. It also shows that the rates of recall varied, depending on the nature of the story and the age and sex of the respondent.

As one would expect from uses and gratifications theories, the disparities between men's and women's recall patterns conform to their different life

Table 5-4   Recall of Specific Information on Unemployment and Inflation (in Percentages)*

Responses	Unemployment							
	Ford				Carter			
	Women		Men		Women		Men	
	O**	Y	Y	O	O	Y	Y	O
Statistics	0%	0%	0%	2%	4%	0%	2%	11%
Policy data	12	8	9	12	3	4	3	5
General information	41	38	44	43	43	41	48	35
Don't know	47	55	47	43	50	55	46	48

Responses	Inflation							
	Ford				Carter			
	Women		Men		Women		Men	
	O	Y	Y	O	O	Y	Y	O
Statistics	1%	0%	1%	0%	0%	0%	1%	0%
Policy data	1	2	2	0	3	2	6	6
General information	38	34	39	42	34	29	29	27
Don't know	59	63	59	58	63	69	64	67

* N = 1,716 replies.
** O stands for older women and men (over age 40).
   Y stands for younger women and men (age 40 and under).

NOTE: "Statistics" means that the respondent was able to cite precise figures for unemployment and inflation rates and/or rate changes. "Policy data" means that the respondent was able to refer to specific proposals made by Ford or Carter to cope with the inflation or unemployment problem. "General information" means that the respondent knew whether general trends were changing or stable, and knew whether action was planned, without being able to give specifics.

SOURCE: Graber, "Agenda-Setting: Are There Women's Perspectives?" p. 22.

styles. It became clear upon further questioning that most women, unlike men, lacked focused interests such as gathering information to help with their jobs or a penchant to learn more about prominent people. Women tended to remember instead interesting or touching details about disparate stories without having a particular use for the story other than its suitability for conversation.[52] Stories about crimes and accidents were recalled more readily than other kinds of stories by both women and men. The chief reasons for not paying attention to stories or forgetting them were lack of interest in the subject matter, unwillingness to struggle with complex matters, or simply skipping over certain stories unintentionally.

The paucity of factual learning by the average individual has disturbed many people because it is one of the axioms of democracy that good citizens

must be well informed. Political scientists Scott Keeter and Cliff Zukin titled their intensive study of voter knowledge gains during the 1976 and 1980 presidential elections *Uninformed Choice.* They argue that citizens are too uninformed to make intelligent political choices.[53] Earlier studies show even less knowledge than the Three Sites Project and the Keeter-Zukin studies indicated. In many of them informedness was gauged largely by ability to name prominent politicians and to recite facts from the U.S. Constitution. Such factual information tests are inappropriate for judging political knowledge and competence. What really matters is that citizens understand major political issues—not that they can recite names of political figures or the length of the term of a U.S. Supreme Court justice.

Are people aware of major political issues and their significance? Are they able to place them in the general context of current politics? When these genuinely important questions are asked, the picture of public political competence brightens considerably. People may not remember election facts very well but, as we have already noted, they are aware of a wide range of current issues. Moreover, when interviewers probe for understanding, rather than knowledge of specific facts, they often find considerable political insight. For instance, people who cannot define either "affirmative action" or "price deregulation" may have fairly sophisticated notions about these matters. Panelists in the Three Sites Project and others who had very little formal education knew about government controls of the prices of some goods and services and fully understood the burdens faced by people hampered in finding a job because of their race or sex.[54]

Table 5-5   Stories for Which Specific Details Were Recalled
(in Percentages)*

| | Women | | Men | |
Story Topic	O**	Y	Y	O
Women's issues	0%	4%	8%	20%
Medical/health care	2	2	11	9
Education	6	2	11	6
Economy in general	3	3	2	0
Unemployment	13	5	9	15
Inflation	8	3	8	14
Celebrities	18	4	13	18
Entertainment	0	10	14	16
All news stories (including group above)	5	4	14	13

* N = 5,421 stories.
** O stands for older women and men (over age 40).
   Y stands for younger women and men (age 40 and under).

SOURCE: Graber, "Agenda-Setting: Are There Women's Perspectives?" p. 25.

Learning General Orientations

Some media stories leave the audience with politically significant feelings that persist long after facts are forgotten. Although many details of the assassination of President Kennedy have been forgotten, Americans retain vivid feelings of sympathy, grief, shame, and moral indignation. Often stories that impress few factual memories on people's minds may leave them with generalized feelings of trust or distrust. For instance, prominently featured stories of serious corruption in government may lower the public's esteem for governmental integrity. This was demonstrated by a 1974 national survey that showed that people who had been exposed to newspapers that had severely criticized various governmental actions trusted government significantly less than respondents exposed to more favorable views. People who had not gone beyond grade school seemed to be particularly susceptible to erosion of trust in the wake of mass media criticism.[55] A number of laboratory and field experiments demonstrate similar linkages, positive as well as negative. Favorable publicity enhances esteem for government; unfavorable publicity diminishes it. Cynical people, in turn, tend to participate less than others in activities such as voting and lobbying.[56]

As political scientist Murray Edelman has noted, media stories may produce an overpowering sense of a world out of control, or they may reassure the audience that all is going well. Feelings of both insecurity and security may make people quiescent because they become fearful of interfering with crucial government actions or else complacent about the need for public vigilance. Fear that dissension weakens the government may decrease tolerance for dissidents. Edelman also warns that political quiescence leads to acceptance of faulty public policies, poor laws, and poor administrative practices—significant political effects.[57]

On a more personal level, for millions of people the media are a way to keep in touch with their environment. This helps to counter feelings of loneliness and alienation because information becomes a bond among individuals who share it.[58] Media may also arouse desires that can change the course of life of individuals and societies. The models of life depicted by the media create wants and expectations as well as dissatisfactions and frustrations. These feelings may become powerful stimulants for social change for the society at large or for selected individuals within it. Whether media-induced changes are considered positive, negative, or a mixture of both depends, of course, on one's sociopolitical preferences.

Deterrents to Learning

Media exposure produces more political enlightenment than has been generally revealed through survey research. Nevertheless, the average individ-

ual's political knowledge and understanding remains quite limited. Lack of motivation for political learning and distrust for the media, as well as deficiencies in the information supply, provide explanations. Most people do not need detailed knowledge of current affairs for either their jobs or their social relationships. Rather than discussing politics, which they see as a touchy topic, they prefer to talk about sports, or the weather, or the local gossip. People scan the news for major crises without trying to remember specific facts. When they sense that events will greatly affect their lives, or when they need information to make voting choices, political interest and learning perk up quickly and often dramatically.[59]

Occasionally, serious programs on radio and television become highly popular. Most of them involve themes of corruption, violence, or other wrongdoing, which may account for their popularity. Examples are "Sixty Minutes," which probes a variety of social ills; "The Winds of War," a made-for-TV movie that recapitulated World War II; and documentaries dealing with rape, child-snatching, and prison violence. Programs such as the televising of the Watergate hearings or broadcast of the Panama Canal debates also fall into this category. These are exceptions, however.

Like a straw fire, widespread public interest in most political crises dies almost as quickly as it flares. For instance, attention to stories about the Watergate scandal peaked only briefly. Most people tired of the matter after a few weeks and began to complain that it usurped too much media time. Attention spans are erratic and brief, even though most Americans believe that, as good citizens, they ought to be well informed about political news and feel guilty, or at least apologetic, if they are not.[60]

Learning is further inhibited by the alienation of many population groups from the media. Some white ethnics and police and union members, for instance, consider most mass media to be opposed to them. They believe that the media lie and distort, either in general or in certain particulars. Overall, public opinion polls in the 1980s showed considerable erosion of public confidence in the trustworthiness of the media. On a scale ranging from "a great deal," to "some," to "very little," late 1983 Gallup and Harris polls found high confidence in television and newspapers in less than one-quarter of the public.

The presentation of media information also contributes to the difficulty people experience in learning from the media. First of all, there is the sheer bulk of new information. People are deluged day after day with important and trivial news, most of which is touted as significant. The constant crisis atmosphere numbs excitement and produces boredom. The presentation of stories in disconnected snippets further complicates the task of making sense out of them and integrating them with existing knowledge. This is especially true when stories are complex.[61] People who feel that they cannot understand what is happening are discouraged from spending time reading or listening.[62]

Featuring conflicting stories and interpretations, without giving guidance to the audience, also deters learning.

Television news, which is watched by half of the adult population on an average day, deters learning because it carries little information. The average half-hour television news program covers the equivalent in words of only one newspaper page. If several newscasts are watched, about half the material is repetitive. Even within a single newscast, a large proportion of every item is background information that must be furnished to put the item into perspective for viewers seeing it for the first time. Moreover, as Tony Schwartz points out in *The Responsive Chord,* most television programs are not primarily designed "to get stimuli across, or even to package ... stimuli so they can be understood and absorbed." Rather, television tries "to evoke stored information ... in a patterned way" to make use of what the audience already knows.[63] These deterrents to learning are not outweighed by positive factors such as the interest generated by the picture and sound combination and the high confidence in familiar newscasters. Viewing purposes are also important. Because most people watch television news largely as entertainment, and because it is structured according to show business guidelines, audiences are not likely to try hard to learn much from it. "Happy-Time" news formats and exciting film footage encourage the feeling that news should be viewed as lighthearted diversion. Of course, an entertaining format does not preclude learning—people do learn even from pure entertainment fare. Still, this kind of format reduces motivation to learn.[64]

The internal structure of television newscasts also impedes learning. In the average news program, disparate items are tightly strung together with few pauses to allow the viewer to absorb information. Pauses are essential for learning. In their absence, it is not surprising that half the audience, after the lapse of a few hours, cannot recall a single item from a television newscast. The fact that television news viewing is often combined with distracting activities, such as cooking dinner or playing games, does not help either.[65]

Some social scientists even contend that the availability of television, per se, has destroyed learning incentives because television takes the place of personal interactions and real life experiences. People who participate in life passively, watching the world through a television set, do not need to acquire information for talking with others and do not learn through action.[66]

Having said this much about slim knowledge and the reasons for it, we still can end the discussion of political learning and socialization from the mass media on a positive note. Compared with other people in the world, Americans rank quite high in political information levels. With the increasing education of the population, which heightens the need for and salience of information, this record should improve even further. Americans are also well socialized into the American system. Despite the negative publicity given to political stories, the underlying support for the political system and culture that

pervades the news is shared by most Americans. They may be disappointed and cynical about particular leaders or policies, but relatively few question the legitimacy of the government, object to its basic philosophies, or reject its claims to their support. If one believes in the merits of the system, this finding is, indeed, cause for satisfaction with current political socialization.

Learning Effects: Behavior

If the media shape people's political knowledge, attitudes, and feelings, they obviously influence political behavior, since it is based to a great extent on attitudes and feelings. To illustrate behavioral effects, we will examine media impact in two areas: imitation of crime and violence, particularly among children, and stimulation of development in underdeveloped regions. Both have long been areas of great political concern. In Chapter 6 we will discuss the effects of media coverage on voting behavior, and in Chapter 9 the impact of the media on behavior in various societal crises will be analyzed.

Crime and Violent Behavior in Children

Many Americans, including many social scientists, believe that violence and crime portrayed in the media, particularly in television entertainment, lead to learning and imitation. Children are presumed to be particularly impressionable. Because crime and violence are serious problems in American society, considerable public and private money and effort have been expended to investigate the possible link between television exposure and deviant behavior. Several surgeon generals' commissions have produced a bookshelf of information in support of corrective legislation, should it be needed.[67] Congressional committees have spent countless hours listening to conflicting testimony by social scientists about the impact of television violence. Meanwhile, violent content, particularly in fiction programs, has escalated. In 1983 the National Coalition on Television Violence reported on violence in popular programs. "Police Squad" averaged 34 violent acts per hour; "Dukes of Hazzard," 23; and the "ABC Sunday Movie," 21. Prime time network programs averaged 8 violent acts per hour; the Home Box Office cable television channel averaged 20.

What have studies of the impact of television violence revealed? Despite the strong inclination of many of the researchers to find that crime fiction causes asocial behavior, research evidence provides only modest support. As the "Born Innocent" incident discussed at the beginning of this chapter demonstrates, some children do copy violent behavior. This is especially true when they have watched aggression that was left unpunished or was rewarded, and when countervailing influences from parents and teachers were lacking.[68]

But, aside from immediately copying television examples when tempted to do so, children do not ordinarily become habitually violent after exposure to violence in the mass media. Most children lack the predisposition and usually the opportunity for violence, and their environment discourages asocial behavior. In fact, exposure to crime makes some children more sympathetic toward the suffering of crime and violence victims.[69] A crude cause and effect model is therefore obviously invalid.

The percentage of imitation-prone children in the vast child population exposed to televised violence is not known at this time. We do know that the wide dispersion of television throughout American homes makes it almost certain that the majority of susceptible children will be exposed. We also know that many other triggers to violence could arouse these children, even in the absence of television. Whatever the source of arousal, even if the actual number of very susceptible children is tiny and statistically insignificant, the social consequences still may be profound.

Other confounding factors in assessing the impact of television on children are age-linked comprehension differences. Younger children may not be able to comprehend many of the events presented by the media in the same way that older children do. Several studies of preschool-age and early grade-school-age children suggest that much of what adults consider to be violent does not seem so to children. Cartoon violence is an example. When an enemy drops Donald Duck on his head, or shoots Mickey Mouse, or flattens Mrs. Flintstone with a boulder, most children view it as funny make-believe.[70] For them, it is not a behavior model for action in the real world. If this is true, many of the programs that adults consider to be potentially dangerous may actually be harmless.

Children not only see things differently from adults, but they also draw different inferences. The complex social reasoning that adults often ascribe to even young children does not develop until youngsters reach their teens. For instance, after seeing a series of shows with the implied message that the big bully who hits everybody always wins, children presumably conclude that similar behavior on their part will yield similar results. Although young children often imitate what they have seen, they are rarely able to generalize or respond to implied messages. Until we understand better how the average child at various stages of development interacts with the stories presented by the media, we cannot completely assess media effects on subsequent behavior. Nor can we plan program content with any assurance that it will encourage approved or inhibit disapproved behaviors.

Behavior Change in Adults

What about imitation of socially undesirable behavior by adults? The same broad principles apply as in the case of children. Imitation of the

"I remember we got into this heated argument about whether TV causes violence. . . . The rest is a blur."

Reprinted, courtesy of the *Journal Herald.* © 1982 Summers.

behavior depends on the setting at the time of exposure and on the personality and attitudes the viewer brings to the situation. Widespread societal norms seem to be particularly important. For instance, studies by the presidential Commission on Obscenity and Pornography found that exposure to aberrant sexual behavior led to comparatively little imitation. In fact, there was some evidence that greater availability of obscene and pornographic materials might reduce sex crimes and misdemeanors because vicarious experiences were substituted for actual ones.[71] By comparison, there was a great deal more evidence that exposure to criminal behavior encourages imitation. The difference may be more apparent than real, however, since crime is more likely to be reported while sexual perversions remain hidden.

Given our lack of knowledge about the precise linkage between exposure to media images and corresponding behavior, legislative tampering with media offerings appears premature. It will take a great deal more research and experimentation to determine how media fare can be presented to produce desirable results and avoid undesirable ones. Even assuming that this goal could be reached—which may be an unrealistic assumption—it is questionable whether a democratic society should attempt to manipulate the minds of its citizens to protect them from temptations to violate social norms. If there should be any control of content of entertainment programs it should spring from widely based informal social pressures rather than from legislation. Whether such pressures should be allowed to interfere with reporting real world violence poses even more difficult dilemmas.

Socioeconomic Modernization

The assumed potential of the media to guide people's behavior has led to great efforts to use media as tools for social and political development. The results have been mixed—some successes and many failures. We will try to explain why this is so.

Psychic Mobility. The hope of using the media to bring about industrialization, improved social services, and greater political participation in underdeveloped areas of the industrialized nations, such as parts of the South in the United States or in Third World nations, ran very high at mid-century. The psychological key to human and material development was then assumed to be a personality characteristic that political scientist Daniel Lerner labeled "empathic capacity." The media were thought to be the stimuli; when media present new objects and ideas, they presumably stimulate people to empathize and imagine themselves as involved with these objects and ideas. For instance, when the media show how slum dwellers have converted old tires into sandals, or how flood victims have purified their polluted water supply, audience members begin to wonder "How would this work for me?"

Before mass media became widely available to average people, this "psychic mobility" was generated when people came into direct contact with strangers with different life styles and experiences. Because such contacts usually were limited to relatively few people, changes spread very slowly to wider groups. The broad diffusion of mass media, however, made it possible for the first time in human history to reach millions of people with comparative ease and to expose them to developmental stimuli, either directly or through contact with others reached by the media. Transistor radios and satellite television have opened even remote and inaccessible regions to modern communication and brought news of current life styles to isolated communities.

Social scientists who assign to the media a major role in modernization have made three assumptions. First, they believe that the mass media are, indeed, able to create interest and empathy for unfamiliar experiences. Second, they contend that the mass media not only present people with alternatives to their traditional life styles, but also with graphic examples of new practices, which are then readily understood and copied. For instance, movies can show people how to build novel structures, how to prepare food scientifically, or how to raise children in a technological society. Third, social scientists argue that development, once started, creates an incentive for more and more people to become more skilled and informed. Where formal education is not readily accessible, the media provide information and enhance the capacity to learn. Proof of the validity of these assumptions is seen in the fact that advances in media development in many regions have been followed by advances in urbanization, industrialization, per capita income, and literacy.[72]

Psychological Barriers to Modernization. While many poor and technologically underdeveloped regions have shown measurable progress, with the media apparently serving as a catalyst, modernization has been far slower and more sporadic than expected. A number of psychological and physical obstacles have kept the dreams of the development theorists from coming true. Most damaging has been outright hostility by individuals or communities to change and an unwillingness to alter long-established patterns. In this situation mass media may actually become a negative reference point; people condemn the modern life style depicted by the media.

For instance, when several federal government agencies attempted in the 1960s to improve poverty conditions in Knox County, Kentucky, where per capita income was one-fourth of the U.S. average, they found great resistance in tightly knit, homogeneous communities. Mass media programs designed to change health, child-rearing, and employment practices fell on deaf ears. In more heterogeneous communities in the county, success was moderate.[73]

In the absence of overt hostility to change, people may still be totally uninterested in changing. This has been called the "housewife syndrome" because it happens most frequently with women who are isolated in their homes. Or it may spring from insecurity about ability to cope with changes and reluctance to further complicate a difficult life. Women and men exhibiting this mental state cannot be reached by the mass media without the intervention of a trusted person, such as a priest, physician, or family member. Mass media influence then becomes a "two-step" flow reaching its targets through selected opinion leaders.

Putting modern skills into words and concepts that people with little formal education can understand has also turned out to be exceedingly hard. For instance, teaching people new ways to keep baby food pure, or to apply for aid from a government agency, or to construct cinder block houses, all involve concepts and terminologies that may be tough to grasp for people who have had little or no schooling. The disparity in social background between the journalists and their audiences further confounds the problem of communication. It creates "heterophily"—a gap in social background, which complicates communication—rather than "homophily"—similarity in backgound, which eases it.

Changes that require adopting new social values or abandoning old habits are the most difficult of all and the least likely to occur. For example, people whose religious and social values favor large families are unlikely to be persuaded by mass media information that they should settle for small ones. Ingrained habits, such as driving without seatbelts, are almost resistant to change. In the 1970s the Insurance Institute for Highway Safety broadcast advertisements in a number of cities about the importance of wearing seatbelts. Even though these public service commercials were shown on prime time television more than 100 times each month, roughly 70 percent of the people who had seen and agreed with them did not use car seatbelts.[74] In the absence of penalties for noncompliance, the National Highway Traffic Safety Administration, which spends nearly $10 million annually on its seatbelt campaign, has been able to raise usage by only 4 percentage points, from 11 to 15 percent.

Adoption of Changes. How can the mass media bring about socially desirable changes? We will outline the five steps involved in change and indicate how the mass media fit into the picture.

The first step is an awareness of the possibility for change. Here the media are especially helpful. Radio can inform people about new energy-saving devices or new child-rearing methods. Television and movies can show new technologies and new styles of political participation.

The second step is understanding how to accomplish the suggested changes. For example, people may be aware that public assistance is available, but they may not know how to apply for it. Mass media usually fail to supply detailed information. On the average, only one-third of all stories that might inspire action of various types, such as environmental protection or energy conservation, contain implementing information.[75] Unless this gap is filled, the chain leading to the adoption of innovations is broken.

The third step involves evaluation. People assess the merits of the innovation, given their circumstances, and decide whether they want to adopt it. Innovations often fail to take root because prospective users consider them bad, inappropriate, too risky, or too difficult. Media messages alone may not be persuasive enough. It may be crucial to have a trusted person urge or demonstrate adoption of the innovation.

The fourth step is trial. The effect of the media in getting people to try innovations is limited. Factors beyond media control are more important, such as social and financial costs of the change as well as the audience's willingness to change. Generally, young men are most receptive to innovations; older people are most skeptical and cautious.

Finally, trials may be followed by adoption. The media contribute most to this phase by encouraging people to stick with the changes that they have made part of their life and work styles. For example, adoption of birth control is useless unless it is continuous. The same holds true for many health and sanitation measures or improved work habits. To ensure continuity, mass media must cover a topic regularly, stressing long-range goals and reporting progress.

Predicting which media campaigns designed to change behavior will succeed and which will fail has proved to be difficult. The federal government, which spends millions of dollars each year on public service advertisements and consumer education programs, has reaped little from these efforts. A number of carefully planned projects to motivate poor people or elderly shut-ins to listen to vitally needed information about nutrition, medical care, and social security benefits have failed. On the other hand, campaigns to get people to study pesticide labels more carefully, to learn about employment for the mentally retarded, or to win support for environmental protection programs have succeeded. Despite careful study, the explanation for these differences in success has thus far eluded researchers in most cases.[76]

Douglas S. Solomon, who studied health campaigns conducted by private and public institutions, believes that four factors account for success or failure. To succeed, campaigns must set well-specified, realistic goals, tailored to the needs of various target groups. They must carefully select appropriate media and media formats and present them at key times and intervals. Messages must be carefully designed for greatest persuasiveness. There also must be continuous evaluation and appropriate readjustments.[77]

In some instances, mass media efforts to mobilize people for change have produced unanticipated attitudes and changes in behavior. For instance, when television was introduced in several Canadian Eskimo communities in the 1970s, programs were designed to show the viewers how to modernize their living conditions and to acquaint them with Canadian affairs generally. Instead of anticipated results, Eskimo adults in the television communities turned their eyes to the past. Rather than aspiring to further modernization of their life styles, they wanted to return to traditional Eskimo ways. It is not clear whether this attitude, which was not apparent in localities without television, sprang from nostalgia for the past or aversion to the life style changes foreshadowed by television. Yearning for traditional life styles went along with a spectacular rise in aspirations for a modern life style for their children.[78]

Above all, the success of the mass media in bringing about change hinges on the receptivity for change. Ongoing efforts to use the media to modernize underdeveloped areas or bring socially helpful information to the poor, the elderly, or the handicapped must concentrate therefore on identifying the specific circumstances most likely to bring success. Responding to locally initiated requests, rather than designing information campaigns from the outside, and integrating local traditions into modern approaches, seem to hold the most promise.[79]

Summary

The mass media play a major role in political socialization—the learning and accepting of norms and rules, structures, and environmental factors that govern political life. Contrary to earlier findings that indicated limited impact, the mass media significantly influence this process. Given the importance of continuous political socialization, this alone, quite aside from other political functions, makes the mass media a tremendously powerful political force.

However, the impact of the media on political socialization and other aspects of political learning is not uniform for all members of the media audience. Individuals of different life styles and circumstances are affected by mass media information in different ways. Psychological, demographic, and situational factors influence perceptions and the ensuing political consequences.

While many factors contribute to diversity in socialization and learning, there are also powerful unifying forces. As a result of these, most Americans are exposed to similar information and develop roughly similar outlooks on what it means and ought to mean to be an American and live one's political life in the United States.

In this chapter we also looked at major theories that explain why and how individuals select particular information to remember. Factual learning of specific media information is sparse. Nonetheless, people become aware of many political problems and sense their basic significance, even without remembering details about them. Equally important, exposure to the media produces politically significant moods, such as apathy, cynicism, fear, trust, acquiescence, or support. These moods condition people's participation in the political process, which may range from total abstinence to efforts to overthrow the government by force.

The media may also produce or retard behavior that affects the quality of public life. We assessed the role of the media in fostering socially undesirable behavior, particularly the controversy over the impact of crime and violence in the media on the behavior of children and adults. We also looked at the role that media play in the political and social development of poor and industrially backward population groups. Media influence is greatest in informing people and creating initial attitudes, and it is least effective in changing attitudes and ingrained behaviors.

Given the many largely uncontrollable variables that determine what influence media offerings will have on individual behavior, concerted efforts to manipulate media content to foster societal goals are risky at best. They could set dangerous precedents for inhibiting the free flow of controversial ideas or for using the media as channels for government propaganda.

Notes

1. Impact differences between print and electronic media are discussed in Peter Clarke and Eric Fredin, "Newspapers, Television and Political Reasoning," *Public Opinion Quarterly* 42 (Summer 1978): 143-160; Lee B. Becker, Idowu Sobowale, and William E. Casey, "Newspaper and Television Dependencies: Their Effects on

Evaluations of Public Officials," *Journal of Broadcasting* 23 (Fall 1979): 465-475; and Robert D. McClure and Thomas E. Patterson, "Print vs. Network News," *Journal of Communication* 26 (Spring 1976): 23-28.

2. Ronald Mulder, "Media Credibility: A Use-Gratifications Approach," *Journalism Quarterly* 57 (Fall 1980): 474-477.

3. Jacob Jacoby and Wayne D. Hoyer, "Viewer Miscomprehension of Televised Communications: Selected Findings," *Journal of Marketing* 46 (Fall 1982): 12-26.

4. Stephen D. Reese and M. Mark Miller, "Political Attitude Holding and Structure: The Effects of Newspaper and Television News," *Communication Research* 8 (April 1981): 167-188.

5. George Comstock, "Social and Cultural Impact of Mass Media," in *What's News: The Media in American Society,* ed. Elie Abel (San Francisco: Institute for Contemporary Studies), p. 246.

6. Gary Coldevin, "Internationalism and Mass Communications," *Journalism Quarterly* 49 (Summer 1972): 365-368.

7. M. Margaret Conway, A. Jay Stevens, and Robert G. Smith, "The Relations Between Media Use and Children's Civic Awareness," *Journalism Quarterly* 52 (Autumn 1975): 531-538; Steven H. Chaffee, H. L. Scott Ward, and Leonard P. Tipton, "Mass Communication and Political Socialization," *Journalism Quarterly* 48 (Winter 1970): 647-659.

8. Leo Bogart, *Press and Public: Who Reads What, When, Where, and Why in American Newspapers* (Hillsdale, N.J.: 1981), p. 1. See also Suzanne Pingree, "Children's Cognitive Processes in Constructing Social Reality," *Journalism Quarterly* 60 (Fall 1983): 415-422 and Charles K. Atkin, Bradley S. Greenberg, and Steven McDermott, "Television and Race Role Socialization," *Journalism Quarterly* 60 (Fall 1983): 407-414.

9. For a good review of the political socialization literature, see Sidney Kraus and Dennis Davis, *The Effects of Mass Communication on Political Behavior* (University Park: Pennsylvania State University Press, 1976), pp. 8-47. See also Charles K. Atkin, "Communication and Political Socialization," in *Handbook of Political Communication,* ed. Dan D. Nimmo and Keith R. Sanders (Beverly Hills, Calif.: Sage, 1981), pp. 299-328 and sources cited there.

10. Jean Piaget, *The Language and Thought of the Child,* 3d ed. (New York: Harcourt Brace, 1962).

11. George Comstock, Steven Chaffee, Natan Katzman, Maxwell McCombs, and Donald Roberts, *Television and Human Behavior* (New York: Columbia University Press, 1978), pp. 261-287. See also W. Andrew Collins, "Cognitive Processing in Television Viewing," in *Television and Behavior: Ten Years of Scientific Progress and Implications for the Eighties,* vol. 2, ed. David Pearl, Lorraine Bouthilet, and Joyce Lazar (Rockville, Md.: National Institute of Mental Health, 1982).

12. This research is summarized in Comstock et al., *Television and Human Behavior,* pp. 172-287.

13. Alexander Szalai et al., eds., *The Use of Time* (The Hague, Netherlands: Mouton, 1972) and John P. Robinson, *Changes in Americans' Use of Time: 1965-1975* (Report published by Cleveland State University, August 1977).

14. John P. Robinson, "Television and Leisure Time: A New Scenario," 31 (Winter 1981): 120-130.

15. George Gerbner et al., "Cultural Indicators: Violence Profile No. 9," *Journal of Communication* 28 (Summer 1978): 176-207, at 178, 193. See also George Gerbner et al., "Charting the Mainstream: Television's Contributions to Political Orientations," *Journal of Communication* 32 (Spring 1982): 100-127.

16. George Comstock, "The Impact of Television on American Institutions," *Journal of Communication* 18 (Spring 1978): 12-28.
17. Paula M. Poindexter, "Non-News Viewers," *Journal of Communication* 30 (Autumn 1980): 58-65.
18. Doris A. Graber, *Processing the News: How People Tame the Information Tide* (New York: Longman, 1984), pp. 75-78.
19. Reese and Miller, "Political Attitude Holding," p. 182.
20. L. Erwin Atwood, Ardyth B. Sohn, and Harold Sohn, "Daily Newspaper Contributions to Community Discussion," *Journalism Quarterly* 55 (Autumn 1978): 570-576; Harold G. Zucker, "The Variable Nature of News Media Influence," in *Communication Yearbook 2,* ed. Brent D. Ruben (New Brunswick, N.J.: Transaction Books, 1978): pp. 225-240.
21. Frederick T. Steeper, "Public Response to Gerald Ford's Statements on Eastern Europe in the Second Debate," in *The Presidential Debates: Media, Electoral and Policy Perspectives,* ed. George F. Bishop, Robert G. Meadow, and Marilyn Jackson-Beeck (New York: Praeger, 1978), pp. 81-101. For additional evidence of changes in political opinions produced by commentary, see Michael J. Robinson, "The Impact of 'Instant Analysis,' " *Journal of Communication* 27 (Spring 1977): 17-23.
22. Comstock et al., *Television and Human Behavior,* pp. 307-309. For evidence that similarity in exposure leads to similar socialization, see Alexis S. Tan, "Media Use and Political Orientations of Ethnic Groups," *Journalism Quarterly* 60 (Spring 1983): 126-132.
23. Frederick Williams, Herbert S. Dordick, and Frederick Horstmann, "Where Citizens Go for Information," *Journal of Communication* 27 (Winter 1977): 95-99.
24. Comstock et al., *Television and Human Behavior,* pp. 295-306.
25. Sheldon G. Levy, "How Population Subgroups Differed in Knowledge of Six Assassinations," *Journalism Quarterly* 46 (Winter 1969): 685-698.
26. Bogart, *Press and Public,* pp. 76-79.
27. Bradley Greenberg and Brenda Dervin, "Mass Communication Among the Urban Poor," *Public Opinion Quarterly* 34 (Summer 1970): 224-235. For partly contradictory evidence, see Tan, "Media Use."
28. Bogart, *Press and Public,* p. 77. See also Leo Bogart, "Negro and White Media Exposure: New Evidence," *Journalism Quarterly* 49 (Spring 1972): 15-21 and George Comstock and Robin E. Cobbey, "Television and the Children of Ethnic Minorities," *Journal of Communication* 29 (Winter 1979): 104-115 and sources cited there.
29. Bogart, *Press and Public,* p. 56.
30. Ibid., p. 66.
31. Ibid., p. 56.
32. Jack M. McLeod and Lee B. Becker, "The Uses and Gratifications Approach," in *Handbook,* ed. Nimmo and Sanders, pp. 67-99.
33. Lee B. Becker, "Two Tests of Media Gratifications: Watergate and the 1974 Election," *Journalism Quarterly* 53 (Spring 1976): 28-33. See also Bogart, *Press and Public,* p. 112 and Philip Palmgreen, Lawrence A. Wenner, and J. D. Rayburn II, "Relations Between Gratifications Sought and Obtained: A Study of Television News," *Communication Research* 7 (April 1980): 161-192.
34. Graber, *Processing the News,* pp. 113-115. For a discussion of how a person's life style influences media use, see Stuart H. Schwartz, "A General Psychographic Analysis of Newspaper Use and Life Style," *Journalism Quarterly* 57 (Autumn

1980): 392-401.

35. Lewis Donohew and Philip Palmgreen, "A Reappraisal of Dissonance and the Selective Exposure Hypothesis," *Journalism Quarterly* 48 (Autumn 1971): 412-420. See also Michael A. Milburn, "A Longitudinal Test of the Selective Exposure Hypothesis," *Public Opinion Quarterly* 43 (Winter 1979): 507-517 and Steven H. Chaffee and Yuko Miyo, "Selective Exposure and the Reinforcement Hypothesis: An Intergenerational Panel Study of the 1980 Presidential Campaign," *Communication Research* 10 (January 1983): 3-36.

36. Percy H. Tannenbaum, "The Indexing Process in Communication," *Public Opinion Quarterly* 19 (Fall 1955): 292-302.

37. Donald L. Shaw and Maxwell E. McCombs, *The Emergence of American Political Issues: The Agenda-Setting Function of the Press* (St. Paul: West Publishing Co., 1977) and sources cited there. See also Maxwell E. McCombs, "The Agenda-Setting Approach," in *Handbook*, ed. Nimmo and Sanders, pp. 121-140.

38. Doris A. Graber, "Agenda-Setting: Are There Women's Perspectives?" in *Women and the News*, ed. Laurily Keir Epstein (New York: Hastings House, 1978), pp. 15-37.

39. Zucker, "The Variable Nature of News Media Influence," p. 227. See also James H. Watt, Jr., and Sjef van den Berg, "How Time Dependency Influences Media Effects in a Community Controversy," *Journalism Quarterly* 58 (Spring 1981): 43-50 and Doris A. Graber, *Crime News and The Public* (New York: Praeger, 1980).

40. The importance of personal and contexual factors in news selection and evaluation is discussed in Lutz Erbring, Edie Goldenberg, and Arthur Miller, "Front-Page News and Real World Cues: Another Look at Agenda-Setting by the Media," *American Journal of Political Science* 24 (February 1980): 16-49.

41. Graber, *Processing the News*, pp. 20-30.

42. For details on processing, see Ibid., chaps. 7-9.

43. David Krech and Richard S. Crutchfield, "Perceiving the World," in *The Process and Effects of Mass Communications*, rev. ed., edited by Wilbur Schramm and Donald F. Roberts (Urbana: University of Illinois Press, 1971), pp. 235-264.

44. Walter Lippmann, *Public Opinion* (New York: Harcourt Brace, 1922), p. 31.

45. Phillip J. Tichenor, George A. Donohue, and Clarice N. Olien, "Mass Media Flow and Differential Growth in Knowledge, *Public Opinion Quarterly* 34 (Summer 1970): 159-170. For evidence of shared reactions to television programs, irrespective of educational level, see W. Russell Neuman, "Television and American Culture: The Mass Medium and the Pluralist Audience," *Public Opinion Quarterly* 46 (Winter 1982): 471-487.

46. Eliot Freidson, "Communication Research and the Concept of the Mass," in *The Process and Effects of Mass Communication*, ed. Schramm and Roberts, pp. 197-208. See also Steven H. Chaffee, "Television and Social Relations, Introductory Comments," in *Television and Behavior*, ed. Pearl, Bouthilet, and Lazar, pp. 260-263.

47. Roberta S. Sigel, "Effects of Partisanship on the Perception of Political Candidates," *Public Opinion Quarterly* 28 (Summer 1964): pp. 488-496. See also Graber, *Processing the News*, pp. 147-177.

48. A brief review of recent effects studies is in Comstock, "The Impact of Television." See also Kraus and Davis, *The Effects of Mass Communication on Political Behavior*. A general discussion of learning factors is presented in Albert Bandura, *Social Learning Theory* (Englewood Cliffs: Prentice Hall, 1977).

49. The chances of becoming a crime victim are small in real life, but 30 to 64 percent in TV life. See Gerbner et al., "Cultural Indicators," pp. 106-107 and Paul Hirsch, "The 'Scary World' of the Nonviewer and other Anomalies: A Reanalysis of Gerbner et al.'s Findings on Cultivation Analysis," Parts 1 and 2, *Communication Research* 7 and 8 (Winter 1980 and Spring 1981): 403-457 and 3-37; Michael Hughes, "The Fruits of Cultivation Analysis: A Re-examination of the Effects of Television Watching on Fear of Victimization, Alienation, and the Approval of Violence," *Public Opinion Quarterly* 44 (Summer 1980): 287-303.

50. Graber, *Processing the News,* pp. 81-99 and John Stauffer, Richard Frost, and William Rybolt, "The Attention Factor in Recalling Network Television News," *Journal of Communication* (Winter 1983): 29-37.

51. Graber, "Agenda-Setting," p. 23.

52. Goal-oriented information seeking is discussed in Charles Atkin, "Instrumental Utilities and Information Seeking," in *New Models for Mass Communication Research,* ed. Peter Clarke (Beverly Hills: Sage, 1973), pp. 205-242.

53. Scott Keeter and Cliff Zukin, *Uninformed Choice: The Failure of the New Presidential Nominating System* (New York: Praeger, 1983).

54. V. O. Key, with the assistance of Milton C. Cummings, Jr., *The Responsible Electorate* (Cambridge, Mass.: Harvard University Press, 1965), p. 7, reached the same conclusion.

55. Arthur H. Miller, Edie N. Goldenberg, and Lutz Erbring, "Type-Set Politics: Impact of Newspapers on Public Confidence," *American Political Science Review* 73 (March 1979): 67-84.

56. Michael J. Robinson, "Public Affairs Television and the Growth of Political Malaise: The Case of 'The Selling of the Pentagon,' " *American Political Science Review* 70 (June 1976): 409-432. See also Garrett J. O'Keefe, "Political Malaise and Reliance on Media," *Journalism Quarterly* 57 (Spring 1980): 122-128.

57. Murray Edelman, *Politics as Symbolic Action* (New York: Academic Press, 1976).

58. Comstock et al., *Television and Human Behavior,* pp. 289-309.

59. For news selection criteria, see Graber, *Processing the News,* pp. 59-80.

60. Doris A. Graber and Young Yun Kim, "Why John Q. Voter Did Not Learn Much from the 1976 Presidential Debates," in *Communication Yearbook 2,* ed. Ruben, pp. 414-419.

61. James W. Tankard, Jr., and Stuart W. Showalter, "Press Coverage of the 1972 Report on Television and Social Behavior," *Journalism Quarterly* 54 (Summer 1977): 293-298 and Philip Palmgreen, "Mass Media Use and Political Knowledge," *Journalism Monographs,* No. 61 (May 1979): 20-33.

62. Edwin Diamond, *The Tin Kazoo: Television, Politics, and the News* (Cambridge, Mass., MIT Press, 1975), pp. 50-56.

63. Tony Schwartz, *The Responsive Chord* (Garden City, N.Y.: Anchor Press, Doubleday, 1974), p. 25.

64. C. Richard Hofstetter and Terry Buss, "Motivation for Viewing Two Types of TV Programs," *Journalism Quarterly* 58 (Spring 1981): 99-103 and Mihaly Csikszentmihalyi and Robert Kubey, "Television and the Rest of Life: A Systematic Comparison of Subjective Experience," *Public Opinion Quarterly* 45 (Fall 1981): 317-328.

65. Richard M. Perloff, Ellen A. Wartella, and Lee B. Becker, "Increasing Learning from TV News," *Journalism Quarterly* 59 (Spring 1982): 83-86.

66. Jarol B. Manheim, "Can Democracy Survive Television?" *Journal of Communica-*

tion 26 (Spring 1976): 84-90.

67. None of these studies focuses on the effects of exposure to nonfictional violence in the media since the First Amendment would be a strong bar to censorship of news. Surgeon General's Scientific Advisory Committee on Television and Social Behavior, *Television and Growing Up: The Impact of Televised Violence* (Washington, D.C.: U.S. Government Printing Office, 1971) and the 1981 follow-up in *Television and Behavior*, ed. Pearl, Bouthilet, and Lazar. For a critical review of the report see Thomas D. Cook, Deborah A. Kendzierski, and Stephen V. Thomas, "The Implicit Assumptions of Television Research: An Analysis of the 1982 NIMH Report on 'Television and Behavior,'" *Public Opinion Quarterly* 47 (Spring 1983): 161-201. See also Richard A. Dienstbier, "Sex and Violence: Can Research Have It Both Ways?" *Journal of Communication* 27 (Summer 197): 176-188.

68. George A. Comstock, *The Evidence on Television Violence* (Santa Monica, Calif.: Rand Corporation, P-5730, 1976).

69. Herbert H. Hyman, "Mass Communication and Socialization," in *Mass Communication Research,* ed. W. Phillips Davison and Frederick T. C. Yu (New York: Praeger, 1974), pp. 36-65.

70. Robert P. Snow, "How Children Interpret TV Violence in Play Context," *Journalism Quarterly* 51 (Spring 1974): 13-21.

71. Commission on Obscenity and Pornography, *Report of the Commission on Obscenity and Pornography* (New York: Bantam Books, 1970). See also Dienstbier, "Sex and Violence," pp. 177-180.

72. David O. Edeani, "Critical Predictors of Orientation to Change in a Developed Society," *Journalism Quarterly* 58 (Spring 1981), 56-64.

73. Lewis Donohew, "Communication and Readiness for Change in Appalachia," *Journalism Quarterly* 44 (Winter 1967): 679-687 and Lowndes F. Stephens, "Media Exposure and Modernization Among the Appalachian Poor," *Journalism Quarterly* 49 (Summer 1972): 247-257.

74. Leon S. Robertson, "The Great Seat Belt Campaign Flop," *Journal of Communication* 26 (Autumn 1976): 41-45.

75. James B. Lemert, Barry N. Mitzman, Michael A. Seither, Roxana H. Cook, and Regina Hackett, "Journalists and Mobilizing Information," *Journalism Quarterly* 54 (Winter 1977): 721-726.

76. Rodolfo N. Salcedo, Hadley Read, James F. Evans, and Ana C. Kong, "A Successful Information Campaign on Pesticides," *Journalism Quarterly* 51 (Spring 1974): 91-95; Dorothy F. Douglas, Bruce H. Westley, and Steven H. Chaffee, "An Information Campaign that Changed Community Attitudes," *Journalism Quarterly* 47 (Autumn 1970): 479-487.

77. Douglas S. Solomon, "Health Campaigns on Television," in *Television and Behavior,* ed. Pearl, Bouthilet, and Lazar, pp. 316-319.

78. Sheldon O'Connell, "Television and the Canadian Eskimo: The Human Perspective," *Journal of Communication* 27 (Autumn 1977): 140-144 and Gary O. Coldevin, "Anik I and Isolation: Television in the Lives of Canadian Eskimos," *Journal of Communication* 27 (Autumn 1977): 145-153.

79. Everett M. Rogers, "The Rise and Fall of the Dominant Paradigm," *Journal of Communication* 28 (Winter 1978): 64-69 and Wilbur Schramm and Daniel Lerner, eds., *Communication and Change: The Last Ten Years—and the Next* (Honolulu: University Press of Hawaii, 1976).

Readings

Altheide, David L., and Robert P. Snow. *Media Logic.* Beverly Hills, Calif.: Sage, 1979.

Bogart, Leo. *Press and Public: Who Reads What, When, Where, and Why in American Newspapers.* Hillsdale, N.J.: Lawrence Erlbaum, 1981.

Frank, Ronald E., and Marshall G. Greenberg. *The Public's Use of Television: Who Watches and Why.* Beverly Hills, Calif.: Sage, 1980.

Graber, Doris A. *Processing the News: How People Tame the Information Tide.* New York: Longman, 1984.

Stover, William James. *Information Technology in the Third World: Can It Lead to Humane National Development?* Boulder, Colo.: Westview Press, 1984.

Winick, Mariann Pezzella, and Charles Winick. *The Television Experience: What Children See.* Beverly Hills, Calif.: Sage, 1979.

Withey, Stephen B., and Ronald P. Abeles, eds. *Television and Social Behavior: Beyond Violence and Children.* Hillsdale, N.J.: Lawrence Erlbaum, 1980.

Elections in the Television Age

In the fall of 1978, the Senate reelection campaign of Charles H. Percy of Illinois was in trouble. Alex Seith, the Democratic challenger, had pulled ahead, and the polls were predicting a defeat for the two-term Republican incumbent. Then, during the final days of the campaign, Chicago's media saved the day for Percy. Three tough columns by famed *Chicago Sun-Times* columnist Mike Royko linked Seith to corrupt machine politicians allied with the Chicago crime syndicate and blasted him for racist appeals to black voters. Percy, sensing the punch that these columns carried, reprinted them as full-page newspaper advertisements and mailed them throughout the state. Seith's strength in the polls began to drop sharply. Then, just four days before the election, another media event delivered the knockout blow. Percy and Seith got into a verbal brawl in the lobby of a Chicago television station, just before they were scheduled for a joint broadcast. Walter Jacobson, the station's news anchor and commentator, kept the verbal battle going while the candidates were before the cameras. Later on that night, the film became part of a 75-minute news special. It created an image of Percy, the dignified political professional, defending himself against an undeserved attack by a vicious, unprincipled challenger. The voters sided with Percy.

That, at any rate, was the story making the rounds among Chicago's political pundits who were trying to explain the changing fortunes of candidates Percy and Seith. The trouble with the Percy-Seith story and many others like it is that they do not prove beyond a doubt that the media stories turned the tide. Other significant events were taking place at the time in Illinois politics and in the campaign of both senatorial candidates. Although the link between media and elections has been studied more thoroughly than other media-politics linkages, we still lack definite answers for most cause-effect questions such as those posed by the Percy-Seith contest.

The State of Research

Understanding the role of the mass media in elections is hampered by imbalances in research. Presidential elections have been extensively studied, but we know far less about the media's role in congressional and gubernatorial elections and practically nothing about their impact on local, judicial, or school board elections. The limited evidence available thus far suggests that the role of the mass media varies substantially, depending upon the particular office being contested, even when the manner of coverage is fairly constant.[1]

Even at the presidential level, comparatively little research has been done to point up differences in the role of the media as candidates and issues change from one election to the next.[2] Nor has the influence of factors such as incumbency, three-way competition, or major national crises been thoroughly investigated. It stands to reason that the impact of the media will vary depending on the changing political scene, the type of coverage chosen by newspeople, and the fluctuating interests of voters. Comparable studies of media impact on elections in Canada, Britain, France, Germany, and elsewhere are plagued by similar problems.[3]

Another serious obstacle to understanding is the dearth of analyses of media content. Election news content and its setting within the context of general news have been examined only rarely because content analysis is very costly. But without knowing the exact content of news, it becomes impossible to test what impact, if any, it had on the images held by media audiences. Another problem is failure to ascertain media exposure accurately. Investigators frequently assume that people have been exposed to media without checking the accuracy of that assumption. They fail to ascertain precisely which stories have come to the attention of various individuals and what these individuals learned from these stories. High costs have also discouraged studying media and other political influences throughout the entire campaign, from the preprimary period to the primaries and the general election. The crucial early stages in the campaign, when candidate selection takes place, have been ignored most often.

A shortage of good data also prevents us from isolating the effects of political advertising on political campaigns.[4] Candidates and their supporters spend a large share of their campaign budgets on political advertising displayed on bumper stickers and billboards, printed in newspapers, or broadcast with clockwork regularity on radio and television. The precise impact of these advertisements on target audiences is uncertain because it is difficult to untangle effects of commercials from the effects of other types of campaign publicity.

In their investigation of the impact of television commercials during the 1972 presidential campaign, Thomas Patterson and Robert McClure found that major campaign issues were covered more extensively in television commercials than in network newscasts.[5] For instance, between September 18 and November 6, 1972, more than 65 minutes of advertising time was used to tell about Nixon's policies regarding Vietnam, China, Russia, and America's allies. The average television network spent only 15 minutes on these stories.[6]

Most viewers—particularly those who did not read newspapers and were poorly informed—remembered more from the commercials, which each took only five minutes or less of air time, than from the television news. Simplicity of content, expert eye-ear appeal, and repetition of the message combined to produce this result.

Although people learned about campaign issues from them, the commercials apparently failed to influence viewers' evaluations of the candidates. Commercials are perceiver-determined. People see in them pretty much what they want to see—attractive images for their favorite candidates and unattractive ones for the opponent. If attempts to glamorize political actors and hide their weaknesses succeed, the effect lasts for only a short time. Commercials of opposing candidates see to that. Commercials did not alter ultimate voting choices in the 1972, 1976, or 1980 presidential campaigns.[7] The claims that television commercials can manufacture fairyland candidates and make them believable to credulous audiences apparently are vastly exaggerated when voters have alternative means for knowing the candidates.[8]

At the lower levels of political office, where such means are lacking, the story is different. The impact of commercials can be decisive. Wisely spent advertising funds can, indeed, buy elections.[9] Michael Robinson concluded that commercials for congressional candidates "can work relative wonders," especially when they are not challenged by the other side. "A well-crafted, heavily financed, and *uncontested* ad campaign does influence congressional elections—1980 is substantial proof." [10]

Television commercials add substantial chunks of information to the flow of news about candidates and issues. They often provide the only chance to gain information about the many candidates who are ignored by the media.[11] Substantively, commercials deal primarily with the same kinds of issues that are already covered by newspapers, radio, and television, albeit often in different proportions and from different perspectives. Although commercials often present expertly crafted images of candidates and their positions, these images frequently fail to penetrate viewers' protective shielding against being gulled by "propaganda." This is especially true when audiences are familiar with the candidates or have alternative sources of information.

The Consequences of Media Politics

The advent of television and its ready availability in every home, the spread and improvement of public opinion polling, and the use of computers in election data analysis have combined to bring major political changes that have vastly enhanced the role of the mass media in elections. In this era of "media politics," what major changes have been wrought by the new technologies?

Decline in Party Influence

Foremost among the changes is the decline of the influence of political parties, particularly in presidential elections. During the 1940s, when social scientists first investigated the impact of the mass media on the outcome of presidential elections, party allegiance was the most important determinant of the vote, followed by group allegiance, assessment of the candidate's personality, and consideration of issues, in that order.

Since the full flowering of the electronic age, the order has been reversed. The candidate as a personality has become the prime consideration at the presidential level. Second are issues associated with the candidate, followed by party affiliation and group membership.[12] When voters base their decisions on candidate personality or issues, the media become more important because they are the chief source of information about these matters.

Correspondingly, political parties take on less importance. When voters can see and hear candidates in their own living rooms, they can make choices that differ from those made by the party. Split ticket voting, that is, voting for candidates of different parties, has become common. Candidates can also defy party control because radio and television give them direct access to voters. More candidates can enter the race and campaign on their own strengths, raising their own money and building their own organizations. New candidates, with the aid of the media, can gain a wide following rapidly. This new independence of voters and candidates makes primary and general election races more crowded and less predictable than in the past. Party regulars who have groomed themselves over long periods of time for positions of power may find themselves bypassed.

Party affiliation remains very important at the state and local levels where the average person knows little about most candidates and media information is scanty, particularly on television. This is not true, however, when candidates run without overt or covert party designation and endorsement, or when candidates of the same party compete against each other in primary elections. When party choice criteria are lacking and personal experience or advice from opinion leaders is unavailable, people turn to whatever guidance the media may offer. Some will follow expressed or implied endorsements; others will take them as cues to vote the opposite way. In either case, whether the endorsements are accepted or rejected, what the media say about the candidates becomes the information base for decisionmaking.

Media as Kingmakers

A second and related consequence of the new media politics is the sharp increase in the power of media personnel to influence the selection of candidates and issues. Candidates, like actors, depend for their success as much on the roles into which they are cast as on their acting ability. In the television age, media people usually do the casting for presidential hopefuls, whose performance is then judged according to the assigned role. Strenuous efforts by campaign directors and public relations experts to dominate this aspect of the campaign have been only moderately fruitful.

Casting occurs early in the primaries when newspeople, on the basis of as yet slender evidence, must predict winners and losers in order to narrow the field of eligibles. Concentrating on the front-runners makes newspeople's tasks more manageable, but it often forces out of the race those who have been labeled losers. As *New York Times* political writer R. W. Apple conceded after appraising the presidential candidates' chances in January 1976, "Such early calculations are highly speculative.... But early calculations have a life of their own because they are the backdrop against which politicians and the media tend to measure the performance of the various candidates in their early confrontations." [13]

For instance, in the 1976 Democratic primaries, when almost a dozen candidates were running, the media covered Jimmy Carter far more heavily and favorably than other contenders. Coverage began months before the primaries, with above average numbers of newspaper stories assiduously sought out by the Carter campaign staff. Ample television coverage followed after the New Hampshire primary in February in which Carter received 30 percent of the Democratic vote. NBC's Tom Pettit called Carter "the man to beat." *Time* magazine labeled his campaign as the only one "with real possibilities of breaking far ahead of the pack." It featured him on its front cover, as did *Newsweek*. Along with the front cover picture in *Time* went a 2,630-line feature story, compared with 300 lines devoted to all other Democrats in the race. Television news and newspaper front-page coverage were equally generous, giving Carter three and four times the attention his opponents received.

Sen. Henry Jackson and Rep. Morris Udall, who did well in the early Democratic primaries, between them got less than a third of the coverage that Carter received. Subsequent primary defeats, such as Carter's poor showing in Massachusetts in early March, were characterized as exceptions that merely slowed his momentum, rather than as disastrous defeats. Gallup poll ratings in early February that credited Carter with only five percent of the national vote were ignored. [14]

Carter earned his "winner" spurs because he had managed to outrun the expectations newspeople had established for his political success. Such expectations, based on poll results, projections from past campaigns, and more or less educated guesses, are the uncertain yardsticks by which newspeople measure winners and losers. Carter won his prized and priceless status after less than five percent of the primary delegates had been selected. The emphasis that the media placed on these early victories created the kind of psychological momentum that enhances a candidate's chances for winning successive primaries and getting the nomination. Media legitimation is particularly important for political unknowns, such as Democratic hopeful Gary Hart in 1984. The winner or loser image may become a self-fulfilling prophecy because supporters and money flow to the front-runner. In Hart's case, the flow of money and support needed for a full-scale campaign effort became ample only after his victories in New England states had attracted press attention. But, even then, the boost was insufficient to match the resources of front-runner Mondale whom news stories continued to designate as the likely winner of the presidential primary sweepstakes, albeit with lowered odds.

Media predictions and public opinion polls also move in tandem. For instance, all 1980 presidential candidates designated as losers by the media lost support in the polls, while all who were designated as winners gained support.[15] The media role as kingmaker or killer of the dreams of would-be kings is often exercised over a long span of time. Image-making for presidential elections now begins on a massive scale more than a year before the first primary. The "pre-pre-campaign," on a more limited scale, begins shortly after the finish of the previous election. By the end of 1981, for instance, 30 Democrats and 14 Republicans had already been mentioned as potential presidential candidates for 1984.[16] Senators who receive favorable publicity over many years may gradually come to be thought of as likely presidential nominees. On the basis of such media boosts, people may decide to vote for them irrespective of an official party nomination. The perennial public support for a presidential candidacy by Sen. Edward Kennedy of Massachusetts is a case in point.

Media giants have often been able to use their personal influence and the power of the media under their control to support nominations for their favorites and to harm opponents. For instance, the late publisher Henry Luce enticed popular war-hero Dwight Eisenhower to run for the presidency in 1952. Luce put his publications, such as *Time* and *Life,* at Eisenhower's service. Kyle Palmer and the Chandler family, through their control of the *Los Angeles Times,* were instrumental in getting Richard Nixon a seat in the House of Representatives in 1946 and a U.S. Senate seat in 1950. Col. Robert McCormick used the powerful *Chicago Tribune* to defeat policies of the Roosevelt and Truman administrations and to put Republican politicians into office in Illinois.[17]

On the other hand, Sen. Thomas Eagleton's crushed chances for the vice-presidency illustrate the problems faced by public officials whose public and private difficulties make headlines. When the media reported that the Missouri senator had a record of traffic arrests and treatment for mental breakdowns, Sen. George McGovern, who had chosen him as his running mate in the 1972 election, felt forced to drop him from the ticket. Publicity for even trivial incidents may nip presidential aspirations. Stories about Sen. Edmund Muskie's tears over an insult to his wife and Gov. George Romney's offhand remark that he had been "brainwashed" by the military establishment during a trip to Vietnam are examples.

Media images can also become vastly important during the general election campaign. For instance, media events such as the Kennedy-Nixon television debates of 1960 and the Carter-Reagan debate of 1980 helped to remove public impressions that John F. Kennedy and Ronald Reagan were unsuited for the presidency. Kennedy was apparently able to demonstrate through the debates that he was capable of coping with the presidency despite his youth and inexperience. Reagan conveyed the impression that he was neither trigger-happy nor physically or mentally decrepit. No other medium could have equaled the reach and impact of television.

In fact, the risks of televised debates so awed presidential candidates after the 1960 encounter that a repeat performance did not occur for 16 years. When debates reemerged in 1976, they lacked the drama of the 1960 encounter. No Prince Charming here, battling against a sweaty, gray-looking opponent. Candidates Gerald Ford and Jimmy Carter were devoid of the kind of charisma that had generated so much audience appeal. In all-important visual attractiveness, they were fairly well matched. Still, many political observers believe that President Ford might have won reelection in 1976 had he been able to look substantially more presidential than Jimmy Carter in the debates. Likewise, in 1980, Ronald Reagan might have been unable to overcome public concern about his level-headedness in international crises had television not pictured him as a friendly, grandfatherly type.

Presidents Lyndon Johnson and Jimmy Carter saw their chances for a second term diminish sharply because they were unable to use the media effectively to make a good case for unpopular policies. Carter's case reflects the now common practice of the media to subject incumbents to such scathing criticism that reelection becomes all but impossible.[18] A comparison of the full record of Johnson's public statements justifying his Vietnam policies with the statements that were actually publicized shows that the bulk of his most telling messages were never transmitted. Media message selection had gutted the case he needed to make himself a strong second-term candidate for the presidency in 1968.[19] Unlike Carter, Johnson decided not to seek another term.

Media-owned and operated public opinion polls are yet another weapon in the arsenal for king-making. The CBS-*New York Times* poll, the NBC-Associated Press poll, and the ABC-*Washington Post* poll all conduct popularity ratings and issue polls throughout presidential elections. In fact, 73 percent of the polls reported on television in 1980 were media-generated.[20] These widely publicized poll results become bench marks for voters, telling them who the winners and losers are and what issues should be deemed crucial to the campaign. Depending on the nature of the questions formulated by the pollsters and the political context in which the story becomes embedded, the responses spell fortune or misfortune for the candidates.

Polls may determine which candidates enter the fray and which keep out. Ronald Reagan apparently was encouraged to enter the 1976 presidential race because President Ford's poll ratings were low prior to the Republican presidential nominating convention of that year.[21] With these low poll ratings as backdrop, Ford's subsequent rise in the polls was widely interpreted as a show of real political strength. Similarly, President Carter's poor poll ratings early in the 1980 campaign encouraged Edward Kennedy's candidacy and gave Carter an image of political weakness that he was unable to shed even when his ratings improved. A Harris poll reported by ABC News in June 1980 boosted financial and volunteer support for Republican John Anderson when it showed that 31 percent of the respondents would vote for him "if the polls showed" that he had a real chance of winning the election. Ironically, poll predictions hastened Anderson's political downfall when he dropped below expected support in the crucial primary in his home state of Illinois. Good ratings in polls also increase media coverage, and vice versa, setting in motion a spiral of support or defection.

Television-Age Recruits

A third important consequence of the new politics is the change it has wrought in the types of candidates likely to be politically successful. Because television can bring the image of candidates for high national and state office directly into the homes of millions of voters, political recruiters have become extremely conscious of a candidate's ability to look impressive and to perform well before the cameras. People who are not telegenic have been eliminated from the pool of available recruits. Abraham Lincoln's rugged face probably would not have passed muster in the television age. President Harry S. Truman's "Give 'em Hell, Harry," homespun style would have backfired if presented to nationwide groups rather than small gatherings. Franklin D. Roosevelt's wheelchair appearances would have spelled damaging weakness, as did George Wallace's in the 1970s. Roosevelt, in fact, was keenly aware of the harmful effects that a picture of himself in a wheelchair might have and never allowed photographs to be taken while he was being lifted to the speaker's rostrum.

Actors and celebrities from other walks of life who are adept at performing before the public now have a much better chance than ever before to be recruited for political office. Ronald Reagan, a former actor, John Glenn, an ex-astronaut, and Jesse Jackson, a charismatic preacher, are

Reprinted by permission. Tribune Media Services, Inc., 1984.

examples of typical television-age recruits whose chances for public office would have been much smaller in an earlier era. As columnist Marquis Child has put it, candidates no longer "run" for office; they "pose" for office.[22]

Candidates who are short on television performance skills now spend considerable time with professionals to remedy their shortcomings. In recent years television advisers have become regular members of presidential and gubernatorial staffs. Names of media experts such as John Deardourff, Gerald Rafshoon, Tony Schwartz, David Garth, Charles Guggenheim, or Joseph Napolitan have become as well known as the political bosses of yesteryear. They guide candidates in creating commercials and in generating and handling general news coverage of the campaign.

Largely because of the high costs of television commercials and the costs of gaining news exposure, media expenses have become a crucial factor in politics. Media coverage of campaigns currently takes 30 to 50 percent of the budget spent by all candidates and parties in elections at all levels. In 1976, total campaign spending was $540 million.[23] In 1980, Carter and Reagan each had $29.4 million to spend on just the general election campaign. Of this amount, each man spent more than half on commercials, mostly 30- and 60-second spots, and a few 5-minute telebiographies and 30-minute campaign night specials.[24] In addition, various political action committees (PACs) and other groups spent $13.7 million on behalf of the 1980 presidential candidates, most of it for media exposure. Ronald Reagan was the beneficiary of most of the PAC money. PACs spent even more heavily on congressional campaigns, primarily to defeat liberals and promote conservatives.[25]

Given the high cost of campaigns, a candidate's ability to raise money remains an important consideration, even when federal funding is available. Wealthy candidates who can draw on personal resources have an advantage. Activities and statements likely to alienate donors are shunned. While there is evidence that the best-financed candidates do not always win, folklore says they do. Hence falling behind in the race for money to finance media exposure is a sharp brake on political aspirations. The political consequences in recruitment and postelection commitments that spring from such financial considerations are enormous.

Campaigning for the Media

A fourth major aspect of the new politics is the fact that mass media coverage has become the campaign's pivotal point. Campaigns are expressly arranged for the best media exposure before the largest suitable audience. To attract media coverage, candidates concentrate on press conferences, talk show appearances, or trips to interesting locations. Even when candidates meet voters personally through rallies, parades, or shopping center visits, they generally time these events to attract the media and dovetail with news publication schedules. Campaigns thus are carefully tailored to suit media coverage opportunities and to orchestrate the kinds of images that candidates like the media to project for them.

Incumbents have a distinct advantage over challengers in this effort to attract coverage because journalists need exciting stories, preferably from candidates of proven newsworthiness. The official status and public activities of incumbents make them intrinsically attractive. Therefore they usually get more and better coverage than challengers. Incumbents may also be able to dictate time and place for media encounters. When an incumbent president schedules a meeting for reporters in the White House Rose Garden, ample coverage is ensured. There even is a quasi-incumbency status for promising challengers. Once they have attained wide recognition as front-runners, newspeople compete for their attention. Their power to grant or withhold it can be translated into influence over quality and quantity of coverage.

Candidates often plan their schedules to dovetail with media plans. For instance, when it became apparent during the 1976 prenomination period that the media would cover the January presidential caucuses in Iowa as a weather vane for the presidential campaign, candidates hurriedly rearranged their schedules to make a good Iowa showing. Rep. Morris Udall, who had planned to campaign only in New Hampshire, Massachusetts, and Wisconsin, felt that "Iowa justifies the expense. It will be covered like the first primary always has been in the national press. If we can emerge as the clear liberal choice in Iowa, the payoffs in New Hampshire will be enormous." [26] Udall committed $80,000 of his scarce funds and 10 days of valuable time to the Iowa effort, but the anticipated payoffs did not materialize. Nonetheless, 1980 and 1984 hopefuls responded in similar manner to prospective media coverage for straw polls and caucuses in places such as Iowa, Florida, and Maine, where campaigning might otherwise have been light.

To keep a favorable image of their candidates in front of the public, campaign managers arrange newsworthy events to familiarize potential voters with their candidates' best aspects. Television reporter Lesley Stahl thus described efforts to make Carter appear as the people's friend in 1980:

> What did President Carter do today in Philadelphia? He *posed,* with as many different types of symbols he could *possibly* find.
> There was a picture at the day care center. And one during the game of bocce ball with the senior citizens. Click, another picture with a group of teenagers. And then he performed the ultimate media event—a walk through the Italian market.
> The point of all this, *obviously,* to get on the local news broadcasts and in the morning newspapers. It appeared that the President's intention was not to say anything controversial. . . .
> Simply the intention was to be seen, as he was, and it was photographed, even right before his corned beef and cabbage lunch at an Irish restaurant with the popular mayor Bill Green. . . .
> There were more symbols at the Zion (black) Baptist church. . . .
> Over the past three days the President's campaign has followed a formula—travel in a must-win state, spending only a short time there but ensuring several days of media coverage. . . .[27]

Even though talking is the staple of campaigners, most television producers do not like "talking heads," which means merely showing the faces of speakers. Candidates therefore may engage in some fairly meaningless activities merely to provide attractive pictures. Most of these pictures are deliberately packed with symbols to convey stock messages quickly and easily. In fact, over the years a complete language of picture stereotypes has developed, and candidates adapt their own styles to fit into this mold. For instance, showing candidates with old people, or black workers, or college students proclaims affinity for these groups. Showing candidates in informal settings, surrounded by family members, attests to their being "regular" folk and good family people.

Most major campaign events are now staged as prime time, live coverage television spectacles. Aside from occasional presidential debates, nominating conventions have been the biggest single media event of a presidential campaign. Both major parties have selected the convention cities with an eye to effective television coverage. Convention managers have tried to keep a tight rein on speakers and demonstrations to make certain that desirable images are conveyed and that major presentations appear when the television audience is likely to be at a peak. For their part, media people have tried to structure the flow of their words and pictures to cover unfolding events and still tell a coherent dramatic story with a central theme, a beginning and end, and a climax. But after presenting almost gavel-to-gavel coverage of the 1980 conventions on all three networks, network executives became disenchanted about the newsworthiness of the presidential nominating conventions. Thanks to the preceding media coverage, the conventions had become little more than ratifications of foregone conclusions. Hence plans called for substantial reduction of coverage in future conventions.

Structuring and staging campaign activities such as conventions to make them newsworthy by the standards of modern American media has enhanced showmanship at the expense of substance. As California governor Jerry Brown's campaign manager put it: in 1976, "newsworthy" means featuring disagreement, conflict, and contrast. It means painting campaign participants as heroes and villains. It means making one's point briefly, at the start of a speech, and using popular, emotionally stirring symbols. It means tailoring one's speech to the needs of the moment and capturing the audience's fancy.[28] Conspicuous by its absence from this definition is any mention that "newsworthy" means saying something important or enlightening to the audience.

Because conflict is deemed attractive and memorable, journalists often goad campaigners into confrontations by asking questions that point up existing conflicts or that may lead to new battles. During the 1980 presidential campaign, for instance, the media encouraged challengers to attack President Carter's energy policies and his handling of cabinet appointments. When journalists select the battlegrounds for the presidential contest, they shape the political agenda not only during the campaign but afterwards as well. Campaign statements may be subsequently construed as commitments to act.

Campaign stories are judged by general news criteria. Therefore minor candidates and newcomers whose chances for success are questionable do not get much coverage. Their efforts to attract the media are apt to fail since they simply are not "big news" to the mass audience. Lack of coverage, in turn, makes it extremely difficult for them to become well known and increase their chances of winning elections. This is another example of unintentional bias built into media coverage that redounds to the benefit of established political forces.

Media Content

We are now ready to examine the kinds of newspaper and television coverage that recent elections have received. We will focus first on the media's evaluation of candidates' qualifications and issue positions in four presidential elections from 1968 to 1980. Was enough information made available about the issues that would be likely to require attention from the new president? Were adequate criteria supplied to enable voters to decide which of several policy options would best suit their priorities? Were people informed about each viable candidate's positions on the issues? Did they receive sufficient information about each candidate's personality, experience, and ability to evaluate his likely performance as president? All of these questions assess the adequacy of the information supply for making voting choices in the manner that democratic theorists consider most rational and desirable.

From the media's perspectives, it is extremely difficult to mesh the general public's preference for simple, dramatic stories with the need to present sufficient information for issue-based election choices. Information that may be crucial for voting decisions may also be unappealing to much of the potential audience, which will therefore ignore it. Hence newspeople feel compelled to feature exciting, humanly touching aspects of the election, even when they are trivial, without totally neglecting essential, unglamorous information useful for issue-based decisionmaking. Any evaluation of how the media perform their task must take these conflicting demands into consideration.

Patterns of Coverage

The information on mass media output comes from an extensive content analysis of newspapers and national and local television newscasts of the presidential campaigns in 1968, 1972, 1976, and 1980.[29] In three of the four elections, the data were collected during the final 30 days of the campaign. Content analysis for the entire year showed only minor variations in news coverage patterns between the early and late parts of the campaign.[30] Therefore we shall talk about election coverage in general for the entire campaign, noting in passing some of the differences that characterize various stages. To simplify the presentation, most tables focus on newspaper data, thereby tapping the richest election data source. Three out of four voters use newspapers, often along with television, during a presidential campaign.

Prominence of Election Stories.   In a presidential election year, election stories are major foci of news attention, on a par with foreign affairs news and crime coverage. In 1968, 1972, 1976, and 1980, they constituted roughly 13 percent of all newspaper political news and 15 percent of television political news. But election stories do not dominate the news. It is quite possible to read the daily paper without noticing election news and to come away from a telecast with the impression that election stories are just a minor part of the day's political developments. Election news must compete for audience attention with many other types of stories; this fact accounts, in part, for its limited impact.

Treatment of election stories in terms of prominence criteria, such as headline size, front page or first story placement, and picture treatment, substantiates that elections share the "limelight" with other news. In all of these categories, election stories received average treatment. However, the space or time allotted to them generally was longer than for other stories. Consequently, election stories could provide more detail.

Uniformity of Coverage Patterns.   One of the most striking findings in all presidential election years is the uniformity of patterns of coverage. Media personnel everywhere selected the same kinds of stories and emphasized the same types of facts, despite the wealth of diverse materials available to them. The only difference was that smaller newspapers carried fewer election stories and that news stories varied in the evaluation of candidates, issues, and campaign events. Newspapers in small or large communities, endorsing Republicans or Democrats, all showed the same pattern. Television news was also uniform.

Content analysis studies during congressional, state, and local campaigns show similar patterns.[31] For example, during the 1983 mayoral campaign in Chicago, all major television stations and the three major local newspapers displayed nearly identical patterns, even though the need to compete against each other and the controversial nature of the race would suggest diverse treatment. Table 6-1 illustrates the similarity in patterns of coverage of the primary and general elections by the *Chicago Tribune* and *Chicago Sun-Times,* the city's two major competing dailies, which are owned and operated by distinct enterprises, and the *Defender,* a paper owned and operated by black business leaders, which caters to Chicago's large black community.

The finding that election news patterns are quite stable in successive elections and uniform for all media covering a particular election is politically

Table 6-1   Distribution of Coverage Areas in the 1983 Chicago Mayoral Primary and General Elections (in Percentage of Story Themes)

	Primary Election			General Election		
	Tribune	Sun-Times	Defender	Tribune	Sun-Times	Defender
Campaign	43%	46%	53%	42%	41%	44%
Policy	28	24	19	20	21	23
Ethics	13	11	7	8	8	8
Qualities	11	14	19	19	19	14
Party	5	5	3	12	13	11
(N)	(639)	(748)	(303)	(1,133)	(1,288)	(635)

SOURCE: Doris A. Graber, "Media Magic: Fashioning Characters for the 1983 Mayoral Race," in *The Making of the Mayor: Chicago 1983,* ed. Melvin G. Holli and Paul Green (Grand Rapids, Mich.: Eerdmans Publishing Co., 1984), p. 84. Tables 6-1, 6-2, and 6-4 are reprinted by permission.

very significant. It means that Americans are supplied with similar information bases for political decisionmaking during election campaigns. Criteria for judging remain constant and uniform, although actual appraisals differ. There are benefits as well as drawbacks to this similarity of coverage. It introduces a large degree of homogeneity into the electoral process. This is an advantage in a heterogeneous country, where it might otherwise be difficult to develop political consensus. But it also means that the same topics and judgment criteria are neglected. Joint knowledge is marred by joint ignorance. Uniformity throttles needed diversity.

Uniformity in evaluation criteria obviously has not produced uniform political views throughout the country. These differences in political evaluations, even when audiences share the same news, must be attributed to the various interpretations that news commentators put on the same facts and to the outlook that audiences bring to the news. As pointed out in the previous chapter, the impact of news frequently is perceiver- rather than stimulus-determined.

Of the factors that encourage uniform coverage, the common professional socialization of journalists is apparently the most important. As we discussed in Chapter 3, newspeople share a sense of what is newsworthy and how it should be presented. Pack journalism also is the rule in reporting elections, as Timothy Crouse pointed out so vividly in *The Boys on the Bus,* a tale of reporters accompanying candidates on their odysseys.[32] Several other possible explanations can be ruled out, such as universal use of wire service stories, quotes from the same speeches, or shared columnists. In the presidential elections that we examined extensively, only a fourth of all campaign stories were based on similar wire service stories or relied on quotes to make their main points. Papers that use very few wire service stories for campaign coverage still showed the same news patterns. The small percentage of campaign stories that were based on the writings of columnists (15 percent) involved a wide array of writers.

Uniform coverage patterns might also be produced if the media followed what has been called the "campaign model" of reporting.[33] In this model—the utopia of campaign managers—the rhythm of the campaign as produced by the candidates and their staffs determines what is covered. Reporters dutifully take their cues from the candidates. But comparisons of campaign activities with media coverage show that this model does not prevail. Press coverage conforms instead to an "incentive model." Whenever exciting stories provide an incentive for coverage, they are published in a rhythm dictated by the needs of the media and the tastes of their audiences. The needs and tastes of the candidates may be ignored. Media coverage routinely lags behind the acceleration of campaign activity just prior to nominations and primary and general elections because newspeople are waiting to cover the outcome.

The incentive model also explains the handling of news substance.

Producing exciting stories means concentrating on conflicts, real or manufactured, keeping score about who is ahead or behind in the race, and digging out tidbits about the personal and professional lives and foibles of the actors in the political drama. Complex election stories, stuffed with statistics and strange names, may be shunned.

Election coverage by specialized media further illustrates the use of the incentive model. News patterns differ from those in the general audience media. For instance, papers geared to ethnic audiences focus on the aspects of the campaign that are of primary concern to them and ignore the rest. Business and labor publications put extraordinary emphasis on the campaign's relation to the economy, featuring stories that may be totally lacking in general audience publications.

Political and Structural Bias. Does election coverage give a fair and equal chance for all viewpoints to be expressed in a manner that allows the media audience to make informed decisions? Are the perennial charges of bias leveled by disappointed candidates merely reactions to coverage that did not advance their cause, or are they evidence that newspeople always show favoritism?

The answer is that media people generally try very hard to produce balanced coverage for all major candidates for the same office. This holds true for print journalists, who have no legal obligation to keep coverage balanced, as well as for broadcasters, who, although they are obliged to give equal coverage for special election programs, are free to indulge in unequal exposure in regular news programs. There are no universally accepted standards of fairness and balance. Newspeople traditionally aim for rough parity in the number of stories about each candidate and rough parity in the balance of overtly favorable and unfavorable stories. Fairness does not mean discussing the candidates from the same perspectives, quoting their friends and enemies in equal proportions, or giving their stories similar time, space, or placement.

The 1983 Chicago mayoral primary elections demonstrate the unfairness that may result. Table 6-2 reveals the imbalance that ensues when the media give the lion's share of coverage to those candidates who have a realistic chance for election. Hence the Republican contender in Chicago's mayoral primary election, Bernard Epton, received practically no coverage compared with that received by the candidates fighting for the Democratic nomination, incumbent Jane Byrne, Cook County Prosecutor Richard M. Daley (the son of the longtime mayor), and U.S. Rep. Harold Washington. Even during the general election, when his chances for victory had risen dramatically because he was running against a black challenger in a racially polarized city, Epton lagged substantially behind his opponent. Table 6-4 shows imbalance in another coverage aspect—the choice of friendly and hostile sources.

Implementing the prevailing notions of fairness and balance may be impossible. For instance, in the McGovern-Nixon campaign of 1972, George

Table 6-2 Coverage for Each Candidate in the 1983 Chicago Mayoral Primaries (in Percentage of Story Themes)

	Candidates					
	Jane Byrne	Richard M. Daley	Harold Washington	Other Democrats	Bernard Epton	*(N)*
Chicago Tribune						
Campaign	20%	26%	24%	28%	2%	(251)
Policy	41	16	16	27	—	(153)
Ethics	42	9	21	28	—	(76)
Qualities	15	39	17	26	3	(66)
Party	26	17	22	22	13	(23)
(N)	(161)	(127)	(116)	(154)	(11)	
Sun-Times						
Campaign	38	18	20	21	3	(313)
Policy	35	26	15	23	2	(170)
Ethics	53	14	10	22	1	(73)
Qualities	24	23	23	30	1	(102)
Party	20	30	27	10	13	(30)
(N)	(247)	(141)	(126)	(156)	(18)	
Defender						
Campaign	24	14	55	7	—	(149)
Policy	39	27	31	4	—	(52)
Ethics	21	32	32	16	—	(19)
Qualities	10	12	69	10	—	(52)
Party	50	—	50	—	—	(4)
(N)	(66)	(47)	(142)	(21)	(0)	

NOTE: The total N, which may be tallied horizontally and vertically, equals 569 for the *Chicago Tribune*, 688 for the *Chicago Sun-Times*, and 276 for the *Defender*.

SOURCE: Graber, "Media Magic," in *The Making of the Mayor*, ed. Holli and Green, p. 66.

McGovern, a new face on the presidential scene, challenged an incumbent who lacked rapport with most newspeople. McGovern was saying all sorts of newsworthy things, while Nixon stayed out of the media limelight claiming to be too busy in the oval office. Quite naturally, the media quoted Senator McGovern more often than President Nixon. In the Chicago mayoral campaign Harold Washington was a charismatic candidate, while his Republican challenger was lackluster. There was keen interest in exploring the changes that a black mayor might bring about for the city. No wonder the media found Washington far more newsworthy than his opponent.

One may even question whether it is fair to attempt to balance coverage when the situation surrounding candidates is not comparable. Reducing an incumbent's coverage to that accorded to a challenger seems unfair and inappropriate when the public needs to know what officeholders are doing. It would be equally inappropriate to expand a challenger's coverage to an incumbent's proportions. In 1972, when McGovern met more often with reporters and used more quotable phrases than his opponent, it would have been unfair to suppress these quotes for the sake of balance. Imbalanced coverage, in these instances, resulted from "structural bias," which is caused by the circumstances of news production. This differs from "political bias," which would involve slanting the news for partisan reasons. Structural bias, though devoid of partisan motives, may nonetheless have profound effects on the perceptions people form about campaigns.[34]

Explicit bias, by contrast, is highly unusual. Outright editorial comment in news stories is practically nil. Veiled criticism is somewhat more common and can be detected in 1 to 4 percent of the stories, if one considers all types of media and all types of elections. At times, it is also difficult to judge to what extent structural bias is fueled by explicit bias. In the Chicago election, for instance, newspeople could argue that the heavy emphasis on negative stories about incumbent Jane Byrne was structural: there were many misdeeds to be laid on her doorstep. One could also make a good case for claiming that newspeople revelled in digging up negative news about her, while seeing and hearing comparatively little evil about her challengers. Editorials, of course, are biased, since it is their primary function to express opinions.

As part of the editorial function, many news sources endorse candidates. On the presidential level, endorsements do not seem to be very influential. Even though Republican presidential candidates have received the bulk of endorsements in this century, by 1980, 10 out of 21 elections had been won by Democrats. Endorsements for less exalted offices have been far more influential, particularly in elections in which voters had little information available to make their own decisions.[35] Influential papers, such as the *Los Angeles Times*, William Loeb's Manchester *Union Leader*, or the *Washington Post*, can be extraordinarily successful in promoting the election of candidates they have endorsed and in defeating unacceptable contenders. These three papers were credited, respectively, with sending Richard Nixon to the House of Representatives in 1946 and the Senate in 1950, electing Republican John Sununu governor of New Hampshire in 1982 (despite a nationwide trend sweeping Democrats into governorships), and winning the mayoral primary in Washington, D.C., in 1978 for City Councilman Marion Barry, who had been trailing in the polls. At the presidential level, news coverage tends to be essentially evenhanded, regardless of the candidate endorsed. Below the presidential level, there is some evidence that media give more coverage to their endorsed candidates than to those they have not endorsed.

The effort to keep coverage balanced does not extend to third-party candidates. Anyone who runs for the presidency outside of the Republican or Democratic party is out of the mainstream of newsworthiness and slighted or even ignored by the news profession. Ed Clark, the Libertarian party's candidate in 1980, for example, was almost totally ignored by the media. Exceptionally newsworthy third-party candidates, such as George Wallace of the American Independent party, Robert La Follette of the Progressive party, and John Anderson of the National Unity Campaign, were notable exceptions. Newsworthiness considerations also account for the sparse coverage of vice-presidential candidates, despite the importance of the office. Vice presidents frequently become president, but that possibility always seems remote until it happens. Hence these candidates receive very little media attention. Ninety-five percent of the coverage in a typical presidential election goes to the presidential contenders and only 5 percent to their running mates.

Substance of Coverage: Candidates

We now turn to specific coverage characteristics. How are candidate qualifications and positions delineated, and how are campaign events and issues described and analyzed?

Judging from the highly consistent patterns of the 1968-1980 period, it is clear that the media discuss the qualifications of presidential candidates more amply than campaign events and issues. On an average, 60 percent of the comments refer to personal and professional qualifications of the candidates and 40 percent to issues. Actually, emphasis on issues is somewhat greater than these figures indicate, since a moderate portion of the discussion of professional qualities relates to ability to cope with issues.

The qualifications highlighted by the media fall into two broad groups: those that are generally important in judging a person's character and those more specifically related to the tasks of the office. Personal capacities include personality traits, such as integrity, reliability, and compassion. They also encompass style characteristics, such as forthrightness or folksiness, and image characteristics, such as the ability to appear productive and fiscally responsible. Professional capacities at the presidential level include the capacity to conduct foreign and domestic affairs, the ability to mobilize public support, and a flair for government reorganization. The candidate's political philosophy is also a professional criterion.

Within these broad categories some 40 qualities were mentioned repeatedly, in quite similar proportions, in all the news sources that we examined for presidential election coverage. However, only 10 qualities were stressed heavily, and better than half of these involved primarily personal capacities. Over the years, presidential candidates have been most frequently assessed in terms of their trustworthiness, strength of character, leadership capabilities, and compassion. As one wit has phrased it, the crucial question is, "Would you buy a used car from him?" For the media and the public as well, the question of trustworthiness has been paramount because of the tremendous amount of unchecked power in the hands of American political executives, especially presidents. Style and image characteristics, although important, pale before the prominence given to personality traits.[36]

When it comes to professional capacities—the very qualities that deserve the fullest discussion and analysis—media coverage in recent presidential elections has been comparatively scanty and often vague. This held true even when an incumbent was involved, and there was ample opportunity to assess professional qualifications. Only a handful of professional qualifications have been mentioned with any frequency. These include general appraisals of the capacity to handle foreign affairs, which has been deemed crucial throughout the twentieth century, and the capacity to handle domestic affairs. The latter has primarily involved the capacity to sustain an acceptable quality of life for all citizens by maintaining the economy on an even keel and by controlling crime and internal disorder.

Although the same kinds of qualities and even the same specific qualities reappear from election to election, treatment of individual candidates varies. For instance, in the 1983 Chicago mayoral campaign, the proportions of stories allotted to various candidates in major areas of concern varied widely. The *Chicago Tribune,* for example, devoted 42 percent of its discussion about candidate ethics to incumbent Byrne, compared with 21 and 9 percent, respectively, for her chief rivals, Washington and Daley. Each of the other papers had its unique allotments of space: all of them treated the candidates unequally. One must wonder about the impact of such disparate coverage, which makes it very difficult for the electorate to compare and evaluate the candidates on important dimensions. Effective comparisons are also hindered by the major contradictions among remarks reported about the candidates. Bound by current codes of objective reporting and neutrality in electoral contests, the media rarely give guidance to the audience for judging conflicting claims.

Choices usually involve selecting lesser evils, since candidate coverage is quite negative, especially for the incumbents. Table 6-3 shows the negative treatment 1980 presidential candidates received on CBS television. Toward the end of the campaign, even John Anderson and George Bush moved into the negative column. The score each candidate received constitutes the balance between all explicit positive and negative references to the candidate's personal and professional qualities during the campaign. The score leaves out neutral comments and remarks about winning and losing. The lead paragraph in a *Time* magazine story at the end of the campaign sums up the mood:

> For more than a year, two flawed candidates have been floundering toward the final showdown, each unable to give any but his most unquestioning supporters much reason to vote for him except dislike of his opponent.[37]

Newspeople's comments are a comparatively minor reason for the negative cast of the news. The main reason lies in story selection and choice of sources to quote. Newspeople dwell on stories that make candidates look bad and quote amply from hostile sources. Table 6-4 provides an example from the

Table 6-3 CBS News Candidate Evaluations, January to Election Day, 1980

Candidate	Total Scores
John B. Anderson	+4
George Bush	+2
Howard H. Baker, Jr.	−1
John B. Connally	−1
Ronald Reagan	−5
Jimmy Carter	−7
Total score	−18

NOTE: Scores are based on explicit references only. Qualities evaluated: competence, integrity, consistency, general quality. Candidates not explicitly evaluated: Edmund G. Brown, Jr., Edward E. Clark, Philip M. Crane, Robert Dole, Gerald R. Ford, and Larry Pressler. There were no complete stories about Benjamin Fernandez, Lyndon H. LaRouche, Harold E. Stassen.

SOURCE: Michael Jay Robinson, "A Statesman Is a Dead Politician: Candidate Images on Network News," in *What's News: The Media in American Society,* ed. Elie Abel (San Francisco: Institute for Contemporary Studies, 1981), p. 162. Reprinted by permission.

1983 Chicago mayoral election. It shows the orientation of identifiable sources to which reporters attributed their information. Throughout the primary and final elections, the Jane Byrne story in the three newspapers, with one minor exception, reflected predominantly the views of her enemies. Her challengers were treated far better. The outcome was heavily negative coverage for Byrne and much more favorable treatment of Daley and Washington.

On the whole, television coverage resembles newspaper patterns in concentrated form. If newspapers stress personality qualities heavily, television stresses them even more. If newspapers concentrate on comparatively few qualities, television concentrates on even fewer. The usual one- or two-minute story gives little chance for in-depth reporting and analysis. It does permit creation of simple, graphic images that illustrate selected themes about the candidate and the campaign. Viewers can readily absorb and use such interpretive portrayals as a basis for decisionmaking.

To conserve their limited time, television newscasters create stereotypes of the various candidates early in the campaign and then build their stories around these stereotypes by merely adding new details to the established image. During the 1972 primaries, for instance, television stereotyped Sen. Hubert Humphrey of Minnesota as "the politician of the past." Television's Humphrey had old supporters, was linked to the bygone Johnson presidency, and represented the old politics confronted by the new. Sen. Edmund Muskie of Maine was stereotyped as the "front-runner," and Sen. George McGovern was depicted as the "anti-establishment populist." Alabama governor George Wallace was "the creator of division and discord" who was trying to ride into the presidency on the controversial school busing issue.

During the 1980 presidential campaign, Ronald Reagan was typecast as an amiable dunce stumbling into the presidency almost by mistake.[38] Report-

Table 6-4 Source Orientation in the 1983 Chicago Mayoral Primary and General Elections (in Percentage of Story Themes)

Source Orientation	Primary Election			General Election		
	Tribune	Sun-Times	Defender	Tribune	Sun-Times	Defender
Byrne						
Pro	17%	27%	12%	9%	9%	2%
Anti	29	26	17	11	14	7
Daley						
Pro	23	24	10	1	1	—
Anti	8	2	6	—	—	1
Washington						
Pro	20	21	52	34	38	74
Anti	2	1	3	19	11	2
Epton						
Pro	1	1	—	18	20	5
Anti	—	—	1	8	8	10
(N)	(639)	(748)	(303)	(714)	(828)	(508)

SOURCE: Graber, "Media Magic," in *The Making of the Mayor*, ed. Holli and Green, p. 62.

ers dwelled on his frequent misstatements of facts and mangling of names and statistics. They focused extensively on his much ridiculed comments that the volcanic eruption of Mt. St. Helens and trees in forests had caused more pollution than cars and industries. Jimmy Carter, typecast in the 1976 race as the decent small-time loner who had ventured into a hostile Washington, had become, by 1980, the J. R. Ewing candidate. He was constantly portrayed as mean, petty, and manipulative. John Anderson was pictured as a twentieth century Don Quixote, battling all sorts of evils in hopeless struggles. His running mate, Pat Lucey, was cast in the role of Sancho Panza, an admiring but ineffectual sidekick to his master.

A few excerpts from television broadcasts during the 1972 primaries indicate how television produces these kinds of stereotyped images. Relevant passages are italicized. Here is a typical characterization of Humphrey as "the politician of the past."

The television report on Humphrey begins with these comments by the reporter: "While Senator McGovern flew off to New Mexico, Senator Humphrey stumped the state from San Francisco to San Diego in *the sort of wind-up that has become traditional in California campaigns.* And perhaps nothing illustrated the difference between the two campaigns more than that McGovern has done the unusual, the unexpected, while *Humphrey has followed the old paths and done the things that have brought him victory in the past.*" An applauding, mainly black crowd was then shown with Humphrey at the front of the room behind a podium. "His campaign has been hampered by lack of money and a shortage of workers. *The old coalition, labor and the blacks, has not jelled this time* and the California Poll this week showed him trailing McGovern with both groups. Even Humphrey's own poll, released yesterday, showed him trailing McGovern among blacks. Because of that, *Senator Humphrey has had to spend a great deal of time appealing to past loyalties."*

Then the camera zoomed in on Humphrey who said: *"I remember marching with Dr. Martin Luther King, Jr.,* on that day in August 1963, down Pennsylvania Avenue. I was down there marching. I was sitting there on the steps with him on the Lincoln Memorial, and I brought him on over to the White House." At this point, the reporter cut in: *"Senator Humphrey has been a national leader for a long time.* That may help him with some voters, but it could cost him votes among *other people who view him as the politician of the past."* [39]

Senator Muskie suffered in 1972—as did Walter Mondale in 1984—because in the early primaries the media pictured him as "the front-runner," who could be expected to win by wide margins. Candidates try to peg their goals low to avoid the risk of falling below predictions, but the press often preempts this strategy. If candidates fail to live up to expectations set by the press, they are automatically typed as "losers." The problem that the front-runner image created for Muskie quickly became apparent in the New Hampshire primary, the first primary in presidential election years and, as such, billed nationwide as the harbinger of success and failure. Proportionate to the number of delegates elected, it receives at least 10 times the coverage of later primaries. Muskie polled 38 percent of the New Hampshire vote, compared with 37 percent for McGovern. Although Muskie won the primary—unlike Mondale who lost it in 1984 by a substantial margin—the media called him a loser because his slim, one percentage point lead did not comport with the front-runner image.

Here is how one broadcaster handled the "defeat" of front-runner Muskie in New Hampshire. "Edmund Muskie's presidential campaign took off and flew like a paper airplane built by somebody who does not know how to build paper planes. It went straight up, did a strange unexpected loop, and came straight down again. And now Muskie is working desperately at the controls, trying to avoid a crash and trying to avoid an appearance of panic." While winner Muskie received the loser label, loser McGovern received the winner label. He was described as "leaving New Hampshire feeling, he said, like a winner. Numerically he had not won, but compared to what people had expected of him, compared to what they had been writing about him, and saying about him for two years, compared to all of that, he felt he had won." His new momentum meant that "the money comes in, volunteers start calling, the staff works with new zeal, the candidate is lifted. Momentum is fragile and very important. And George McGovern feels that he and his campaign as they head to Florida now have it."

In 1984, Senator Hart, the dark-horse winner of the New Hampshire primary, temporarily benefited from similar glowing media rhetoric at the beginning of the campaign. But the benefits derived from Mondale's long hold on the front-runner image enabled him to quickly regain momentum and reassume the front-runner title.

The potential impact of typecasting on television is vast because television reaches nearly every voter in national and state-wide campaigns. Typecasting is particularly influential in contests between candidates of the same party during primaries because voters cannot use party affiliation as a cue for voting. Candidates with a loser image lose momentum and may well be finished because funds dry up, as does the enthusiasm of actual and potential campaign workers.

During the general election, when party cues are available, typecasting is less consequential, even though earlier images persist from the primaries of previous campaigns. Once Jimmy Carter had been tagged as "fuzzy" in the 1976 campaign, for instance, there was, according to his press secretary Jody Powell, "no way on God's earth we could shake the fuzziness question . . . no matter what Carter did or said. He could have spent the whole campaign doing nothing but reading substantive speeches . . . and still have had the image in the national press." [40] The general feeling in such cases seems to be that leopards do not change their spots.

Substance of Coverage: Issues and Events

Issue and events coverage usually lags behind coverage of personal characteristics. This imbalance bothers social scientists, who contend that the electorate ought to judge the candidates on their issue positions. It also runs counter to the common impression that the print media put primary emphasis on issues, leaving it to television to show off personalities. Actually, electronic and print media display surprisingly similar patterns, although television lags behind print media in the range and depth of issue coverage.

The overriding consideration in choosing issues, as in other political coverage, is newsworthiness rather than intrinsic importance. This is why the changing record of happenings on the campaign trail, however trivial, receives extended coverage. Even when ample time is available to explore serious issues in depth, as happens when presidential nominating conventions are covered in full, the emphasis is on brief, rapidly paced, freshly breaking trivial events. In fact, the amount of coverage for particular issues often seems to be in inverse proportion to their significance. For instance, during the 1976 campaign the media extensively covered Ford's questionable statement that "there is no Soviet domination of Eastern Europe" and Carter's indelicate remark that ethnic purity might be desirable for neighborhoods, as well as his comments about lust and sex during an interview with *Playboy* magazine.

Three major features stand out in coverage of issues and events during the 1968, 1972, 1976, and 1980 presidential campaigns. Most significantly, the media devoted the bulk of their stories to campaign hoopla and the horse-race aspects of the contests. They slighted political, social, and economic problems facing the country and said little about the merits of the solutions proposed, unless these issues could be made exciting and visually dramatic. Information about issues was patchy because the candidates and their spokesmen addressed only issues that would help their campaigns and that would not alienate any portion of the huge and disparate electorate from which all were seeking support. Newspeople, in turn, focused selectively on controversial issues that lent themselves to appealing stories. They rarely attempted systematic coverage of all important issues. The issue positions of vice-presidential candidates remained virtually unexplored.

Table 6-5 shows the proportions of stories allotted to various types of issues and events during the final months of these four campaigns.[41] Stories about campaign incidents dominated, except in 1968 when election-related Vietnam War stories captured the most coverage. In 1972, 1976, and 1980, emphasis on foreign affaris campaign issues dropped sharply. The Iranian crisis, which might have boosted foreign affairs coverage in 1980, had the reverse effect. Candidates shied away from attacking the president while the crisis continued, fearing that the public might consider criticism to be unpatriotic. Next to campaign events, election issues concerning general domestic politics normally receive the heaviest coverage. They consist of reports about the candidates' views concerning ongoing activities of government at all levels. Such stories, which are available from regular beats, are generally tied to familiar names and widely salient events. Therefore they require little background information, and pictorial coverage is easily arranged. All of these considerations make it very tempting to report domestic politics stories.

Table 6-5 Newspaper Issue Coverage in the Last Month of the 1968, 1972, 1976, and 1980 Presidential Campaigns

	1968	*1972*	*1976*	*1980*
Campaign Events	14%	42%	51%	52%
Domestic Politics	21	24	19	29
Foreign Affairs	30	18	14	5
Economic Policy	13	10	11	7
Social Problems	22	7	5	6

NOTE: Percentages are based on the following numbers of issues: 1968: 3,538; 1972: 11,187; 1976: 11,027; 1980: 147. The 1980 data come only from the *New York Times.* Data for the earlier elections come from 20 newspapers. Because news distribution patterns are quite similar among all papers, the data for a single paper are representative.

SOURCE: Doris A. Graber, "Hoopla and Horse-Race in 1980 Campaign Coverage: A Closer Look," in *Mass Media and Elections: International Research Perspectives,* ed. Winfried Schulz and Klaus Schönbach (München: Verlag Olschläger, 1983), p. 286. Reprinted by permission.

Social problems, like poverty or the plight of the elderly, usually lack novelty and are complex to describe. They frequently involve highly controversial and emotionally charged policies about which candidates and media keep silent for fear of alienating large segments of the public. Social issues therefore receive scanty coverage in election stories, except when they erupt into violence, as happened in 1968 when racial tensions turned into racial riots.

Coverage of economic issues, like unemployment, inflation, and taxes, is also limited because these issues are hard to explain and dramatize and rarely produce exciting pictures. Skimpy coverage may seem puzzling because these are issues of personal concern to the average voter.[42] The explanation is that most people, although concerned, are unwilling to wrestle with a difficult subject that newspeople have not yet learned to simplify and dramatize. Rather than risk writing complex campaign stories that most of the audience probably would ignore, newspeople prefer to feature the horse-race glamour of campaign developments. Jimmy Carter analyzed it well when he commented in an interview in 1976:

> ... the traveling press have zero interest in any issue unless it's a matter of making a mistake. What they are looking for is a 47-second argument between me and another candidate or something like that. There's nobody in the back of this plane who would ask an issue question unless he thought he could trick me into some crazy statement.[43]

From the Republican side, David A. Keene, national political director of Bush for President, echoed the complaint in 1980:

> It doesn't matter how much or how long or how often a candidate talks about issues to small groups in Iowa, or answers issue-oriented questions, or talks in terms and substance of why he ought to be nominated, if the coverage is on the momentum and the horse race.[44]

Nevertheless, candidates continue to emphasize issues, as Tables 6-6 and 6-7 indicate; the dearth of issue information should not be blamed on them. The tables are based on a content analysis of the candidates' campaign rhetoric by Darrell M. West of the University of Pennsylvania.[45] Five of eleven major-party candidates devoted better than half of their rhetoric to issues. Reagan and Kennedy topped 70 percent. The rest of their campaign statements were devoted to campaign developments or other subjects. After the nominations, rhetoric by all three presidential candidates and one vice-presidential candidate exceeded 50 percent issue content.

Overall, some 25 issues surfaced constantly in the press and some 20 on television in recent presidential campaigns. Typically, only half of these received extended and intensive attention, so that media issue coverage is considerably narrower than party platforms, which cover well over 50 issues. The media omit many important policy questions likely to surface during the forthcoming presidential term. While candidates like to talk about broad policy issues like war and peace or the health of the economy, newspeople

Table 6-6   Issue Mention by Presidential Candidates During the 1980 Primaries (in Percentages)

	Candidates					
	John Anderson	Howard Baker	George Bush	John Connally	Philip Crane	Robert Dole
Issues	49%	44%	53%	67%	0%	0%
Campaign Events	29	26	25	17	0	68
Other	22	30	22	16	100	32
(N)	(186)	(137)	(315)	(107)	(2)	(44)
	Ronald Reagan	Jerry Brown	Rosalyn Carter	Walter Mondale	Edward Kennedy	
Issues	72	57	38	42	72	
Campaign Events	10	20	10	11	13	
Other	18	23	52	47	15	
(N)	(396)	(128)	(131)	(128)	(957)	

NOTE: Rosalyn Carter and Walter Mondale acted as presidential surrogates. Percentages are based on campaign statements reported in the *New York Times*.

SOURCE: Darrell M. West, "Rhetoric and Agenda-Setting in the 1980 Presidential Campaign" (Paper presented at the annual meeting of the Midwest Political Science Association, Milwaukee, Wisconsin, April 1982), p. 5. Reprinted by permission. This table also appeared in *Mass Media and Elections,* ed. Schulz and Schönbach, p. 289.

prefer to concentrate on clear-cut issues on which the candidates disagree sharply.[46] Comparisons of candidates' speeches with television newscasts show that two-thirds of the issues mentioned by candidates are broad, designed to attract wide support from an anxious electorate. By contrast, only one-quarter of the issues featured on television are broad. The rest deal with controversial matters like abortion, or busing, or military aid for a specific country.[47]

In successive elections many issues reappear in the media, such as effectiveness of the incumbent administration, defense policies, race and ethnic relations, the meaning of public opinion polls, and campaign strategies. Like presidential qualifications, issues discussed in connection with individual candidates vary, however. For instance, in the 1972 presidential campaign newspapers quoted President Nixon most fully on foreign affairs and economic policy. By contrast, his opponent was quoted most on domestic policies. When newspeople discussed the campaign without quoting the candidates, none of these policy areas were emphasized. Instead, reporters chiefly stressed campaign hoopla. Voters received little aid from the media in appraising and comparing the candidates on the issues. Therefore they were more likely to rest their voting decisions on general personality characteristics, which were more amply presented and far easier to evaluate.

Compared with the print media, television news displays more uniform

Table 6-7 Issue Mention by Presidential and Vice-Presidential Candidates During the 1980 General Election (in Percentages)

	Candidates					
	Ronald Reagan	George Bush	Jimmy Carter	Walter Mondale	John Anderson	Patrick Lucey
Issues	71%	44%	59%	65%	61%	37%
Campaign Events	5	27	14	16	15	53
Other	24	29	27	19	24	10
(N)	(549)	(216)	(574)	(175)	(392)	(19)

SOURCE: West, "Rhetoric and Agenda-Setting," p. 8. Reprinted by permission. This table also appeared in *Mass Media and Elections,* ed. Schulz and Schönbach, p. 290.

patterns of issue coverage for all the candidates and involves a more limited range of issues. The drama of campaigning receives even heavier emphasis than in the print media. Television stories are briefer, touch on fewer aspects of each issue, and contribute to the stereotypic images developed for particular candidates.

Stripping information to its bare bones and covering what is left as a theatrical event apparently appeals to the public. Television news and commercials have become the primary sources of presidential election information for the majority of people, ranking well ahead of newspapers. Television images of the candidates are more appealing because they are far simpler and more positive, with fewer conflicting appraisals than their newspaper counterparts. Readers who find newspaper coverage confusing and depressing can turn to television for a simpler and more encouraging image of the unfolding electoral scene.

Substance of Coverage: Medialities

Normal content-analysis procedures weigh stories evenly, but in actuality all stories are not equal. Therefore, media coverage should be assessed in terms of its political significance in addition to assessments in purely quantitative terms. Story substance must be examined as well as the political context in which the story appeared and the play it received from various news channels throughout the country. There are times when the public and politicians are particularly vulnerable to campaign stories, and a few stories carry extraordinary weight. Rapid diffusion of the stories throughout the major media enhances their impact. Michael Robinson calls such featured events "medialities"—"events, developments, or situations to which the media have given importance by emphasizing, expanding, or featuring them in such a way that their real significance has been modified, distorted, or obscured." [48]

During the 1980 presidential campaign, medialities included:

● a television interview on November 4, 1979, in which Sen. Edward Kennedy hemmed and hawed painfully and could not explain why he wanted to be president;

● the networks' in-depth review of the year-long hostage ordeal on the last day of the 1980 campaign. The review showed Carter unable to stop a small country from deliberately mistreating American citizens;

● media focus in the spring of 1980 on the spectacular rise of interest rates and the deepening economic recession;

● media intrusion into the vice-presidential choice by first raising and then scuttling the chances for a Reagan-Ford ticket.[49]

It stands to reason that such key stories should be singled out in content-analysis interpretations. They are likely to have a far more profound impact on the campaign than thousands of routine stories.

Adequacy of Coverage

We will conclude our discussion of media content by considering the adequacy of current election coverage. How helpful are the media for making voting decisions in the manner preferred by democratic theorists? On the basis of close examination of the 1983 Chicago mayoral election, the 1968, 1972, 1976, and 1980 presidential elections, and preliminary studies of the 1984 campaign, one would have to conclude that appraisal of candidates and issues is not made easy for voters. In presidential contests, information is ample on personal qualifications of the major, mainstream candidates and on day-to-day campaign events. It is sketchy and often confusing on most professional qualifications, on substantive issues, and on the policy options involved in these issues. Most primary contenders, candidates of minor parties, and the vice-presidential candidates are largely ignored. The prevalence of negative information makes it seem that all of the candidates are mediocre, or even poor, choices. This negative cast appears to be a major factor in many voters' decisions to stay home on election day. In the mayoral election, issue coverage was more complete and less confusing primarily because many issues at that level are less complex and closer to the voters' personal experiences.

In presidential contests, the deficiencies of media coverage are most noticeable during the primary period when a large slate of same-party candidates is running in each primary. The media solve the dilemma of covering a multitude of candidacies by giving uniformly skimpy treatment to all candidates except for those designated as front-runners. For instance, during the spring and summer primaries in 1976, 74 percent of all mentions of presidential contenders referred to the campaigns of Republicans Gerald Ford and Ronald Reagan and Democrat Jimmy Carter. The remainder were divided among 10 less-favored candidates. In 1980, the combined average for

Carter, Reagan, and Kennedy was 71 percent. If Anderson is added, that figure mounts to 81 percent. The remaining 19 percent of the coverage was shared by six second-tier contenders—Bush, Baker, Brown, Connally, Crane, and Dole. Figure 6-1, based on coverage of the candidates by CBS news, demonstrates the pattern graphically. The figure includes former president Ford, who was not a candidate in 1980, and several contenders whose coverage was almost nonexistent.

Similar trends have been demonstrated for congressional elections, in which challengers generally receive only a fraction of the coverage bestowed on incumbents. Even that pittance lags in substantive quality. Table 6-8 compares the major content themes raised in 14 tight congressional races in which an incumbent was running.

Remarks about personal qualifications generally are so scant in presidential primary coverage compared with general election coverage that the balance between discussion of qualifications and issues and campaign events is reversed. As Thomas Patterson has noted, "Issue material is but a rivulet in the news flow during the primaries, and what is there is almost completely diluted by information about the race." [50] In 1976, 61 percent of all primary commentary referred to issues and events and only 39 percent to presidential qualities, despite the need to acquaint voters with a host of unfamiliar personalities. Moreover, horse-race and hoopla news predominated, taking up 65 percent of issue coverage, at the expense of more substantive matters. Only 20 percent of the coverage was devoted to domestic and foreign affairs and only 15 percent to economic and social problems. The 1980 figures were comparable: 63 percent for campaign events, 27 percent for domestic and foreign affairs, and 10 percent for social and economic problems.

While the quality of primary coverage may be questionable, the quantity is substantial. A check of the *New York Times* in 1980 showed that 34 percent of all campaign stories appeared from January to March. The Iowa caucuses and the New Hampshire primary were especially well covered. Another 30 percent of all stories covered the April-May-June period. The reduction in coverage is more significant than it seems because 25 primaries, many of them

Table 6-8   Median Number of Local Newspaper Paragraphs Mentioning Selected Themes in 14 Tight Congressional Races, September 27-November 7, 1978

Themes	Incumbent News	Challenger News
Campaign organization	22	27
Personal characteristics	10	13
Political attributes	49	4
Issues/ideology/group ties	29	12

SOURCE: Peter Clarke and Susan H. Evans, *Covering Campaigns: Journalism in Congressional Elections* (Stanford, Calif.: Stanford University Press, 1983) p. 61. Reprinted by permission.

Figure 6-1 Total News Seconds Given to All Candidates Receiving Time on CBS Evening News, January 1 - November 3, 1980 (campaign stories only)

Seconds (in thousands)

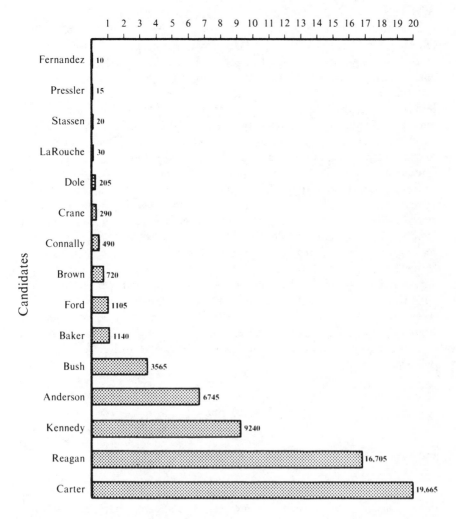

SOURCE: Michael Jay Robinson, "A Statesman Is a Dead Politician: Candidate Images on Network News," in *What's News: The Media in American Society*, ed. Elie Abel (San Francisco: Institute for Contemporary Studies, 1981), p. 176. Reprinted by permission.

involving large states, occurred in this period. They thus received substantially less coverage than the 12 primaries that fell into the initial primary period.

The July-August time span, following the primary season, includes the nominating conventions. This is an important period because approximately 25 percent of the voters usually make up their minds in the wake of the conventions. In 1980, 31 percent of the campaign coverage fell within those two months. Most surprising was the dearth of coverage of the final campaign, following the Labor Day holiday in September. Although the last two months of the campaign encompassed two presidential debates in 1980, this period garnered only 5 percent of the campaign coverage. What might have been a last-minute media blitz to rehearse the public for the political climax fizzled into a tired media anticlimax. Issue content did rise by 14 percentage points during the final campaign weeks, and election stories received slightly greater prominence in display as the campaign neared its end. This increased the likelihood that issue information would come to the voters' attention as the day of decision approached.

Although it would be unfair to blame low voter turnout in presidential primary elections entirely on inadequate election news, interviews with voters show that poor coverage does play a significant part. Voters find election stories interesting, but they do not feel that they adequately prepare them to make choices. Media images depict campaigns as tournaments where voters sit on the sidelines and watch the bouts, waiting to see who is eliminated and who remains. Winning and losing are presented as all-important, rather than what winning and losing mean in terms of the political direction of the country in general or the observer's personal situation in particular. Taking its cues from the media, the audience accepts election news as just another story rather than as an important tale about real life with very direct impact on its own welfare.

Media Effects

Learning About Candidates and Issues

What do people learn from campaign coverage? It varies, of course, depending on factors such as interest in the campaign, prior political knowledge, a felt need for information, and political sophistication. But certain general trends emerge from national surveys, such as those conducted biannually by the Survey Research Center at the University of Michigan, and from intensive interviews of smaller panels of voters, such as those conducted by the author of this book.

The foremost impression from interviews with voters is that they learn very little specific information in a presidential campaign. National surveys show that 59 percent of the electorate scores below the mean in election knowledge, and only 16 percent reach genuinely high scores.[51] These figures are based on the numbers of responses people are able to give when asked open-ended questions about parties and candidates. During the 1980 presidential primaries, when learning increments between February and June were measured, an average of only 17 percent of the respondents in the National Election Survey increased their knowledge. An average of 10 percent actually lost ground over the course of the primaries.[52]

The fact that most citizens are interested in the campaign thus does not mean that they learn a great deal about it beyond who is winning and losing, how the candidates look, and how they go about fighting political battles. Interest in the campaign competes with interest in other events and issues. In 1976, for instance, a panel of voters who kept diaries on the important news stories that came to their attention throughout that election year devoted only 11 percent of their entries to election stories. When asked to name "major current events or issues," 38 percent of the panelists never named the primary election in four interviews conducted during the primary season.[53]

A comparison of election information supplied by the media with information mentioned by survey respondents about candidates and issues reveals roughly similar patterns. As Table 6-9 shows, several thousand respondents in a nationwide survey were asked for good and bad points about each candidate that might affect their voting choices. In addition to the qualifications discussed by the media and general comments about liking or disliking candidates, respondents also mentioned party allegiance and personal and economic interests as reasons for casting their votes. The similarity between media content and the public's views is greatest for people who use the media most and who rely most heavily on newspapers. However, there are differences in emphases and specificity between media and public images. The public mentions fewer issues and qualities than the media and is much hazier about image content. For instance, when asked about the reasons for voting for a candidate, a respondent may say, "I like him," but may be unable to name any specific reasons. A query about the issues that figured in the voter's appraisal of the candidates is likely to elicit a broad reference to foreign or domestic policy in general rather than mention of specific issues. Facts and figures are rarely recalled, and a good deal of misinformation surfaces when specifics are mentioned. Complex policy positions are remembered far less often than positions involving simple yes or no choices.

Overall, three out of four answers people give when asked what they have learned about candidates and issues or why they would vote or refrain from voting for a certain candidate concern personality traits. People are interested in the human qualities of their elected leaders, particularly their trustworthiness, principled character, strength, and compassion. The media provide ample data on these traits. In many instances people apparently ignore much available media information. They make their choice first, commonly on the

Table 6-9   Presidential Qualities Mentioned by the Public and by Newspapers in 1976 (in Percentages)

	Likes		Dislikes		Newspapers 1976
	Carter	Ford	Carter	Ford	
Personal Comments					
Personality Traits	49	38	39	18	36
Presidential Image	15	37	21	24	25
Style	5	4	16	10	16
Total:	69	79	76	52	77
Professional Capacities					
Capacities	21	17	16	43	7
Relations with Public	1	—	—	—	3
Philosophy	9	4	8	5	12
Total:	31	21	24	48	22

N = 2,182 for Carter likes, 2,337 for Ford likes; 2,125 for Carter dislikes; 1,747 for Ford dislikes. N = 17,423 mentions of qualities for 1976 newspapers.

NOTE: The percentages are based on responses to the question, "Now I'd like to ask you about the good and bad points of the two major candidates for president. Is there anything in particular about (name of candidate) that might make you want to vote for him? Is there anything about (name of candidate) that might make you want to vote against him? What is that? Anything else?"

SOURCE: Survey data from 1976 Election Survey, Center for Political Studies, Survey Research Center, University of Michigan; newspaper data from author's research.

basis of quick judgments about personality or vague feelings of party allegiance, and then later acquire information to justify that choice.

In a typical election, such as the 1976 presidential race, fully 43 percent of the people in a nationwide poll could comment on only one candidate's strengths and weaknesses. Such limited information prevented them from comparing candidates and choosing accordingly. Less than 20 percent could state three or more likes or dislikes about either candidate. Appraisals commonly were limited to one or two statements. Positive and negative comments about candidates were evenly balanced with a slight tilt toward the positive. This, of course, differs from the more negative tone found in campaign news. Like newspeople, respondents who bothered to learn about several candidates often evaluated them along different dimensions. This reduced the chances for comparisons. During the 1976 primaries, for instance, Ford was appraised more on his issue stands and personality traits and Carter more on his style and image characteristics. Ronald Reagan was judged largely on his political philosophy.

The issues people mentioned as important in the campaign represented a much abbreviated and imprecise version of media issue coverage. As Table 6-10 indicates, people put substantially greater stress on economic and social issues than did the media. This is not surprising; people have personal experiences with these issues that are more salient to them than any media re-ports. The public does not need media coverage to know that inflation, unemployment, poverty, crime, race relations, and environmental pollution are serious problems requiring attention from presidents. Nor is it surprising that people put much less emphasis on campaign hoopla, covered so plentifully by the media. Although they find these fleeting events entertaining, people make little effort to remember them long.

Knowledge Base for Voting

Many social scientists worry about the public's limited preparation for voting and fault the media for doing a poor job, particularly in covering issues. But the worry and blame are largely misplaced. Although election news definitely stresses personality traits over issues, it does supply a fair amount of issue coverage. Voters who want to base their decisions on the candidates' stands on specific issues can usually find that information. When voters are poorly informed about issues, the chief reason is that elections are not important enough for them to take the time and make the effort to learn.

Given the realities of politics, the average voter's choice to concentrate heavily on personal qualities of the candidates can be defended as sound and rational. Forming opinions about complex issues like arms limitation or monetary policies is time-consuming and difficult, particularly when experts differ about the merits of conflicting policy recommendations. People there-fore ignore most issues, paying attention to only a few major ones, like American military involvement in the Middle East and Central America or social security payments and unemployment. Interest in issues is also dimin-

Table 6-10 Comparison of Percentage of Mention of Issues and Events by Newspapers and Television and Rated and Unrated Survey Responses, 1976

	Papers	*Television*	*Rated Responses*	*Unrated Responses*
Campaign events	51%	63%	0%	0%
Domestic politics	19	14	5	5
Foreign affairs	14	10	5	7
Economic policy	11	9	75	63
Social problems	5	4	14	23

Rated responses specify the most important national problem. Unrated responses are based on multiple answers to a question asking for important national problems. N = 11,027 for newspapers, 1,355 for television, 2,263 for rated responses and 5,575 for unrated responses.

SOURCE: Survey data come from the 1976 Election Survey, Center for Political Studies, Survey Research Center, University of Michigan; media data from author's research.

ished because the issue stands discussed during the campaign generally refer to the past. Voters do not know what kinds of issues and issue configurations will actually arise during a president's term. Moreover, once elected, candidates may be unable to keep their campaign promises because of an obstreperous Congress, lack of funding, or other unforeseen problems.

The kind of thing that most people *can* judge, often quite expertly, is a candidate's general ability and integrity. Through personal experience they learn to pick a doctor, clergyman, or repairman without understanding medicine, religion, or machines. They know how to judge people in terms of trustworthiness and general competence. The information that media provide most plentifully is geared toward such evaluations of personal character.

Although the media furnish most people with more information than they are willing or able to use, the media fall short of supplying the needs of political elites. Much of the mass public still depends on opinion leaders to appraise and select candidates and to assess the merits of prospective public policies. These leaders need more information about issues and candidates than most media currently offer. Opinion leaders and the mass public alike would benefit from greater clarity of presentation in the daily press, more point-by-point comparisons of candidates and policies, and more ample evaluations of the political significance of differences found among candidates and their programs.

The finding that little specific knowledge is "learned" should not blind us to the fact that conclusions drawn from facts may be retained. Voting choices often match approval of a candidate's policy positions, even when voters do not remember the candidate's stands or the specifics of the policy.[54] They may convert media facts into politically significant feelings and attitudes, which they will remember long after the facts have been forgotten. Such long-range, cumulative general impressions are likely to have more profound impact than short-term memory. For instance, a general impression, received after a series of elections, that one's party is fielding candidates of poor caliber may ultimately destroy party allegiance. The negative appraisals that candidates receive from each other and from the media may leave a residue of disappointment with politics that drives people away from the polls.

Voting Behavior

Does campaigning via the media change votes? The answer to this perennial question—so dear to the hearts of campaign managers, public relations experts, and social scientists—hinges on the interaction between audiences and messages. Crucial variables include the voter's receptivity to a message urging change, the potency of the message, the appropriateness of its form, and the setting in which it occurs. A vote change is most likely when voters pay fairly close attention to the media and are ambivalent in their attitudes toward the candidates. Messages are most potent if they concern a major and unpredicted event, such as a successful or disastrous foreign policy venture or corruption in high places, and if individuals find themselves in social settings where a change of attitudes will not constitute deviant behavior. This combination of circumstances is fairly uncommon, which explains why changes of voting intentions are comparatively rare. The talk about "electronic ballot box stuffing" is therefore unrealistic.

Although rare, even small numbers of media-induced vote changes may be important. Many elections at all levels are decided by very small percentages of votes, often less than 1 percent. The media may also have a crucial impact on election outcomes whenever they are able to stimulate or depress voter turnout. This is a more likely consequence of media publicity than changes in voting choices.

A recent problem involving turnout and last-minute vote switches concerns the impact of early winner and loser projections in presidential elections. In 1980, for instance, NBC projected Reagan as the winner at 8:15 P.M. Eastern time, several hours before the polls closed on the West Coast. Such declarations appear to reduce the late turnout on the West Coast, but the precise impact on elections is not known. Current evidence indicates that the effects are rarely substantial.[55] Most reform proposals that attempt to stop immediate dissemination of projections of winners and losers run afoul of First Amendment free speech guarantees.

The most important influence of the media on the voter does not lie in changing votes, once predispositions have been formed, but in shaping and reinforcing predispositions and influencing the initial selection of candidates. When newspeople sketched out the Jimmy Carter image and dubbed him a potential winner during the 1976 primaries, ignoring most of his rivals, they made "Jimmy-Who?" into a viable candidate. Millions of voters would never have cast their ballot for the obscure Georgia politician had not the media thrust him into the limelight as a likely winner.

By focusing the voters' attention on selected individuals, their characteristics, and issue stands, the media also determine to a large extent what the crucial issues will be on which the competence of candidates will be judged. Very early in the campaign, often long before formal campaigning starts, media interpretations of the significance of issues can shape the perceptual environment in which the election takes place.[56]

President Carter's chances for reelection in 1980 hinged in no small manner on the images that the media created about his presidency in the previous four years. In the same way, Watergate revelations created public moods that doomed many Republicans in the 1974 elections. Newspeople shape election outcomes by molding the images of political reality that lead to voting decisions rather than by suggesting voting choices to an electorate that prefers to make up its own mind. They "play less of an independent part in creating issues, sketching imagery, and coloring perceptions of the candidates than in getting attention for their candidacies. Newsmen do not write the score or play an instrument; they amplify the sounds of the music makers." [57] Although voters pay most concentrated attention to media coverage just before elections, the crucial attitudes that determine voting choices may already be so firm that the final vote is a foregone conclusion.

Summary

We have examined the general consequences of the powerful and growing role played by the media, especially television, in recent campaigns. Three results are striking: the shrinking contributions of political parties and other political actors, the domination of the campaign strategies and schedules by media demands, and the emergence of the media as kingmakers in political recruiting and sustaining of candidates, particularly at the presidential level.

We also scrutinized newspapers and television election coverage throughout the campaign. General coverage patterns and the problem of political and structural bias, the substance and slant of coverage, and the manner of presentation were considered. Heaviest emphasis is on personal rather than professional qualities of the candidates and on campaign events rather than substantive issues. Stories are chosen for their newsworthiness—not their educational value.

Lastly, we examined the effects of media output on the people who are exposed to it. Although the public complains about the skimpiness and shallowness of election coverage, it absorbs only a small portion of available news. Lack of political understanding or irrational voting does not necessarily result, however. The bits of information that people absorb permit informed choices based on appraisal of a chosen candidate's character. We also pointed out that minute changes brought about by the media in final voting decisions or voter turnout may alter the outcome of a close election and the course of political life.

Claims that the media have only a very limited influence on elections rest on the election studies undertaken in the 1940s and 1950s, which have become obsolete. The early research preceded the age of television dominance and was concerned primarily with changes in the final voting decision. More recent research has cast the net much wider to include media effects on all phases of the election campaign, from the recruitment and nomination stages to the strategies that produce the final outcome. In addition to media impact on the final voting choice, social scientists have looked at political learning during campaigns and the information base that supports the voting decision. Television, in particular, has changed the election game rules, especially at the presidential level. Candidates and media are inextricably intertwined. Those who aspire to elective office must play the "new politics," which is "media politics."

Notes

1. A good review of the literature on presidential elections is presented in Herbert Asher, *Presidential Elections and American Politics* (Homewood, Ill.: Dorsey Press, 1980). For reports on congressional campaigns, see John Carey, "How Media Shape Campaigns," *Journal of Communication* 26 (Spring 1976): 50-57; Peter Clarke and Susan H. Evans, *Covering Campaigns: Journalism in Congressional Elections* (Stanford, Calif.: Stanford University Press, 1983); and Edie N. Goldenberg and Michael W. Traugott, *Campaigning for Congress* (Washington, D.C.: CQ Press, 1984). Gubernatorial contests are covered in John W. Windhauser, "Reporting of Campaign Issues in Ohio Municipal Election Races," *Journalism Quarterly* 54 (Summer 1977): 332-340; Leonard Tipton, Roger D. Haney, and John R. Baseheart, "Media Agenda-Setting in City and State Election Campaigns," *Journalism Quarterly* 52 (Spring 1975): 15-22; Jules Becker and Douglas A. Fuchs, "How the Major California Dailies Covered Reagan vs. Brown," *Journalism Quarterly* 44 (Winter 1967): 645-653; and Jan Pons Vermeer, *"For Immediate Release": Candidate Press Releases in American Political Campaigns* (Westport, Conn.: Greenwood Press, 1982).
2. Comparative information is presented in John H. Kessel, *Presidential Campaign Politics: Coalition Strategies and Citizen Response*, 2d ed. (Homewood, Ill.: Dorsey Press, 1984) and Richard L. Rubin, *Press, Party and Presidency* (New York: Norton, 1981).
3. For examples, see Winfried Schultz and Klaus Schönbach, eds., *Mass Media and Elections: International Research Perspectives* (München: Olschläger, 1983).
4. See Richard Joslyn, *Mass Media and Elections* (Reading, Mass.: Addison-Wesley, 1984), chap. 7. Joslyn is one of the few recent authors who devotes careful attention to campaign advertisements.
5. Thomas Patterson and Robert McClure, *The Unseeing Eye* (New York: G. P. Putnam's Sons, 1976), pp. 102-108. See also C. Richard Hofstetter and Cliff Zukin, "TV Network News and Advertising in the Nixon and McGovern Campaigns," *Journalism Quarterly* 56 (Spring 1979): 106-115 and Richard Joslyn, "The Content of Political Spot Ads," *Journalism Quarterly* 57 (Spring 1980): 92-98.
6. Patterson and McClure, *The Unseeing Eye*, p. 104.
7. Michael J. Robinson, "The Media in 1980: Was the Message the Message?" in *The American Elections of 1980*, ed. Austin Ranney (Washington, D.C.: American Enterprise Institute for Public Policy Research, 1981), pp. 179-180.
8. For contrary views, see Joe McGinniss, *The Selling of the President, 1968* (New York: Trident Press, 1969), p. 31.
9. James D. Nowlan, "Broadcasting Advertising and Party Endorsements in a Statewide Primary," *Journal of Broadcasting* 28 (Summer 1984).
10. Robinson, "The Media in 1980," p. 186.
11. Joslyn, *Mass Media*, chap. 7, and Michael J. Robinson, "Three Faces of Congressional Media," in *The New Congress*, ed. Thomas E. Mann and Norman J. Ornstein (Washington, D.C.: American Enterprise Institute for Public Policy Research, 1981).

12. Walter DeVries and V. Lance Tarrance, *The Ticket Splitters* (Grand Rapids, Mich.: Eerdmans, 1972). Kessel, *Presidential Campaign Politics*, pp. 251-253, defines "issues" very broadly. This leads him to the conclusion that issues are most important in voting.
13. F. Christopher Arterton, "Campaign Organizations Confront the Media—Political Environment," in *Race for the Presidency: The Media and the Nominating Process*, ed. James David Barber (Englewood Cliffs, N.J.: Prentice Hall, 1978), p. 21.
14. Ibid., p. 22. See also Michael J. Robinson, "TV's Newest Program: The 'Presidential Nominations Game,'" *Public Opinion* 1 (May-June 1978): 41-46.
15. Thomas R. Marshall, "The News Verdict and Public Opinion During the Primaries," in *Television Coverage of the 1980 Presidential Campaign*, ed. William C. Adams (Norwood, N.J.: Ablex, 1983), p. 58.
16. Richard Stout, "The Pre-Pre-Campaign-Campaign," *Public Opinion* 5 (December/January 1983): 17-20, 60.
17. Rubin, *Press, Party*, pp. 129, 138.
18. Michael J. Robinson, "A Statesman Is A Dead Politician: Candidate Images on Network News," in *What's News: The Media in American Society*, ed. Elie Abel (San Francisco: Institute for Contemporary Studies, 1981).
19. Walter Bunge, Robert Hudson, and Chung Woo Suh, "Johnson's Information Strategy for Vietnam: An Evaluation," *Journalism Quarterly* 45 (Autumn 1968): 419-425.
20. C. Anthony Broh, "Presidential Preference Polls and Network News," in *Television Coverage*, ed. Adams, p. 32.
21. Ibid., p. 21.
22. Edwin Diamond, *Sign-Off: The Last Days of Television* (Boston: MIT Press, 1982), p. 175.
23. Herbert E. Alexander, *Financing the 1976 Election* (Washington, D.C.: CQ Press, 1979), pp. 166, 372, 373, 411.
24. Diamond, *Sign-Off*, p. 175.
25. Robinson, "The Media in 1980," pp. 186-190.
26. Arterton, "Campaign Organizations Confront the Media," pp. 16-17, quoting an aide to Morris Udall.
27. Michael J. Robinson and Margaret Sheehan, "Traditional Ink vs. Modern Video Versions of Campaign '80," in *Television Coverage*, ed. Adams, p. 18.
28. J. D. Lorenz, "An Insider's View of Jerry Brown," *Chicago Tribune*, February 12, 1978.
29. The 1980 analysis was limited to the *New York Times* because earlier analyses had shown great similarity in coverage patterns among news sources throughout the country. In 1968, 1972, and 1976, the newspaper sample consisted of 20 newspapers from communities of different size and political orientation from all parts of the country. The sample is broadly representative of the American press, although slightly skewed toward papers that media critics consider above average in performance. The papers were the *New York Times, Philadelphia Inquirer, Boston Globe, Bangor Daily News, Chicago Tribune, Cleveland Plain Dealer, Detroit Free Press, Topeka Daily Capital, Houston Chronicle, Miami Herald, Raleigh News & Observer, Atlanta Constitution, Los Angeles Times, Seattle Daily Times, Denver Post, Salt Lake City Tribune, Chicago Daily Defender, National Observer, Wall Street Journal,* and *Washington Post*. Papers were selected with the assistance of a panel of editors to be representative of the American press. Criteria for sample selection included representation of all sections of the United States, diversity of community size, representation of high

and low population density regions, diversity of endorsement and audience political affiliation, reflection of various types of newspaper competition ranging from near-monopoly status to highly competitive markets, and inclusion of papers designed for special interest audiences. The television sample came from the early evening national news presented by ABC, CBS, and NBC, as well as local Chicago area CBS and NBC newscasts. 1980 television data came from CBS and are based on the work of Michael J. Robinson and Margaret A. Sheehan, *Over the Wire and on TV: CBS and UPI in Campaign '80* (New York: Russell Sage Foundation, 1983). Tapes and abstracts for coding broadcasts for 1968, 1972, and 1976 were made available by the Vanderbilt Television News Archive, described in Fay C. Schreibman, "Television News Archives: A Guide to Major Collections," in *Television Network News: Issues in Content Research,* ed. William Adams and Fay C. Schreibman (Washington, D.C.: George Washington University, 1978), pp. 89-110.

30. Doris A. Graber, "Media Coverage and Voter Learning During the Presidential Primary Season," *Georgia Journal of Political Science* 7 (Spring 1979): 19-48.

31. See Carey, "How Media Shape Campaigns"; Windhauser, "Reporting of Campaign Issues"; and Clarke and Evans, *Covering Campaigns.*

32. Timothy Crouse, *The Boys on the Bus* (New York: Ballantine, 1976).

33. C. Richard Hofstetter, *Bias in the News: Network Television Coverage of the 1972 Election Campaign* (Columbus: Ohio State University Press, 1976), pp. 39-41.

34. Wenmouth Williams, Jr., and William D. Semlak, "Structural Effects of TV Coverage on Political Agendas," *Journal of Communication* 28 (Autumn 1978): 114-119 and Hofstetter, *Bias in the News,* pp. 32-36.

35. Michael Hooper, "Party and Newspaper Endorsements as Predictors of Voter Choice," *Journalism Quarterly* 46 (Summer 1969): 302-305 and G. Cleveland Wilhoit and Taik Sup Auh, "Newspaper Endorsements and Coverage of Public Opinion Polls in 1970," *Journalism Quarterly* 51 (Winter 1974): 654-658.

36. The eight most frequently mentioned qualities are trustworthy, principled, compassionate, inspirational, forthright, strong, administratively competent, and capable in foreign affairs.

37. Anthony King, "How Not to Select Presidential Candidates: A View from Europe," in *The American Elections,* ed. Ranney, 305.

38. Typecasts have been extracted from Robinson, "A Statesman is a Dead Politician," pp. 178-182.

39. All quotations of network news coverage of Democratic presidential candidates are taken from Marc F. Plattner, "Introduction," and James R. Ferguson, "Network Coverage of the Major Democratic Candidates," pp. 2-12, 14-89, in Alternative Educational Foundation, *Report on Network News' Treatment of the 1972 Democratic Presidential Candidates* (Bloomington, Ind.: 1972). Reprinted by permission.

40. F. Christopher Arterton, "The Media Politics of Presidential Campaigns," in *Race for the Presidency,* ed. Barber, p. 36.

41. The data are based on coding up to three issues per story. An experiment involving coding of all 1980 issues mentioned in every story showed campaign events at 37 percent, domestic policy at 19 percent, foreign affairs at 12 percent, economic policy at 20 percent, and social problems at 13 percent. This indicates that many stories stressing hoopla and horse-race aspects do have subordinate coverage of more substantive issues. The usual, more limited coding procedures do not capture this. However, it is questionable whether most readers will notice these less obvious story elements.

42. Seymour Martin Lipset and William Schneider, *The Confidence Gap: Business, Labor, and Government in the Public Mind* (New York: The Free Press, 1983), chap. 5.
43. Robert C. Sahr, "Energy as a Non-Issue in 1980 Coverage," in *Television Coverage,* ed. Adams, p. 135.
44. Jonathan Moore, ed., *The Campaign for President: 1980 in Retrospect* (Cambridge, Mass.: Ballinger, 1981), p. 96.
45. Darrell M. West, "Rhetoric and Agenda-Setting in the 1980 Presidential Campaign" (Paper presented at the annual meeting of the Midwest Political Science Association, Milwaukee, Wisconsin, April 1982), pp. 5-8.
46. Benjamin I. Page, *Choices and Echoes in Presidential Elections: Rational Man and Electoral Democracy* (Chicago: University of Chicago Press, 1978), chap. 6.
47. Thomas E. Patterson, "Television and Election Strategy," in *The Communications Revolution in Politics,* ed. Gerald Benjamin (New York: The Academy of Political Science, 1982), p. 28.
48. Robinson, "The Media in 1980," p. 191.
49. Ibid., pp. 196-202.
50. Thomas Patterson, *The Mass Media Election: How Americans Choose Their President* (New York: Praeger, 1980), p. 168.
51. Kessel, *Presidential Campaign Politics,* p. 232.
52. Scott Keeter and Cliff Zukin, *Uninformed Choice: The Failure of the New Presidential Nominating System* (New York: Praeger, 1983), p. 80. The figures are based on Reagan, Kennedy, Bush, Brown, Connally, Baker, and Dole data.
53. Doris A. Graber, *Processing the News: How People Tame the Information Tide* (New York: Longman, 1984), p. 119.
54. Richard W. Boyd, "Popular Control of Public Policy: A Normal Vote Analysis of the 1968 Election," *American Political Science Review* 66 (June 1972): 429-449; Philip E. Converse, "The Concept of Normal Vote," chap. 2, in *Elections and the Political Order,* ed. Angus Campbell et al. (New York: John Wiley, 1966); and Graber, *Processing the News,* pp. 71-74.
55. Paul Wilson, "Election Night 1980 and the Controversy Over Early Projections," in *Television Coverage,* ed. Adams, pp. 152-153; Percy H. Tannenbaum and Leslie J. Kostrich, *Turned-On TV/Turned-Off Voters: Policy Options for Election Projections* (Beverly Hills, Calif.: Sage, 1983).
56. Arthur T. Hadley, *The Invisible Primary* (Englewood Cliffs, N.J.: Prentice-Hall, 1976).
57. Leon V. Sigal, "Newsmen and Campaigners: Organization Men Make the News," *Political Science Quarterly* 93 (Fall 1978): 465-470.

Readings

Adams, William C., ed. *Television Coverage of the 1980 Presidential Campaign.* Norwood, N.J.: Ablex, 1983.

Arterton, F. Christopher. *Media Politics: The News Strategies of Presidential Campaigns.* Lexington, Mass.: D. C. Heath, 1984.

Clarke, Peter, and Susan H. Evans. *Covering Campaigns: Journalism in Congressional Elections.* Stanford, Calif.: Stanford University Press, 1983.

Joslyn, Richard. *Mass Media and Elections.* Reading, Mass.: Addison-Wesley, 1984.

Linsky, Martin, ed. *Television and the Presidential Elections: Self-Interest and the Public Interest.* Lexington, Mass.: D. C. Heath, 1983.

Robinson, Michael J., and Margaret A. Sheehan. *Over the Wire and on TV: CBS and UPI in Campaign '80.* New York: Russell Sage Foundation, 1983.

Weaver, David H., Doris A. Graber, Maxwell E. McCombs, and Chaim H. Eyal. *Media Agenda-Setting in a Presidential Election: Issues, Images, and Interest.* New York: Praeger, 1981.

The Struggle for Control: News from the White House, Congress, and the Courts

Walter Cronkite once remarked, "Politics and media are inseparable. It is only the politicians and the media that are incompatible." [1] There is a love-hate relationship between government officials and the media. To perform their functions adequately, each needs the other. But they have conflicting goals and missions and operate under different institutional constraints. To retain public support and maintain its power, the government wants to influence what information is passed on to the public and to other officials. It wants to be able to define situations and project images in its own way to further its social and political objectives.

The Adversary Relationship

Newspeople often see the world from a different perspective than politicians and want to describe the situation accordingly. As critics of government, they take special pains to expose wrongdoing. They also want to present exciting stories that will attract a large audience. This often means prying into matters that government officials would like to hide because they involve conflict, controversy, corruption, or simple wheeling and dealing. Government wants its portrait taken in its Sunday best, from the most flattering angle. The media, however, want to take candid shots, showing government in awkward poses and off its guard.

In this chapter we will examine more closely the interrelationship of government and the media, considering in turn the executive, legislative, and judicial branches. Casual as well as systematic observations readily establish that the media devote a great deal of attention to the affairs of the national government. A year-long content analysis of three Chicago newspapers in 1976, for instance, showed that 27 percent of all their news stories dealt directly or indirectly with the presidency. Ten percent of the stories were devoted to the 1976 presidential election, bringing total coverage of the presidency to 37 percent. Like the president, Congress was covered either directly or indirectly by 27 percent of all stories. Direct coverage amounted to only 3 percent of all stories, but this was supplemented by stories concerning domestic and foreign policy issues involving Congress. Five percent of all stories focused on the judiciary, primarily Supreme Court coverage. National television averaged 10 percent more coverage of the presidency than the newspapers, if one includes election stories, and slightly less coverage for congressional and judicial affairs.[2]

We shall begin our analysis at the level where the marriage between government and the media is most encompassing—the presidency. Most of what is said about the presidency also applies, although to a lesser degree, to other chief executives such as governors and mayors.[3]

The Media and the Executive Branch

Four Major Functions

The media perform four basic functions for presidents and other chief executives. First, they supply them with information about current events and the political settings for their policies. They highlight problems that then may spur executive action. Not infrequently, media provide daily news faster than bureaucratic channels. President John F. Kennedy, for instance, would read the *New York Times* before beginning his official day because stories about foreign affairs often reached him 24 hours earlier through the *Times* than through State Department bulletins that had to be coded initially and then decoded.

Second, the media give the president a feel for the major concerns of the American people. They do this directly by reporting on public opinion and indirectly by featuring the stories likely to shape public discussion and public opinion. Public officials assume that newspeople are in touch with popular concerns because they want to write stories that are meaningful to their readers and viewers. Readers and viewers, in turn, take their cues about what is important and worthy of discussion from the media.

Third, media furnish chief executives with channels to convey their messages to the general public as well as to political elites within and outside of government. These channels, to which presidents have access almost at will, provide unparalleled opportunities to explain presidential policies and to attack opponents' positions. Political elites need such information as much as or more than the public because there is no effective internal communication system to link government officials who are dispersed throughout the country with each other and with Washington.[4]

Fourth, the media allow chief executives to remain almost continuously in full public view on the political stage, keeping their human qualities and professional skills on constant display. Newspapers, television, and radio supply running commentary about a president's daily routines. Coverage of personal life may be minute. For instance, when President Dwight D. Eisenhower had a heart attack in Denver in 1955, presidential news secretary James Hagerty held five news briefings a day, seven days a week, for three weeks. The media dutifully reported even the most intimate details of the president's condition, including the color of his morning toast and the bowel movements recorded on his medical chart. The purpose of this coverage was more than selling human interest tidbits. It was to reassure the public that it was fully informed about the president's disability and his fitness to continue his official functions. Human interest stories help to forge links of human concern between people and their leaders and may contribute to the relation of trust that turns people into willing followers.

Media Impact

An outline of the functions that media perform for the executive branch fails to convey the full story about the political significance of the relationship. Media coverage is the lifeblood of politics because it shapes the political perceptions that form the reality on which political action is based. Media do more than depict the political environment; they *are* the political environment. Because direct contact with political actors and situations is limited, media images define situations for nearly all participants in the political process.

As we saw in previous chapters, the age of television politics that began in the 1950s has vastly enhanced media impact and hence media power. In the past, a story might have caused ripples on the political seas when thousands of people in one corner of the country read it in the paper or heard it on the radio. Today that same story can cause political tidal waves when millions nation-wide see and hear it simultaneously on television. A politician now can visit with millions of potential followers in their living rooms, creating the kinds of emotional ties that hitherto came only from personal contact. A representative's appearance on television may be far more crucial for his or her political future than service on an important congressional committee.

A large share of the millions who watch these spectacles are people who have never before paid serious attention to politics. Lyndon B. Johnson was right when he called the rising power of television the major change in political life between his early days in Congress and his presidency 30 years later. You've given us a new kind of people, he told a television filming crew, and new kinds of politicians as well. "They're your creations, your puppets. No machine could ever create a Teddy Kennedy. Only you guys, they're all yours. Your product." [5]

In the process of attracting new participant-observers to politics and creating new types of politicians, television has tipped the political scales of power in favor of the presidency. This follows from what have been called the first and second laws of "videopolitics": "Television alters the behavior of institutions in direct proportion to the amount of coverage provided or allowed," and "the more coverage an institution secures, the greater its public stature and the more significant its role." [6]

We have already described how strongly media in general, and television in particular, influence who becomes eligible for presidential office and how profoundly the media affect the conduct and outcome of elections. After elections, the success of presidential policies, the length, vigor, and thrust of a president's political life, and the general level of support for the political system depend heavily on the images that the media convey. For instance, support for the Vietnam War ebbed after television news showed American marines leveling Vietnamese villages and reported the massacres of Vietnamese civilians by American troops. Television news provided "greater receptivity to darker news about Vietnam. . . . It was the end of the myth that we were different, that we were better." [7] Television also gave respectability to vocal

"My son, you have survived the ordeal by fire and the ordeal by water. You now face the final challenge—ordeal by media."

Drawing by Lorenz; © 1982 The New Yorker Magazine, Inc.

opponents of the war by covering antiwar lobbies and teach-ins pitting academicians against officials. President Johnson considered it hopeless to try to recapture public support for the war when Walter Cronkite announced in 1968 that the war could not be won. Accordingly, the president decided to abandon the venture. As David Halberstam put it: "It was the first time in American history a war had been declared over by an anchorman." [8] Although it is difficult to prove conclusively that Vietnam War coverage had the massive effects that Halberstam claims, circumstantial evidence supports the verdict.

The media frequently raise issues that presidents and other public officials would prefer to keep out of the limelight. Many observers believe that publicizing problems created by school busing has kept alive and strengthened opposition to federally mandated racial integration of schools. The Watergate scandal of 1973, which led to the resignation of President Richard Nixon, is a prime example of a damaging issue put at the top of the public agenda by constant media prodding, despite presidential efforts to downplay it. The seemingly endless list of major and minor scandals that the media have highlighted to the government's dismay have included misdeeds of the Central Intelligence Agency, corruption in the General Services Administration, shady dealings by the Environmental Protection Agency, and tasteless jokes by the secretary of the interior.

Media coverage can increase as well as undermine public support for a presidential policy. This is particularly important in national emergencies when substantial congressional and public acceptance is vital. For instance, only 42 percent of the American public supported President Johnson's Vietnam policies in August 1964, raising doubts about his ability to continue to raise men and money for the war. These doubts were apparently dispelled when approval ratings of his Vietnam policies rose to a comfortable 72 percent after he broadcast an explanation. Similarly, President Richard Nixon's dispatch of troops to Cambodia in April 1970 won a 50 percent approval rating after he explained it on television. Prior to the broadcast, only 7 percent of the public had approved. Favorable ratings for President Jimmy Carter's foreign policy jumped by 34 percentage points—from 22 to 56 percent—after the news media announced that the 1978 Camp David meeting had produced a peace settlement between Egypt and Israel. But such steep gains may be short-lived because memories fade quickly. Following the Camp David stories, the ratings dropped steadily by about 4 percentage points a month, until the trend was reversed by a new announcement of Mideast successes six months later.

By highlighting problems, requesting governmental action, or reporting demands for action, media stories may lead to new policies or major changes in existing policies. For instance, a 1982 CBS television documentary called "People Like Us" portrayed three destitute American families as victims of the Reagan administration's budget cutbacks. The three were a man with cerebral palsy who had lost his disability benefits, a mother who was forced to institutionalize her disabled 13-year-old daughter because of Medicaid cutbacks, and a woman who quit her job and went on welfare so that she could qualify for Medicaid. Fearing a major backlash from the documentary, the White House asked the network for time to reply. The network refused, claiming that the administration had received ample time on news programs to explain the cutbacks in social services. Officials of the Department of Health and Human Services then investigated the three cases and governmental wheels were set in motion to make sure that truly needy people could "rest assured that the social safety net of programs they depend on are exempt from any cuts." [9]

There have even been instances where the threat of potential publicity has been used by media personnel to force presidents and bureaucracies to act. They are hard to document. One reported incident occurred in 1950 when publisher Philip Graham of the *Washington Post* forced the White House and Department of the Interior to integrate Washington swimming pools. He did it by threatening to publish a story, which the paper had previously withheld, about rioting in the capital. [10]

Sensational adverse publicity can kill as well as generate programs. For instance, the publicity following an accident at a nuclear plant in Three Mile Island, Pennsylvania, in 1979 inevitably resulted in sharp curbs in the production of nuclear energy. Welfare programs, such as Head Start's prekindergarten training for poor children or financial aid for minority businesses, have been decimated by coverage of inefficient management and corrupt handling of money.

Media publicity can also be crucial in determining whether a candidate for high appointive office will pass Senate scrutiny. Griffin Bell, President Carter's nominee for attorney general, almost missed confirmation in 1977 because of adverse press reports about his racial views. During the Nixon administration, the Senate refused to confirm two prospective Supreme Court justices, Clement F. Haynsworth, Jr., and G. Harrold Carswell. In each instance, knowledgeable observers thought that highly unfavorable media publicity was instrumental in the defeats. In the case of nominee Carswell, the most damaging piece of evidence was a 1948 speech in which he had praised segregation. The speech was unearthed by a reporter for a Jacksonville, Florida, television station affiliated with the *Washington Post*. [11]

A Rocky Marriage

Direct and Mediated Transmission.   Audiovisual and print images about government are conveyed in two modes: directly or indirectly. Direct conveyance allows government officials to transmit their messages verbatim, and often live, with a minimum of media editorializing. President Harry S. Truman was the first to use the direct mode by broadcasting his entire State of the Union message in 1947 to a nationwide audience. In January 1961, President Kennedy initiated live telecasts of news conferences. More than other public officials the president enjoys opportunities for virtually uncontrolled access to the American people. As we saw in Chapter 4, political leaders competing with the president for power and public support have tried for matching privileges with only minimal success.

Of course, even live television and radio broadcasts are not totally devoid of media influence because camera angles and other photographic techniques slant all presentations somewhat. Instant commentary, following the presentation, may further blunt its impact. Likewise, a print news story describing a presidential news conference, followed by a published transcript, involves some shaping by media personnel. It is minimal, however, compared with the great leeway that newspeople usually have in choosing and interpreting information about the presidency.

Indirect or mediated transmission—the shaping of news presentations by media personnel—lies at the heart of the problems of the rocky marriage between media and government because it bestows more power upon the media than governments like to surrender. Mediated transmission permits journalists to pick and choose from among the information given to them, supplementing it with information gathered from other, often hostile sources, and to present it in a framework of their own choosing. It allows them to evaluate people and policies at will and to criticize an administration, frequently when its popularity is already on the downgrade. This has given rise to the charge that mediated coverage is used deliberately, or at the least carelessly, to hurt public officials and their policies.

Media Goals and Tactics.   Media personnel refute the charge that they go out of their way to show incumbent administrations in a bad light. They contend that they are looking for lively, significant stories that will earn them the respect of their colleagues and the acclaim of their readers and viewers. They see themselves as guardians of the public interest, helping to keep or make government more honest and efficient. Newspeople believe that they have a duty to report wrongdoing by public officials. The actors who produced the unfortunate situation, not the newspeople who reported it, should be blamed, they contend. Politicians who attack the media for reporting bad news are accused of resembling the ancient Greeks who often killed bearers of bad tidings. This is what newsman William J. Small had in mind when he entitled his book on government and the media *To Kill a Messenger*.[12]

As we have seen, many of the stories journalists choose to cover deal with socially undesirable or unusual behavior. When this is coupled with the intent to ferret out government misbehavior, many negative stories inevitably will emerge. It is true that media personnel assigned to the presidential beat regularly feature harsh criticism of presidential programs, particularly if such criticism is voiced by politically influential opponents. Examination of television commentaries about President Ronald Reagan in 1983 showed that during a two-month span 58 percent of the coverage was negative, 39 percent was neutral, and only 3 percent was positive.[13] Media also try to present the most sensational story possible, often accenting a comparatively minor point. For example, Martin Plissner, the political editor of CBS news, dug out President Carter's incriminating remarks about the merits of ethnic purity in various neighborhoods from the back pages of the *New York Daily News* and asked one of his reporters to question the president about them at a press conference. Carter fell into the trap and the fat was in the fire.[14]

Strains in the Relationship.   In general, chief executives are unhappy with the coverage that they receive from the media. All presidents profess to believe in a free press and claim to run an open government, but they rapidly develop a distaste for news about their administration. As President Kennedy told a 1962 news conference midway into his term, "(I am) reading more and enjoying it less." [15]

A classic attack on presidential press coverage occurred on November 13, 1969, in Des Moines, Iowa, when Vice President Spiro Agnew lashed out at the media for their instant adverse commentary on a televised address by President Nixon. Agnew charged that a tiny, anonymous group of men based in New York and Washington, who represented nobody but their own privileged fraternity, took it upon themselves to impugn the truthfulness and capabilities of the elected head of the nation. He challenged the networks to give the American people "a full accounting of their stewardship," warning that "we would never trust such power over public opinion in the hands of a small and unelected elite." [16] Media people were outraged, but the many people who called stations to comment on the address sided with Agnew two to one.[17]

Presidential displeasure with media coverage is readily understandable. Media coverage deprives presidents, to varying degrees, of control over the definition of political situations. It forces them to talk in clichés and quotable oversimplifications and, in the process, to put themselves on record in ways that may narrow their options for future action. When secret activities are disclosed, such as an impending military intervention or a planned price freeze, publicity may actually force the president's hand. Bargaining advantages may be lost through premature disclosure of news; trivia, conflict, and public wrongdoing may receive undue emphasis.

In practice, open battles between the press and the president are comparatively rare. Despite traded accusations that the government manipulates and lies and the press distorts and entraps, each side is fully aware of its need for the other. The president controls valuable information that the media must publish quickly while it is fresh. In fact, the president *is* the story in many instances. If presidents deny reporters the privilege of direct access, the story cannot be covered firsthand. Alienating the prime newsmaker and prime source of government news therefore is a major catastrophe for any news organization. There is usually little time to check the facts or consult other sources to balance what the president has said. Even when outside information sources are available, "official" sources are preferred.

The media, for their part, can withhold publicity that the president needs or force publicity that he does not want. They can stress the positive or accent the negative. They can give instantaneous live coverage or delay broadcasts until a time of their choosing. In December 1982, for example, several networks refused a request for live coverage of President Reagan's Oval Office announcement to the press regarding his compromise with congressional leaders on the MX missile system.[18]

The upshot of such an even match between the press and the government is a good deal of fraternizing and cronyism among these two "enemies," often to the dismay of those who would have the press be "pure." Each side works hard to cultivate the other's friendship. They often collaborate in examining political issues and problems. This coziness may reduce journalists' zeal to investigate government misdeeds. Indeed, charges of collusion have been made when media, time and again, have suppressed news at the request of government departments or the White House. Many of these instances have concerned questions of national security. Two examples are the squelching of a 1962 TV documentary about a German attempt to tunnel under the Berlin Wall, and the delay in 1980 in publicizing plans for an American invasion of Iran to rescue Americans held hostage by Iranian militants.[19] Reports about the forthcoming Bay of Pigs invasion of Cuba in 1961 were also held back. With the wisdom of hindsight, President Kennedy acknowledged later that the news suppression might have been a mistake. Publicity might have averted the ill-fated venture.[20]

Cycles in the Relationship. The climate of the relationship between the media and the chief executive often displays three distinct phases.[21] Initially, there is a honeymoon period, a time of cooperation when the media convey the president's messages about organization of the new administration, appointment of new officials, and plans and proposals for new policies. At this early stage, few policies and proposals have been implemented, so there is little opportunity for adverse criticism. Presidents and their advisers, eager to get their story across, make themselves readily available to the media and supply them with ample information.

Once the administration embarks on controversial programs and becomes vulnerable to criticism of its record, the honeymoon ends. Attacks on President Reagan's plans to sell Saudi Arabia billions of dollars worth of arms, and derisive comments about his tax cut proposals passed in 1981, are examples. By mid-term, top officials have become immersed in their work and often delegate contact with the media to lower level officials, particularly those charged with press relations. The administration, stung by adverse publicity, tries to manipulate the media. The media, in turn, try to develop more unofficial sources to supply them with the information that they do not get from the top.

If the rifts between media and the executive branch become particularly severe, there may be a third period in which both sides retreat from their mutually hostile behavior to a more moderate stance. Frequently this phase coincides with a reelection campaign during which newspeople try harder to provide impartial coverage, and presidents are more eager to keep newspeople happy. For instance, relations between President Gerald R. Ford and the news media brightened considerably during his 1976 campaign to retain the presidency.

Administrations differ considerably in their ability to get along with the media. In recent history the Kennedy and Reagan administrations have been particularly good at press relations, while the Nixon administration was especially bad. In fact, there has been speculation that Nixon's Watergate problems might never have developed into a major scandal had he been able to charm the press in the Kennedy manner.

The relationships between the executive and media vary not only from one administration to the next but from one part of the country to another. Frictions are greatest between the White House and the press corps in Washington because they are most strongly interdependent, and familiarity breeds a certain amount of contempt. The northeastern seaboard press, in general, has a reputation of being more critical than the press in the rest of the country. For this reason, most presidents occasionally circumvent the eastern press by scheduling news conferences in other parts of the country and by making major policy announcements away from the East Coast. As Jeb Stuart Magruder explained in his account of the Nixon years, "We were involved in media politics, and we were seeking not only to speak through the media in the usual fashion—press releases, news conferences—but to speak around the media, much of which we considered hostile, to take our message directly to the people...." [22] Similarly, Presidents Carter and Reagan adopted a policy of visiting small communities throughout the country to bask in the adulation of local audiences and local media for the benefit of nationwide television audiences. Reagan even began 10-minute weekly Saturday afternoon radio broadcasts in hopes of front-page coverage in Sunday papers.

Presidential Goals and Tactics. Just as newspeople seek to control the substance and tenor of news, so presidents and their staffs attempt to manipulate what is published. Three approaches are used. First, presidents try to win reporters' favor. This is not difficult because presidents are constantly surrounded by people who must have fresh news to earn their pay. Second, presidents try to shape the flow of news to make good publicity more likely and bad publicity less likely. Finally, they pace and arrange their work schedules to produce opportunities for favorable media coverage.

Chief executives woo reporters through offering them good story material in general as well as occasional scoops that may bring distinction. Presidents cultivate reporters' friendship by being accessible, treating reporters with respect, and arranging for their creature comforts. To keep reporters in line, presidents may threaten them directly or obliquely with withdrawal of privileges. These may include accommodations in the presidential plane, special interviews, or answers to their questions during news conferences. Presidents may attack individual reporters or their organizations for undesirable reporting, as President Kennedy did when he found David Halberstam's reports about Vietnam in the *New York Times* objectionable. The *Times* did not follow Kennedy's suggestion to remove Halberstam from location in Vietnam, and he later won a Pulitzer Prize for his on-the-scene reporting. Kennedy also dispatched Gen. Maxwell Taylor, chairman of the Joint Chiefs of Staff, to complain personally to publisher Henry Luce about reporters who had made inaccurate statements concerning the Bay of Pigs disaster. But the protest was to no avail. No heads rolled in consequence.[23]

To guide the flow of news, presidents try to push the least controversial and sensitive stories rather than the most controversial and sensitive ones that reporters want to cover. Presidents may prohibit their staffs, on pain of dismissal, from publicly disagreeing with presidential politics. They may require administrative departments to clear any interviews through the White House to avoid conflicting pronouncements on matters such as unemployment statistics or oil conservation policies. Or they may assist newspeople in prying loose information from agencies, like the Department of Defense, that have a tight information policy. The Carter administration insisted that members of the White House staff clear any appearances on televised talk shows with the president's top advisers. Similarly, the Reagan administration demanded that officials privy to sensitive information receive approval of their superiors prior to granting interviews to the press. Criticism by the eastern press has been averted by withholding advance copies of speeches or timing them late enough in the evening to preclude adequate coverage in the morning papers in the East.

Presidents also may space out releases so that there is a steady, manageable flow of news. If they want emphasis on a particular story, they may withhold competing news that breaks simultaneously. Sometimes a barrage of news is released or even created to distract attention from sensitive developments. For instance, at the end of the 1976 presidential campaign, Jimmy Carter feared losses in California and New Jersey. To deemphasize them, and to focus media attention on his expected victory in Ohio, he altered his travel plans to campaign primarily in Ohio. He also called Chicago's

Mayor Richard Daley just before a mayoral press conference to emphasize that Ohio would be the key state to win—a message Daley immediately passed on to the press. Carter's staff later claimed credit for deflecting media attention from the California and New Jersey primaries and making Ohio the critical state. As Pat Caddell, Carter's pollster, put it: "We orchestrated that. We were in trouble in New Jersey but we knew we were going to win Ohio. Then Daley did it. Of course, we orchestrated that too!"[24]

Ways of arranging activities to create favorable publicity are numerous. They include the scheduling of campaign events, the heightening of suspense through news blackouts prior to major pronouncements, and the manufacturing of pseudo-events. Timing speeches for broadcast during television hours and at times when there are no competing sports events or television spectacles is another example. Political successes may be coupled with political failures in hopes that publicity for the success will draw attention away from the failure. The announcement of the opening of formal relations with the People's Republic of China late in 1978 was reportedly timed to take the edge off possible failure by the Carter administration to clinch a Mideast peace settlement between Israel and Egypt.

News management may even go to the point of deceiving the press in order to get a smoke-screen message in front of the public. For instance, during the 1961 Bay of Pigs invasion, spokesmen for the executive branch told Miami reporters that 5,000 troops had been dispatched. This news was intended to encourage Cubans to rise up in support of a large invasion force. In actuality, only 1,000 troops had been sent. When the troops ran into trouble, officials circulated stories that only a few hundred American troops had been involved and that their chief mission had been to land supplies for anti-Castro guerrillas in Cuba rather than to invade the country. When reporters discovered that they had been used to spread false stories, they were furious. The inevitable result was a credibility gap between government and the media and between the media and the public.

In a more indirect way, presidents can shape the news through the appointments they make to the Federal Communications Commission (FCC) and other public agencies concerned with the media and through informal contacts with personnel in these agencies. Financial lifelines can be controlled through the Office of Management and Budget, which screens the budgetary requests of all federal agencies, including those related to communications, like the FCC and the Corporation for Public Broadcasting. Control can also be wielded through the Justice Department. For instance, the Antitrust Division can challenge FCC decisions such as the approval of a merger between the American Broadcasting Company and the International Telephone and Telegraph Company. In that case the Justice Department carried a series of appeals through the courts and ultimately to the Supreme Court. The Antitrust Division in the Justice Department has also discouraged monopoly control of prime time programming on television and various types of mergers of diverse media enterprises. Presidents may even involve themselves directly in media policymaking through White House study commissions and task forces.

Institutionalizing Media Access

Organization and Personnel. Because the relationship between the executive branch and the media is so continuous and pervasive, it has become routinized and institutionalized. In 1970, President Nixon created the first permanent agency within the White House to plan communications policy. His Office of Telecommunications Policy took strong stands on a number of policy issues. The Carter administration abolished the office and replaced it with the National Telecommunications and Information Agency, a less powerful organization within the Commerce Department. This was done to lessen the temptation for White House pressure to make the FCC its political tool and to give the impression that the White House had distanced itself from communications policy questions. The position of assistant secretary for national telecommunications and information administration was created in the Commerce Department. Only a small policy planning staff remained in the White House to advise the president. Such diffusion of control, which has been typical in communications policy, has worked to the detriment of strong executive leadership. Moreover, the divorce of policy planning from operations has made it more difficult to plan wisely and to implement policies.

Other White House media agencies include the Office of the Press Secretary and the Office of Media Liaison. By custom, the press secretary meets almost daily with the White House press corps to make announcements and take questions. These briefings supply reporters with the White House interpretation of events. The Office of Media Liaison sets up meetings twice a month between the president and groups of editors, publishers, and non-Washington reporters. White House reporters are excluded from these gatherings and do not get transcripts until those in attendance have had a chance to file their stories. This restraint gives the president an opportunity to get publicity beyond the control of the often hostile Washington press corps. As part of the White House organization, there is also a press release office and a research office that provides information on what the president has said in the past. Furthermore, press secretaries are attached to other parts of the presidential establishment, such as the National Security Council.

In addition to appointing a press secretary, President Carter in 1978 appointed a special assistant for communication. Gerald Rafshoon, a media consultant who had handled advertising and media coverage during Carter's 1976 campaign, was hired to structure the president's activities so that he and his programs could project a desirable image for media coverage. Despite the fact that President Reagan was widely viewed as the "Great Communicator," he, too, appointed a director of communication to polish the presidential image. David R. Gergen held that job during the initial Reagan years.

On the media side, the White House press corps consists of some 70 newspeople who cover the president regularly. Many have considerable experience and reputations to match. Major newspapers, such as the *New York Times, Washington Post, Los Angeles Times, Chicago Tribune,* and *Philadelphia Inquirer,* have full-time reporters exclusively assigned to the president. So do a number of newspaper chains, such as the Scripps-Howard papers, the Hearst press, and the Newhouse papers. Other papers send their Washington bureau chiefs to the White House when there is news of special interest to their region.

Each of the major broadcast networks has three or four reporters at the White House on a regular basis; smaller networks have one. Cable Satellite Public Affairs Network (C-SPAN), a 24-hour cable news operation with a staff of more than 50 people, provides White House coverage as well as gavel-to-gavel coverage of the House of Representatives. C-SPAN sends its signal to more than 1,500 cable systems throughout the country with a potential audience of more than 30 million people, but the actual audience for government coverage has been quite small. Other all-news cable services with White House representation are Satellite News Channels, sponsored by ABC and Westinghouse Broadcasting, and Turner Broadcasting's Cable News Network. There are also regular representatives from the weekly ·news magazines and several periodicals, as well as photographers and their supporting staffs. Much of the photographic coverage of the president, however, is handled by White House staff photographers.[25]

Better than 70 percent of the country's dailies have no regular Washington correspondent or part-time "stringer" to cover the White House. The same still holds true for most of the country's television and radio stations. But lowered news transmission costs, thanks to inexpensive satellite time, are boosting the numbers of stations that can afford direct coverage of the Washington scene, permitting them to view the activities of the national government through the prism of local interests. News organizations without Washington staffs rely heavily on wire service news. Both major American wire services, Associated Press (AP) and United Press International (UPI), have three full-time reporters accredited to the White House who cover the beat continuously, including all presidential trips. Other news organizations alternate coverage of presidential trips, taking turns at assigning a reporter to the "pool" of reporters scheduled to accompany the president. Two foreign wire services, the British Reuters and the French Agence France-Presse, also have one regular reporter each assigned to the White House.

The White House press corps spends much of its time waiting for news from the president's staff. Reporters often find this frustrating and even humiliating. Their press passes give them unlimited access to the White House press room only. Other parts of the White House and executive offices are off limits except by special appointments, which are given out selectively. For public ceremonies in the East Room or Oval Office or Rose Garden, reporters usually are escorted as a group. Some have likened this to being herded like cattle. Many also object to the hero worship and protectiveness that they sense in the president's staff and the frequent occasions when presidents make personal or public moves without first alerting the press corps.

Forms of Contact. The release of news by chief executives or their aides takes a number of routinized forms. Most of these represent a concerted effort to control news output. The most common is the *news release,* a story prepared by government officials and handed to members of the press, usually without an opportunity for questions. It can be used verbatim, and officials hope that it will be. To make sure that the release appears at the most opportune time, it often has a date line that stipulates the earliest time when it may be published. If an administration wants to give the appearance of great activity or to distract reporters' attention from areas of undesired publicity, it may publish a flood of releases simultaneously. The Carter administration also initiated a program of taping 30- to 40-second radio spots to be distributed to stations around the country on request. In this way, stations receive the news in a ready-made version controlled directly by the White House.

In a *news briefing* reporters have an opportunity to ask the press secretary questions about the news releases. But because officials furnish the news for the briefing, they control the substance and tone of the discussion. Although most press secretaries, as well as members of the press, believe that daily news briefings are unnecessary and could be covered just as well by press releases, the briefings have become traditional.

A *news conference* may appear to be a wide-open question period, but most are in fact heavily controlled by the official to be questioned. They are a form of political theater, staged, directed and partially written by top executives to cast themselves in praiseworthy roles. Seemingly spontaneous answers are usually carefully prepared by experts on the executive's staff and rehearsed during extensive briefings that precede news conferences. White House briefings are based on thick volumes of questions and answers submitted to the president by various cabinet departments and agencies.

Presidents usually decide when to call a news conference and when to skip it. They generally make a lengthy statement at the beginning of the conference to set its tone. If the president wants the headlines to focus on particular policies or incidents, he will lead off with these topics, hoping that politically embarrassing issues may be bypassed. Presidents may also plant questions by letting it be known ahead of time that certain types of queries will receive very interesting answers. Pierre Salinger, John Kennedy's press secretary, and Bill Moyers, Lyndon Johnson's press secretary, used this tactic especially well.

Presidents generally know which reporters are likely to ask sympathetic or hostile questions. By recognizing friendly reporters for questions and controlling follow-up questions, presidents can largely dictate the subject and tone of a news conference. But no president has been able to squelch embarrassing questions entirely or to deny' reporters the chance to use their questions as opportunities to express their own views about controversial issues.[26]

Some news conferences are off-the-record *backgrounders.* They are called by high officials to give newspeople important information that may not be publicized at all or may not be attributed to its source. Various forms of vague attribution may be permitted, such as "government sources say" or "it has been reported by reliable sources," or even more specifically, "the White House discloses" or the "Defense Department indicates."

Government officials like the relatively anonymous backgrounder because it permits them to bring a variety of policy ideas before their colleagues and the public without openly identifying with them. Secretary of State Henry Kissinger used backgrounders to submit foreign policy options to public debate and to warn foreign countries that their behavior was unacceptable to the United States. For instance, to discourage the Soviet Union's support of India in a war with Pakistan, Kissinger told reporters in a backgrounder that Russia's policy might lead to cancellation of a trip to Moscow that President Nixon had planned. If the statement had been officially attributed to Kissinger, it would have constituted a threat that might have undermined détente with the Soviet Union.

Similarly, Secretary of Defense Caspar Weinberger summoned reporters to a secret briefing in 1982 to provide them with data on Soviet military capacity that would substantiate the administration's claim that the Soviet Union posed a grave military threat to the United States and Europe. The data—photographs produced by satellites and secret electronic systems—had been withheld because it was feared that disclosure might alert the Soviet Union to U.S. surveillance tactics. Weinberger hoped that in the wake of viewing these photographs, which were not to be described in news stories, reporters would no longer publicly question the administration's claims of danger. Increased press support for Reagan's defense policies might also engender support among the public and among government officials.

Reporters, for their part, are ambivalent about backgrounders. They like having access to news that might otherwise be unavailable, but they dislike being prevented from publishing all aspects of the story or giving the source of the information so that the story can be placed in its proper perspective. At times they have evaded the prohibition on source disclosure by refusing to attend a background briefing and then reporting the story as told to them by reporters who attended. To prevent such leaks, government officials have occasionally solicited written pledges from reporters that they would not reveal information released during briefings. Usually reporters refuse to sign.

In addition to formal encounters, there are countless informal contacts in work and social settings between reporters and the president or White House staff. Frequently, the most probing stories about White House activities come from reporters not ordinarily assigned to cover the president. The regulars would be too vulnerable to retaliation by the White House if they wrote unusually critical reports.

Top government officials, and occasionally the president, may appear on news programs such as "Meet the Press," "Face the Nation," "Today," or "Nightline." Questioning on these shows can resemble a hostile inquisition, but executive officials participate because they provide an excellent opportunity to present the administration's position to an interested nationwide audience. Besides, if questioning becomes excessively harsh, the audience often feels sorry for the targets and sides with them.

An even less formal release of news occurs through *leaks,* the surreptitious release of information by government sources who wish to remain anonymous. Leaks frequently involve information that the officials in question may not be authorized to release or that they may not wish to release formally. Sometimes officials leak information to gain attention from top officials. Leaks may destroy the timing of political negotiations, alienate the parties whose secrets have been betrayed, and cause substantial political harm by disclosing politically sensitive matters. They also may bring important suppressed issues to needed public attention, serve as trial balloons, and permit government officials to release information anonymously. Although presidents frequently leak confidential stories, they passionately hate news leaks by others. Because the source is hidden, personal confrontation and punishment are impossible. All recent presidents have therefore used federal investigative agencies such as the FBI and CIA to find the sources of news leaks.[27]

A typical leak occurred in 1970, when a memorandum by Defense Secretary Melvin Laird warned U.S. commanders to keep silent about the willingness of the United States to sign a treaty with the Soviet Union that would abandon the antiballistic missile (ABM) system. Silence was crucial to preserve negotiating strength. But an unidentified official leaked the memo, which was then printed in full by the *Washington Post* and covered by the *New York Times.* American negotiators were distraught; the leak had impaired their negotiating ability.

The harm that leaks cause must be weighed against their benefits. In a system in which the executive maintains tight control over the formal channels of news flow, leaks provide a valuable counterbalance. The controversial budget proposals made by President Reagan in 1983 are a case in point. Administration insiders, eager to bring their concerns to the public and Congress, resorted to almost daily leaks of economic appraisals that contradicted the president's views. An irate Reagan proclaimed, "I've had it up to my keister with these leaks," but he modified his budget nonetheless.[28]

The Media and Congress

Nature of Coverage

Image vs. Reality. According to political folklore, the presidency basks in the limelight of publicity at all times while Congress waits in the shadows. The television age has permanently altered the balance of political power, making the president dominant and the legislature inferior, political observers claim. As Sen. J. William Fulbright of Arkansas told Congress in 1970, "Television has done as much to expand the powers of the President as would a constitutional amendment formally abolishing the co-equality of the three branches of government." [29]

If one probes beyond these impressions to the underlying facts, the situation appears less clear. Over a period of a year, even a presidential election year, Congress and the presidency receive roughly the same amount of coverage *(see Table 3-2)*. In fact, Congress has a slight edge, if we include stories dealing with the institution in general and individual members and exclude campaign stories. A content analysis of 22 newspapers and the evening news of the three television networks during a typical week in 1978 showed nationwide media coverage of Congress and the presidency to be about the same. In the most influential form of coverage—newspaper stories— Congress held the edge by 54 to 46 percent. For television, the edge was reversed, with the president ahead, 59 to 41 percent. [30] But much television coverage was highly negative, reducing its usefulness as a booster for the president. [31] Why, then, is there the impression of vast presidential advantage from media coverage?

There are several reasons. Most importantly, the presidency is a single-headed institution—readily personified, filmed, and recorded in the visible person of the chief executive. This gives the media and media audiences a single, familiar, easily dramatized focus of attention. Even when stories come from congressional sources, they are generally linked to the executive. Stephen Hess has noted that 71 percent of news stories about the president or Congress come from legislative sources, but only 48 percent credit Congress. Conversely, 52 percent of stories about the executive and legislature are credited to the executive, even though only 29 percent originate there. [32]

The president is like a superstar, surrounded by a cast of supporting actors. As the symbolic personification of the nation, the president can command national television or radio time almost at will, often at prime time, and simultaneously on all major networks. One 1976 study showed that during a 10-year period, 44 out of 45 presidential requests for television coverage were granted, compared with 3 out of 11 for the congressional leadership. [33]

In contrast to the presidency, Congress, like the sparsely covered bureaucracy, is a many-headed hydra with no single widely familiar personal focus.[34] Its activities are conducted simultaneously in more than 100 locations on Capitol Hill. No individual member can command nationwide media coverage at will. Even well-known senators and representatives are viewed as spokesmen for their own or their party's views, or as potential presidential candidates, not as spokesmen for Congress as an institution. Their celebrity status often has little to do with their legislative activity in Congress. In fact, there has never been a single spokesman for Congress in general, or even for the Senate or House, because senators and representatives are loathe to designate one of their number as *primus inter pares*. Consequently, large numbers of stories about Congress deal with individual members or legislative activity on specific issues rather than with the body as a whole.

Another reason why stories on Congress escape wide attention lies in the nature of its work. The legislative branch plans action, makes compromises among conflicting interests, forges shifting coalitions, and works out legal details. Stories about the executive branch that describe what is actually done are far more memorable than reports about the laborious process of hammering out legislation. Besides, the most interesting aspect of the legislative process, the shaping of broad guidelines for policy, is usually reported by the media as part of the work of the executive branch.

Concentration on readily available stories frequently interferes with the usefulness of congressional coverage. In the early stages of the legislative process, when there is still time for citizen input, congressional coverage should be most ample. Yet this is the time when policy proposals generally receive least attention, especially on television. Coverage focuses instead on final action that merely ratifies the work of committees and subcommittees. Citizens learn what the new policies are without being exposed to the pros and cons and the political interplay that led to the ultimate compromise.[35]

Recognizing that legislative floor sessions would present an unedifying, boring spectacle, Congress itself resisted live radio and television coverage of most sessions until the late 1970s. Prior to 1979, only selected committee hearings were televised, primarily those involving spicy topics such as labor racketeering, Communists in government, or high-level corruption. The televised sessions became highly dramatic morality plays, with casts of sinners brought to justice and congressional knights battling evil before the public. Senators such as Harry Truman and Estes Kefauver and beetle-browed Sam Ervin were catapulted into the national limelight by these hearings. Many of the targets of the investigations, on the other hand, were harmed by the damaging publicity, even when they were later officially exonerated of any misdeeds. Few ordinary congressional sessions could provide comparable drama.

In 1979, the prohibition on televising House floor sessions imposed by Speaker Sam Rayburn in 1951 was lifted. The action was prompted in part by the desire to do everything possible to counterbalance the political advantages reaped by the executive branch from heavy media publicity. House sessions began to be telecast, albeit with restrictions. Fearful of negative publicity, the House retained control over filming and specified that only the member speaking could be shown. Except when the leadership orders otherwise, this stipulation bars from public view the typical scene on the House or Senate floor of the near-empty chamber and inattentive members. Commercial, cable, and public television are allowed to plug into the House system to show the procedures live or on tape. They are not permitted to do their own taping.

Senate floor sessions remain off-limits except for special occasions such as the Panama Canal Treaty debate of 1978, portions of which were broadcast live on National Public Radio. Leisurely debate, by senators who are unconcerned about the impression it might make on the public, is deemed a hallmark of the upper house. As one senator put it: "In a representative democracy, the people govern indirectly." Televising legislative sessions "seeks to impose upon the legislative process an aspect of direct democracy that undermines representative government ... (and) would act as a deterrent to the exercise of individual judgment." [36]

The verdict is not yet in on the long-range consequences of coverage, although it is doubtful that televised sessions will change the publicity balance between the president and Congress. For the reasons outlined already, Congress is not likely to become a first-rate "show." A few interesting and unexpected results of congressional coverage have been reported, however. Representatives themselves are apparently among the most avid watchers of House coverage because the television cameras permit them to monitor sessions that they previously missed. Now they can keep up on floor action and issues reported by committees other than their own.[37]

In time, the chance to appear on television and gain valuable publicity may even lure more representatives to the chamber, just as televised committee hearings have attracted above average congressional attendance. There already has been an increase in brief, quotable statements made by members in time to appear on the evening news. Some members have claimed that recent sharp increases in the time spent to pass legislation are largely due to television coverage.[38] The added publicity may make incumbent representatives even more unbeatable for reelection than they are now. As Sam Rayburn had feared, broadcasting also may make it more difficult to reach legislative compromises once representatives have publicly committed themselves to definite positions.

Another possible consequence of broadcasting House sessions is less powerful lobbies. In their efforts to convince the public of the rightness of their views, lobbyists now must compete harder for media attention. Interested observers are tuning in to House sessions and realizing that many issues are far more complex than lobbyists had led them to believe.[39]

Implementation of Coverage Criteria. Newspeople assigned to the congressional beat use general criteria of newsworthiness and gatekeeping to decide who and what will be covered and who and what will be ignored. Exciting, novel, or controversial topics that can be made personally relevant to the public and simply presented have precedence over complex, ongoing problems of a mundane nature, such as congressional reorganization or the annual farm bill. Orderly, dispassionate debate usually is passed over in favor of purple rhetoric and wild accusations that can produce catchy headlines. Heated confrontations are more likely to occur in the more intimate committee hearings than in full sessions. In fact, the chance of headlines may provoke disputes when they might not otherwise occur.[40] Accordingly, committee hearings attract most extensive coverage, particularly on television.

Of all the stories by the Washington press corps, foreign policy receives the largest amount of coverage, especially on television and radio. Economic policies come next. Scandals rank in third place for television and in fourth place for the print media.[41]

Congress is a regular beat, and major media organizations such as the *Washington Post* and the *New York Times,* major newspaper chains such as Gannett, Hearst, and Knight, and the television networks and wire services have full-time reporters covering it. Some are specialists in various policy areas. Among wire service reporters, some concentrate on news from diverse regions, covering, for instance, members of Congress from western states and committees dealing with problems affecting the West. There are also Washington "stringer" bureaus whose reporters serve assorted subscriber news services throughout the country. Specialized news services such as Congressional Quarterly cover the congressional beat in detail for professional audiences. In all, more than 2,000 correspondents are accredited to the press galleries in the House and Senate. About 400 of these cover Congress exclusively.[42]

Congressional press releases and written reports provide news sources without a regular reporter on the Hill with much of the information about Congress. These documents are gathered and distributed by wire service reporters who are unable to attend the many hearings occurring simultaneously. Press releases enable members of Congress to tell their stories in their own words. They give an advantage to members whose offices can turn out interesting public statements.[43]

In general, senators enjoy more press coverage than representatives, even though an equal number of reporters cover both houses. On network television, stories about senators outnumber those about representatives more than two to one, probably because senators have greater prominence and prestige, and their larger constituencies make them of interest to a wider audience. Senators from large states also are more likely to have sufficient staff to turn out good press releases and other publicity.

Table 7-1 Press Coverage of Congress: Subjects (in percent of stories)

Newspaper	Individuals		Institutions		House & Senate Equally	President & Congress	Congress & Bureaucracy*	Other
	House	Senate	House	Senate				
Atlanta Constitution	21%	18%	13%	19%	10%	13%	5%	—
Boston Globe	9	13	27	21	9	17	5	—
Chicago Sun-Times	10	18	15	22	17	15	4	—
Dallas Morning News	13	16	19	19	10	18	4	—
Denver Post	15	16	22	24	9	13	1	—
Los Angeles Times	12	13	17	24	12	19	3	—
Miami Herald	15	17	19	17	12	16	3	1
Minnesota Star	17	17	25	13	8	18	3	—
Philadelphia Inquirer	18	21	14	16	4	15	5	2
Washington Post	14	14	24	16	11	13	3	6

* Stories about relationship between Congress and the bureaucracy.

N = 2,299 stories, including news, analysis, editorials, op-ed items, and cartoons.

SOURCE: Adapted from Charles M. Tidmarch and John J. Pitney Jr., "Covering Congress: An Analysis of Reportage and Commentary in Ten Metropolitan Newspapers" (Paper presented at the annual meeting of the Midwest Political Science Association, Milwaukee, Wisconsin, 1982). Used with permission of authors.

Table 7-1 shows the distribution of news stories about the House and Senate and their members in 10 assorted urban newspapers. The figures are based on content analysis of all Congress-related stories that appeared during one month, spanning parts of July and August 1978. At the time, congressional work involved nothing out of the ordinary. The table shows substantial variations in coverage of specific congressional subjects among individual papers. When comparing coverage of representatives and senators, it should be remembered that representatives are far more numerous and most of them were involved in election contests in 1978. One therefore would expect to see a higher number of stories about representatives as a group than about senators. That this was not the case demonstrates the greater newsworthiness of members of the upper house.

Unlike the president, neither senators nor representatives enjoy automatic coverage of whatever they say and do, even though they issue frequent press releases and call occasional news conferences. However, on certain topics, such as tax policy or investigation of executive activities, congressional spokesmen, rather than the president, are routinely sought out. Additionally, many members of Congress receive regular local coverage through their own news columns, radio, or television programs.

Functions of Media

The functions performed by Congress for the national media and by the national media for Congress parallel press-presidency relations. But there are major qualitative differences in the relationship. Neither Congress nor the media needs the services of the other as keenly as the presidency needs the press. The media can afford to alienate some legislators without losing direct access to congressional news. Similarly, legislators often can ignore national publicity and rely instead on publicity in their districts. News about national events and national public opinion is also somewhat less important to most members of Congress than to the president. Senators and representatives are most interested in news affecting their own constituency. The home media are particularly important to them as sources of news and as channels for transmitting messages back to the district while they are at work in Washington.

National as well as local media provide senators and representatives with a forum to express their views on political issues and to attract public support for themselves and their causes. This publicity reassures constituents that their elected representatives are aware of problems and are trying to solve them. It may produce action to remedy publicized abuses such as faulty tires, unnecessary surgery, or pesticides in food. Publicity by itself may bring about reform without the need for legislation or judicial action.

For a few members of Congress, national media attention may be a springboard to higher office, including the presidency. Once members achieve visibility, their fame often grows by its own momentum. They become regulars on interview shows, and their opinions are solicited when important national issues are debated. However, members rarely receive the intimate personal coverage that presidents get. For most members, media attention may do little more than make them visible targets for lobby groups. This may lead to reelection support from these groups or research support for pet projects. On the other hand, publicity may fuel support for the opposition.

For members of Congress who are not aspiring to higher office, national publicity may be practically irrelevant. But favorable media attention in their districts is essential to let their constituents know what they are doing and to pave the way for reelection. Local publicity is usually easy for members to obtain. Local media are eager to feature news about their Washington activities. Several congressmen own mass media outlets, assuring them of ample coverage. The best known of such owners was Lyndon Johnson, who held extensive broadcast properties in Texas during his years in Congress. Newsletters and individual letters targeted to reach selected constituents help round out the picture.

All legislators have full- or part-time media consultants. Senators and representatives also have studios available on Capitol Hill where they can produce, at low cost, videotapes, films, and audiotapes for distribution to their constituencies. Seventy-five percent of the House membership and 80 percent of the Senate membership use these facilities to make broadcasts for hometown distribution.

A Cautious Marriage

Just as the functions that media perform are similar for the executive and legislative branches so is the love-hate relationship. But it, too, is less ardent for Congress, even though mutual recriminations are plentiful. Senators and representatives, competing with peers for media attention, bemoan lack of coverage of their pet projects and pronouncements. They complain that reporters treat them as if they were scoundrels conspiring to defraud the public. As Table 7-2 indicates, they have reason to lament the little positive coverage they receive. In fact, congressional coverage is considerably more negative than coverage of the presidency or the Supreme Court.[44] Members of Congress resent the crossexaminations that reporters love to conduct with a prosecutor's zeal and an air of infallibility. They charge and can prove that the media emphasize trivia and scandals and official misconduct and internal dissent and often ignore congressional consensus and activities of major significance. They blame the media for the declining prestige of Congress.

The media, in turn, complain with justification about legislators' efforts to manage the news through their professional publicity staffs. They point to

Table 7-2 Press Coverage of Congress: Evaluation (in percent of stories)

Newspaper	Positive	Negative	Neutral	Positive/Negative Editorial Ratio*
Atlanta Constitution	9	34	56	1:2.1
Boston Globe	14	32	53	1:1.8
Chicago Sun-Times	5	26	68	1:3.8
Dallas Morning News	5	18	78	1:1.8
Denver Post	12	32	57	1:1.1
Los Angeles Times	4	20	75	1:10
Miami Herald	6	27	67	1:2.4
Minnesota Star	5	29	66	1:2
Philadelphia Inquirer	8	40	53	1:3
Washington Post	5	21	75	1:2.4

* Ratio of positive to negative editorials with neutral editorials excluded.
N = 2,299 stories, including news, analysis, editorials, op-ed items, and cartoons.

SOURCE: Adapted from Charles M. Tidmarch and John J. Pitney Jr., "Covering Congress: An Analysis of Reportage and Commentary in Ten Metropolitan Newspapers" (Paper presented at the annual meeting of the Midwest Political Science Association, Chicago, Illinois, 1982). Used with permission of authors.

congressmen's lack of candor and to their exclusion of media personnel from many congressional activities. Broadcasters also resent the constraints put on them when they cover congressional sessions.

But senators and representatives realize that they need the media for information and for the publicity that is crucial to their work. They know that the media discreetly ignore their personal foibles so long as no official wrongdoing is involved. Newspeople, in turn, realize they need individual legislators for information about congressional activities and as a counterfoil and source of leaks to check the executive branch. Members are valuable for inside comments that can personalize otherwise dull stories. Congress often creates major story topics for the media by investigating ongoing problems like auto or mine safety. A congressional inquiry may be the catalyst that turns an everyday event into a newsworthy story. The story then may ride the crest of publicity for quite some time, creating its own fresh and reportable events until it recedes into limbo once more. Newspeople do not want to dry up these sources; they do not want to bite the hand that feeds them the news.

Congress and Communications Policy

Additionally, the media, particularly radio and television, are aware of the potential power Congress has over regulatory legislation. In the past, Congress made little use of its power to legislate communications policy, viewing it as a hornets nest of political conflict best left alone. The major exception was the broad grant of authority to the Federal Communications

Commission (FCC) in the 1934 Communications Act and supplementary laws dealing with technical innovations. Periodic attempts to supersede the act have usually floundered, but the power to legislate communications policy remains. If and when strong, unified industry or consumer pressures develop, Congress's legislative powers could become important. Meanwhile, there is a vacuum in both policy formulation and oversight of administration, which neither the president nor the FCC has attempted to fill.[45] Communications industry representatives have partly jumped into the breach. They are in a strong position to push their ideas because they enjoy a near monopoly over the basic information needed to make policy.

The communications subcommittees of the Commerce, Science, and Transportation Committee in the Senate and the Energy and Commerce Committee in the House control communications policy largely through the power of investigation. This power has been used more frequently for the FCC than for most other regulatory bodies. In fact, just since 1970, more than 50 different congressional committees and subcommittees have reviewed various FCC activities. But there have been few dramatic results beyond spending a significant share of the commission's limited resources on responding to these investigations. Investigations have included reviews of specific FCC actions, studies of FCC operations and structures, examinations of broad policy issues such as the impact of television's portrayal of the aged or of alcohol and alcohol abuse, and studies of corruption in television-sponsored game shows. The appropriations committees, too, have wielded their power over the FCC's purse in a desultory way. They occasionally have denied funds for the commission or explicitly directed what particular programs should be funded.[46] However, monetary control may be stricter in the future because Congress switched the FCC in 1982 from the status of a permanently authorized agency to one requiring bi-annual renewal.

The Senate has used confirmation hearings only occasionally to impress its views on new FCC commissioners. This does not mean that the views of powerful senators have been ignored. Prospective commissioners are likely to study past confirmation hearings carefully and take their cues from them. Most presidential nominees have been confirmed. Appointments usually represent political rewards to the faithful.[47] While congressional control over the FCC thus has been generally light, there is always the possibility of stricter control. All the parties interested in communications policy, including the White House and the courts, pay deference to that possibility.

Congressional control over media also includes matters such as postal rates and subsidies, legislation on permissible mergers and chain control of papers, and laws designed to keep failing newspapers alive. Copyright laws, which affect print and electronic media productions, are also involved. So are policies and regulations about telecommunication satellites, broadcast spectrum allocations, and cable television. The vast, congressionally guided changes in the telephone industry are yet another area of major concern to media interests.

Laws regulating media procedures occasionally may have a strong impact on media content and policies. For instance, FCC encouragement of diversification of radio programs was largely responsible for the development of a sizable number of FM rock music stations. These stations were able to provide alternatives to more conventional programs. Congressional scrutiny of documentaries may chill investigative reporting. Congress investigated a documentary on drug use at a major university because the events were allegedly staged, and it also looked into the accuracy of charges of illicit public relations activity by the Pentagon. Former Democratic senator John Pastore of Rhode Island, who was deeply concerned about television violence, helped create the Surgeon General's Advisory Committee on Television and Social Behavior, which has investigated violence in television shows in preparation for congressional action.[48]

Congressional failure to act may also have far-reaching consequences for the mass media. For instance, failure to regulate cable television has left the FCC and the courts in control of this medium. Last but not least, ownership of media outlets or purchase of media time makes senators and representatives part of the media fraternity or valued clients who may receive kid-glove treatment.

News Impact on Reelection

Because of their dependence on Congress, the media treat congressional leaders and Congress as an institution with a fair amount of deference and respect. Media critic Ben Bagdikian has even charged that the media have become an effective propaganda arm for Congress. He credits them with virtually guaranteeing the reelection of any incumbent who is willing to run. "Most of the media are willing conduits for the highly selective information the member of Congress decides to feed the electorate," he argues.[49] This claim is exaggerated; many factors unrelated to media coverage contribute to the high reelection rate of incumbents. Besides, the media often present incumbents in an unfavorable light, and they do not publish the bulk of their self-promoting press releases. For example, in the Third Congressional District in Wisconsin, papers published only 7 percent of the available news release copy from their representative in 1973. Senatorial publicity fared even worse. Many papers did not publish any news releases; the most generous papers published no more than 30 percent of the news release copy they received.[50] Nonetheless, there is some truth to Bagdikian's charges of kid-glove treatment.

Through a thorough analysis of the impact of media coverage on Congress, Michael Robinson detected several major effects. The media have, indeed, increased the reelection chances of incumbents, but only in the House of Representatives where local coverage, which is generally favorable, is most important. In the Senate, the negative tenor of the national media and the greater attention to challengers seeking Senate seats have reduced the reelection chances of incumbents. As is true for the presidency, media adeptness has become a crucial talent for would-be members of Congress. They must know how to "show-boat" to get coverage from newspapers and television.[51]

Compared with the presidency, Congress as a whole has suffered a decline in image and power. This springs partly from stories that picture it routinely as lobby-ridden, incompetent, and slow and partly from the fact that the White House has provided more exciting copy.[52] However, individual presidents, like senators, have been more bloodied by adverse publicity than is true of individual members of the House. Thus the media have fostered a stronger presidency, but weaker presidents, and a weaker Congress, but more durable representatives.

Robinson also points out that direct communications by members of Congress through newsletters, direct mail, and campaign brochures and advertisements often fill gaps left by media coverage. These controlled media serve as a counterweight to the adverse news coming from newspapers and television.

The Media and the Courts

Nature of Coverage

Of the three branches of government, the judiciary receives the least publicity for its officials. At the federal level, aside from initial appointments to the federal bench, judges are rarely in the limelight in a way that would be comparable to chief executives or members of the legislature. Judges infrequently grant interviews, almost never hold news conferences, and generally do not seek or welcome media attention, primarily because they fear their impartiality might be compromised. Remoteness enhances the impression that judges are a breed apart, doling out justice to lesser mortals. At the state and local levels, where many judges are elected rather than appointed to office, media coverage is somewhat more common and the aura of judicial majesty recedes accordingly.

The courts as institutions also receive comparatively little coverage. There are exceptions, of course. The difficulties of the courts in coping with the flood of legal actions, the problems of disparate sentencing policies, and the flaws in the correctional system have all been the subject of sporadic media investigations. Speeches by Supreme Court justices to public bodies such as the American Bar Association have been telecast and reported nationwide. Chief Justice Warren E. Burger has even allowed himself to be questioned routinely about his annual "State of the Judiciary" speech. The news conference before the speech is off the record, however, and the chief justice may not be quoted directly.

Although justices and court systems are not very newsworthy because they generally do not become embroiled in open battles about policies, their products—judicial decisions—do make the news. This is particularly true of U.S. Supreme Court decisions, which frequently have major consequences for the social and political system. For example, *Brown v. Board of Education* (1954) declared unconstitutional the separate schooling of children of different races and *Baker v. Carr* (1962) led to massive changes in electoral districting in the United States.[53] In more recent decisions, the Burger court has made important news with major rulings on abortion, obscenity, capital punishment, and affirmative action.

Impact of Coverage

Publicity about Supreme Court decisions informs public officials at all governmental levels, as well as the general public, about the substance of selected decisions. Choices about which decisions to cover and which to ignore are made by newspeople with little guidance from the legal profession. This significant responsibility rests on the shoulders of the small corps of reporters covering the courts. At the Supreme Court, full- and part-time reporters combined number about 50 people. Of these only the correspondents for the major wire services and four major newspapers are full-time.

Supreme Court coverage is difficult; the reporters must digest a large number of voluminous and often contradictory opinions supporting or dissenting from a given decision. This must be done quickly and without help from the justices who authored the opinions. Advice from outside commentators is usually unavailable initially since they are not allowed to preview the opinions. Leaks of advance information are very rare. The Supreme Court does have a press office, which provides a few reference materials and bare-bones records of the Court's activities. In addition, brief analyses of important pending cases are available to the media through publications sponsored by the legal profession.

Because of the shortage of skilled reporters, much court reporting, even at the Supreme Court level, is imprecise and sometimes even wrong. Justice Felix Frankfurter once complained that editors who would never consider covering a baseball game through a reporter unfamiliar with the sport regularly assigned people unfamiliar with the law to cover the Supreme Court.

This situation has improved considerably in recent years, but it is far from cured.

Baker v. Carr and *Engel v. Vitale,* the latter a 1962 school prayer decision,[54] illustrate faulty reporting. An analysis of stories about these two decisions in 63 metropolitan daily papers showed that headlines were misleading and coverage was sketchy and uninformative.[55] Ill-informed statements by well-known people opposing the Court's decisions made up the major part of the stories. Several stories contained serious errors. For instance, it was reported that the decision outlawing classroom prayer in public schools was based on the religious freedom clause of the Constitution. In fact, it was based on the establishment of religion clause. Arguments made in lower courts were erroneously attributed to Supreme Court justices. Moreover, the media covered the prayer decision most heavily because it was relatively easy to grasp and presented an emotionally stirring story. They slighted the duller reapportionment decision, which was of far greater political significance because it forced states to reapportion legislative districts on a massive scale to meet the one-person, one-vote requirement.

The media also fail to cover many important decisions entirely. A study of *New York Times* coverage of one Supreme Court term showed that one quarter of all written opinions received no mention at all. In the stories about the remaining 112 opinions, 49 lacked essential information. The *Detroit News,* a more typical paper, failed to mention 70 percent of the written opinions.[56]

The thrust of judicial complaints about sketchy, inaccurate reporting is the same as for coverage of the presidency and Congress. However, reporting of court activities seems to be more superficial and flawed than its presidential and congressional counterparts.[57] The reasons are not difficult to understand. The volume of decisions is huge, frequently clustering near the end of a court term. The subject matter is often highly technical, hard for reporters to understand and make understandable. With notable exceptions, stories about judicial decisions lack the potential to become exciting, front-page news. They are hard to boil down into catchy phrases and clichés. The Supreme Court beat tends to be understaffed. All of this makes it very difficult for assigned reporters to prepare interesting, well-researched accounts.

The information supplied to the public may produce respect for the judiciary and compliance with its rulings. Most people, though they know little about the Supreme Court, hold it in high esteem.[58] Occasionally Court publicity has the opposite effect. For instance, widespread adverse publicity about Supreme Court decisions outlawing prayer in the public schools has encouraged individuals and entire school systems to ignore the ban. It also has led to an abortive movement to pass a constitutional amendment to permit prayers in the public schools. Justice Tom Clark, one of the participants in the 1962 prayer decision, complained that popular misunderstanding of the *Engel v. Vitale* case made this ruling unpopular. He blamed inadequate reporting for the misunderstanding.

Public reactions to Supreme Court decisions, in turn, may affect future decisions of the Court. Justices themselves are influenced in their work by what they read and hear from the media. Media reports of crime waves, or price-gouging by business, or public opposition to aid for parochial schools are likely to influence Court decisions and set boundaries to judicial policymaking.[59] Publication of decisions by the Supreme Court and lower courts is by no means the only significant news about the judiciary. General news about crime and the work of the justice system is also important in creating images of the quality of public justice. Here a plentiful media diet is available. For example, a 1976 survey of Chicago newspapers and television stations, as well as national network broadcasts, showed that crime and the justice system in general were discussed in 25 percent of all newspaper stories, 20 percent of all local television stories, and 13 percent of all national television stories. Even if the large number of stories reporting individual crimes are subtracted from the totals, the figures are impressive, particularly when compared with stories about other social problems. The combined total of stories about health issues and minorities, for example, received less than one-third of the coverage given to crime and the justice system. Like stories about other governmental activities, crime and justice system stories tend to focus on sensational events, often at the expense of significant trends and problems in the legal system that might benefit from greater public attention.[60]

Judicial Censorship

Although crime and justice system news in general is amply covered by the media, there are a number of prohibited areas. The Supreme Court bars reporters from all of its deliberations prior to the announcement of decisions. On the few occasions when information about a forthcoming decision has been leaked ahead of time, justices have reacted with great anger and have curtailed the contacts between newspeople and court personnel. Television cameras are barred from the Supreme Court and other federal courts, and proceedings may not be broadcast directly.

Below the federal level, courts in many states still prohibit radio and television reporters from covering trials and other proceedings. The rationale for this restriction is that electronic equipment might produce a carnival atmosphere that would intimidate participants and harm the fairness of the proceedings. Sensational coverage of the Lindbergh kidnapping trial in 1935 spawned such bans. Now, however, they appear to be on the decline. By 1983, 40 states permitted electronic coverage of judicial proceedings in state courts, but some of the permissions were on a trial basis.

Restraints on live audio and video coverage are not the only limitations on judicial publicity. In the interest of ensuring fair trials, courts also limit the information that may be printed about court proceedings. These types of restrictions were discussed in Chapter 4.

Communications Law

Judges are also of interest to media personnel for their views on communications law. Because the public interest standard established for the FCC is vague, and judges have clashed over the interpretation of the First Amendment's free press provisions, federal courts are frequently asked to interpret compliance with constitutional and statutory restraints. Media lobbies have therefore attempted to influence the appointment of federal judges. In appeals from FCC licensing and rules change decisions, they have tried to have the cases submitted to sympathetic judges and often have provided testimony.

In an average year, 15 to 20 appeals involving various aspects of communications policy are brought from the FCC to the courts, most often to the Court of Appeals for the District of Columbia. The law permits any person who is "aggrieved" or whose interests are "adversely affected" by the orders of the FCC to seek a court review, and these provisions have been loosely interpreted. Such liberal access policies have enhanced concern about the potentially large role of the courts in communications policymaking

The majority of FCC rulings have been upheld in the federal Court of Appeals, although this may be changing. In the late 1970s, the court frequently substituted its own policy analysis and preferences for those of the commission.[61] The limited number of cases that have reached the Supreme Court, usually because violation of First Amendment rights was alleged, have generally upheld the FCC's rulings. While influence over the FCC itself thus seems more important for policy impact than control over the courts, it is difficult to gauge how much impact the prospects of judicial review have on FCC activities. Agencies frequently modify their behavior to avoid reversals by the judiciary.

The vagueness of the power granted to the FCC provides immense leeway to the courts as well as to the commission. As Daniel Polsby and Kim Degnan have observed, "If 'the public interest' leaves the FCC in a trackless normative wilderness in which it is free to make up the rules of the game, the court's discretion to pass on those rules for reasonable or substantial correspondence with record evidence is not less broad." [62] Interpretation of the scope of the FCC's mandate therefore inevitably involves the courts in shaping communications policy.

Summary

In this chapter we have examined the relationship between the media and the three branches of the national government. Coverage is ample, but the goals of the media differ from those of government officials. Officials want stories that report them and their work accurately and favorably. They also wish to dominate the news sifting process so that published news mirrors their sense of what is important and unimportant. Newspeople, on the other hand, want stories that are newsworthy, judged by the usual criteria. They believe that their publics are more interested in exciting events and human interest tales than in academic discussions of public policies, their historical anteced- ents, and their projected impact, expressed in statistics. Newspeople also feel a special mission, like Shakespeare's Mark Antony, "to bury Caesar, not to praise him." And, like Brutus, they claim that their criticism is not disloyalty. They do not love the government less; they only love the nation more.

Each side in this tug of war uses wiles and ruses as well as clout to have its own way. The outcome is a see-saw contest in which both sides score victories and suffer defeats, but each is most attuned to its own failures rather than its victories. The public interest is served in equally uneven fashion. If we equate it with a maximum of intelligible information about important issues and events, media presentations fall short. But coverage is good in that it is continuous, often well-informed, with sufficient attention to audience appeal to make dry information palatable. Investigative reporting has brought to light many shortcomings and scandals that otherwise might have remained hidden. The fear of exposure by the media has undoubtedly kept government officials from straying into many questionable ventures, although this effect is hard to document. On the negative side, fear of media coverage and publicity have probably inhibited desirable actions.

Because the contacts between officials of the national government and the media are so constant, a formal institutional structure has been established to handle these interactions. The fairly elaborate setup at the presidential level and the simpler arrangements for Congress and the Supreme Court have been described. We also have indicated some of the problems that newspeople face in covering a flood tide of complex news expeditiously, accurately, and with a modicum of critical detachment and analysis.

Problems in communications policymaking remain. All three branches of government shape communications policy, but there is little coordination among them. Even within the executive and legislative branches, where most policy should be made, control is dispersed among so many different committees and agencies that drift rather than direction has resulted. Few major policy decisions have been made except in times of crisis, and even then the weaknesses of governmental structures have made it easy for industry spokesmen to dominate the decisionmaking process.

Governmental weakness in this area may be a blessing in disguise and in the spirit of the First Amendment. Because the Constitution commands that Congress shall make no law abridging the freedom of the press, it may be well to keep all communications policymaking to the barest minimum. As Chief Justice John Marshall warned the nation at the start of its history, the power to regulate is the power to destroy.[63] Policymaking and regulation overlap. A uniform, well-articulated communications policy, however beneficial it may seem to many people in public and private life, still puts the governmental imprint indelibly on the flow of information.

Notes

1. James F. Fixx, ed., *The Mass Media and Politics* (New York: New York Times Arno Press, 1971), p. ix.
2. See Table 3-2, pp. 82-83.
3. One of the best accounts of the effects of media coverage of the presidency is Newton Minow, John B. Martin, and Lee M. Mitchell, *Presidential Television* (New York: Basic Books, 1973). A more recent source is William C. Spragens, *The Presidency and the Mass Media in the Age of Television* (Lanham, Md.: University Press of America, 1978). Books about the relations of individual presidents with the press include Kenneth W. Thompson, ed., *Ten Presidents and the Press* (Lanham, Md.: University Press of America, 1983); William C. Spragens, *From Spokesman to Press Secretary: White House Media Operations* (Lanham, Md.: University Press of America, 1980); and James Deakin, *Straight Stuff: The Reporters, the White House and the Truth* (New York: William Morrow, 1984).
4. John Kenneth Galbraith has noted: "Nearly all of our political comment originates in Washington. Washington politicians, after talking things over with each other, relay misinformation to Washington journalists who, after further intramural discussion, print it where it is thoughtfully read by the same politicians. It is the only completely successful system for the recycling of garbage that has yet been devised." Quoted in William L. Rivers, *The Other Government: Power & The Washington Media* (New York: University Books, 1982), p. 19.
5. David Halberstam, *The Powers That Be* (New York: Alfred A. Knopf, 1979), p. 6.
6. Michael J. Robinson, "A Twentieth Century Medium in a Nineteenth-Century Legislature: The Effects of Television on the American Congress," in *Congress in Change: Evolution and Reform,* ed. Norman J. Ornstein (New York: Praeger, 1975), pp. 241, 256.
7. Halberstam, *The Powers That Be,* p. 49.
8. Ibid., p. 514.
9. Tony Schwartz, "Protest on CBS Show: 'Fairness' Dispute Renews," *New York Times,* April 23, 1982.
10. Halberstam, *The Powers That Be,* p. 161.
11. William E. Porter, *Assault on the Media: The Nixon Years* (Ann Arbor: University of Michigan Press, 1976), p. 61.
12. William J. Small, *To Kill a Messenger* (New York: Hastings House, 1970).
13. Michael Robinson, Maura Clancey, and Lisa Grand, "With Friends Like These . . . ," *Public Opinion* 6 (June/July 1983): 3.
14. Jules Witcover, *Marathon: The Pursuit of the Presidency, 1972-1976* (New York: Viking, 1977), p. 302.
15. *Kennedy and the Press: The News Conferences* (New York: Thomas Y. Crowell, 1965), p. 239.
16. *Collected Speeches of Spiro Agnew* (New York: Audubon Books, 1971), p. 89.
17. Porter, *Assault on the Media,* p. 47.

18. Sally Bedell, "Networks Explain Shift in Coverage of President," *New York Times*, December 15, 1982.
19. Small, *To Kill a Messenger*, p. 29.
20. Ibid., p. 102.
21. Michael Baruch Grossman and Martha Joynt Kumar, "The White House and the News Media: The Phases of Their Relationship," *Political Science Quarterly* 94 (Spring 1979): 37-53.
22. Jeb Stuart Magruder, *An American Life* (New York: Atheneum, 1974), p. 101.
23. William J. Small, *Political Power and the Press* (New York: W. W. Norton, 1972), p. 162.
24. F. Christopher Arterton, *Media Politics: The News Strategies of Presidential Campaigns* (Lexington, Mass.: D. C. Heath, 1984), p. 181.
25. John Herbers, *No Thank You, Mr. President* (New York: W. W. Norton, 1976).
26. For a thorough analysis of press conferences, see Jarol B. Manheim, "The Honeymoon's Over: The News Conference and the Development of Presidential Style," *Journal of Politics* 41 (February 1979): 55-74 and Frank Cormier, James Deakin, and Helen Thomas, *The White House Press on the Presidency: News Management and Co-Option* (Lanham, Md.: University Press of America, 1983).
27. Small, *Political Power and the Press*, p. 163.
28. Steven R. Weisman, "Reagan, Annoyed by News Leaks, Tells Staff to Limit Press Relations," *New York Times*, January 11, 1983.
29. Robert O. Blanchard, ed., *Congress and the News Media* (New York: Hastings House, 1974), p. 105.
30. Stephen Hess, *The Washington Reporters* (Washington, D.C.: The Brookings Institution, 1981), p. 98. The figures are based on 921 newspaper and 87 television stories.
31. Robinson, Clancey, and Grand, "With Friends Like These."
32. Hess, *The Washington Reporters*, p. 99.
33. Alan P. Balutis, "Congress, the President and the Press," *Journalism Quarterly* 53 (Fall 1976): 509-515.
34. For a more detailed description of bureaucracy coverage, see Rivers, *The Other Government*, pp. 50-68.
35. Hess, *The Washington Reporters*, pp. 104-105, and Michael J. Robinson and Kevin R. Appel, "Network News Coverage of Congress," *Political Science Quarterly* 94 (Fall 1979): 410-411.
36. Quoted in Stephen Frantzich, "Communication and Congress," in *The Communications Revolution in Politics*, ed. Gerald Benjamin (New York: The Academy of Political Science, 1982), p. 98.
37. Ibid., p. 99.
38. Ibid., p. 100.
39. Effects reported by California Representative Lionel Van Deerlin's office to a panel on the "Politics of Broadcasting," International Communications Association, Philadelphia, 1979.
40. Warren Weaver, Jr., *Both Your Houses* (New York: Praeger, 1972), p. 12.
41. Hess, *The Washington Reporters*, p. 109.
42. Blanchard, *Congress and the News Media*, p. 240. For a detailed content analysis of television coverage of Congress, see Robinson and Appel, "Network News Coverage of Congress," pp. 407-418.
43. Blanchard, *Congress and the News Media*, pp. 169-239.
44. Arthur Miller, Edie Goldenberg, and Lutz Erbring, "Type-Set Politics: Impact of Newspapers on Public Confidence," *American Political Science Review* 73 (March 1979): 70.

45. Daniel D. Polsby and Kim Degnan, "Institutions for Communications Policymaking: A Review," in *Communications for Tomorrow: Policy Perspectives for the 1980s*, ed. Glen O. Robinson (New York: Praeger, 1978), pp. 501-514. See also Erwin G. Krasnow, Lawrence D. Longley, and Herbert A. Terry, *The Politics of Broadcast Regulation*, 3d ed. (New York: St. Martins, 1982), pp. 87-132.
46. Krasnow, Longley, and Terry, *The Politics of Broadcast Regulation*, p. 99.
47. Ernest Gellhorn, "The Role of Congress," in *Communications for Tomorrow*, ed. Robinson, pp. 445-457.
48. For a full account of congressional investigations of television violence, see Willard D. Rowland, Jr., *Policy Uses of Communication Research* (Beverly Hills, Calif.: Sage, 1983).
49. Ben H. Bagdikian, "Congress and the Media: Partners in Propaganda," *Columbia Journalism Review* 12 (January-February 1974).
50. Leslie D. Polk, John Eddy, and Ann Andre, "Use of Congressional Publicity in Wisconsin District," *Journalism Quarterly* 52 (Autumn 1975): 543-546.
51. Michael J. Robinson, "Three Faces of Congressional Media," in *The New Congress*, ed. Thomas E. Mann and Norman J. Ornstein (Washington, D.C.: American Enterprise Institute for Public Policy Research, 1981), pp. 55-96.
52. Robinson and Appel, "Network News Coverage," p. 412. See also David L. Paletz and Robert M. Entman, *Media Power Politics* (New York: The Free Press, 1981), pp. 79-98.
53. 347 U.S. 483 (1954); 369 U.S. 186 (1962).
54. *Engel v. Vitale*, 370 U.S. 421 (1962).
55. Chester A. Newland, "Press Coverage of the United States Supreme Court," *Western Political Quarterly* 17 (1964): 15-36.
56. David Ericson, "Newspaper Coverage of the Supreme Court: A Case Study," *Journalism Quarterly* 54 (Autumn 1977): 605-607. See also Michael E. Solimine "Newsmagazine Coverage of the Supreme Court," *Journalism Quarterly* 57 (Winter 1980): 661-664.
57. David L. Grey, *The Supreme Court and the News Media* (Evanston, Ill.: Northwestern University Press, 1968).
58. Paletz and Entman, *Media Power Politics*, pp. 106-109.
59. Robert E. Drechsel, *News Making in the Trial Courts* (New York: Longman, 1983), pp. 19-22.
60. A detailed account of coverage of crime and justice system news is presented in Doris A. Graber, *Crime News and the Public* (New York: Praeger, 1980).
61. Krasnow, Longley, and Terry, *The Politics of Broadcast Regulation*, pp. 65-66.
62. Polsby and Degnan, "Institutions for Communications Policymaking," p. 513.
63. *McCulloch v. Maryland*, 4 Wheaton 316 (1819).

Readings

Blanchard, Robert O., ed. *Congress and the News Media*. New York: Hastings House, 1974.

Drechsel, Robert E. *News Making in the Trial Courts*. New York: Longman, 1983.

Graber, Doris A. *Crime News and The Public*. New York: Praeger, 1980.

Grossman, Michael Baruch, and Martha Joynt Kumar. *Portraying the President: The White House and the News Media*. Baltimore: The Johns Hopkins University Press, 1981.

Hess, Stephen. *The Washington Reporters*. Washington, D.C., 1981.

Paletz, David L., and Robert M. Entman. *Media Power Politics*. New York: The Free Press, 1981.

Rivers, William L. *The Other Government: Power & the Washington Media*. New York: Universe Books, 1982.

Rubin, Richard. *Press, Party, and Presidency*. New York: W. W. Norton, 1981.

Spragens, William C. *From Spokesman to Press Secretary: White House Media Operations*. Lanham, Md.: University Press of America, 1980.

The Media as Policymakers   8

In his autobiography Lincoln Steffens, who has been called "America's greatest reporter," tells how a history professor introduced him to an audience as "the first of the muckrakers." Steffens corrected the professor. "I had to answer first that I was not the original muckraker; the prophets of the Old Testament were ahead of me, and—to make a big jump in time—so were the writers, editors, and reporters (including myself) of the 1890s who were finding fault with 'things as they are' in the pre-muckraking period." [1]

Steffens was right. Public exposés of evil and corruption in high places have been with us throughout recorded history. They rest on the assumption that exposure will shame the wrongdoers and lead to public condemnation of their deeds and possibly punishment. Ultimately, major reforms may ensue. [2] Exposés have always been and will continue to be an important feature of American social responsibility journalism. They are a major part of the "deliberate manipulation of the political process" mentioned in Chapter 1 as one of the chief functions performed by the media.

In this chapter the muckraking process will be examined to show how it really works, with particular attention to the role played by public opinion. Then we will look at agenda-building, another widely used strategy for manipulating politics. We will illustrate how it works in different situations, such as leadership crises, the development of science policy, and the support of interest group goals. Next, we will assess the political impact of nationally broadcast factual and fictional documentaries that deal with current political issues. Our study of manipulative journalism concludes with reflections on the responsibility of newspeople to refrain from questionable methods in their zeal to reform society.

Like other manifestations of the social responsibility ethic, manipulative journalism raises philosophical, ethical, and news policy questions. Do newspeople jeopardize important professional values when they help shape the events that they report? If newspeople fail to be objective, neutral reporters of the passing scene, do they sacrifice credibility? Where can media audiences turn for a reasonably unbiased view of the complexities of political life if

259

media sources, like government officials, are partisans? Claims by newspeople that their political activities reflect the wishes of their audiences are questionable as long as the selection and activities of journalists are not subject to public control.

Despite the questions it raises, the role of the journalist as political actor is currently popular. This is evidenced by the many instances of outright collaboration between official policymakers and media personnel. It is also shown by the widespread practice of "leaking," where dissatisfied insiders, rather than attempting reforms on their own, enlist media support to gain their ends. Moreover, citizens routinely contact the media with problems concerning public affairs. In fact, just as the media have taken over many functions formerly performed by political parties during elections, so they have assumed many of the ombudsman, reform and law enforcement functions traditionally performed by other institutions in society. Whether this is the cause or consequence of the weakening of these other institutions remains a hotly debated question.

Manipulative Journalism in Perspective

The extent of newspeople's efforts to participate in policymaking has fluctuated as philosophies of newsmaking have changed. The turmoil of the sixties, which raised the social consciousness of American youth, and the shift toward accepting a social responsibility ethic in journalism schools have once again raised manipulative journalism from a position of disdain to a position of high esteem. Approval is not unanimous, to be sure, but it is widespread, especially in elite media circles. Reporters and media institutions whose investigations have led to important social and political reforms frequently win prizes for high journalistic achievement. Given the prestige accorded to investigative journalists and the political successes attributed to them, it is no surprise that investigative units began to thrive in major print and electronic media institutions during the 1970s.

Independent investigative units that collaborate with media institutions have flourished as well. The nonprofit, foundation-subsidized Center for Investigative Reporting, set up in San Francisco in 1977, is an example. The center consists of free-lance reporters who collectively conduct investigations and who can be hired by various media to undertake projects that cannot be readily handled internally. The Community Information Project in Los Angeles and the Better Government Association in Chicago are other institutions that do similar investigative work.[3]

Collaboration between independent government watchdog bodies and media is mutually beneficial. It ensures that the investigations of interest to these institutions will be publicized, thereby increasing the chances for corrective action. Tapping into media resources also helps cover the costs of complex investigations that can run into hundreds of thousands of dollars apiece. This added financial support can be crucial. The media, in turn, gain collaborators who are skilled in investigating public issues and who often have excellent connections in government and in the community. The prestige and credibility of the organization may also enhance the credibility of a jointly issued report.

The substance and style of most investigative stories reflect three major objectives. The first is to produce exciting stories that will appeal to media audiences. Second, investigative reporters hope to gain plaudits from the journalism profession. Third, in addition to these routine journalistic goals, many reporters want to trigger political action or be part of it. Even when political consequences are not initially envisioned, most reporters feel highly gratified when their stories lead to actions that accord with their political and social preferences.

Sometimes the line between deliberate attempts to produce political changes and incidental sparking of reforms is too fine to distinguish. For example, when the media follow up on a report of a rash of deaths in nursing homes, and discover and describe deplorable conditions that led to these deaths, is this a case of muckraking designed to manipulate political events and bring about reform? Or does the idea that reform is needed arise naturally and purely incidentally from a routine news story? Was Lincoln Steffens telling the truth when he claimed: "I did not intend to be a muckraker; I did not know that I was one till President Roosevelt picked the name out of Bunyan's *Pilgrim's Progress* and pinned it on us." [4] Could Steffens specialize in writing sensational exposés of corruption in state and local government and in private business for the sheer joy of delving into the muck, with no thought given to the major reforms that followed in the wake of some of these stories?

From the standpoint of the political reformer it may not matter whether reform was intended or was an unintended byproduct of investigative reporting. But the distinction matters to newspeople because it raises controversial issues about the proper role of journalism in American society. It is therefore not surprising that journalists, even when they favor social responsibility journalism in the abstract, will rarely admit that their stories were designed to produce social and political reforms.

Muckraking Models

How does investigative journalism lead to political action? There are three ways. Journalists may write stories about public policies in hopes of engendering a massive public reaction that will lead to widespread demands for political remedies. Alternatively, journalists may write stories to arouse

Reprinted with special permission from King Features Syndicate.

political elites who are officeholders or who have influence with officeholders. These elites, eager to forestall public anger, then may attempt to resolve the problems, often even before the media report is actually published. Finally, action may be the result of direct collaboration between investigative journalists and public officeholders. They may coordinate news stories and supportive political activities to bring about desired reforms. We will trace the rate of success in each of these different types of situations.

The process can be pictured in the form of three models: the simple muckraking model, the leaping impact model, and the truncated muckraking model.[5] Social scientists Harvey Molotch, David Protess, and Margaret Gordon, and their coworkers who developed these models, tested them in investigative situations involving muckraking—sensational exposés of corruption usually involving high status individuals. But the models are equally illustrative for other types of manipulative journalism.

The *simple muckraking model* begins when journalists investigate a serious societal problem that could be ameliorated through political action. The investigation leads to published news that stirs the public. Aroused public opinion then mobilizes policymakers who act to solve the problem. Schematically, the process usually looks as pictured below, although the sequence of the elements in the model may vary:

Investigation—> Publication—> Public Opinion Arousal—> Elite Arousal—> Elite Action—> Correction

When some elements in the model are skipped entirely, the *leaping impact model* is at work. For instance, following investigation and publication of the story, elites may be aroused without prior public opinion pressure, or they may act even though their interest in the matter is not linked to the investigative stories. Publication of stories may lead to correction as a consequence of public opinion arousal, even without elite intervention.

In the *truncated muckraking model,* the simple muckraking sequence may be aborted at any point so that the investigation fails to lead ultimately to correction of the problem. This occurs frequently and can happen in several ways. The investigation may not lead to published stories because the evidence is insufficient or too hot to handle. Published stories may not stir public opinion. An aroused public may not move the elite. A stirred elite may, nonetheless, fail to act. Elite action, even if it is not purely symbolic, still may not lead to any substantial correction of the problem.

Several examples of muckraking will illustrate these models. Most of the examples come from intensive studies of muckraking conducted by groups of scholars in the Chicago area. The scholars had been alerted to forthcoming media exposés. This permitted them to interview approximately 400 citizens and 60 policymakers concerned with the issue under investigation, both before and after publication of the stories. In this way, the impact of the story could be assessed far more accurately than is usually possible when stories come as a surprise and permit only ex post facto measurement. Actual changes in public policy also were monitored for a period of several months following the exposés. The journalists' motives and methods in conducting the investigations were assessed as well.[6]

Simple Muckraking

A story about reform of a school for the mentally retarded in Staten Island, New York, illustrates simple muckraking: the media arouse the public which then demands and receives action. Geraldo Rivera, a well-known television commentator, was asked by a friend to visit the Willowbrook State School for the mentally retarded to observe shocking conditions in the facility that housed 5,000 children. Rivera did so, concurred that conditions were horrible, and prepared a seven-minute television report that was shown by a station near the school. Some 700 viewers called the station after the broadcast to express their concern. Parents, shocked by the report, later gathered at the school and solicited promises of help from local public officials. The Staten Island Chapter of the Society for the Prevention of Cruelty to Children began hearings and asked the state and national government to investigate.[7] But the flurry of activity was short-lived and largely unproductive. Only minor reforms in the school's handling of children resulted from these investigations.

Such modest outcomes are typical in situations that reflect the simple muckraking model. Researchers rarely find solid evidence that media-aroused public opinion is a force for major change. There are several reasons why political reform is seldom linked to public opinion arousal. First, it is difficult to spur average Americans to take action on public problems, even those directly affecting them. For example, extensive efforts to alert the public to the realities of energy shortages and to the need for conservation have largely proved futile.[8] Because most Americans' major interests lie outside of politics, they ignore or assign little importance to investigative news stories, or forget them quickly. Disinterest in politics is bolstered by the fact that many Americans are complacent about the political status quo. They either trust that politicians will cope satisfactorily with serious problems, or they are cynical about politicians' willingness to respond to needs and views expressed by various publics. Either view often suppresses the desire to think seriously about political issues and to become involved in political action.

On the other end of the interest spectrum, media investigative stories may be about an issue that is already a matter of high public concern. The investigative story then confirms that concern but does not raise it substantially to the point where it might prompt political action. For example, a five-part newspaper series in the *Chicago Sun-Times* in 1982 on "Rape: Every Woman's Nightmare" dealt with the incidence and consequences of rape in the Chicago area. The stories did little to change the views of general and elite media audiences. Interviews conducted prior to the series had shown that the public was already greatly concerned about the problem; there was little room for escalation of concern and increased motivation to fight the crime. But an interesting, unexpected byproduct of the rape stories was that they heightened the sensitivity of the newspaper staff to the problem. Following the series, *Sun-Times* stories on rape more than doubled in number, and coverage became more insightful.[9]

Although it is difficult for the media to arouse public opinion, some investigative stories do. The Willowbrook School case is an example. The elements that brought about its success included an emotional issue—the treatment of disabled children—in the audience's locality; a flamboyant, well-known reporter; and a local group of citizens directly and profoundly affected by the alleged misbehavior of public officials. When such a story captures people's interest, and they have little prior knowledge about the situation, they may learn much and become highly concerned. As we have noted, however, corrective action remains unlikely.[10]

Leaping Impact Muckraking

The leaping impact model is exemplified by a media exposé called "Arson for Profit" that was aired by ABC's "20/20" program in 1979. That investigation indicated that extensive fire damage in Chicago's Uptown neighborhood resulted from arson planned by a group of real estate owners. The group would buy dilapidated buildings, insure them heavily, and then burn them down to collect the insurance. Following the exposé, government elites voiced concern but failed to act. Yet corrections occurred anyhow. The arson-for-profit perpetrators obviously had taken heed of the media's message. In the month following the broadcast, fires declined by 27 percent in the area where arson for profit had flourished. It was the first decline in five years. Insurance payments for arson also dropped by more than 20 percent in the year following the arson stories. This occurred at a time when no other metropolitan area showed comparable drops. The Illinois legislature failed to act until all of these corrections were already under way. Then it instituted minor policy reforms. There were no criminal indictments of the parties implicated in the fraud. This story exemplifies the leaping impact model because the leap was from publication directly to correction; elite arousal and, by and large, elite action and public opinion pressures were nonexistent.

The most common "leaping impact" situation takes place when newspeople and public officials openly collaborate. This type of activity has been called "coalition journalism." It may be initiated either by media or government personnel, or it may arise fortuitously without initial formal contacts between media personnel and policy actors. Newspeople are very eager to involve government officials in investigative stories because it lends credibility and significance to their stories and increases the chances of substantial policy consequences. Although it may jeopardize the media's zealous pursuit of the watchdog role, coalition journalism gets results.

A good example of coalition journalism concerns the events following an NBC "Newsmagazine" story, "The Home Health Hustle," broadcast May 7, 1981, which exposed fraud and abuse in home health-care programs. Public opinion polls showed that the broadcast aroused the concerns of many viewers who previously were unaware of problems with these programs. But public opinion apparently was not instrumental in the introduction of appropriate reform legislation in Congress. In the fashion of leaping impact models, the legislative results seemed to flow directly from collaboration between investigative reporters and members of the U.S. Senate that preceded airing of the story by several months.

Journalists had met with officials of the Senate's Permanent Subcommittee on Investigations to plan a series of hearings on home health-care fraud and to coordinate their broadcasts with the Senate's activities. The hearings were then announced during the broadcast. Subsequently, senators credited media personnel with major contributions to the investigation of home health-care fraud. However, it is uncertain to what degree the knowledge of the forthcoming telecast and its projected impact on public opinion influenced the senators to collaborate with the media. The combined investigative activities of the media and the Senate ultimately led to a number of proposals for corrective legislation.[11]

Similarly, when the rape series appeared in the *Chicago Sun-Times,* newspeople had already alerted policymakers. This permitted the policymakers to time announcements of previously planned measures, such as creation of a rape hotline, to coincide with the investigative series. When a story about unnecessary and illegal abortions in state clinics was about to break in Illinois, the governor associated himself with the media investigators immediately prior to publication. This made it possible to make reform proposals part of the original story. It also enhanced the governor's image as an effective leader.

Truncated Muckraking

The truncated muckraking model is well illustrated by the Mirage investigation, conducted in 1977 by the *Chicago Sun-Times* and CBS's "Sixty Minutes" program with the help of Chicago's civic watchdog Better Government Association. Hoping to demonstrate extensive graft in the city's regulatory agencies, the partners in the investigation opened a bar in Chicago, appropriately named the *Mirage*. The bar was wired to record transactions that might take place between its personnel and city officials. In a brief period of time, ample evidence of bribery and fraud was accumulated.[12] After the story about the illegal transactions was published, public opinion polls recorded that large numbers of citizens were outraged. Nonetheless, no serious corrective action was taken to prevent similar graft in the future. Schematically, the model ended with the arousal of public opinion, skipping elite arousal and action, and final corrective activities.

The Role of Public Opinion

The major role attributed to public opinion in producing political action is greatly exaggerated, as our examples of muckraking suggest. More often than not, the media fail to arouse the public, even when investigative stories are written to produce public excitement. When stories do agitate the public, little happens as a rule. Politicians and journalists have learned that public concern, like a straw fire, flares brightly but dies quickly. Usually it is ignored, unless it can be used to support other pressures for reform. Corrective action is more likely to come through the concerns of publicity-shy wrongdoers or through media impact on, or collaboration with, political elites.

Thus, the role of the media in prompting government officials to take corrective action does not differ substantially from the role played by other powerful pressure groups that manage to get consideration for their concerns. The media's great influence springs from their control over publicity, often an essential ingredient in putting issues on the civic agenda. Other interest groups who need this ingredient may fail when they cannot get it.

It is clear that the media's role in muckraking is generally not well understood. The idea persists that media influence works via the public opinion process, with thoughtful publics determining which of the issues brought to their attention deserve action by public officials. If public opinion is, in fact, largely irrelevant, this raises questions about the role of the media as a handmaiden to the democratic process. Do the media use the façade of public opinion support to enhance their already powerful position as a public interest pressure group?

Beyond Muckraking:
Power Plays and Surrenders

Direct media intervention in the governmental process may take a number of forms other than muckraking. Three types of situations are usually involved: media power plays, media acting as surrogates for public officials, and media acting as mouthpieces for government officials or interest groups.

Least common are media *power plays* in which newspeople bully government officials into action by threatening to publicize stories that officials would prefer to conceal. The *Washington Post's* use of such a threat to bring racial integration to the capital's swimming pools is a case in point *(see Chapter 7)*. In addition to overt threats, which are rare, there are numerous instances of implied or anticipated threats with major political consequences. Politicians may act, or refrain from action that might otherwise take place, because they know that newspeople have damaging information that may surface if they are highly displeased with particular officials.

Even less frequently, news personnel may act as *surrogates* for public officials by becoming active participants in an evolving situation, such as a prison riot or a diplomatic impasse. The solution, developed with the assistance of news personnel or at their initiative, may then significantly shape subsequent government action. Walter Cronkite's impact on relations between Egypt and Israel, discussed in Chapter 10, is a famous example of diplomacy conducted by journalists.

To prevent future tragedies and solve existing cases, journalists have also become involved in broadcasts about kidnapped children and in "crime stopper" programs, which feature reenactments or recountings of unsolved crimes. The programs use media stories, coupled with financial rewards, to elicit information from citizens that may help in solving the crime. They are featured in nearly 500 communities in the United States and Canada and have helped to clear up thousands of felonies.[13]

A far more common form of interaction occurs when the media become a *mouthpiece* for government officials or interest groups, either because of belief in their causes or in return for attractive stories and other favors. This type of interaction often involves leaks. Government officials who are disgruntled with current policies or practices for personal, professional, or political reasons may leak information to sympathetic journalists in hopes of enlisting their support. Journalists may cooperate and publish the allegations, or they may investigate the situation, often with the cooperation of the individuals who leaked the information. As we saw in Chapter 7, the political impact of leaks may be profound.

When newspeople and officials collaborate, the boundary between ordinary reporting and manipulative journalism often becomes blurred. It is difficult to tell when one merges into the other because a correct diagnosis involves establishing motivations. In many instances the available evidence strongly suggests that newspeople acted as political partisans who used their powers of publicity to foster preferred causes and harm others. In other cases the main objective in publicizing leaked information is mercenary. Newspeople put their services at the command of anyone who promises to be a fertile source for future news or who can provide an attractive story, no matter what its merits. The television networks are particularly vulnerable to the enticement of exciting scoops during "sweeps"—the periods when audience ratings are measured.

That the media are used by public officials and political interest groups as a tool to attain political objectives is often quite obvious. The NBC television interview of an American hostage in Iran in the spring of 1979 is a good example. NBC broadcast an interview with Cpl. William Gallegos who had then been held hostage in the U.S. Embassy in Teheran for 36 days. CBS and ABC refused to interview Gallegos because access to him was subject to restrictions imposed by his Iranian captors. NBC agreed to the conditions, laying itself open to the charge of acting as a propaganda conduit for the Iranian militants who had seized the embassy. Most observers agreed that the controlled interviews were a ploy by the Iranians to gain access to American public opinion via the American media. When the issue was raised in Congress, Rep. Robert Bauman of Maryland angrily suggested that NBC should be given "the Benedict Arnold award for broadcasting." NBC defended its broadcast, saying that it had produced greater understanding of the crisis. But the impression lingered that it had allowed itself to be used for the enemy's purposes and that this was an improper and disgraceful position for a responsible media institution.

Agenda-building

In many instances the media manipulate the political scene by creating a climate for political action. They thus become a major contributor to agenda-building, the process whereby news stories influence how people perceive issues and evaluate the appropriateness of proposed policies. Agenda-building goes beyond agenda-setting. The media set the public agenda when they are successful in riveting attention on a problem. They build the public agenda when they supply the context that determines how people will think about the issue and evaluate its merits.

When elites agree on matters of public policy, newspeople rarely stir up controversy. The absence of reported conflict then leads to a general impression that elites as well as the public agree about the unchallenged policies.[14] But when an issue becomes a matter of controversy among political elites, the media zero in on it. They "supply the context that, by making the problem politically relevant, gives people reasons for taking sides and converts the problem into a serious political issue. In this sense the public agenda is not so much set by the media as built up through a cycle of media activity that transforms an elite issue into a public controversy." [15] The role of the media in policymaking thus is symbiotic. They are an essential part of the operation, but ultimate success hinges on major roles played by other political actors as well.

Molotch, Protess, and Gordon make this clear in the conclusion of their study of the role of investigative journalism in the Watergate affair. The resolution of the issue was not, as popularly believed, a triumph for unaided media power:

> We therefore disagree with those who would assign "credit" for the Nixon exposures to the media just as we would disagree with those who would assign it to the Congress or the U.S. system of checks and balances. Nor should credit go, in some acontextual, additive sense, to both of these sectors. Instead, the Watergate "correction" was the result of the ways in which news of the Nixon scandals fit the goals and strategic needs of important media and policy actors. All of these actors, each with some degree of "relative autonomy" . . . , are part of an evolving "ecology of games," part of a "dance" . . . in which actors have, by virtue of their differential skills and status positions, varying access to participate. Because they so continuously anticipate each other's moves, their activities are, *as a matter of course,* mutually constituted.[16]

Political Scandal

Sociologists Kurt and Gladys Lang reached similar conclusions. Their study of the role of the media in Watergate traces the precise part played by the media in this "ecology of games" in which the disparate interests of various political actors are blended to create and develop political scenarios. The Langs outlined the steps through which political agendas are usually constructed.[17] A look at the steps makes it clear that there is ample opportunity and often strong temptation for newspeople to guide agenda-building deliberately.

Agenda-building begins when newspeople decide to publish a particular story. In most instances this is a matter of free choice since few stories are so blatantly significant that omission is unthinkable. The second decision concerns the degree of attention to be given to the story. This is the point where ordinary agenda-setting activities can most readily turn into deliberate agenda-building. If newspeople determine that a story should become prominent, they must feature it conspicuously and often enough to arouse the attention of the elite media, including national television, and the attention of political elites. The Watergate story, for instance, received extensive and sustained publicity in the *Washington Post* before it finally "caught on" and gained nationwide publicity.

Capturing national attention usually requires several other media-controlled steps. Issues must be put into a context that arouses the concern of media audiences. For instance, as long as the media put Watergate into the context of the 1972 presidential election, the story was discounted by media audiences as just another partisan squabble. Once the media were able to depict it as an issue of pervasive corruption and dishonesty at the highest levels of government, it generated widespread concern. Without this climate of public concern, severe penalties for the Watergate offenders, including the president, would never have been considered as an acceptable policy option. In the course of putting issues into a conceptual framework, language choice becomes an important tool. When newspeople switched from writing and talking about the Watergate "caper" or the "bugging incident" and began to discuss the Watergate "scandal" and "tragedy," what had been perceived as a fairly trivial incident became transformed into a very serious matter.

In their study of how political agendas are built, the Langs emphasize the importance of the particular sources through which stories are told. The selection of sources involves more than the skewing that inevitably takes place when newspeople tap one human mind, rather than another, for information and interpretation. In the case of major public policy issues, the spokespeople who are selected become symbols that indicate to media audiences whether a particular position is or is not meritorious. When the media featured prominent Republicans and members of the judiciary acknowledging the gravity of the issues at stake and the need for an investigation, Watergate became a major political crisis justifying drastic action.[18]

Scientific and Technological Innovations

Media agenda-building is not limited to political scandals. There are many other types of issues in which the media play similar roles. We will discuss two areas in which agenda-building is of vast importance for American political life: science policy and social movements.

The merits of various types of scientific endeavors are matters of deep political concern in twentieth-century America. Government support and regulation of science operations have become highly controversial public policy issues.[19] The fate of nuclear energy in the United States provides a particularly interesting example because major public opinion shifts have been recorded and can be compared with the thrust of media stories. Public opinion regarding the safety and desirability of nuclear energy dropped sharply in the seventies, before as well as after the Three Mile Island nuclear accident in 1979. While only 20 percent of Americans were opposed to locating a nuclear plant in their community in 1956, 56 percent were opposed in 1979. Since then, opposition has risen. Sentiment for building more nuclear energy plants has dropped precipitously, and nuclear energy now is rated as the least preferred energy source.

Social scientists attributed this loss of public support to perceptions among the general public, as well as portions of the scientific community, that scientists involved with nuclear power had lost faith in it. No one seemed to know for sure how this perception started and whether the science community was indeed disillusioned with nuclear power as an energy source.[20] Political scientists Stanley Rothman and S. Robert Lichter decided to investigate. They interviewed scientists who were selected to represent the science community in general as well as scientists whose work related closely to the issues posed by nuclear energy. The latter group was subdivided into scientists whose work touched on the nuclear energy field in a broad sense, such as atmospheric chemistry, solar energy, conservation, and ecology, and nuclear energy experts involved more directly with nuclear energy science through expertise in radiation genetics, radiation health, nuclear engineering, and reactor physics. A total of 1,092 scientists were interviewed. Of these, 279 worked in nuclear energy related fields while 72 were nuclear specialists.

A large array of questions was then used to identify scientists who wished to proceed with nuclear development and those who wished to halt it. All of the nuclear experts (79) wanted to proceed with nuclear development; 92 percent urged rapid rather than slow progress. Ninety-five percent of the experts from related fields (279) also urged continuance of development; 70 percent favored rapid progress. In the remainder of the sample (734), with no ties to the nuclear industry, only 10 percent urged that development should be halted. Ninety percent favored proceeding with nuclear development, albeit at a somewhat slower pace. Clearly, the widespread perceptions of science community opposition to developing nuclear energy were wrong.

A probe of the reasons for these faulty perceptions pointed to mass media stories. When pro- and antinuclear statements were counted in newspapers and television, the balance was on the negative side. A study by the Battelle Human Affairs Research Center showed that a slight predominance of positive statements in the early 1970s had shifted to a negative predominance thereafter. By 1976, negative articles outnumbered positive ones by a two-to-one margin.

The attitudes of journalists toward the issue of nuclear energy development matched the tone of their stories. The vast majority of science writers, especially those working for elite media and television, were hostile to the use of nuclear energy. On a scale ranking support of nuclear energy development from -9 (strong opposition) to $+9$ (strong support), nuclear experts ranked at $+7.9$ and scientists in related fields at $+5.1$. By contrast, science journalists at the *New York Times, Washington Post,* and the television networks ranked at $+0.5$. Rothman's and Lichter's figures for television reporters as a group were in minus territory, at -1.9. Public television journalists were most strongly opposed with an average score of -3.3.

A major factor in the predominantly unfavorable coverage was the choice of sources.[21] The small corps of reporters who specialize in science writing drew much of their information from enemies of nuclear development. For instance, television broadcasts between 1968 and 1979 quoted the Union of Concerned Scientists more than any other source. The union, an organization of antinuclear scientists, represents only a tiny fraction of the scientific community. Ralph Nader was the most widely quoted individual "nuclear expert" during the period in question. In the month following the Three Mile Island accident, pronuclear views were never featured prominently.

Although the antinuclear views of newspeople may have been the main reason for searching out and featuring compatible views expressed by scientists, other factors, many of them typical in news production, also played a part. Among them, the economies of news supply are very important. Journalists are more likely to select stories that are readily available to them with comparatively little effort. In the 1970s, antinuclear information was more readily available in easy-to-use formats. A look at the publication patterns of nuclear scientists showed that the vast majority did not publish their work in general circulation journals. Most felt that dissemination of their views in popular outlets in laymen's terms was inappropriate until these views had stood the test of scientific scrutiny through publication in professional journals. The comparatively small number of scientists who frequently published their views in the popular literature were less inclined to believe that initial publication should be in scientific journals. They were also less disposed to limit their published remarks to the areas of their specific training and research. As a group, those scientists were far more inclined to oppose nuclear energy development.

When journalists who oppose nuclear development find that a preponderance of stories published in general circulation sources support the views that they prefer, it is not surprising that they draw heavily on these sources. This allows them to develop an exciting theme—the danger of nuclear power and the lack of adequate safety concerns of a major industry—and support it with views that can be designated as "expert." Relying on science articles in general circulation journals is far easier than delving into arcane scientific journals and making contact with scientific leaders who may be reluctant to supply the absolute statements of doom or salvation that make exciting headlines. In the words of David Paletz and Robert Entman, "When values are shared by source and press and probably readers too, there is no felt need on the part of reporters to seek countervailing information elsewhere." [22]

As yet no one has definitely proven that skewed selection of sources for nuclear energy stories accounts for the public's current hostility to nuclear energy. However, studies of public opinion polls on science issues show that extensive media coverage of scientific controversies is followed by increased public opposition to the highlighted technology, even when the coverage is not particularly hostile. When media coverage of the controversy diminishes, opposition diminishes as well. The public, it seems, opts against any technology when doubts are raised about its safety. It is especially sensitive to heavily negative safety reports. Political elites, in turn, are loathe to challenge scientific findings that the media have labeled as "expert" opinion, and they are loathe to take actions that may engender widespread fears among the citizenry. [23]

Firm proof is also lacking that the current decline of the nuclear energy industry can be attributed in large part to this hostile opinion climate. But even without such proof, the evidence strongly suggests that the predominantly negative images of the nuclear industry featured in numerous media stories played a major part in undermining the growth of the industry. The situation has been similar in other fields of science, including bio-medical research. [24] Only a few scientists, distinguished by their controversial positions on public issues, are steady sources for news about new drugs, new medical procedures, and various aspects of genetic engineering. The rest of the science community has remained largely excluded. Similarly, only a few potentially risky technologies have been scrutinized by science reporters, with choices determined haphazardly or mirroring the interests of selected pressure groups. Many other science topics have been ignored and thereby kept off the public agenda, even though they involve significant aspects of public health and safety.

Social Movements and Interest Groups

Just as the media regularly boost selected public policy issues, so they can and do promote selected groups that are working for specific public policy causes. Whenever a group needs wide publicity to reach its goals, a decision by media personnel to grant or withhold publicity becomes crucial for the group's success. Many decisions about granting publicity are made without explicit political motivations to boost a movement or suppress it. But in some instances the sympathies of newspeople for particular causes guide their choices of news content in hopes of influencing the course of politics. This is what happened with Students for a Democratic Society (SDS), one of the left-wing movements of the 1960s. The story is particularly interesting because it demonstrates that attention from sympathetic newspeople may boomerang and produce unintended, highly destructive consequences.

SDS, part of what came to be known as the "New Left," had been active on American university campuses since 1960. But the movement received little media attention until *New York Times* reporter Fred Powledge wrote a long supportive story that appeared in the *Times* on March 15, 1965.[25] Coverage by a national news medium amounted to symbolic recognition that student radicalism had become an important political issue. When SDS sponsored an anti-Vietnam War protest march on Washington in the spring of 1965, the event received nationwide coverage. Major articles on the New Left appeared in national news magazines and in large circulation weeklies such as the *Saturday Evening Post* and the *New York Times Magazine.*

Although many newspeople sympathized with the gamut of left-liberal reforms advocated by SDS and knew that sensational publicity might be harmful, they decided, in line with media prescriptions for exciting stories, to focus on the movement's most extreme leaders and goals. News stories pictured SDS as a single-issue extremist group rather than as a group concerned with a broad array of issues ranging from civil rights to socialism and anti-imperialism.

This distorted image, besides misleading media audiences, also affected the self-perceptions of SDS members. Individuals singled out by the media as spokespersons for the organization became celebrities. With this new-found status, many no longer felt accountable to their rank and file. To maintain the flow of publicity that they deemed essential for their survival, SDS members stressed those elements in the organization that conformed to the media image. In turn, this brought in new members whose outlook was in tune with the media image and who expected the organization to perform as pictured. These new Leninist and Maoist elements began to take over the leadership of the organization, turning it away from its long-range reformist goals to radical, immediate action policies focusing primarily on opposition to the war in Vietnam.

Sociologist Todd Gitlin contends that the media's decision in 1965 to give wide publicity to SDS ultimately destroyed the movement and with it much of the power of the New Left. In his colorful metaphor, the media spotlight became a magnifying glass that burned everybody to a crisp. Media efforts to bestow legitimacy on the movement totally failed. But, as is true in other instances of agenda-building, political forces besides the media contributed to the turn of events. Radicalization of the SDS movement was also enhanced by the Johnson administration's escalation of the Vietnam War and by the growing alienation from mainstream society that it produced among many Americans.[26]

Many critics of American media contend that the fate of SDS is typical for groups that pose major challenges to the established order. Paletz and Entman argue:

Organizations that accept establishment rules, and pursue incremental goals discretely, benefit from journalists' needs and practices. Groups whose methods violate convention, whose objectives require a significant alteration of the structure of power, usually find their radical activities distorted or condemned, their radical analyses and proposals ignored or scorned. Any publicity they receive tends to isolate them from the mass of citizens, encouraging them to moderate their ways until they either fade from sight or shade into the establishment.[27]

Of course, many movements, interest groups, and lobbies have been helped by media coverage, as long as they did not deviate too far from mainstream values. The civil rights movement is a memorable case. Sympathetic nationwide media coverage of freedom marches and of the battles fought for civil rights in Little Rock, Arkansas; Selma, Alabama; and Oxford, Mississippi, helped ready lawmakers and the nation for passage of the Civil Rights Act in 1964. Support for consumer organizations and environmentalist groups constitutes another success story. Media publicity has legitimized these organizations in the eyes of the public and in the eyes of political elites.[28] Their activities now are covered regularly and favorably. Ralph Nader, the most prominent consumer advocate, has become a media celebrity and a respected, much-consulted guru. The concerns of consumer interest groups and of general public interest lobbies such as Common Cause have become the subject of legislation, implemented through newly created public agencies.

Publicity is likely to benefit high status groups most. Newspeople are apt to ignore the claims of low status organizations whose goals encompass routine human concerns.[29] Political scientist Edie Goldenberg studied the attempts of four citizen groups in Massachusetts to attract newspaper coverage to the problems of welfare mothers, senior citizens, low-income tenants, and people deprived of fair treatment by the courts. Finding that these groups had little success, she concluded: "There is bias in the system that consistently favors some and neglects others." The favored groups are "haves," those who possess the resources to make and maintain contact with the press and to arrange their operations so that they complement the needs of the press. The unfavored ones are those "most in need of press attention in order to be heard forcefully in the political arena" yet "least able to command attention and . . . least able to use effectively what few resources they do control in seeking and gaining press access." Goldenberg warns: "If intensely felt interests go unarticulated and therefore are unnoticed and unaffected by policy makers, one important aspect of rule of, for, and by the people is weakened."[30] In the eyes of social critics such as Goldenberg, a free press must be responsive to the needs of all segments of society.

Documentaries and Docudramas

To influence public policy, newspeople are not limited to straight news and feature stories. Fictional productions, such as docudramas shown to millions of viewers on prime time national television, are used as well. The political goals of many documentaries and docudramas are obvious. As Oscar Gandy has pointed out: "Too frequently to be mere coincidence, serial dramas, or the made-for-television movies we describe as docudrama, have been aired simultaneously with the discussion of related issues in Congress." [31] An example of a widely publicized docudrama that coincided with related political events was "The Day After," a two-hour ABC dramatization of a nuclear attack on Kansas City and its aftermath. It was broadcast on Sunday, November 20, 1983, following an extensive prebroadcast advertising campaign that included an eight-page viewer's guide. The drama was replete with scenes of cremated bodies, faces rotting from radiation sickness, and smoldering rubble.

At the time of broadcast, nuclear weapons policy was in the limelight because the Reagan administration was attempting to gain support in Europe and the United States for deploying American missiles in European NATO countries. Antinuclear groups in Europe and the United States were working feverishly to stop the deployment. The docudrama was aired a few days before the decision to place the missiles was to be approved by the West German legislature.

Supporters of missile deployment feared that the program would lead to massive public demonstrations designed to force a change in nuclear deployment policies. When the Reagan administration was invited to send a representative to participate in a postbroadcast discussion of the lessons of the docudrama, it symbolized its profound concern by sending Secretary of State George P. Shultz. Throughout the furor raised by the broadcast, ABC denied that the timing had been politically motivated. The November date was chosen, it claimed, to raise ABC's ratings during a "sweeps" month, when ratings would be taken that would then be reflected in advertising prices.

What, then, was the political impact of "The Day After," which was seen in millions of homes and in many schools, churches, and town halls that had arranged for group watching and subsequent group discussion? (The *New York Times* reported that more than 100 million people had watched.)[32] It appears that the broadcast boosted the activities of antinuclear groups and engendered public controversy about the role that "The Day After" and the attendant publicity and discussion might play in generating a defeatist attitude among Americans. But public opinion polls after the broadcast did not show massive shifts of public attitudes about nuclear missile policies. In Europe, where immediate drastic political consequences had been feared, the missile deployment went off without major obstacles.

A number of analysts ascribed the lack of impact to flaws in the docudrama, which left the rationale for the nuclear attack uncertain. Others felt that the public had gained knowledge and awareness from the film, but had learned to remove itself psychologically from fictional disasters and therefore failed to empathize fully with the stricken residents of Kansas City.

Even though the apparent consequences of "The Day After" were less than expected, concern—or hopes—remain high that such broadcasts may have major political consequences in the long or short run.[33] This potential obligates a responsible press to take greater pains to present all sides of an issue and be more accurate in its depiction, even in a fiction program. Many felt the drama understated the likely consequences of atomic attack, which are apt to be far more serious than those shown in the film. Moreover, the appropriate contextual background was lacking. Viewers were not told that the option of a U.S. nuclear freeze is severely constricted by knowledge that it may not be reciprocated by other world powers with nuclear arsenals.

Methods: Fair and Foul

The fairness and accuracy of news presentations and the appropriateness of news gathering techniques become important issues when one considers the media as potential actors in the political process. In recent years the media have frequently been accused of improper methods. Law suits filed against them have multiplied.

Confirming Prejudgments

A famous, $120-million libel suit, discussed earlier in Chapter 4, illustrates concerns about the legitimacy of media tactics. The suit was brought by Gen. William C. Westmoreland against CBS for statements made about him in a 90-minute documentary on the Vietnam War called "The Uncounted Enemy: A Vietnam Deception." The principal message of the documentary was that the general, while he was the commander of American forces in Vietnam, had deliberately manipulated information about the strength of enemy troops during the war. He had allegedly done so prior to the 1968 Tet offensive to show the president and Congress that American troops under his command were winning the war.

This case is ideal for examining questionable media practices because the results of an internal CBS review of production methods were made public through a court order. The evidence obtained through the network's own investigation indicated that the producers of the documentary believed in Westmoreland's guilt from the very start and organized the production to support their preformed conclusions. According to the internal report, CBS made 11 major procedural errors while putting together the documentary. These included failure to adequately support the charge that a conspiracy was involved, choosing to interview mostly witnesses who supported the program's overall conclusions, reshooting unsatisfactory testimony after allowing a witness to hear what others had said, and "coddling sympathetic witnesses." [34]

The report, which was prepared by senior CBS producer Burton Benjamin prior to the Westmoreland suit, contained portions of unedited transcripts of interviews in which witnesses were apparently coached by interviewers. At times, interviewers asked witnesses loaded questions such as whether they agreed that there had been "a full-fledged conspiracy to fake intelligence reporting." If witnesses failed to agree, their remarks were omitted from the final broadcast. Materials that might have undermined the documentary's principal conclusions about General Westmoreland's activities ended up on the cutting room floor.

In the final documentary, eight of the ten persons whose testimony was featured sided against Westmoreland. One of the two who did not, Lt. Gen. Daniel Graham, was given a mere 21 seconds of air time, even though he had been the chief of the army's current intelligence and estimates division in Vietnam in the late 1960s. Overall, Westmoreland and his supporters spoke for only 5 minutes and 59 seconds, while his accusers were given 19 minutes and 19 seconds, a ratio of better than three-to-one for the accusers.

Van Gordon Sauter, president of CBS News, acknowledged that CBS policies and standards had been violated during the making of the documentary, but he argued that these flaws did not undermine the editorial integrity of the broadcast. According to him, it was an accurate and important account of the distortion of enemy strength estimates by the military in Vietnam.

After two years of legal sparring, the substantive issues involved in Westmoreland's libel suit had not yet been resolved by final court action. But the issue of media policy is clearer. There is little disagreement about the standards of fairness and accuracy that should be applied in broadcasts involving important public issues. The standards by which CBS judged its own conduct make this apparent. But—and this is the disturbing aspect—these standards are breached all too often. Such breaches raise questions about the sense of responsibility of high-level media personnel. When important public matters are at stake, are the media, especially the influential electronic media, exercising sufficient care to make sure that the preconceptions of media personnel do not taint their stories and mislead media audiences?

With investigative journalism growing in popularity, the problem of inaccurate reports has mounted. In many instances, reports have permanent economic, professional, and social consequences for the individuals and institutions whose story is told. In the Westmoreland case, for example, the reputation of a prominent general is at stake. In another case, one involving the Kaiser Aluminum and Chemical Corporation, potential business losses could run into millions of dollars. An investigative report had accused the company of knowingly selling dangerous household electrical wiring under false pretenses. Substantial economic damage to the company was likely.

The serious injuries inflicted when publicity is careless or biased have become a deep concern for civil libertarians. As Ira Glasser, executive director of the American Civil Liberties Union, has warned: "justice by press release and summary political punishment are methods we should have by now learned to avoid." [35] The problem is made worse by the fact that rebuttals, if permitted at all by the networks, have been subject to their editorial control. Network representatives have argued that documentaries, unlike ordinary news, are edited productions so that uncensored rebuttals need not be permitted.[36]

Entrapment

Serious ethical issues are also raised when newspeople become involved in undercover operations or bogus enterprises created to entrap potential and actual wrongdoers. The story told earlier about the Mirage, the tavern set up to elicit and record bribery by city officials, illustrates the practice. A far more massive crime trap was set by Canadian media to expose organized crime in North America. The investigation resulted in a three-and-a-half hour documentary broadcast by the Canadian Broadcasting Company (CBC) on March 27, 1979.

CBC reporters and agents who were planted inside organized crime circles used hidden microphones and cameras to obtain dramatic film footage of gangsters discussing their activities. In one instance a reporter arranged meetings with a woman suspected of helping gangsters to buy real estate in Atlantic City. The reporter pretended to represent a person in Italy who wished to export several million dollars from Italy to Canada. The money was then to be funneled into Atlantic City real estate under the guise that it belonged to legitimate Canadian investors. Through this initial contact, another meeting was set up between a disguised reporter, who had had previous experience as an informant for law enforcement agencies, and underworld figures involved in the illegal real estate deals. All of these meetings were taped and some parts were filmed.[37]

Such sting operations raise serious civil liberties issues even when they are conducted by regular law enforcement agencies, often under the watchful eyes of the courts.[38] The concerns about protecting the rights of suspects are even greater when the sleuths are acting without an official mandate and without supervision by a responsible public body. Quite aside from civil liberties issues, sting operations raise fundamental questions about the proper functions of the press. Should its watchdog role be carried to the point where it becomes a quasi-police force, tracking down selected offenders when a good story promises to be the likely reward?

Summary

This chapter examined direct involvement by journalists in the conduct of governmental affairs. We began with an analysis of the process of muckraking, comparing reality to a series of models of the process. The findings were significant because they showed that the media's power to arouse public opinion with exposés of corruption is far less than popularly believed. Even if the public becomes highly concerned, political action is not guaranteed. The belief that muckraking commonly produces reforms when journalists arouse the public, and public opinion then pressures successfully for political action, is wrong.

The most propitious road to reform is via direct liaison between newspeople and government officials. When officials provide story leads in areas where they would like to produce action, or when newspeople can interest officials in taking action on issues that have come to the media's attention, successful political activities are apt to occur. On rare occasions the media are also able to produce action by using the club of potential unwanted publicity to force officials to act or by becoming participants in political negotiations.

The Watergate scandal provided an illustration of the many instances in which political action emerges from the interplay of various social institutions. The media, through a series of agenda-building steps, created the climate in which it became possible to force the resignation of a president. Agenda-building examples from science policy and from the realm of interest group politics demonstrated the impact of the media on developments in these fields. The media serve as catalysts that precipitate the actions of other elements within the society. They make the course of events possible, but the ultimate outcome may defeat their political purposes because it is beyond their control.

The various public policymaking roles played by the media more or less directly are important for American politics in general as well as for the lives of many individuals and institutions. How sensitively and accurately they are performed therefore becomes a matter of concern. Newsgathering and news production can be substantially flawed, even when media institutions profess to believe in high standards. How often these standards are violated, and what the costs are to people caught in the net of inaccurate publicity, is a matter for conjecture.

One major cause lies at the heart of most flawed productions and of most instances when newspeople allow themselves to be used as mouthpieces for politicians and interest groups. That cause is the desire to produce exciting news stories. This is not surprising. Journalism requires the art of telling stories that will attract audiences. That journalists face the temptation to be good story-tellers above all, even at the expense of other goals, should give pause to those who advocate that they should play the political game actively and regularly. If one grants that newspeople should attempt to influence what gets on the crowded political agenda, one must ask whether their professional standards equip them to guide politics wisely and well. To put it another way: When issues are selected for attention, should their newsworthiness be the controlling factor? If the answer is "no," then the heavy hand of the media in policymaking may be very dangerous.

Notes

1. Lincoln Steffens, *The Autobiography of Lincoln Steffens* (New York: Harcourt Brace, 1931), p. 357.
2. A brief review of the history and tactics of muckraking can be found in William L. Rivers, *The Other Government: Power and the Washington Media* (New York: Universe Books, 1982), pp. 119-143.
3. Frank J. Prial, "Coast Freelance Unit Thrives on Reporting for TV," *New York Times,* September 10, 1983.
4. Steffens, *Autobiography,* p. 357.
5. Harvey Molotch, David L. Protess, and Margaret T. Gordon, "The Media Policy Connection: Ecologies of News" (Occasional paper, Center for Urban Affairs and Policy Research, Northwestern University, Evanston, Illinois, 1983).
6. Fay Lomax Cook, Tom R. Tyler, Edward G. Goetz, Margaret T. Gordon, David Protess, Donna R. Leff, and Harvey L. Molotch, "Media and Agenda Setting: Effects on the Public, Interest Group Leaders, Policy Makers, and Policy," *Public Opinion Quarterly* 47 (Spring 1983): 16-35. See also David L. Protess, Donna R. Leff, Stephen C. Brooks, and Margaret T. Gordon, "News Media Investigations of Social Problems: The Effects of Exposés on the General Public, Policymakers, Policymaking, and the Press," *Public Opinion Quarterly* 48 (1984).
7. Robert Muccigrosso, "Television and the Urban Crisis," in *Screen and Society,* ed. Frank J. Coppa (Chicago: Nelson-Hall, 1979), pp. 44-45.
8. Chris T. Allen and Judith D. Weber, "How Presidential Media Use Affects Individuals' Beliefs about Conservation," *Journalism Quarterly* 60 (Spring 1983): 98-104, 196.
9. Protess et al., "News Media Investigations."
10. In some instances alerting the public to difficult situations is the chief point of a program with little immediate action expected. For example, PBS officials made their documentary "Crisis at General Hospital" to create public awareness about the development of a two-tier health system in which people of means will be served by excellent private hospitals while the remainder of the population receives second-rate care in inferior public hospitals. Kenneth R. Clark, "Hospital Dilemma: The System Sends Poor Home to Die," *Chicago Tribune,* January 17, 1984.
11. Cook et al., "Media and Agenda Setting," p. 31.
12. The full story is told in Pamela Zekman and Zay Smith, *The Mirage* (New York: Random House, 1979).
13. Wayne King, "Houston Finds that Dramatizing Crime Does Pay," *New York Times,* January 23, 1984.
14. David L. Paletz and Robert M. Entman, *Media Power Politics* (New York: Free Press, 1981), p. 184.
15. Gladys Engel Lang and Kurt Lang, *The Battle for Public Opinion: The President, the Press, and the Polls during Watergate* (New York: Columbia University Press, 1983), p. 58.
16. Molotch et al., "The Media Policy Connection," pp. 38-39, citing Peter Dreier, "The Position of the Press in the U.S. Power Structure," *Social Problems* 29

(February 1982): 298-310; Todd Gitlin, *The Whole World is Watching: Media in the Making and Unmaking of the New Left* (Berkeley: University of California Press, 1980); Norton Long, "The Local Community as an Ecology of Games," *American Journal of Sociology* 64 (1958): 256; and Harvey L. Molotch, "Media and Movements," in *The Dynamics of Social Movement,* ed. Mayer Zald and John D. McCarthy (Cambridge, Mass.: Winthrop, 1979), pp. 71-93.

17. Lang and Lang, *The Battle for Public Opinion,* pp. 59-60.
18. The agenda-building role of the media in local conflicts is explored in detail in Phillip J. Tichenor, George A. Donohue, and Clarice N. Olien, *Community Conflict and the Press* (Beverly Hills, Calif.: Sage, 1980). For a brief discussion of the influence of the media on controversial national defense policies, such as SALT II, nuclear weapons policy, the sale of AWACS planes to Saudi Arabia, and U.S. policy in El Salvador, see Bernard C. Cohen, "The Influence of Special-Interest Groups and Mass Media on Security Policy in the United States" (Paper presented at the annual meeting of the American Political Science Association, 1982).
19. Oscar H. Gandy, *Beyond Agenda Setting: Information Subsidies and Public Policy* (Norwood, N.J.: Ablex, 1982), pp. 149-162.
20. Stanley Rothman and S. Robert Lichter, "The Nuclear Energy Debate: Scientists, the Media and the Public," *Public Opinion* 5 (August/September 1982): 47-48.
21. For a more general discussion of the problem of sources of science information, see Alan Mazur, "Media Coverage and Public Opinion on Scientific Controversies," *Journal of Communication* 31 (Spring 1981): 106-115 and Sharon S. Dunwoody, "The Science Writing Inner Club: A Communication Link Between Science and the Lay Public," *Science, Technology & Human Values* 5 (Fall 1980): 14-22.
22. Paletz and Entman, *Media Power Politics,* p. 144.
23. Patrick Leahy and Alan Mazur, "The Rise and Fall of Public Opposition in Specific Social Movements," *Social Studies of Science* 10 (1980): 191-205 and Mazur, "Media Coverage and Public Opinion."
24. For a symposium on science news, see the spring 1981 issue of *Journal of Communication,* vol. 31: 2.
25. Gitlin, *The Whole World,* pp. 25-26.
26. For a more general discussion of the role played by media in shaping social movements, see Joey Reagan, "The Uses of Media and Communication for Social Movements" (Paper presented at the annual meeting of the Midwest Political Science Association, 1981).
27. Paletz and Entman, *Media Power Politics,* p. 146.
28. Gitlin, *The Whole World,* p. 284.
29. Paletz and Entman, *Media Power Politics,* p. 144.
30. Edie Goldenberg, *Making the Papers* (Lexington, Mass.: D. C. Heath, 1975), pp. 146-148.
31. Gandy, *Beyond Agenda Setting,* p. 88.
32. Sally Bedell Smith "Film on a Nuclear War Already Causing Wide Fallout of Partisan Activity," *New York Times,* November 23, 1983.
33. For a discussion of the subtle yet significant consequences that are often missed, see Don D. Smith, "Cognitive Psychology, Information Processing, and 'The Day After'" (Paper presented to the American Association for Public Opinion Research, 1984).
34. Richard Bernstein, "CBS Releases its Study of Vietnam Documentary," *New York Times,* April 27, 1983.
35. Deirdre Carmody, "The Role of the Press in the U.S. Corruption Inquiry," *New York Times,* February 5, 1980.

36. For a typical case involving denial of the right to unedited rebuttal, see Sally Bedell, "ABC Backs Off Charge it Made Against Mobil, *New York Times,* June 22, 1982.
37. Andrew H. Malcolm, "TV Film Links to Mob in Toronto," *New York Times,* March 28, 1979.
38. Bennett L. Gershman, "Abscam, the Judiciary, and the Ethics of Government," *Yale Law Journal* 91 (July 1982): 1565-1591.

Readings

Gitlin, Todd. *The Whole World is Watching: Media in the Making and Unmaking of the New Left.* Berkeley: University of California Press, 1980.

Goldenberg, Edie. *Making the Papers.* Lexington, Mass.: D. C. Heath, 1975.

Lang, Glady Engel, and Kurt Lang. *The Battle for Public Opinion: The President, the Press and the Polls During Watergate.* New York: Columbia University Press, 1983.

Miller, Susan Heilmann. *Reporters and Congressmen: Living in Symbiosis.* Columbus, Ohio: Journalism Monograph Series No. 53, 1978.

Rivers, William, and Wilbur Schramm. *Responsibility in Mass Communication.* New York: Harper and Row, 1980.

Steffens, Lincoln. *The Autobiography of Lincoln Steffens.* New York: Harcourt, Brace, 1931.

Zekman, Pamela, and Zay Smith. *The Mirage.* New York: Random House, 1979.

Crisis Coverage   9

You awake at 4:00 A.M. Outside the civil defense sirens are screaming. What could be wrong? Has it happened? Or is it about to strike? What are you supposed to do to cope with this as yet unknown menace? You turn on your radio, almost instinctively. Sounds of soft music. Just hearing them is reassuring. At least the radio is working. If there are things you must do immediately, the radio announcer will tell you. You wait for the music to stop, anxious to know what is happening. But you also hope it won't stop for a while—the longer it plays, the less chance that you're in real danger. They wouldn't play music if disaster were imminent.

Finally the announcer breaks in. A tornado has been sighted nearby. "Take shelter," says the voice on the radio. "Keep away from windows. Stay indoors until the sirens stop. There will be further news bulletins at five-minute intervals." You heave a sigh of relief as you dress quickly, pick up your apartment keys and a small transistor radio, and head for the basement. Nothing has happened yet, and if it does, officials are obviously prepared to deal with the crisis. They already woke you, warned you about the potential menace to your life and property, told you how to protect yourself initially, and promised to shepherd you through the dangers of the hours to come.

The Nature of Crisis Conditions

This is just one small scenario of a periodic public crisis. Public crises are natural or man-made events that pose an immediate and serious threat to the lives and property or to the peace of mind of large numbers of citizens. Examples are assassinations of major public figures, terrorist attacks, particularly when hostages are taken, or major accidents, like train wrecks or spectacular fires. They trouble the public's peace of mind even when they threaten no personal harm to most observers. When such disasters happen, people expect to be informed and protected by the appropriate government agencies.

In times of crisis the media, particularly radio, become a vital arm of government. They perform their usual functions of selecting, shaping, and reporting the news to people in and out of government. But, in addition, they provide a ready channel for government officials to address the public directly or indirectly through media personnel. These official messages keep endangered communities in touch with essential information and instructions. People are reassured and may be less likely to panic.

The rapid transmission of information and commentary is most crucial in those areas that are immediately and directly affected by the disaster and must cope with its disruptions. Our analysis will focus on on-the-scene crisis coverage. However, many of the problems faced locally also have ramifications for remote areas. The coverage of a racial riot in Los Angeles may have effects on readers and viewers in Detroit or Chicago when similar background conditions exist or similar situations occur. Publicity for airplane crashes or radiation leaks may affect the future of these industries throughout the country, not only at the disaster scene.

A dramatic example of the nationwide impact of a local event occurred in 1970 when four students were killed during an antiwar demonstration at Kent State University in Ohio. Wide publicity for the event kindled protest demonstrations on campuses from coast to coast. Classes stopped, antiwar rallies were held, and thousands of students rushed to Washington to lobby against the Vietnam War and the Kent State slayings.

Besides the intrinsic importance of crisis coverage, it also serves to highlight the major philosophical and policy issues that confront the government-media interrelationship. When physical survival of large numbers of ordinary citizens is at stake, sensitivity to the significance of media publicity becomes heightened. The media's responsibility to serve public needs and the government's responsibility to control, direct, and even manipulate the flow of news for public purposes become issues viewed from the perspective of self-preservation. The Olympian view yields to a vision of danger at eyeball distance.

Four Crisis Situations

In this chapter we will examine media coverage of four crises: the assassination of President John F. Kennedy in Dallas, Texas, November 22, 1963; race riots in Winston-Salem, North Carolina, November 2-5, 1967; Israel's Yom Kippur War, October 6-28, 1973; and a series of recent natural and man-made disasters.

The Assassination of John F. Kennedy

The facts of the assassination of President Kennedy in the third year of his first term are familiar. A young, vigorous president, who had created an aura of political freshness and idealism, was struck down by a sniper's bullets while traveling in an open limousine in a motorcade in Dallas. The president died in a hospital several hours after the attack. Initially, there was uncertainty about his physical condition. The extent and severity of his injuries were unknown. The exact procedures that would be followed in filling the presidential office without delay were unclear. Rumors mushroomed that the assassination was part of a larger plot by domestic or foreign political enemies of the president to kill prominent government officials. There were countless unanswered questions about the impact the disaster might have on American politics and policies. All these uncertainties compounded the grief and anger that touched millions of Americans in a very personal way.[1]

North Carolina Racial Rioting

In Winston-Salem in 1967, a black man was arrested on the street for drunkenness. He was taken to a local police station where a white policeman clubbed him for being unruly. Several days later the victim died of a fractured skull. Because this incident occurred during a period of racial unrest and mounting opposition to harsh police action, particularly against minority groups, the police apparently tried to hush up the story. But rumors of the incident circulated in the black community, and a brief story appeared in one local newspaper. The National Association for the Advancement of Colored People (NAACP) planned a march to protest police brutality but was persuaded to cancel it for fear that it would provoke rioting.

After the victim's funeral, rioting began: rocks were thrown, windows were broken, small fires were started. Ultimately, 500 people were involved, and the governor called out 1,000 National Guard troops. There were rumors of bomb threats and looting and sniping. A curfew was then imposed, and the National Guard was supplied with ammunition, in case the situation got out of control. It did. Fighting lasted for four days. Fortunately, no one died, but more than 100 people were injured, 200 people were arrested, and there was $750,000 worth of property damage.[2]

The Yom Kippur War

The Yom Kippur War, or the War of Ramadan as the Arabs call it, began at 2:00 P.M. on October 6, 1973, with a surprise attack by Egyptian and Syrian forces on Israeli troops along Israel's frontiers. Fighting was confined to the border regions, and there were no large-scale attacks on civilian populations. Although this was the fourth time in Israel's 26-year history that the country found itself at war, the suddenness of the outbreak surprised most Israelis. There had been no political and little military warning of the attack, and hence few preparations had been made to cope with the initial crisis. On the day of the attack, people were busy with religious ceremonies of the Yom Kippur holiday, the most sacred day for members of the Jewish faith. Because of the holiday, the Israeli media were totally shut down.

The wailing of the air raid sirens at 2:00 P.M. jolted the nation back to worldly affairs. Radio and television immediately resumed broadcasting. Their first tasks were to summon military units through coded information, to broadcast civil defense instructions, and to inform an anxious public about ongoing events. In the days that followed, the media's initial responsibilities were expanded to include keeping up the morale of the soldiers and the home front, directing propaganda broadcasts to the Arab world, and interpreting the conduct of the war so that the public could put unfolding events into perspective and understand and support the policies of their government.[3] Stories that raised doubts about public policies were censored.

Natural or Man-made Disasters

Disasters are akin in many ways to first strikes in war. In the case of floods and tornadoes or chemical or radiation pollution, the physical impact of water or wind or man-made substances suddenly wipes out or threatens to wipe out lives and property and disrupt communication and transportation. People fear for their own survival and welfare and that of their loved ones and communities.

The cases on which our analysis of disaster coverage is based involve four flood and three storm disasters in several cities and the threatened radiation calamity in March 1979 at the Three Mile Island nuclear plant near Harrisburg, Pennsylvania. In two of the floods, nearly the entire city was submerged in the wake of a hurricane; in the other two, flash floods wiped out part of the city. In the storm disasters, tornadoes hit and destroyed major portions of towns in Georgia, Texas, and Iowa. Homes were leveled, burying people under the rubble. Telephone lines were broken, and live electric wires posed hazards of electrocution and fire. Streets became impassable even to rescue vehicles. Television stations, bereft of power, stopped broadcasting.[4]

Unlike the floods and storm disasters, no actual destruction occurred in the Three Mile Island nuclear plant mishap. Nonetheless, news stories covering the dangers of radiation that might accompany a meltdown of an overheated nuclear reactor led to major disruptions in community life. More than 150,000 people fled the area. In the actual disasters, radio became the major source for emergency information. It is the most likely medium to have emergency power supplies if regular power is disrupted and, thanks to transistors, it is the most likely to be received by large numbers of the public when electricity is unavailable.

Media Response and Role

During crises, the public depends almost totally on the media for news that may be vital for survival and for important messages from public and private authorities. The mass media are the only institutions that can collect this massive amount of information and disseminate it quickly. Therefore when people become aware of a crisis, they turn on their radios or television sets, often on a round-the-clock basis, to monitor the event.

Table 9-1 presents data on sources on which people relied for disaster information in three communities hit by recent disasters. People in the disaster-free control community speculated about the potentially most useful sources. The table demonstrates people's heavy reliance on electronic media and the comparatively small role played by interpersonal communication and direct experience, even after living through similar disasters. Community A, located on the Gulf Coast, had experienced numerous hurricanes. Communities B and C, in the Midwest, had suffered two tornadoes and two major floods, respectively. Community D had no experience with a major natural disaster. A sample of residents in each of these communities was asked: "From what sources have you obtained the greatest amount of information concerning natural disasters?" Several sources could be cited in response.[5]

Table 9-1 Principal Sources of Disaster Information (in percent of responses)*

Sources of Information	Site A	Site B	Site C	Site D
Electronic media	66%	59%	75%	75%
Newspapers	24	20	40	64
Magazines	3	7	8	15
Nonfiction books	10	10	11	4
Other persons	17	12	14	9
Direct experience	37	32	20	6
Public education	9	6	5	—

* Multiple answers were permitted.

N = 290 for Site A, hurricane disasters; 281 for Site B, tornado disasters; 209 for Site C, flood disasters; 341 for Site D, disaster-free control.

SOURCE: Dennis E. Wenger, "A Few Empirical Observations Concerning the Relationship Between the Mass Media and Disaster Knowledge: A Research Report," in *Disasters and the Mass Media: Proceedings of the Committee on Disasters and the Mass Media Workshop* (Washington, D.C.: National Academy of Sciences, 1980), p. 244. Reprinted by permission.

The audience for crisis information is massive and loyal. In the days immediately after the Kennedy assassination, the average television set was turned on for nearly 32 hours of broadcasts about the unfolding events. In the United States alone, 51 million homes were tuned in. During the Yom Kippur War, the entire Israeli population used both radio and television. Sixty-eight percent of the population listened to radio all day long to catch the hourly news bulletins.

Besides information, the public looks to the media to explain and interpret the situation, since media personnel are often the first ones on the scene collecting reports and trying to fit them into a coherent story. Official investigations generally come much later. The media also guide the public about appropriate behavior during the crisis. This may be a warning to retreat to an air raid shelter, an announcement of escape routes, information on purification of polluted food and water, news of missing persons, or schedules to be maintained by schools and work places. Outside the immediate crisis area, news stories may mobilize relief operations.

Stages and Patterns of Crisis Coverage

Stage One.   The typical scenario of crisis coverage has three stages. During the first stage, the crisis or disaster strikes or is announced as impending. Media people, officials, and onlookers rush to the scene. This immediately produces a flood of uncoordinated messages, largely transmitted over the airwaves. Radio and television stations interrupt regularly scheduled programs with bulletins announcing the crisis, or they may preempt the entire program for reports from the scene.

During the storm and flood disasters, emergency messages generally were broadcast within minutes after the disaster struck, often by a sharply limited corps of stations that had survived the immediate impact of the catastrophe. The stations rapidly became information collection centers. People would phone them with reports to be broadcast or call them to find out information. The most important broadcasts in the early hours of the disaster were messages describing what had happened, directing people to places where aid was available, summoning National Guard units and other security forces, and coordinating appeals for survival supplies, such as food, blankets, blood donations, and medical equipment.

In the early phase the number of news broadcasts rises steeply. During the Yom Kippur War, radio and television doubled broadcast time to a 24-hour schedule and replaced many regular programs with war-related news and interviews. News bulletins were issued hourly on radio and five times daily on television. After a major earthquake in 1964 ravaged Anchorage, Alaska, radio stations remained on the air continuously and asked people to stay tuned in for emergency messages.[6]

Reprinted by permission. Tribune Media Services, Inc.

Once the initial announcements have been aired, many people who have heard the broadcast will relay the information to others by word of mouth, either in person or by telephone. This in turn stimulates those who have been alerted to tune in to subsequent broadcasts. For instance, when the news of the assassination of President Kennedy was first broadcast, a larger than average daytime audience heard it within minutes from the media because the shooting took place at the noon hour when many people in the East and Midwest were listening to radio during lunch. Each person who heard the news told it to five or six other people on the average.[7] More than two-thirds of the American public—nearly 150 million people—received the news within one-half hour after the shooting. Similarly, on March 30, 1981, it took approximately 90 minutes to diffuse the news of the attempted assassination of President Ronald Reagan to 90 percent of the public. The average person then told three others.[8]

The striking characteristic of this first stage is the rapidity of the communication. Television and radio can focus the public's attention almost instantaneously on the developing situation. In many cases news about the crisis replaces most other stories. Whatever else happens in the world during the crisis period, regardless of its importance, may be totally blocked out.

At this early stage the media are the major source of information, even for public officials concerned with the crisis. Media reports serve to coordinate public activities. During the Anchorage earthquake, for example, the radio stations that were able to function became the focal point for coordinating information on casualties, property damage, and available supplies so that officials could determine priorities for relief work. At a later stage, direct communication among officials and other affected parties may supplement or even supersede media communication.

Next to reaching the disaster site, the chief problem for newspeople during the first stage is getting accurate information. Public and private officials involved in the crisis may be reluctant to talk. Rumors abound. During the Yom Kippur War, stories about damage done by the initial attack, the preparedness of the Israeli army, and advance warning about the forthcoming attack were garbled. During the Alaska earthquake, many buildings were evacuated unnecessarily because of false reports that they had been condemned or were about to collapse. The number of dead and the extent of injuries were frequently exaggerated. In the case of the Kennedy assassination and the racial disturbances, there were intimations of conspiracies to commit more violence. Newspeople were faced with many conflicting reports and not enough time to check their accuracy.

If highly technical matters are involved—as happens in explosions, structural failures, and radiation disasters—it may be impossible to present a coherent story. Reporters may lack the expertise to make sense out of baffling technical data and the skill to simplify the information so that laymen can comprehend it. Sources of news are often deliberately obscure, tight-lipped, and even hostile. Confusion prevailed during the week-long Three Mile Island incident.[9] At one news conference, the Nuclear Regulatory Commission's chief spokesman, Harold Denton, attempted to correct a false report that the hydrogen bubble in the reactor was in imminent danger of exploding. Here is what he said:

> The oxygen generation rate that I was assuming yesterday when I was reporting on the potential detonation inside the vessel is, it now appears to have been, too conservative. There's an emerging consensus of technical opinion that the—for situations such as this where there's high oxygen overpressure in a vessel, that the oxygen evolution rate is very low, and our numbers for the rate of oxygen yesterday—I think I quoted a number on the order of one per cent a day—is very, very conservative, and the actual rate is much lower than that.[10]

If you are baffled about what he meant, so were the reporters.

To provide continuous crisis coverage, television and radio stations must suddenly produce a steady stream of interesting stories to fill hours instead of minutes of broadcast time. Pressure for fresh accounts often tempts media personnel to interview eyewitnesses and commentators of doubtful knowledge, who may lend a local touch without adding to the known facts about the crisis. It also leads to reporting information that has not been adequately verified or that may be atypical.[11] By focusing on the destruction of a tornado, for instance, the audience may be left with the wrong impression that the entire community is in ruins.[12] The pressure for news encourages reporters and public officials alike to speculate about what happened. At times, these speculations involve spinning past prejudices into a web of scenarios that cast blame for the disaster or its aftermath on socially outcast groups. "Outsiders" or ethnic minorities or political deviants in the community often become the hapless scapegoats. The racial riots of the 1960s were routinely attributed to "outside agitators" who were depicted as common criminals, bereft of moral dignity and social consciousness. The Winston-Salem case is in point.[13]

Stage Two. During the second stage the media try to make sense out of the situation. At this point enough time generally has elapsed so that the chief dimensions of the crisis are emerging. For instance, in a natural or man-made disaster, the full extent of the damage has been ascertained. Names of most victims and the degree of their injuries are known. Plans have been made for repairs and reconstruction. In the Kennedy assassination, it became clear how the death occurred, even though the persons responsible for the crime were not yet known. Plans were made for the funeral ceremonies and for the transfer of power.

In general, print media are able to do a more thorough job during this stage in pulling together the various events and fitting them into a coherent story. Compared with radio and television, print media have larger staffs for investigation and more room to present background details that make the events understandable. For instance, in the hours and days following the assassination of John F. Kennedy, the *New York Times* probed into the motives for the assassination, the possibility of conspiracy, and the involvement of foreign agents—questions that the government's Warren Commission investigated only later and at a far slower pace.

Stage Three. The third stage overlaps with the other two. It involves attempts by media personnel to place the crisis into a larger, long-range perspective and to prepare people to cope with the aftermath of the initial events and modifications in initial policies. For instance, information on evacuation routes and ways to protect people and property may be updated with an eye to ultimate restoration of normal conditions. In wartime, the third stage may involve broadcasting news, patriotic features, and action-adventure or comedy shows designed to relieve tensions and sustain morale. In the case of the Yom Kippur War, it also required structuring messages so that they would not give aid and comfort to the enemy, who could readily listen to broadcasts intended for Israeli consumption.

A concerted effort may have to be made to prevent panic. After the Anchorage earthquake, the mayor and other city officials made frequent radio reports describing the damage and assuring people that the authorities had the situation under control. Similarly, following the assassination of Martin Luther King, Jr., in 1968, live camera facilities were set up to permit local mayors throughout the United States to communicate with city people. In Washington, D.C., for example, Mayor Walter Washington and other black leaders addressed the public repeatedly urging people to stay calm. Network tributes to Dr. King were designed to stress peaceful behavior as a genuine tribute to the civil rights leader's memory.

During the Three Mile Island incident, efforts to calm the population involved centralization of news releases to halt disquieting conflicting reports. All information furnished by government and plant officials about the disaster had to be cleared through a press center operated by the federal government's Nuclear Regulatory Commission near the site of the accident. Officials of the stricken plant protested about the censorship but complied with President Jimmy Carter's order. Later a formal investigation of how 43 newspapers and network evening newscasts reported the accident credited the media with providing balanced treatment in a highly confused and confusing situation.[14]

To reassure a shaken public after President Kennedy's assassination and to reorient people to the new administration, news about Lyndon B. Johnson's inauguration and assumption of presidential responsibilities was featured. Immediately after Kennedy's death, a greater than average effort was made to inform the public concerning the whereabouts and activities of the new president and to convey the impression that the political life of the nation was continuing with only minor disruptions.

In the storm and flood disasters, after the initial relief activities had been organized, stations switched their emphasis to morale-building activities. The general theme of these efforts was that the community had shown its strength by coping heroically with the disaster and that it would now unite and rapidly build a better future. "Belmond is coming back," proclaimed the front page of the local newspaper in the Iowa town paralyzed by a tornado. "Belmond is looking ahead. It had received perhaps the cruelest blow ever dealt an Iowa town in the way of a natural catastrophe. But it is far from being beaten." [15]

Which medium—radio, television, or newspapers—performs best in crisis situations? Public opinion surveys from the Yom Kippur War provide some answers. More than half of the people who were interviewed about their media preferences said that radio had been best in providing initial information. Television was rated second best for information but best for interpreting events. As interpreter, radio ranked second, followed by interpersonal communication and newspaper coverage, in that order. Television also was called the best medium for tension release, followed by interpersonal communication. Only 5 percent of the respondents credited newspapers with providing relief from tension.

Less educated people relied more heavily on television and interpersonal communication for news and interpretation, while the better educated relied more on radio and newspapers. Less educated people also felt the highest levels of tension and found it most difficult to get relief. Without comparable information from other crisis situations, one can only guess that these reactions to crisis coverage by various media are probably representative of what occurs in similar crises in other countries.

Effects of Media Coverage

Positive Effects. Media coverage of crisis situations usually has both positive and negative effects. On the positive side, information, even if it is bad news, relieves disquieting uncertainty and calms people. The mere activity of watching or listening to familiar reporters and commentators reassures people and keeps them occupied. It gives them a sense of vicarious participation, of "doing something." To maintain this quieting effect, media personnel may avoid showing gruesome crisis details. For instance, photos of President Kennedy's injuries were not shown initially, although they were available. In the Three Mile Island accident, conjectures about possible effects of a nuclear explosion were avoided. To lessen the chance for panic, local media even rejected advertisements by merchants for "evacuation sales" and radiation detectors.

News stories may be able to create the reassuring feeling that grief and fear are not borne alone. After seeing the same disaster pictures and listening to the same broadcasts, people can discuss the crisis with neighbors, friends, and coworkers who have shared their experiences. This gives the feeling of mutual support. Watching John F. Kennedy's funeral on television and witnessing the grief of his young family made Americans feel that they were participating with millions of others in a national catharsis of grief. Many were able to cry to relieve their personal tensions.

If the news conveys the idea that the authorities are coping properly with the disaster, this, too, is reassuring. Scenes of a train or bus or plane crash become less frightening if the police, firefighters, ambulances, and medical personnel are on the scene. Watching the mayor or governor tour a disaster site provides further reassurance. Finally, directions about appropriate behavior may save lives and property and ensure that the stricken community continues to function.

While benefits of coverage are readily apparent in most disasters, the case is not always clear. In the riots following the King assassination, for instance, looting and rioting erupted or continued despite broadcasts intended to cool the tense situation. The broadcasts may have reduced the amount of violence and television coverage may have restrained assaults by rioters or police, but we do not know for sure.

Negative Effects. Media coverage also may have adverse effects. It is this possibility that raises serious questions about the responsibility of media personnel to consider the societal consequences of freedom to publish. The government's responsibility to prevent harm-producing coverage, possibly by strict censorship, also becomes a major political issue.

Careless or even carefully prepared news messages may disturb people to the point that they cannot act rationally. In the face of crisis news, people may panic, endangering themselves and others. For instance, a precipitous mass exodus of frightened people during an impending flood or wind calamity may clog roads and overcrowd shelters; it may lead to injuries and death for those caught beyond the safety of their homes and work places. Pictures of violence may lead to a terrifying multiplication effect. Audiences frequently believe that the violent act is merely one of many. One house on fire or the sight of one victim's body may lead to visions of whole neighborhoods on fire and scores of victims killed. Police may be ordered to shoot lawbreakers on sight and citizens may resort to excessive violence to protect themselves.

Statements provoking unwise reactions are more likely to be publicized in times of crisis because the exceptionally large demand for news and guidance reduces gatekeepers' vigilance. Pack journalism may run rampant when all available news is shared to provide as much coverage as possible. If mistakes are made by news sources or reporters, they appear in all the media. During the Kennedy assassination crisis, Dallas police made many incautious comments about Lee Harvey Oswald, Kennedy's accused slayer. The remarks were widely publicized and would have impaired Oswald's chances for a fair trial, had he lived. After the nuclear mishap at Three Mile Island, workers complained that erroneous media reports, based on conflicting assessments by government officials about the explosiveness of a hydrogen bubble, frightened their families into needless evacuation of the area and threatened the survival of the plant and their job security.

Crisis and disaster news frequently attract crowds of citizens and reporters to the site, impeding rescue and security operations. It is arguable that Jack Ruby, who killed Lee Harvey Oswald while he was being taken into custody in full view of millions of television watchers, could never have trailed Oswald had it not been for the reporters cluttering Dallas police premises. News coverage of physical disasters routinely attracts looters to the scene.

Media coverage also may incite riots or spur rioting that already has erupted. For instance, during the racial riots in the Watts neighborhood of Los Angeles in 1965, police reported that violence peaked wherever television cameras were in evidence. Rioters actually seemed to "perform" for the cameras. Racial rioting in which whites attacked blacks in Washington, D.C., and in Chicago and East St. Louis, Illinois, in 1919 was attributed to sensational coverage of crimes by blacks against whites.[16]

Media coverage of racial riots may let people know where police forces are deployed, permitting looters and arsonists to avoid those areas. Potential riot participants use news reports to learn where most of the action is so that they can join in the fray. In this manner the disturbance may be enlarged. During racial rioting in Detroit in 1967, live coverage of looting and shooting seemed to so arouse viewers that some who had never before resorted to lawlessness took part in the violence.[17]

Even a small number of publicized riot scenes may produce adverse results because acts of violence generally are noticed and remembered much more clearly than other aspects of riot coverage. Four hundred ninety-nine men who had been among those arrested in the Detroit race riots were asked what they had seen on television about race riots. Seventy-one percent of the respondents spoke first about seeing killings, shoot-outs, police brutality, arson, looting, rock throwing, fighting, screaming, and other violent acts. Yet the Special Advisory Commission on Civil Disorders, appointed by President Lyndon B. Johnson in 1967, and headed by Illinois governor Otto Kerner, found that, overall, violent behavior constituted less than 5 percent of total television coverage of race riot incidents.[18]

Wide publicity for heinous crimes, such as random distribution of poisoned food supplies or sabotage of transportation facilities, may lead to so-called "copycat crimes." While these are few in number, their impact in terms of human suffering and widespread fear is vast. The case of copycat crimes throughout the United States in 1982, in the wake of seven fatal poisonings caused by cyanide-laced Tylenol tablets, is an example.

Planning Crisis Coverage

Because media play such a crucial role in keeping the polity going during crises, most media organizations have more or less formal plans to cope with crisis coverage problems. This is particularly true for electronic media. In one sample of 72 radio and television stations in 12 U.S. cities, 70 percent of the stations had plans for reporting natural disasters, and 73 percent had plans for reporting civil disturbances.[19] The plans generally were more detailed for natural disasters because needs are more predictable and there is greater consensus about the objectives to be pursued. In addition to media-sponsored plans, most stations were tied into the Federal Emergency Broadcasting System (EBS) that provides a network for relaying news during a national emergency.

Crisis coverage planning involves two aspects: preparation for the crisis and deciding how to present ongoing events. Plans to avoid crises are rare, probably because media focus on short-range happenings and because crisis prediction is difficult. Nonetheless, the media often have been blamed for neglecting preventive coverage. The Public's Right to Information Task Force of the President's Commission on the Accident at Three Mile Island blamed the Edison company, the Nuclear Energy Commission, and the media for ignoring problems at the Three Mile Island plant prior to the accident and for overemphasizing the safety of nuclear power.[20]

The Kerner Commission's 1968 report is another example. The commission condemned the media for their silence about the plight of blacks in the United States. It claimed that ample early coverage might have prevented violence in the mid-1960s. It is difficult to argue the case for preventive coverage under most circumstances because there is usually disagreement about whether or not specific sets of social indicators herald a crisis at some future time. Besides, even if newspeople could accurately forecast an impending crisis, there is no assurance that increased publicity would prevent it. As we saw in Chapter 5, publicity does not necessarily produce behavioral changes, however easy and obviously beneficial they may be.

Preventive coverage to stop the government from involving the nation in dangerous hostilities, including war, raises several serious issues. We already have mentioned the willingness of major media to suppress advance publicity about the disastrous Bay of Pigs invasion in Cuba in 1961. Had the media published the story, the invasion might have been aborted. Alternatively, it might have taken place anyhow, but with greatly reduced chances for success and much heavier losses of human life. Would publication have been a patriotic or a traitorous act? It is hard to tell.

In 1980, when columnist Jack Anderson wrote a column claiming that an election-minded Carter administration was planning a major military invasion of Iran to counteract the humiliation of the ongoing hostage crisis, the vast majority of the subscribers to the column printed it. Most papers also printed government denials. As one paper editorialized, "The recklessness of a politically motivated invasion would be far more dangerous than reckless journalism." [21] No major invasion ever took place. The nature of the invasion plans, if any, and the impact of the Anderson column have not been clarified yet.

Natural Disasters. Rodney Kueneman and Joseph Wright, who explored the natural disaster coverage plans of 72 radio and television stations, found that the plans were generally predicated upon the assumption that people tend to panic and that coverage must be designed to forestall this. The management of 72 percent of the stations, particularly those that had previous experience with natural disasters, assumed that panic would occur.[22]

Preparation for predicted natural disasters may involve the publication of news tracing the path of a storm or reporting geological studies that forecast the likelihood of earthquakes in an area. Official warnings and plans in case of disasters may be publicized along with information about protective measures that individuals can take. Stories that are graphic enough to arouse a lethargic population to prepare for the disaster, however, may cause panic or may be so scary that people shut them out of their minds. Such ostrich tactics may explain why, despite frequent warnings about the danger of serious earthquakes in southern California, few residents have taken recommended precautions.

Civil Disorders. Interviewees at 83 percent of the stations in the previously mentioned Kueneman-Wright study assumed that there would be a contagion effect from broadcasts of civil disturbances that would increase the number of people flocking to the scene to commit violent acts. Broadcasters with previous experience covering riot situations reported that "respected members of the community, who had jobs, who lived in pretty decent homes, joined the rioting and became looters and snipers because all of a sudden there was an unleashing of . . . hatred." [23] By contrast, social scientists who study disasters deny that panic and contagion occur frequently.[24] Whether or not they are correct, the important fact is that media personnel expect these reactions and act accordingly.

In Winston-Salem, advance preparations for civil disturbances were made following race riots elsewhere. The 1965 riots in Watts had led many observers to conclude that rioting was started by outsiders who expected few penalties for law infractions. Accordingly, the local papers in Winston-Salem, which were generally liberal on civil rights, decided to print stories pointing out that the city planned to treat rioters harshly. The preparatory stories also implied that rioters would most likely be outside agitators rather than local people. This type of publicity was intended, first of all, to discourage would-be rioters by warning them that they faced stiff punishment, and second, to increase public support for harsh suppression of disturbances. If, as the mayor of Winston-Salem put it, rioting would be done by "thugs and hoodlums who see a chance to profit from looting," the local community would feel no sympathy for these offenders.

The Problem of News Suppression

In natural as well as man-made crises, major policy questions are posed by plans for temporary or permanent news suppression. How much coverage should be presented immediately, at the risk of telling an inaccurate story, spreading panic, and attracting bystanders and destructive participants to the scene? What facts should be withheld initially or permanently? Eighty percent of the newspeople in the sample of radio and television stations mentioned earlier said that they would temporarily withhold information that might provoke troublesome reactions. Many would go further, indicating that they would withhold live coverage entirely, particularly in civil disturbances, because they believed that coverage increases the intensity and duration of crises. Such a self-imposed blackout of live television and radio coverage occurred in Winston-Salem during the first day of rioting. The story was reported solely in the print media, making it less immediate and graphic. Similarly, in 1979, television networks avoided coverage of demonstrations involving Iranian students in the United States. It was feared that coverage would spur more disturbances, further straining tense U.S.-Iranian relations and endangering American citizens held hostage in Iran.

Some news outlets plan to delay live coverage until officials have the situation under control. Others believe that suppression of live coverage will allow the spread of rumors that may be more inciting than judicious reporting of ongoing events. We do not know which of these views is most correct or how different circumstances affect reactions to media coverage of crises.

Deciding whether or not to suppress coverage becomes particularly difficult when a crisis involves terrorists, prison rioters, assassins of political leaders, or maniacal mass murderers who crave publicity. Granting exposure to them by live coverage may encourage them or others to commit further outrages. As the *New Yorker* commented in 1977 in the wake of live coverage of terrorist acts by Hanafi Moslems in Washington, D.C., and lurid stories about a mass murderer in New York, known as Son of Sam: "By transforming a killer into a celebrity, the press has not merely encouraged but perhaps driven him to strike again—and may have stirred others brooding madly over their grievances to act." [25] At an international conference on terrorism, participants accused the press of "subtle collusion" and of doing "more than the terrorist organizations themselves to make organized political violence glamorous and successful." [26]

Such accusations highlight the dilemma the press faces. Publicity does play into the hands of individuals willing to spread terror through indiscriminate killings and other abuses of the rights of fellow human beings. On the other hand, if the press fails to cover the terrorist acts, it can be accused of infringing on the public's right to know. If the press follows the government's official line in describing terrorists and their motives, it becomes a government propaganda tool. [27] If it dwells on either the human strengths or the frightful human frailties of the violent actors, it will be accused of making saints out of villains or villains out of hapless victims of society's malfunctions.

Several rules for cautious reporting during crises have been widely adopted. For instance, television newspeople learned from filming the Watts uprising that they must keep their equipment inconspicuous. Consequently, when rioting broke out after the assassination of Martin Luther King, Jr., camera crews traveled to riot scenes in unmarked vehicles and kept camera equipment unobtrusive. They used available light rather than floodlights. The development of small videotape equipment that does not require floodlighting has helped immeasurably to keep coverage discreet.

Newspeople have also learned to avoid inflammatory details or language in their reports. For instance, editors in Winston-Salem instructed reporters in advance of the crisis to identify the troubled area precisely and to indicate that surrounding areas were quiet. This was intended to reduce the multiplication effect. Reporters were asked to keep details of the incident that led to the rioting to a minimum. Exaggerated language or unconfirmed reports of violence were to be avoided. The rule to follow was "When in doubt, leave out."

In the Winston-Salem case, the media heeded these rules. The scope of rioting was minimized, for example, by reporting that "As the rioters moved through downtown last night, most of the city went about its business as usual. Many people probably never knew what was going on." [28] The riots were described as occurring "in connection with unrest created by the recent death," rather than murder, of a man "who died after injuries sustained when he resisted arrest and was hit," rather than clubbed, by a police officer. A detailed story of the incident was not published until several days after the rioting ended. Wire service copy, which was used in other cities, had said that the victim died "after he was blackjacked by a white policeman."

Words such as "rioting mobs" or "murder" or racial designations were largely avoided by the Winston-Salem press. Photographs showed black and white law enforcement officials working together to quell the riots, assisted by both black and white citizens. They showed arrests of looters and confiscation of their loot. There were no predictions of future trouble or further threats and no unconfirmed reports on dead and wounded and property damage. After the riots ended, most newspeople and community leaders felt that the press had handled the crisis as planned, with good results.

Nonetheless, a preference for muted coverage, particularly in civil disturbances and instances of political terrorism, raises some serious political and philosophical questions. Muted coverage generally leads to presentation of the official story only and suppression of unofficial views. The perspectives of law enforcement officers, preoccupied with controlling criminal activities, become paramount. In fact, stories are frequently cleared with the police before being published. As a result, they stress peace-keeping aspects rather than the causes of violent behavior and the political and social changes that might prevent future violence.

In the Winston-Salem case, the initial stories did not show that many blacks supported the riots as a social protest against unfair treatment of blacks by the white community. The media reports suppressed or failed to vent the feelings and ideas of militant black leaders. Instead, they concentrated on portraying blacks who supported the policies of the established local governing elites. In the short run this helped keep the situation under control, but the long-run effects of carefully limited coverage are more problematic. In terrorist incidents or prison riots, failure to air the grievances of terrorists and prison inmates may deprive them of a public forum for voicing their grievances. Their bottled up anger may lead to more violent explosions. Needed reforms may be aborted.

Some observers feel that muted reporting reduces the potential for arousing hatred and unbridgeable conflicts. Delayed coverage, they feel, can be more analytical and thus more likely to produce reforms. Others argue that the drama of an ongoing crisis raises public consciousness much better and faster than anything else. People will act to remedy injustice only if the situation is acute. If the heat of battle is already over, action may seem pointless. A permanent news blackout will make reforms highly unlikely. Those opposed to muted coverage or news suppression are willing to risk paying a very high price in lost lives, personal injuries, imprisonment, and property damage in hopes that immediate, complete coverage will shock the community to undertake basic social reforms. Most American political leaders, as well as most newspeople, have hitherto opted for muting conflict rather than bringing it to a head.

Finally, there is the unresolved philosophical question about the wisdom and propriety of news suppression in a free society. The true test of genuine press freedom does not come in times of calm. It comes in times of crisis when the costs of freedom may be dear, tempting government and media alike to impose silence. If a free press is a paramount value, then the die must be cast in favor of unrestrained crisis coverage, moderated only by the sense of responsibility of individual journalists.

Summary

In American political culture, the normal feuds of politics are suspended when the nation is in danger. Although this unwritten rule has been mentioned most often in connection with foreign policy, where "politics stops at the water's edge," It applies equally to domestic crises of the types we have discussed in this chapter. When there is widespread danger to life and property or when sudden death or terror have taken a large toll, when well-known leaders are in serious trouble or have fallen by the wayside, people and their government pull together far more than in normal times. Although there are many instances when sensational media coverage has hindered governmental efforts to maintain calm, it is increasingly true that the media abandon their adversarial role during crises: They become teammates of officialdom in attempts to restore public order, safety, and tranquility.

In this chapter we have described the indispensable functions that media perform during crises in diffusing vital information to the public and officials, in interpreting the meaning of events, and in providing emotional support for troubled communities. In major disasters radio is particularly helpful because its technical requirements are most adaptable to makeshift arrangements. It can broadcast without regular electric power supplies to people who have only a pocket transistor radio and are otherwise isolated.

Because the media play such a large part in public communication during crises, the manner in which they discharge their responsibilities has been of great concern to public officials and to the community at large. Information gaps, misinformation, and the dissemination of information that makes the effects of the crisis worse have led to demands that the information flow be controlled to ease crisis management. Many media institutions have formal plans that temporarily set aside the usual criteria for publishing exciting news in the interest of calming the public.

We have questioned the wisdom of muted coverage, particularly during civil disturbances and incidents of political terrorism, because it may drown out explicit and implicit messages about unmet societal needs. We have not questioned the need to plan for crisis coverage. Modern society faces crises of various sorts so frequently that policymakers in the media and in government would be remiss were they to make no plans to cope with emergencies.

Notes

1. Wilbur Schramm, "Communication in Crisis," in *The Kennedy Assassination and the American Public: Social Communication in Crisis,* ed. Bradley S. Greenberg and Edwin B. Parker (Palo Alto, Calif.: Stanford University Press, 1965), pp. 1-25.
2. David L. Paletz and Robert Dunn, "Press Coverage of Civil Disorder: A Case Study of Winston-Salem, 1967," *Public Opinion Quarterly* 33 (Summer 1969): 329-345.
3. Tsiyona Peled and Elihu Katz, "Media Functions in Wartime: The Israel Home Front in October 1973," in *The Uses of Mass Communications: Current Perspectives on Gratifications Research,* ed. Jay G. Blumler and Elihu Katz (Beverly Hills, Calif.: Sage, 1974), pp. 49-69.
4. The incidents are reported in Jerry J. Waxman, "Local Broadcast Gatekeeping During Natural Disasters," *Journalism Quarterly* 50 (Winter 1973): 751-758 and Russell R. Dynes, *Organized Behavior in Disaster* (Lexington, Mass.: D. C. Heath, 1970), pp. 41-43, 88-89, 127-128.
5. Dennis E. Wenger, "A Few Empirical Observations Concerning the Relationship Between the Mass Media and Disaster Knowledge: A Research Report," in *Disaster and the Mass Media: Proceedings of the Committee on Disasters and the Mass Media Workshop* (Washington, D.C.: National Academy of Sciences, 1980), pp. 242-244.
6. Daniel Yutzy, *Community Priorities at the Anchorage, Alaska Earthquake, 1964* (Columbus, Ohio: Ohio State University Disaster Research Center, 1969), p. 127.
7. Schramm, "Communication in Crisis," pp. 1-25.
8. Walter Gantz, "The Diffusion of News About the Attempted Reagan Assassination," *Journal of Communication* 33 (Winter 1983): 56-65.
9. Mitchell Stephens and Nadyne G. Edison, "News Media Coverage of Issues During the Accident at Three-Mile Island," *Journalism Quarterly* 59 (Summer 1982): 199-204, 259.

10. Casey Bukro, "How Accurate Was Press About Three Mile Island?" *Chicago Tribune,* March 30, 1980.
11. T. Joseph Scanlon, "Media Coverage of Crises: Better than Reported," Worse than Necessary," *Journalism Quarterly* 55 (Spring 1978): 68-72.
12. Wenger, "A Few Empirical Observations," pp. 252-253.
13. David L. Paletz and Robert M. Entman, *Media Power Politics* (New York: The Free Press, 1981), pp. 114-117.
14. Deidre Carmody, "News Media Defended in Inquiry on Reports of Three Mile Island," *New York Times,* October 31, 1979, and Peter Sandman and Mary Paden, "At Three Mile Island," *Columbia Journalism Review* (July/August 1979): 43-58.
15. Dynes, *Organized Behavior in Disaster,* pp. 127-218.
16. Paletz and Dunn, "Press Coverage of Civil Disorder," p. 329.
17. Benjamin D. Singer, "Mass Media and Communication Processes in the Detroit Riot of 1967," *Public Opinion Quarterly* 34 (Summer 1970): 236-245.
18. Ibid., p. 238.
19. Rodney M. Kueneman and Joseph E. Wright, "News Policies of Broadcast Stations for Civil Disturbances and Disasters," *Journalism Quarterly* 52 (Winter 1975): 670-677.
20. Sharon M. Friedman, "Blueprint for Breakdown: Three Mile Island and the Media Before the Accident," *Journal of Communication* 31 (Spring 1981): 116-128.
21. Douglas A. Anderson, "Handling of Controversial 'Merry-Go-Round' Columns," *Journalism Quarterly* 59 (Summer 1982): 295-298.
22. Kueneman and Wright, "News Policies," p. 671.
23. Ibid., p. 672.
24. See the report on the work of the Disaster Research Center at Ohio State University reported in E. L. Quarantelli and Russell R. Dynes, eds., "Organizational and Group Behavior in Disasters," *American Behavioral Scientist* 13 (January 1970): 325-456.
25. *New Yorker,* August 15, 1977, p. 21.
26. Jonathan Institute Jerusalem Conference on International Terrorism, "Political Violence and the Role of the Media: Some Perspectives," *Political Communication and Persuasion* 1 (1980): 79-99. The comments are by Lord Chalfont and Norman Podhoretz.
27. Alex P. Schmid and Janny de Graaf, *Violence as Communication: Insurgent Terrorism and the Western News Media* (Beverly Hills, Calif.: Sage, 1982), p. 98.
28. Quoted in Paletz and Dunn, "Press Coverage of Civil Disorder," p. 336.

Readings

Clarke, James W. *American Assassins: The Darker Side of Politics.* Princeton, N.J.: Princeton University Press, 1982.
Disasters and the Mass Media: Proceedings of the Committee on Disasters and the Mass Media Workshop. Washington, D.C.: National Academy of Sciences, 1980.
Greenberg, Bradley S., and Edwin B. Parker. *The Kennedy Assassination and the American Public: Social Communication in Crisis.* Palo Alto, Calif.: Stanford University Press, 1965.
Howitt, Dennis. *The Mass Media and Social Problems.* Oxford: Pergamon Press, 1982.
President's Commission on the Accident at Three Mile Island. *Report of the Public's Right to Information Task Force.* Washington, D.C.: U.S. Government Printing Office, October 1979.
Schmid, Alex P., and Janny de Graaf. *Violence as Communication: Insurgent Terrorism and the Western News Media.* Beverly Hills, Calif.: Sage, 1982.
Tichenor, Phillip J., George A. Donohue, and Clarice N. Olien. *Community Conflict and the Press.* Beverly Hills, Calif.: Sage, 1980.

Foreign Affairs Coverage

On November 22, 1978, after eight years of acrimonious debate and many months of intensive negotiations, the 146 states that are members of the United Nations Educational, Scientific and Cultural Organization (UNESCO), including the United States, finally endorsed a Declaration on the Media. The document consists of 11 brief articles and bears the rather pompous full title, "The Declaration of Fundamental Principles Concerning the Contribution of the Mass Media to Strengthening Peace and International Understanding, the Promotion of Human Rights and to Countering Racialism, Apartheid, and Incitement to War." Article III is typical in mapping out a wide area of political responsibility for the mass media. It states that "the mass media, by disseminating information on the aims, aspirations, cultures and needs of all people, contribute to eliminate ignorance and misunderstanding between peoples." The media also "make nationals of a country sensitive to the needs and desires of others," thereby ensuring "the respect of the rights and dignity of all nations, all peoples and all individuals." By drawing "attention to the great evils which afflict humanity, such as poverty, malnutrition and diseases," the media promote "the formulation by states of policies best able to promote the reduction of international tension and the peaceful and equitable settlement of international disputes." A tall order: Can, do, and should American media fill it? How are they organized to do this job?

To throw light on such questions, we will discuss the overall significance that American media and Americans assign to news about foreign countries. The types of foreign news most common in American media also will be examined. Foreign news gathering is quite different from domestic reporting, so we will consider the qualifications of foreign correspondents and the unique problems they face. Partly as a result of these problems, and partly because news about foreign countries reflects American foreign policy interests and is designed to satisfy American newsworthiness criteria, the world image presented by the American media is often distorted. A number of examples and their consequences for U.S. foreign policy will be assessed. Finally, media performance will be analyzed in light of UNESCO's high hopes for the press.

The Foreign News Slice in the News Pie

Newspeople and social scientists commonly assume that the American public is highly ethnocentric, interested primarily in what goes on in the United States. Newspaper and broadcast news editors routinely judge audience interest in foreign news to be less than interest in local and national news, sports, and comics. Americans themselves profess somewhat greater interest, but their claims are not matched by their behavior.[1] When given a choice, they do not seek out foreign policy news.

A number of studies have confirmed the accuracy of the ethnocentrism assumption. For instance, when the *Indianapolis News* polled readers and editors, asking them to name the top 10 stories in 1976, no foreign stories were mentioned by the readers. The editors, on the other hand, ranked six foreign affairs stories among the top 10. These included major events such as political changes in China, conflict in southern Africa, civil war in Lebanon, the murder of two U.S. soldiers by North Koreans, CIA foreign activities, and several earthquakes in foreign countries.[2]

The assumption of limited interest has put a damper on foreign affairs news coverage. On an average, in periods when there are no major crises, it constitutes only 11 percent of all stories in American newspapers and about 16 percent of the stories on national newscasts. By contrast, foreign affairs news takes up 17 percent of the newspaper space in Russian papers, 23 percent of the space in the press of Third World countries, 24 percent in Western European papers, and 38 percent in papers in Eastern European countries. Foreign affairs coverage is limited even in elite American newspapers. For instance, a comparative analysis of the world's press reported in 1977 that only 16 percent of the *New York Times* coverage was devoted to foreign affairs, compared with 22 percent in the *London Times,* 25 percent in the *Times of India,* 38 percent in Soviet *Pravda,* and 44 percent in the German *Die Welt.*[3] These figures have remained quite constant over the years.[4]

Besides being limited in number, foreign news stories generally receive comparatively brief space and time, and modest display. The standards that lead to publication for foreign news items are more rigorous than is true for domestic news. Foreign news must be more consequential, involve people of more exalted status, and entail more violence or disaster, for instance.[5]

Although interest in foreign affairs is limited, it does wax and wane with the shifting political currents. It was high during the Vietnam War, various Middle East crises in the 1970s and 1980s, and during presidential trips to China, starting in 1972. It also peaked during the seizure of the U.S. Embassy in Teheran by Iranian militants in 1979, and at various times during the period that ended in January 1981, when the American hostages were released. The 1983 bombing of Marine headquarters in Beirut, Lebanon, killing 241 U.S. servicemen, also focused attention on events abroad, as did the landing of U.S.

troops on the tiny island of Grenada at almost the same time. Even during periods when interest is at a low ebb, television has made more Americans than ever before aware of foreign affairs news. In pretelevision days, many who would have skipped such news if they encountered it in newspapers now are exposed to it on television. Thus while exposure to foreign affairs information is massive, lack of interest still keeps learning at a relatively low level.[6]

When the spotlight shifts away from foreign news, the number of foreign correspondents usually declines. There were 637 accredited U.S. correspondents in South Vietnam in 1968. As American involvement in the war dwindled, the number dropped to 392 by 1970 and 295 by 1972. By mid-1974, only 33 remained. Even though this small corps of correspondents filed relatively few stories from Vietnam, it became difficult to induce editors to use Vietnam stories in daily newscasts and papers because the public had presumably lost interest. When this happens, a spiral effect sets in. Presumed lack of interest leads to less coverage. Reduced coverage further lessens interest in foreign news. An upward spiral of domestic news takes up the slack. This pattern prevails in most of the country's newspapers and television newscasts whenever foreign crises subside.

Compared with average papers and newscasts, prestige papers such as the *New York Times,* the *Washington Post,* and the *Los Angeles Times* provide fairly extensive, thorough, and steady foreign affairs coverage. The country's foreign policy elites, including government officials, depend heavily on these media. A comment from a State Department official is typical: "The first thing we do is read the newspaper—*the newspaper*—the *New York Times.* You can't work in the State Department without the *New York Times.*"[7] Members of the U.S. Congress, particularly those concerned with foreign affairs, and foreign officials in the United States have made similar comments. All feel that elite newspaper reports keep them informed faster and often better than their own official sources.

Making Foreign News

Although differences between newsmaking for domestic stories and newsmaking for foreign stories are substantial, there are also many similarities. To make comparisons easier, we will discuss foreign newsmaking following the organization of our discussion of domestic newsmaking and news reporting in Chapter 3. First we will consider the gatekeepers—the corps of foreign correspondents who are the front-line echelon among foreign affairs news gatherers. Then we will discuss in turn the setting for news selection; the criteria for choosing stories and the means of gathering them; the constraints on news production; and finally the effects of gatekeeping on foreign affairs coverage.

The Gatekeepers

Concentration of Control.   A striking aspect of foreign news coverage is the extreme degree of concentration of the newsgathering process. Most foreign news for the American press is collected by only seven newspapers, the two wire services, and the three national television networks, along with an occasional story from syndicated columnists and news feature services. The papers are the *New York Times, Washington Post, Los Angeles Times, Baltimore Sun, Chicago Tribune, Wall Street Journal,* and *Christian Science Monitor.*[8] Most coverage comes from the wire services. They ferret out the stories that make up the pool from which other gatekeepers select complete reports or find leads to pursue stories more fully. Because wire service reporters work for a vast variety of clients—UPI alone goes to 113 countries in 48 languages—their news must be bland, emphasizing fast and ample reports of ongoing events, not interpretation. Interpretation and follow-up depend on other foreign correspondents.

The stories gathered by the small corps of initial gatekeepers reach a huge audience. During the mid-1970s, the *New York Times* syndicate supplied news for 330 papers in the United States and 97 abroad; the *Los Angeles Times-Washington Post* feature service supplied 290 papers in the United States and 60 abroad.[9] Although subscribers generally use only a limited portion of the coverage made available by the syndicates, what they do use mirrors the story patterns and interpretation of the pace-setting foreign news sources. For instance, when the *New York Times* labeled a 1958 Soviet note to Britain, France, and the United States as an "ultimatum," the American press almost universally followed the lead, even though the facts were questionable and some papers had originally adopted different interpretations.[10] "Once the main stories of the day have been identified and defined, the media can be like a stampeding herd, hard to turn toward a new interpretation of an issue." The stories chosen set the scene for follow-up stories. "The news of today sequels the news in the news of yesterday. Only a relatively small number of journalists are able or allowed to open up new areas of concern."[11] Stereotypes become fixed; countries and leaders whom gatekeepers depict as friendly or antagonistic to the United States may retain those characterizations long after the reality has changed.

Surveillance of the Foreign Scene.   In 1975, 676 full-time overseas correspondents served the American media, including 429 Americans and 247 foreigners. Six years earlier, there had been 929 foreign correspondents, including 563 Americans and 366 foreigners. Between 1969 and 1975 the foreign correspondent corps declined by 27 percent.[12] Several reasons account for this. The winding down of the Vietnam War is one. The ability to dispatch correspondents quickly from an American home base to foreign countries is another. Air travel has made it possible for each American correspondent to reach and cover many more countries than ever before. But physical mobility is not matched by the psychic mobility that would allow reporters to feel at home in more countries. Nor is it accompanied by sudden spurts in knowledge that would permit reporters to cover a new area with insight.

High costs also have led to reduced numbers. During the late 1970s, it cost up to $150,000 a year to keep one correspondent abroad, a steep price considering the limited demand for foreign affairs stories. Using stringers instead of regular employees was much cheaper. Stringers, usually citizens of the country from which they report, are paid for each story they produce.[13] At best, they may have keener insight into local problems than American reporters sent there.

Correspondents are unevenly distributed. More are stationed in friendly countries and areas than in neutral or hostile ones. Table 10-1 tells the story. In 1975, two-thirds of the Middle East correspondents were stationed in Israel and Lebanon, for instance. Correspondents accredited to Western Hemisphere countries served primarily in Canada, Brazil, and Argentina. Asian correspondents were concentrated in Hong Kong, Japan, and Australia. Africa was the most understaffed, with full-time reporters in only four countries. However, their reports were supplemented through news from Reuters and Agence France-Presse, the British and French news agencies respectively, which had more ample representation in Africa. With the decline in the number of foreign correspondents, the number of countries in which newsmen were stationed narrowed as well. In 1972, 64 countries had one American journalist or more, but by 1975 this had dropped to 54 countries.

Table 10-1 Distribution of Foreign Correspondents in 1975

	Distribution of Americans		Origin of Foreigners Covering U.S.	
	N	%	N	%
Western Europe	345	51	(465)	(54)
Central/East Asia	155	23	(132)	(15)
Latin America	101	15	(77)	(9)
Middle East	54	8	(53)	(6)
Africa	34	5	(8)	(1)
East Europe, USSR	20	3	(46)	(5)
Australia/New Zealand	13	2	(33)	(4)
Canada	7	1	(42)	(5)
Worldwide	—	—	(9)	(1)

For Americans covering foreign countries, N = 676; for foreigners covering United States, N = 865. Figures add to more than 100 percent because some correspondents cover more than one area. (Figures for foreigners covering the United States have been added for comparison.)

SOURCE: Foreign data from Hamid Mowlana, "Who Covers America?" *Journal of Communication* 25 (Summer 1975): 87; U.S. data from John A. Lent, "Foreign News in American Media," *Journal of Communication* 27 (Winter 1977): 49.

What kinds of people are these journalists who select the foreign news for American elites and publics? What are their biases? And how do they compare with the correspondents who cover the United States for the benefit of foreign nationals?

A typical American journalist abroad is a white male in his forties, college educated, with more than 10 years of foreign news reporting under his belt. Many have remained at the same locations for several years, so that they are fully familiar with the areas.[14] As Table 10-2 shows, however, this does not necessarily mean language competence. In Western Europe and Latin America, more than 80 percent of American reporters read and speak the native languages fluently or with easy facility. But in Eastern Europe and Africa, these figures are cut in half. The poorest showing is in Central and East Asia, where only 9 percent of American reporters are able to read the intricate written characters, and only 18 percent can speak the languages well. Deficient reading skills hamper American reporters in local interviews and investigations. They must depend on translated newspaper reports and on handouts to the foreign press. This sharply curbs their effectiveness as reporters.

Contacts with local people and personal ties that may supply good insights are also sparse. In Western Europe, 33 percent of the correspondents say that most of their close friendships and social contacts are with nationals of the country. In Latin America, this is true for 23 percent. The figure drops to 16 percent for Eastern Europe, and 15 percent for Central and East Asia.[15] When more casual contacts are added, these figures double, but they still spell a gap in integration into the local setting.

By their own identification, 54 percent of American foreign correspondents lean to the left in their politics, 32 percent are middle-roaders, and 14

Table 10-2   Foreign Language Fluency of American Reporters

	Western Europe		Latin America		Asia		East Europe, Africa, Middle East	
	Read	Speak	Read	Speak	Read	Speak	Read	Speak
Native Fluency	62%	51%	70%	56%	3%	6%	21%	20%
Easy Facility	23	31	19	30	6	12	17	28
Partial	10	16	11	14	23	33	28	32
Slight	3	2	—	—	3	15	10	8
None	1	—	—	—	65	33	24	12

N = 174. The question was: [If English is not the local language] "How familiar are you with the language spoken in the country in which you are stationed?"

SOURCE: Adapted from Leo Bogart, "The Overseas Newsman: A 1967 Profile Study," *Journalism Quarterly* 45 (Summer 1968): 300.

Table 10-3   Agree/Disagree on "U.S. Adds to Third World Poverty" (in percentages)

Media Institutions	Agree	Disagree
Print		
New York Times	61%	39%
Washington Post	61	39
Wall Street Journal	33	67
Newsweek	56	44
Time	35	65
U.S. News & World Report	28	72
Television		
ABC	64%	36%
CBS	45	55
NBC	57	43
PBS	83	17

N = 234. The statement was: "American economic exploitation has contributed to Third World poverty."

SOURCE: S. Robert Lichter, "America and the Third World: A Survey of Leading Media and Business Leaders," in *Television Coverage of International Affairs*, ed. William C. Adams (Norwood, N.J.: Ablex, 1982), p. 75. Reprinted by permission.

percent lean to the right. These figures closely parallel those for staff people generally in prominent American news organizations.[16] When the views of media people in prominent news organizations are compared with the views of business leaders, the gap is vast. For instance, on the question of whether American exploitation adds to Third World poverty, 55 percent of the media people said yes, compared with 22 percent of the business people.[17]

Table 10-3 shows how newspeople from various elite media answered this question. Political orientations among people affiliated with different news organizations obviously vary considerably. Reports on general trends mask these differences. For instance, the fact that an average of 49 percent of people in all the print media in the sample take the liberal stance (that is, agree that the United States adds to Third World poverty), compared with an average of 64 percent in the television media, masks the fact that *New York Times* personnel have a more liberal score than CBS or NBC personnel.

Surveillance of the American Scene. Altogether, 865 correspondents from foreign countries covered the United States in 1975. As Table 10-1 shows, most of them came from nations friendly to the United States. Just as Americans receive most news about friendly foreign countries, so most news about America goes to her friends. Communication with countries outside the friendship circle is far less ample.[18] The foreign journalists stationed in the United States represent various regions and countries unevenly. In 1975, the foreign press corps included no correspondents from black Africa. Israel was represented by 23 correspondents, while the Middle Eastern Arab countries combined had only 13 journalists, including 3 from Egypt. Taiwan in 1975 had 23 registered correspondents, while the People's Republic of China had none. India was represented by 10 newspeople, Pakistan by 1. Canada's media sent 43, compared with 8 from Mexico, the other next-door neighbor of the United States. With the exception of Argentina and Brazil, few Latin American countries had correspondents stationed in the United States.

Foreign reporters are an extremely well-educated group. In 1975, about half had advanced degrees, and 13 percent had Ph.D.s. On the average, they spoke three languages. Nevertheless, close contacts with Americans were limited. Only 7 percent said that their best and closest contacts were Americans. In political orientation, foreign newspeople covering the United States were further to the left than most American reporters. Seventy percent claimed to be left-leaning, 14 percent preferred a middle position, and 17 percent leaned to the right.[19]

It is difficult for foreign reporters to cover the whole United States adequately. Most correspondents are kept busy in Washington and New York. They rarely travel to other parts of the country, except to cover special events such as the Summer Olympics in Los Angeles or a political convention in Dallas. Thus the impressions that foreigners receive about Americans, their views and their politics, are largely official Washington views. The leftward orientation of most reporters from foreign countries produces a substantial amount of criticism of the American economic scene and interventionist foreign ventures and often makes the conduct of foreign relations rocky. Hostile coverage is only partially balanced by the influx of news from American media and government broadcasts, such as those of the Voice of America.

The Setting for News Selection

Cultural Pressures.   As is true in covering domestic news, American correspondents abroad must operate within the context of current American politics and current American political culture. Although their personal leanings may be to the left of the political spectrum, they aim for the middle ground in their stories because that is what their audiences presumably want. Keeping in touch with the American scene is deemed so important that news organizations bring their reporters back to the United States periodically to refresh their feel for what is going on at home.

Stories not only must reflect the American value structure, but also must conform to established American stereotypes. Accordingly, stories by U.S. correspondents in Peru about reforms initiated there by a military government were rejected as lies because they contradicted the stereotype that military regimes support the status quo.[20] Similarly, the credibility of stories about the problems of Peruvian youth might be questioned unless these same problems were plaguing American youth.[21] On the other hand, U.S. correspondents abroad have greater leeway than their domestic counterparts to evaluate and interpret news for domestic audiences because there is less likelihood that large numbers of people or powerful interest groups will be offended.

Intra-organizational norms and pressures also influence news selection. The news is gathered by a small enough group of reporters so that personal contacts and cooperation are common. The wire services perform the initial gatekeeping tasks for most newspapers and electronic media. Elite papers, such as the *New York Times,* then fashion the norms for presentation and interpretation which editors and reporters throughout the country adapt for their media.

Political Pressures.   Overt and covert political pressures play a greater role in foreign news production than on the domestic scene. Pressures are negative—to refrain from covering certain stories—as well as positive—to give publicity that otherwise might be denied. Foreign correspondents are more or less welcome guests in the countries from which they are reporting and often must do their hosts' bidding. Many of these hosts are dictators whose political survival depends on ensuring supportive publicity for their regimes and squelching unfavorable coverage. Foreign correspondents, like their own newspeople, are heavily censored. If foreign correspondents want to remain in the country, they must write dispatches acceptable to the authorities. Otherwise they face severe penalties—expulsion, confiscation of their notes and pictures, closure of transmission facilities, refusal of contact by public officials, and the like. This has led to the strange phenomenon that the most totalitarian countries often receive the least criticism while more open societies are freely reproached.

Censorship can take the form of denying visas. In 1975 alone, 21 countries denied entry to American reporters. Some countries, such as Cambodia, Laos, and Vietnam, have completely shut out all foreign correspondents for years on end. Expulsions of correspondents are also common.[22] Reporters may be prevented from covering certain stories. When the Chinese city of Tangshan was destroyed by an earthquake on July 28, 1976, and more than 655,000 people were killed, reporters stationed in Peking, barely 100 miles away, were denied permission for more than a year to visit the scene.[23] Britain kept foreign reporters away from the embattled Falkland Islands in 1983. Israel repeatedly has imposed tight censorship on coverage of its activities in Lebanon. During the Iran-Iraq hostilities in the early 1980s, reporters were permitted at the front only whenever the host country thought it had won an engagement. South Africa has made it illegal to quote "banned" people or to describe prison conditions. In the Soviet Union, reporters who interview dissidents are harassed.

Bureaucratic hurdles abound. In Moscow, television reporters depend on the Novosti Press Agency for camera crews and access to various sites. Cameras are made available only after a story proposal has been approved by the Foreign Ministry's Press Department. Once a proposal has been filed, no deviations are allowed. Promised camera crews frequently arrive late or not at all. Pictures often are deliberately out of focus, and transmission equipment may be disconnected if events do not proceed as planned.

Reporters in some countries may even face physical danger. Not infrequently, they have been jailed, manhandled, and sometimes murdered. During the Nicaraguan revolution of 1979, for instance, a national guardsman, angry over American support of revolutionary forces, shot and killed an American television reporter. Several murders of newspeople in Lebanon in the 1980s have been attributed to the wrath of Syrian authorities about stories attributed to these journalists.[24] The Helsinki Accords of 1975, in which many countries promised free and safe access to each other's newspeople, have done little to improve the situation.

When previously closed countries suddenly open their borders to newspeople, the foreign press may be totally unprepared for insightful coverage. The opening of the People's Republic of China in 1972 is an example. Reporters arrived with President Richard Nixon and Secretary of State Henry Kissinger. During their short stay in China, they dutifully shot those pictures that the Chinese allowed them to shoot and reported those stories that the Chinese arranged for them to report. The resulting coverage was a romanticized travelogue rather than solid political analysis.

Media Diplomacy.   A recent development in foreign news production is "television diplomacy"—attempts by television correspondents in the United States and abroad to inject themselves directly into the political process and attempts by U.S. and foreign leaders to use television to further their causes. The Middle East situation in the late 1970s presents a number of dramatic examples. CBS anchorman Walter Cronkite became a peacemaker on November 14, 1977, during a television satellite interview, when he drew from Egypt's President Anwar el Sadat a public promise to go to Jerusalem if this would further peace. In a separate interview, Cronkite secured a pledge from Israeli Prime Minister Menachem Begin that he would personally welcome Sadat at Ben Gurion airport, should he come. With such mutual commitments, the scene was set for the historic meeting.

When Sadat arrived in Israel on November 19, anchorpersons from the three American networks were in his entourage. Among the welcoming crowds at the airport were an additional 2,000 journalists from all over the globe. Again this was media diplomacy in the broadest sense. The event was covered live on American television and radio, giving the principals a chance to woo American television audiences. In the weeks to come, more than 30 million Americans and millions worldwide would watch and judge the peacemaking process. Television alone devoted 24 hours of broadcasts to the spectacle, supplemented by radio and print news.

When the Arab-Israeli peacemaking scene moved to the United States in the following spring, media diplomacy continued. President Sadat, fully aware of the importance of wooing the American public, made himself available for a television interview immediately after arrival for the 1978 Camp David meeting. The next day he appeared before the National Press Club for a public address in which he accused the Israelis of stalling the negotiations. Israel countered this propaganda move by promptly dispatching Foreign Minister Moshe Dayan on a 10-day speaking tour of major American cities to garner favorable publicity for the Israeli side.[25] The media covered it all with relish, proud of the role newspeople had played in bringing about encounters between Israeli and Egyptian officials. Little thought was given to the political ramifications that ensue when foreign heads of state readily use the American press as a public relations tool.

The lessons learned by Sadat and Begin have not been lost on other world leaders. For instance, in 1979 Iran's revolutionary leader, Ayatollah Ruhollah Khomeini, rebuffed official emissaries from the United States who were sent to negotiate the release of the American embassy personnel held hostage by Iranian students. Khomeini preferred to discuss the situation instead with American television correspondents. A series of interviews were arranged. By requiring prior approval of questions, the Iranian government carefully controlled what was discussed. To ensure maximum exposure for the Ayatollah's views, Iranian leaders permitted an especially lengthy interview for the highly popular CBS program "60 Minutes." At the same time they assigned low priority to an interview to be aired on low-audience public television. The Iranian embassy also bought full-page advertisements in the *New York Times* and other American newspapers to acquaint the American public with Iran's version of the hostage story.

For their part, reporters used interviews with Iranian officials to suggest policies that might resolve the crisis and to elicit Iranian views and counterproposals. Placing these views before a worldwide audience made them part of the agenda of international politics. Media diplomacy had the advantage of facilitating negotiations that had broken down at the diplomatic level. A number of excellent proposals were generated. Nonetheless, media diplomacy is fraught with disadvantages and dangers. Government officials, who have far more foreign policy expertise than journalists, may be maneuvered into untenable positions. Foreign policy then may become incoherent and inexpert, with serious consequences for the nation.

Economic Pressures. Economic considerations, like cultural and political pressures, strongly influence foreign news selection. First, there is the usual pressure to present appealing stories that attract wide audiences and keep the media profitable. This pressure is even more burdensome for foreign correspondents than for their domestic counterparts because their stories must be exceptionally good to attract large audiences. Second, there is the pressure to avoid or minimize huge production costs. Reporting events such as President Nixon's trip to China or the Yom Kippur War cost each network in excess of $3 million per event. Leasing cables for news transmission is expensive and so is telephone communication. Satellite transmission is also costly, especially for short messages. Networks therefore normally avoid satellites unless they have several important stories to transmit. Networks may pool stories to save on transmission expenses. In the process, some stories may be shut out because they cannot be transmitted cheaply and quickly while others may be included merely because they happened while satellites were in use.

Gathering the News: The Beat

The international beat system is quite similar to local beats. Originally, newspapers established their foreign news bureaus in major capitals of the world, primarily in Western Europe. From there correspondents covered entire countries rather than particular types of stories: London, Paris, Bonn, and Rome were the main newsgathering spots. In the wake of the Vietnam War, Saigon and other Far Eastern points, such as Tokyo and Hong Kong, became important news centers. China moved into focus with the opening of diplomatic relations in 1972.

The average newspaper bureau abroad has one or two correspondents, one or two film crews staffed by foreigners, perhaps a radio correspondent, and a few stringers. Correspondents from these bureaus jet to spots within easy flying range whenever big stories break. For local news, they rely heavily on national news services that exist in two-thirds of the countries of the world. Countries without such services, and without satellite transmission facilities, are far less likely to receive coverage than countries that have them.

The major Western wire services and the three American television networks have overseas news bureaus in the main news centers of the world. However, for nonvisual news the networks rely heavily on wire and newspaper services. Seventy to 80 percent of foreign news copy read on the air comes directly from the wire services.[26] In this way "the major international news agencies and elite newspapers set the agenda for international affairs coverage by other media, including U.S. network television." [27]

The bulk of foreign affairs news for American media actually originates in Washington from various beats in the executive branch. Such stories may be hard to get because officials are reluctant to discuss foreign affairs whenever delicate negotiations or the prestige of the United States are at stake. A further common drawback to Washington stories is their lack of exciting pictures to dramatize them for television. Like domestic newspeople,

Reprinted by permission. Tribune Media Services, Inc.

foreign correspondents prefer predictable stories, like elections or summit conferences, so that coverage can be planned well in advance. The decision to film particular foreign stories abroad is usually made in the United States because the media's home offices consider themselves in closer touch with the interests of American audiences. Foreign bureaus do the actual filming.

Foreign news bestows unequal attention on various countries just as domestic news covers regions of the United States unequally. Neither is there any correlation between size of population and amount of coverage.[28] In general, beats cover America's closest political allies and the major Communist countries. Specifically, this means England, France, West Germany, Italy, and the Soviet Union in Europe; Israel and Egypt in the Middle East; and, more recently, the People's Republic of China and Japan in the Far East. Africa and Latin America are lightly covered, except when Americans become involved in hostilities there. Asian coverage was light until the Vietnam War, when for several years it replaced most stories from other parts of the world.

Table 10-4 provides data on coverage of major regions of the world during two four-year periods, 1972-1975 and 1976-1979. It demonstrates the consistently heavy emphasis on Western Europe and the shifting focus of attention depending on the world's patterns of war and unrest.[29]

Table 10-4 Network Coverage of Major Regions, 1972-1975 and 1976-1979
(in percentages)

Region	1972-1975	1976-1979
Eastern Europe and USSR	16%	19%
Western Europe	30	30
Middle East	20	30
Africa (Sub-Sahara)	2	13
South Asia	2	2
Southeast Asia and Pacific	34	9
East Asia	10	12
Latin America	7	14
Canada	2	4
(N)	(2,680)	(2,798)

NOTE: Measured by the percentage of sampled stories in which one or more nations from the region are mentioned. Percentages sum to more than 100 percent.

SOURCE: James F. Larson, "International Affairs Coverage on U.S. Evening Network News, 1972-1979," in *Television Coverage of International Affairs,* ed. William C. Adams (Norwood, N.J.: Ablex, 1982), p. 37. Reprinted by permission.

Criteria for Choosing Stories

As is true of domestic stories, particular foreign news items are selected primarily for audience appeal rather than for political significance. This means that they must have an angle that is of interest to Americans. Sociologist Herbert Gans, who examined foreign affairs news in television newscasts and in news magazines, has compiled a list of seven subjects that are most often aired.[30] They include, first, American activities in foreign countries, particularly when presidents and secretaries of state visit there. Second, they encompass events that affect Americans directly in a major way. Wars or oil embargoes are examples, along with problems that transcend national boundaries, like unemployment and inflation.

A third area of interest concerns relations of the United States with Communist countries. Internal problems of these countries that relate to their political and military power are emphasized. Elections in non-Communist countries where strong Communist parties are involved, such as those in France and Italy, are also part of the routine coverage of the "Communist menace." Fourth, foreign elections in other parts of the world are covered if they involve a change in the head of state. There also is a sentimental attachment for following the major activities of European royalty.

The fifth subject area entails stories about dramatic political conflicts. Most wars, coups d'état, and revolutions are reported; protests, as a rule, are covered only when they are violent. Left-wing coups receive more attention than right-wing coups. Disasters, if they involve massive loss of lives and destruction of property, are a sixth area of interest. There is a rough calculus by which severity is measured: "10,000 deaths in Nepal equals 100 deaths in Wales equals 10 deaths in West Virginia equals one death next door." [31] In general, the more distant a nation, the more frequently a newsworthy event must happen to be reported.

The seventh area of coverage involves the excesses of foreign dictators, particularly brutality against political dissidents. The deeds of Uganda's ruler Idi Amin and the leaders of Latin American death squads are examples of such news.[32] Noticeably absent from American broadcasts and papers are stories about ordinary people and ordinary events abroad. These would be news to Americans, but, except for occasional special features, they are not "news" in the professional dictionary of journalists.

Foreign news stories also must have an appealing format. Emphasis on violence, conflict and disaster, timeliness or novelty, and familiarity of persons or situation are the major selection criteria. For instance, stories from Western Europe and other culturally related areas are more likely to be published than stories from other parts of the world. When news from countries with unfamiliar cultural settings is published, the rule of "uncertainty absorption" comes into play. This unwritten rule requires that information of uncertain accuracy, coming from remote sources, be eliminated by foreign news gatekeepers. They must publish plausible stories only.[33] The impact of such cumulative biases makes it very difficult to change images of culturally distant countries. Stories from far-off parts of the world are rarely covered except when they report highly exciting events such as violence and disaster or involve major events and personalities, preferably in a negative context.[34] Moreover, the high costs of covering news abroad force news organizations to limit the sites where full-scale news operations can be maintained.

The need to produce stories that have recently surfaced has led to concentration on rapidly breaking news in accessible places, regardless of its intrinsic importance. Long-range developments, which lack a recent climax— like programs to improve public health or reduce illiteracy or develop new political parties—do not fill the bill. Pressure for recentness and novelty also makes news presentation fragmented, with little follow-through. This gives major events an unwarranted air of suddenness and unpredictability. They have neither a past nor a future—merely a brief presence in the parade of current events.

For example, when war-torn El Salvador held elections in March 1982, the press was there in full force, grinding out stories day after day. Coverage dwindled abruptly after the election, even though little had changed in El Salvador and the Reagan administration continued to claim that the United States had important interests in that country. Most American media failed to explain the consequences of the election. When questioned about the exodus of newspeople, news executives said that other crises and events beckoned: the Falkland Islands War, fighting in Lebanon, and the foreign journeys of President Ronald Reagan and Pope John Paul II.[35]

At times, coverage errs in the opposite direction. The Iran hostage story was vastly overcovered, with its dramatic visual scenes of young Americans held captive in a strange land, angry anti-American crowds, and anxious kinfolk at home. During the first six months of the crisis, nearly one-third of each nightly network newscast was devoted to the story.[36] With media attention riveted on developments in Iran, most other foreign news was slighted.

News Production Constraints

The problems of producing domestic news are magnified for foreign newsmaking. Staffs are smaller, research facilities are more limited, language barriers are troublesome, and transmission difficulties may be enormous. Then, once the story finally reaches the audience, it may not be heard because of basic disinterest or ignorance of the setting in which it originated.

Production constraints are particularly severe for television news, which presents the bulk of foreign news to the average American. The quest for good pictures is often frustrated by restrictions on access or because facilities for taking and processing pictures are inadequate.[37] Pictures are especially important for foreign news because they bring unfamiliar sights, which might be hard to imagine, directly into viewers' homes. Starvation in India or Nicaragua, the lifestyles of primitive tribes in New Guinea or Australia, or street riots in Spain or Hungary are better understood if they can be visually experienced.

However, not even words and pictures combined can tell the whole story if the audience is unfamiliar with the setting in which the reported events are happening. Television news showed Buddhists rioting in Saigon and Da Nang during the Vietnam War, but "the pictures could not show you that a block away from the Saigon riots the populace was shopping, chatting, sitting in restaurants in total normalcy. The riots involved a tiny portion in either city; yet the effect of the pictures in this country, including the Congress, was explosive. People thought that Vietnam was tearing itself apart, that civil war was raging. Nothing of the sort was happening."[38] When gripping visuals appear at a time of crisis and uncertainty about current policies, their impact can be extraordinarily great.

The need to keep news stories brief is particularly troubling for foreign correspondents because foreign news is often unintelligible without adequate background information or interpretation. Complexity therefore becomes a major enemy, and avoidance or oversimplification the defensive strategy.

Stories must be written simply and logically even if the situation defies logic. Usually a single theme must be selected to epitomize the entire complex story.

For instance, in January 1972 British Prime Minister Edward Heath went to Brussels to sign an agreement that would bring Britain into the Common Market.[39] A four-minute mini-documentary on television devoted one minute and thirty seconds to the signing ceremony, explaining that Britain and three other countries were beginning a period of integration into the market. The remaining two minutes and thirty seconds were used to explain why agricultural products had created the greatest stumbling block to Britain's entry. Pictures of horse and plow farmers in France and more mechanized farming elsewhere were used as backdrops. The basic theme was that each country was trying to protect its own farmers while keeping the price of farm products low for consumers. This was a gross oversimplification of the highly complex issues involved in Britain's entry, but it made an appealing story, comprehensible to the average listener and viewer.

Effects of Gatekeeping

The various factors that determine the selection of foreign news stories result in foreign affairs coverage that is ample, dramatic, and up-to-date. But it lacks depth and breadth, it stereotypes and oversimplifies, and it often distorts facts in the interest of timeliness. Officials and publics who rely on foreign affairs news may be misled, and faulty policies may ensue. The stories that preceded United States intervention in the Dominican Republic in 1965 are a case in point. While they should not be taken as the norm, they are indicative of the dangers inherent in current news practices.

The Dominican Republic Case. When dispatches reached the United States in late April and early May 1965 that a military coup was in progress in the Dominican Republic, American correspondents were hastily sent to the scene. Upon arrival, they were not allowed by Dominican Republic authorities to visit the cities and countryside because of the military activities. Instead, they received a briefing from the American ambassador based on second-hand information. Because of pressure to meet the earliest publication deadlines, stories were sent out before they could be verified. Since they had come from an authentic source—the American ambassador—no disclaimers were made.

The *Los Angeles Herald Examiner* reported on April 30 that Cuban Communists had arranged the insurrection and that the loss of life was horrifying. "There are about 2,000 casualties, and about half of them are dead. In one street alone, there were at least 90 people dead or dying. There are children dying on the streets with their stomachs ripped open, and nobody to bury their bodies. It is carnage. It is real civil war. The streets are almost literally running with blood." [40] One week later, on May 7, *Time* magazine still reported that "No one had an accurate count of casualties as frenzied knots of soldiers and civilians roamed the streets, shooting, looting and herding people to their execution. . . . The rebels executed at least 110 opponents, hacked the head off a police officer and carried it about as a trophy." *U.S. News & World Report* on May 10 spoke of victims being "dragged from their homes and shot down while angry mobs shouted, 'To the wall!'—the same cry that marked mass executions in Cuba in the early days of Fidel Castro." [41]

On the basis of such reports, President Lyndon B. Johnson, with the approval of the Organization of American States, sent more than 1,000 Marines to the Dominican Republic to quell the rebellion, stop the bloodshed, and halt the march of communism. When the correspondents were finally allowed to visit the cities and countryside, they discovered that none of the horror stories that they had reported had been true. Instead of the 1,000 and 1,500 bodies which, according to President Johnson, had made the intervention imperative, there were fewer than a dozen. There was no looting either, and no display of severed heads. Only a small number of the forces seeking to overthrow the established government were Communists. But by that time it was too late to undo the severe political damage that the American intervention had done to the Dominican Republic and to the reputation of the United States.

Typecasting the Lebanon Invasion.   Judging from public opinion polls and the pronouncements of highly placed American officials, America's love affair with the state of Israel cooled considerably during the early 1980s. The Israeli government and other supporters of Israel believed that the change in public opinion had much to do with biased newspaper and television coverage of what happened in Lebanon during the summer of 1982. Pictures of wartime horrors stirred emotions and produced revulsion without telling the whys and wherefores of the fighting. It was high drama, sans information. To undo the damage attributed to hostile coverage and set the record straight about Israeli military actions in Lebanon, a Jewish group prepared a documentary for American television. It was called "NBC in Lebanon: A Study in Media Misrepresentation," and it aired in February 1984. The documentary deals with the period from June 4 to August 31, 1982, a time span in which NBC Nightly News devoted 600 minutes of air time to Lebanon.

The documentary makes a good case that much of the news about Israel's invasion of Lebanon and the aftermath was distorted because it came from biased sources that were not adequately checked by the networks. The impact of the news clips from Lebanon was heightened because prominent commentators, using overblown rhetoric, severely condemned Israel. For example, on June 10, NBC anchorman Roger Mudd said that 10,000 civilians had died, attributing the figure to the Lebanese Red Crescent—a Red Cross relief organization. Israeli sources at the time claimed 460 civilian deaths. Shortly afterwards, NBC correspondent Jessica Savitch reported that fighting had left 600,000 civilians without food and other essential supplies. The corresponding Israeli figure was 20,000. Additionally, Israeli sources indicated that fewer than 600,000 civilians actually lived in the combat area. At the time when the Lebanese Red Crescent figures were accepted, the brother of PLO leader Yasir Arafat, according to Israeli accounts, was the head of the Red Crescent.

Failure to present background information was another source of potentially serious misperceptions. NBC correspondents, for example, showed film of ruined buildings, accompanied by commentary that these were not military positions. The implication was that Israeli artillery was indiscriminately leveling civilian targets. NBC failed to mention that the PLO frequently stored ammunition in densely populated areas presumably to deter Israeli attacks. If this failed, the attacks were expected to turn the tide of world public opinion against Israel.

That there was anger, indeed, in important quarters can be judged from comments by NBC commentator John Chancellor. Chancellor accused Israel of becoming "imperial" and turning into a "warrior state, using far more force than is necessary to solve its problems." He also compared the bombing of Beirut to the bombing of Madrid during the Spanish Civil War. In his words: "Israel can't go on much longer horrifying the world by its brutal siege of West Beirut." [42] Coupled with pictures of dead and wounded civilians, including many women and children, and sites of destroyed villages and crumbled city streets, such emotional commentary was apt to leave its mark.

Other Television Wars. There is a growing belief among politicians and other political observers that fighting lengthy wars has become nearly impossible for democratic societies in the age of full-color, battle-front television. When battle scenes are broadcast nightly in gruesome color in the nation's living rooms, public support for wars is quickly lost. The political consequences can be vast. The ability of democratic societies to enforce their international goals may be diminished, especially compared with countries that are not subject to similar restraints. The depiction of Israel's invasion and siege of Beirut presents a case in point. In the wake of footage of human carnage, Israel lost measurable amounts of support from its closest allies. This loss reduced its ability to pursue the war and undermined its bargaining position.

In the Falkland Islands War between Great Britain and Argentina from April 2 to June 16, 1982, a Democratic nation and its authoritarian antagonist both resorted to the kind of censorship usually associated only with authoritarian regimes. Like the Russians in Afghanistan or the Syrians in Lebanon, the British and the Argentines curbed and delayed pictorial coverage of the war to reduce possibly adverse consequences at home. Similarly, no reporters were permitted to witness the first phases of the U.S. invasion of Grenada, staged by the Reagan administration in 1983 *(see discussion on page 115)*. At this point in time it is difficult to judge whether the one potentially beneficial consequence of television wars—the reduction in unwarranted armed conflict—has materialized to any degree, large or small.

Distortions and Their Consequences. Just like domestic news, foreign news neglects major social problems, particularly political and economic development issues. In 1977, only 11 percent of foreign affairs coverage dealt with social problems.[43] The reasons are readily apparent. Social problems are difficult to describe in brief stories, visual materials are often lacking, and changes come at a glacial pace. Some of them, like the story of the European Common Market, are extremely complex. Most reporters are ill-equipped to understand let alone describe them. When they do describe them, the focus is on their dramatic negative aspects: shortages, famines, conflicts, and breakdowns. As Rafael Caldera, former president of Venezuela, told a press conference at the National Press Club in Washington, D.C., "the phrase 'no news is good news' has become 'good news is no news'. . . . Little or nothing is mentioned about literary or scientific achievements" in American media or "about social achievements and the defense against the dangers which threaten our peace and development." Instead, "only the most deplorable incidents, be they caused by nature or by man, receive prominent attention." [44]

Negative and conflictual news is more prevalent in the U.S. media than in the media of many other societies, especially those of the Socialist world. Comparisons of U.S. and Canadian news coverage furnish examples drawn from a society that is culturally close to America. The rate of violence on Canadian television news is half the U.S. rate.[45] When the people of Quebec voted in 1980 on the question of separatism from Canada, the *Washington Post* warned that civil war might erupt. American papers featured stories about serious rioting by separatists in English sectors of Montreal. By contrast, the *Toronto Globe and Mail* buried a small story about minor unrest in Quebec in the back pages. The prospect of civil war was never mentioned and was characterized as "ludicrous" by knowledgeable observers.[46] During the Iranian hostage crisis, *New York Times* coverage was dominated by stereotypical portrayals of Moslems and by tales of violence. Substantially different, far more peaceful images emerged from reading the French paper *Le Monde*.[47]

By and large, all Western news media feature more conflict than media in authoritarian and totalitarian societies. In part, this happens because government-controlled news organizations find it comparatively easy to shun dramatic negative news since governmental subsidies relieve them of the need to secure large audiences. Regardless of the reasons for the difference, the approach used by American news media draws attention to conflict rather than to peaceful settlement and makes much of the world outside of the United States seem chaotic. While ordinary foreign news languishes in the back pages or is condensed into the briefest broadcast accounts, stories concerned with civil disorder and revolutions are featured prominently. Usually they are oversimplified and told from an American perspective that may be totally inappropriate. Instead of interpreting what the conflict means to the country and its people, the dominant concern ordinarily is whether the leaders are pro-West or pro-Communist and how this tilt will affect the international balance of power. Similar distortions plague domestic news coverage, but they are less deceptive because American audiences are more familiar with the situation. Past experiences and socialization provide corrective lenses for the domestic scene; the foreign scene, by contrast, is viewed without correction for myopia and astigmatism.

Finally, the thrust of foreign news, like its domestic counterpart, provides basic support for the policies and personalities of the current American administration. The media generally accept official designations of who are America's friends and enemies and interpret their motives accordingly. When relationships change, media coverage mirrors the change. Editorials and news stories about India and the People's Republic of China provide many examples of ebbs and flows in media appraisals that matched changes in official relationships.[48]

If the media are generally supportive of government policy, how can their adverse comments about the Vietnam War be explained? The answer is that the media emphasized the government's positions until respected sources widely voiced their dissent. At that point, the media continued to give the largest amount of coverage to the administration's views. But they coupled it with coverage of the story of growing dissent in America about the merits of Vietnam policies, including ample attention to antiadministration voices and to antiwar demonstrations.[49]

News emphases stabilize perceptions about the international status quo. Preoccupation with the developed powers reinforces many Americans' beliefs about the importance of these nations. Similarly, portrayal of less developed countries incapable of managing their own internal affairs makes it easy to believe that they do not deserve higher status and the media attention that accompanies it.

Support of the status quo also means that newspeople usually are willing to withhold news and commentary when publicity would severely complicate the government's management of foreign policy. Withholding sharp criticism of Iranian leaders during the 1979 hostage crisis to avoid angering them and throttling information about America's breaking of Japanese military message codes during World War II are examples in which major political interests were at stake. Likewise, news of delicate negotiations among foreign countries may be temporarily withheld to avoid rocking the boat before agreements are reached. This has happened when East and West Germans have been engaged in discussions about border crossings and when the Soviet Union has expressed willingness to negotiate arms limitations that it had previously refused to consider.[50]

Appraising the Foreign Newsmaking Process

Clearly, foreign news in the American press does not meet the high standards that UNESCO has set for it. It does not "eliminate ignorance and misunderstanding between peoples." It is too sparse for that and too unbalanced, focusing on the wealthier and more powerful countries. It assesses foreign countries largely in terms of U.S. interests, with little attempt to explain their culture and their concerns from their own perspective. It does not sensitize Americans to "the needs and desires of others" and foster "respect of the rights and dignity of all nations." Rather, it reinforces Americans' preexisting assumptions and stereotypes. Major problems abroad, such as hunger, disease, and poverty, are ignored except when unusual disasters dramatize them temporarily.

These deficiencies must be assessed in light of the basic philosophy of news in a free society. As discussed in Chapter 1, American journalists by and large do not see themselves as extensions of the government, carrying out and keeping in tune with public policies. Although they may sympathize with UNESCO's goals, their first priority is to report exciting news to the American public. In a society that firmly believes in the independence of the press from government, this is a tolerable consequence.

Just as the press does not serve UNESCO's objectives, it fails to serve many objectives of the American government and many needs of the American public. Much foreign news totally lacks a sense of history and a sense of the meaning of successive events. It therefore confuses the public. A good example is the widely believed story that China turned to communism because of American foreign policy failures. This interpretation ignores the long-range forces that made revolution in China inevitable. It vastly exaggerates the power of the United States to change the course of Chinese politics. The news does not even provide sufficient information to permit most Americans to understand the rationale for major foreign policies such as the renegotiation of the Panama Canal treaties or the necessity for international economic cooperation.

Some stories, even those directly involving U.S. security, are ignored until events reach crisis proportions or until there is a precipitating incident. For instance, stories about the relative military strength of the United States and the Soviet Union did not receive prominent coverage until the Strategic Arms Limitation Treaty (SALT) negotiations in 1977. Before that time, news was "so spotty and lopsided that it failed to provide the essential facts for understanding U.S. defense and military issues, the Soviet definition of détente, or the forward surge in Soviet military might." [51] *New York Times* correspondent James Reston put the problem this way:

> We are fascinated by events but not by the things that cause the events. We will send 500 correspondents to Vietnam after the war breaks out, and fill the front pages with their reports, meanwhile ignoring the rest of the world, but we will not send five reporters there when the danger of war is developing. [52]

Adds *Washington Post* assistant managing editor Phil Foisie, "We are surprised more often than we ought to be and need to be." [53] This leaves the country unprepared for twists and turns in foreign affairs that might have been foreseen and for which plans might have been made.

As with domestic news, there is also a continuous debate about whether the "right" foreign news issues have been covered in the proper way. Conservative critics complain about too much disparagement of U.S. activities to restrain communism abroad, too much sympathy for leftist regimes, and too little stress on military security. Liberal critics say the opposite. [54] Others point to distorted coverage during major foreign policy crises that allegedly has misled the American public and harmed foreign policy. Debate about the adequacy of Vietnam War coverage has been especially heated. [55]

If one assumes that better information leads to better policies, then deficiencies in news coverage are grave. When President Jimmy Carter complained that he was ill-informed about unrest in Iran prior to the overthrow of the shah in 1979, he intimated that American policymaking and public support for policies would have benefited from more accurate news. In this case the CIA was blamed as well as the media, which perform what has been called a "massive overt intelligence operation." [56] Coverage of the Bay of Pigs invasion also raises questions about the chance for better policies if the media had told the story more fully and avoided ideological blinders. The media's stress on conflict, and on force as the solution for conflict and as a tool for conflict avoidance, contributes to feelings of insecurity.

Although the media are exceedingly important in providing the information base for policy formation, their explicit input into foreign policymaking is muted. When journalists give policy advice or criticize ongoing policies, their influence is generally weaker than the influence of formal government agencies. In fact, Reston claims that press advice has great influence on American foreign policy only when things are obviously going badly, as they did in the Vietnam War. [57] When policy failures are not readily apparent and the president alleges that all is going well, contrary media claims are not likely to be believed by officials and the mass public.

Impact on Public Opinion

Because most Americans rely primarily on television for foreign news, and lack interest and knowledge about the subject, they are easily swayed by what they see and hear. Television thus has spawned a new, impressionable public, highly susceptible to cues from the tube. In the past, interest in foreign policy was largely confined to a newspaper-reliant elite whose education, interests, and experiences made them far more immune to media influence. Several decades ago, "the public probably would never have heard of El Salvador, much less cared about it. Today the sheer volume of exposure to new information created by television assures a more involved public. Television has created a vast, inadvertent audience for news about foreign policy." [58] Along with it, television has strengthened the president's hand when policies coincide with the tenor of news stories and limited the options when news and policies conflict.

Public support for defense spending, for example, more than doubled between 1978 and 1980, going from 26 to 90 percent. Televised foreign news may well be the explanation. It drove home the message that America's foes were gaining while the country was incapable of defending itself. The Iranian hostage crisis, the Soviet assault on Afghanistan, the upheaval in Poland, and the uncontrollable warfare in Central America were powerful scenes in this melodrama. [59]

As is true of most media effects, it is difficult to obtain convincing proof that public opinion about foreign countries mirrors the images media stories present. Nonetheless, available data are suggestive. William C. Adams, on the basis of careful content analyses of television coverage of the Arab-Israeli conflict in the 1970s and 1980s, concluded that five important changes should have taken place in public opinion if it, indeed, reflected media coverage. Opinions should have become (1) more favorable to Egypt, (2) more sensitive to differences among Arab nations, (3) less favorable to Israel, (4) more sympathetic to Palestinians, and (5) slightly more pro-Arab overall. [60] All of these changes have occurred, although Adams's data, which cover the 1972-1980 period, did not yet reflect the later shift against Israel.

Between 1976 and 1980, favorable opinion of Egypt rose by 25 percentage points, from 46 percent to 71 percent. While attitudes toward Arab countries were largely undifferentiated in 1976, by 1980 Gallup polls showed sizable differences in opinions about various countries. Similarly, opinions had become more sympathetic to the Palestinians and more pro-Arab overall by 12 percentage points. However, opinion about Israel had not dropped, as predicted, by 1980. In fact, it had risen by 9 percentage points. The likely explanation is that supportive opinions were firmly entrenched because of the massive amounts of favorable coverage the country had received since its creation in 1948. In the 1980s the public's favorable views of Israel finally began to tarnish, suggesting that media images were beginning to take their toll.[61]

Exporting News

Although the American public seems reasonably content with the foreign news it receives, Third World countries are unhappy with the thrust of foreign news in the United States. Their disappointment about the world images presented to Americans is compounded by resentment that these images are exported to other countries throughout the globe. Eighty percent of the non-Communist world's political and economic news comes from only four huge American enterprises: the Associated Press (AP), United Press International (UPI), the *New York Times* News Service, and the *Los Angeles Times-Washington Post* News Service.[62] Most of the remainder is produced by Britain's Reuters, France's Agence France-Presse, and Russia's *Tass*. Four countries thus dominate the world's news supply.[63]

This concentration has given rise to charges of media imperialism—the dependence of domestic media systems on dominant foreign media systems.[64] Dependence on foreign news resources is particularly galling for developing countries because they believe that the flow of news is primarily one way—into the developing world but not out of it. Western news producers slight Third World happenings and the information needs of people in developing nations. Foreign affairs journalism, according to these critics, should play an educational role in the Third World; it should inspire and mobilize people to work hard to develop their countries. Instead, it fosters cynicism and dejection over the way Third World leaders manage their problems. If press freedom leads to such results, it is a luxury developing countries cannot afford.[65]

Third World critics also decry the corrupting effects of Western news for Americans, other Westerners, and Third World people. Entertainment programs contain too much violence and too many sexually explicit episodes. Such broadcasts allegedly damage the cultural identity of poorer nations, especially those that are vulnerable because of colonial exploitation.[66] Imported news offerings draw people away from their own heritage and create false expectations about easily attainable affluence. All this is done for the benefit of industrial monopolies in the United States that are eager to sell their merchandise through television. They lure the rich to buy luxury goods that drain their country's resources.

Marxist interpretations of the motives and role of Western media are widely believed in the Third World. These interpretations seem quite plausible because the international news market is indeed dominated by a few giant corporations that have their headquarters in New York and other major

Western cities. These organizations sell news, as well as more tangible goods, for profit. However, scientific proof is lacking that the Marxist interpretation of the causes and consequences of Western dominance of Third World news and media entertainment is correct.

As we noted in Chapter 5, people do not automatically learn new ways of life from the media, even when offerings are designed to educate. Certain conditions must first be met to provide an appropriate context. Hence claims that exposure to Western news automatically indoctrinates the audience are false. Content analyses of Western media, including wire service news, show that many of the charges of deliberate discrimination against the Third World are either groundless or exaggerated. Negative treatment of the Third World and lack of attention to many small nations appear to be natural consequences of treating the Third World according to the same criteria used for the more developed portions of the globe. Chinese officials complain that American media report their political squabbles and economic problems rather than their excellent cotton harvest, but the media apply the same newsworthiness criteria to news about China as they do to news about France or the Soviet Union or the United States. The consequences may differ, but the treatment is the same.[67] The media's emphasis on conflict in the Third World reflects a reality: Third World countries are areas of major social change and therefore bear a disproportionate burden of conflict.

Elite newspapers in America, in sharp contrast to smaller, less prominent papers throughout the country, have paid considerable attention to Third World news in recent years.[68] A 1979 study of foreign news in the *New York Times, Washington Post,* and *Christian Science Monitor* showed that an average of 65 percent of their foreign news coverage was devoted to the Third World. The Third World also fared well in the proportion of front-page stories, editorials, opinion-page articles, and letters to the editor.[69]

Early entry into the media business has given the major news producers an economic edge of size and scale that makes it well-nigh impossible for Third World nations to set up viable competing enterprises.[70] The high cost of television programming and the comparatively low cost of purchasing foreign television entertainment—roughly one-fourth of the cost of original programming—also have discouraged Third World countries from creating their own television industries. Forty-five percent of the developing countries have no facilities for producing television shows. Those that do, still import an average of 55 percent of their programs, particularly those shown in prime time.[71] They also rely on Western technicians and Western money for installation and maintenance.

Current structures and patterns of telecommunications give price advantages to large producers and consumers that hurt less developed countries. News transmission rates are cheaper when volume is high, making it extremely costly for poor countries to send their messages out. It also costs more to transmit news from underdeveloped countries than vice versa. In fact, all the economies of scale benefit the rich and hurt the poor.

As a consequence of their dissatisfaction with the status quo and in recognition of the political importance of news, Third World countries have been lobbying in UNESCO for worldwide agreement that the influx of foreign news should be more strictly controlled. It has been largely a dialogue of the deaf. The United States and other Western countries have strongly resisted these attempts, deeming them an infringement of the right to a free press guaranteed by the Universal Declaration of Human Rights, which the United Nations approved in 1948. The trend toward controlled news in the developing world is making headway nonetheless. UNESCO has been involved in planning for a code of journalistic ethics that would define "responsible" reporting. It also has investigated ways to make journalism a government-licensed profession. The United States has threatened to withdraw from UNESCO if such efforts become the organization's official policy.

Third World countries are also contesting the control of the United States and other Western powers over world radio and satellite facilities. Just as the domestic broadcast spectrum is limited, so is the international spectrum. In the past, frequencies were allocated on a first-come-first-served basis. This has given the developed nations, including the United States, the lion's share of the broadcast spectrum—nearly 90 percent—and the bulk of satellite facilities. Third World nations want to change this. As they made clear at the World Administrative Radio Conference (WARC), which met in Geneva, Switzerland, in the fall of 1979, they want to divide the spectrum equally among all nations and bar radio and television satellite transmissions across national borders unless the receiving country has given permission. They are also demanding more control over satellites.

The United States has resisted Third World demands. It believes that nations with the capability to use advanced telecommunications facilities should control these facilities. Granting them to nations that are not prepared to use them immediately, or in the near future, seems to make little sense. The United States is the world's number one international broadcaster.[72] In the past, it has used international broadcast facilities for important foreign policy objectives. In the late 1970s, United States agencies and several private broadcasters were sending 2,534 program hours weekly throughout the world. (This compared with 1,998 hours for the Soviet Union.)

The Voice of America (VOA) broadcasts constitute an integral part of the federal government's foreign information program, which is handled by the International Communication Agency (ICA). These broadcasts portray American society and its problems and policies abroad and provide Western news to countries unlikely to receive it. VOA's largest service goes to the Soviet Union, to which it broadcasts 168 hours weekly in Russian, Ukrainian, Estonian, Latvian, Lithuanian, Armenian, Georgian, and Uzbek.[73] Other

Eastern European countries receive 87 hours of broadcasts. The international broadcast spectrum is also used for Radio Liberty (RL), which broadcasts foreign internal news, mainly to the Soviet Union; Radio Free Europe (RFE), which does the same for Poland, Czechoslovakia, Hungary, Romania, and Bulgaria; and RIAS, Radio in the American-Sector Berlin, which covers all of Berlin and East Germany. Efforts by Third World nations to gain greater control over international broadcasts threaten the foreign information programs of the United States and the image the United States wants to project.

Summary

The quality of U.S. foreign policy and the effectiveness of U.S. relations with other countries are crucial to the welfare of people throughout the world. Sound policy and relations require a solid information base. As this chapter has shown, the foreign affairs information base on which Americans depend leaves much to be desired. The reasons are complex and, in part, inevitable. They involve the people who produce foreign policy news, the sociopolitical setting in which they must work, and the audiences to whose world views and tastes the news must cater.

Foreign correspondents are a well-trained, able group. But there are too few of them to cover the world. America's correspondents work within a narrowly controlled organizational structure consisting of a handful of giant newsgathering institutions that supply the news and entertainment needs of the United States and much of the rest of the non-Communist world. If one distrusts giant information conglomerates that collect and shape the news for much of the world, the present situation is frightening.

Most Americans are reasonably well satisfied with the foreign news produced by these conglomerates. Many of the foreign clienteles, particularly political leaders in the Third World, are not. They complain that agents of monopoly capitalism are guilty of "electronic rape" of their people through decadent entertainment and Western political propaganda.

Foreign affairs news often must be produced under trying conditions. Strange locations and inadequate technological facilities can make a nightmare of the physical aspects of getting to the scene of the action, collecting information, and transmitting it. These technical difficulties are compounded by political difficulties. They include the reluctance of officials in the United States and abroad to commit themselves publicly on foreign affairs matters and the harassment of correspondents venturing into places where they are unwanted. Expulsion, imprisonment, and physical harm are common. With so much territory to cover and such limited personnel to cover it, newspeople frequently avoid areas where news is hard to get and devote their efforts instead to areas where public attitudes are supportive. This effectively removes many regions from media scrutiny and contributes to unevenness of news flow from various parts of the world.

How good is the foreign affairs news that reaches the United States and other clients of Western international news transmission facilities? The picture is mixed. Foreign correspondents must produce news that is at once timely, exciting, personalized, and brief yet understandable for an American audience that is not intensely interested in most events abroad. Given the problems of foreign affairs news production, correspondents dwell heavily on negative and sensational news. They write stories from an American perspective that follows the current administration's foreign policy assumptions and the American public's stereotyped views of the world. They primarily cover the most important countries, keeping American national interests and policy objectives in mind. Despite these shortcomings, Americans can obtain a reasonably accurate view of salient political events abroad, particularly if they turn to prestigious newspapers that generally give thorough exposure to controversial American foreign policies. However, these papers rarely challenge the merits of foreign policy actions.

In recent years, television commentators occasionally have become active diplomats through interviews that set the stage for subsequent political developments. Aside from these adventures, media influence on foreign policy has been largely indirect, exercised primarily through surveillance activities, the power to choose what to report and what to omit, and the ability to interpret the meaning of events. There has been little investigative or adversary journalism except when foreign affairs were obviously going badly, as happened toward the end of the Vietnam War. Political controversy has largely stopped at the water's edge.

Notes

1. David H. Weaver and John B. Mauro, "Newspaper Readership Patterns," *Journalism Quarterly* 51 (Spring 1978) and David H. Weaver, *Recent Trends in Newspaper Readership Research* (Bloomington, Ind.: School of Journalism, Indiana University, Research Report No. 5, June 23, 1978).
2. Barry Rubin, "International News and the American Media," in *International News: Freedom Under Attack,* ed. Dante B. Fascell (Beverly Hills, Calif.: Sage, 1979), p. 192.
3. George Gerbner and George Marvanyi, "The Many Worlds of the World's Press," *Journal of Communication* 27 (Winter 1977): 55-56. The analysis was based on 1970 data.
4. S. M. Mazharul Haque, "Is U.S. Coverage of News in Third World Imbalanced?" *Journalism Quarterly* 60 (Fall 1983): 521-524.
5. Sophia Peterson, "International News Selection by the Elite Press: A Case Study,"

Public Opinion Quarterly 45 (Summer 1981): 143-163.
6. Doris A. Graber, *Processing the News: How People Tame the Information Tide* (New York: Longman, 1984), pp. 89-90.
7. Bernard C. Cohen, *The Press and Foreign Policy* (Princeton, N.J.: Princeton University Press, 1963), pp. 164-165.
8. Rubin, "International News and the American Media," p. 187.
9. William H. Read, "Multinational Media," *Foreign Policy* 18 (Spring 1975): 55-67.
10. J. Herbert Altschull, "Khrushchev and the Berlin 'Ultimatum': The Jackal Syndrome and the Cold War," *Journalism Quarterly* 54 (Fall 1977): 545-551.
11. Rubin, "International News and the American Media," p. 214.
12. John A. Lent, "Foreign News in American Media," *Journal of Communication* 27 (Winter 1977): 46-50.
13. Rubin, "International News and the American Media," pp. 197-198.
14. Leo Bogart, "The Overseas Newsman: A 1967 Profile Study," *Journalism Quarterly* 45 (Summer 1968): 293-306.
15. Ibid., p. 299.
16. See Chapter 2, pp. 57-61.
17. S. Robert Lichter, "America and the Third World: A Survey of Leading Media and Business Leaders," in *Television Coverage of International Affairs,* ed. William C. Adams (Norwood, N.J.: Ablex, 1982), p. 71. The data were collected in the fall of 1979 and winter of 1980.
18. Hamid Mowlana, "Who Covers America?" *Journal of Communication* 25 (Summer 1975): 86-91. Table 9-1 shows that countries most heavily covered by the United States send the largest number of reporters to the United States.
19. Ibid., pp. 89-90.
20. Peterson,"International News Selection," p. 159.
21. Robert M. Batscha, *Foreign Affairs News and the Broadcast Journalist* (New York: Praeger, 1975), p. 156.
22. *New York Times,* January 14, 1976.
23. Sean Kelly,"Access Denied: The Politics of Press Censorship," in *International News,* ed. Fascell, p. 249.
24. John Kifner, "Reporter's Notebook: Fear is Part of Job in Beirut," *New York Times,* February 22, 1982.
25. Bob Wiedrich, "Sadat Has Invented a New Diplomacy," *Chicago Tribune,* February 9, 1978.
26. Batscha, *Foreign Affairs and the Broadcast Journalist,* p. 122.
27. James F. Larson, "International Affairs Coverage on U.S. Network Television," *Journal of Communication* 29 (Spring 1979): 147.
28. For example, Jeff Charles, Larry Shore, and Rusty Todd, in "The New York Times Coverage of Equatorial and Lower Africa," *Journal of Communication* 29 (Spring 1979): 151, report that only 5 out of 18 countries in that region received substantial coverage.
29. James F. Larson, "International Affairs Coverage on U.S. Evening Network News, 1972-1979," in *Television Coverage of International Affairs,* ed. Adams, p. 37.
30. Herbert J. Gans, *Deciding What's News: A Study of CBS Evening News, NBC Nightly News, Newsweek and Time* (New York: Pantheon Books, 1979), pp. 30-36. See also Peterson, "International News Selection," pp. 144-149, and Johan Galtung and Mari H. Ruge, "The Structure of Foreign News," *Journal of Peace Research* 2 (1965): 64-91.
31. Edwin Diamond, *The Tin Kazoo: Television, Politics, and the News* (Cambridge, Mass.: The MIT Press, 1975), p. 94.

32. Gans, *Deciding What's News,* pp. 30-36.
33. Susan Welch, "The American Press and Indochina, 1950-1956," in *Communication in International Politics,* ed. Richard L. Merritt (Urbana, Ill.: University of Illinois Press, 1972), pp. 227-228.
34. Galtung and Ruge, in "The Structure of Foreign News," have developed a much quoted scheme for rating the newsworthiness of various types of foreign affairs events. See also Einar Ostgaard, "Factors Influencing the Flow of News," *Journal of Peace Research* 2 (1965): 39-63.
35. Jonathan Friendly, "El Salvador Overlooked as Most of Press Turns to Other Crises," *New York Times,* July 10, 1982.
36. William Adams and Phillip Heyl, "From Cairo to Kabul with the Networks, 1972-1980," in *Television Coverage of the Middle East,* ed. William C. Adams (Norwood, N.J.: Ablex, 1981), p. 26.
37. Rubin, "International News and the American Media," p. 227.
38. Batscha, *Foreign Affairs News and the Broadcast Journalist,* pp. 67-68.
39. Ibid., pp. 136-137.
40. Paul Bethel, "Anarchy in Domingo: City Without Food, Water, Medicine in Civil War," in *Mass Media and the Mass Man,* ed. Alan Casty (New York: Holt, Rinehart & Winston, 1968), p. 218.
41. Theodore Draper, "Contaminated News of the Dominican Republic," in *Mass Media and the Mass Man,* ed. Casty, pp. 212-214.
42. John Corry, "TV: View of NBC Coverage of Lebanon Invasion," *New York Times,* February 18, 1984.
43. Gertrude J. Robinson, "Foreign News Conceptions in the Quebec, English Canadian, and U.S. Press: A Comparative Study" (Paper presented to the International Communications Association Convention, Philadelphia, Pa., May 1-5, 1979).
44. Fernando Reyes Matta, "The Latin American Concept of News," *Journal of Communication* 29 (Spring 1979): 169.
45. Benjamin D. Singer, "Violence, Protest, and War in Television News: The U.S. and Canada Compared," *Public Opinion Quarterly* 34 (Winter 1970-71): 611-616 and Chris J. Scheer and Sam W. Eiler, "A Comparison of Canadian and American Network Television News," *Journal of Broadcasting* 16 (Spring 1972): 156-164.
46. James P. Winter, Pirouz Shoar Ghaffari, and Vernone M. Sparkes, 'How Major U.S. Dailies Covered Quebec Separatism Referendum," *Journalism Quarterly* 59 (Winter 1982): 608.
47. Edward W. Said, *Covering Islam: How the Media and the Experts Determine How We See the Rest of the World* (New York: Pantheon, 1981), chap. 2.
48. Lent, "Foreign News in American Media." See also Haluk Sahin, "Turkish Politics in *New York Times:* A Comparative Analysis," *Journalism Quarterly* 50 (Winter 1973): 685-689.
49. Robert M. Entman and David L. Paletz, "The War in Southeast Asia: Tunnel Vision on Television," in *Television Coverage of International Affairs,* ed. Adams, pp. 181-201.
50. W. Phillips Davison, "Diplomatic Reporting: Rules of the Game," *Journal of Communication* 25 (Autumn 1975): 138-146.
51. Ernest LeFever, *T.V. and National Defense* (Chicago: Institute for American Strategy, 1974), p. 139.
52. James Reston, *Sketches in the Sand* (New York: Knopf, 1967), p. 195.
53. Rubin, "International News and the American Media," p. 216.
54. Thomas M. McNulty, "Vietnam Specials: Policy and Content," *Journal of*

Communication 25 (Autumn 1975): 173-180. See also Ernest W. LeFever, "CBS and National Defense," *Journal of Communication* 25 (Autumn 1975): 181-185.

55. Peter Braestrup, *Big Story: How the American Press and Television Reported and Interpreted the Crisis of Tet 1968 in Vietnam and Washington* (Garden City, N.J.: Anchor Press/Doubleday, 1978).

56. Rubin, "International News and the American Media," p. 193.

57. Ibid., p. 182.

58. William Schneider, "Bang-Bang Televison: The New Superpower," *Public Opinion* 5 (April/May 1982): 13-14.

59. Larson, "International Affairs Coverage," pp. 34-35.

60. Adams and Heyl, "From Cairo to Kabul," p. 16.

61. Ibid., pp. 19-22.

62. Mustapha Masmoudi, "The New World Information Order," *Journal of Communication* 29 (Spring 1979): 172-185.

63. Oliver Boyd-Barret, "Media Imperialism: Towards an International Framework for the Analysis of Media Systems," in *Mass Communication and Society,* ed. James Curran, Michael Gurevitch, and Janet Woolacott (London: Edward Arnold, 1971), pp. 117, 129.

64. For a discussion of media imperialism, see Jeremy Tunstall, *The Media Are American* (New York: Columbia University Press, 1977) and Herbert I. Schiller, *Communication and Cultural Domination* (White Plains, N.Y.: International Arts and Science Press, 1976).

65. *New York Times,* August 12, 1977.

66. The impact of foreign television is assessed in David E. Payne and Christy A. Peake, "Cultural Diffusion: The Role of U.S. T.V. in Iceland," *Journalism Quarterly* 54 (Fall 1977): 523-531.

67. Wilbur Schramm and L. Erwin Atwood, *Circulation of News in the Third World: A Study of Asia* (Hong Kong: Chinese University Press, 1981) and David H. Weaver and G. Cleveland Wilhoit, "Foreign News Coverage in Two U.S. Wire Services," *Journal of Communication* 31 (Spring 1981): 55-63. For a contrary view, see Daniel Riffe and Eugene F. Shaw, "Conflict and Consonance: Coverage of Third World in Two U.S. Papers," *Journalism Quarterly* 59 (Winter 1982): 617-626.

68. Coverage by smaller media is discussed in G. Cleveland Wilhoit and David Weaver, "Foreign News Coverage in Two U.S. Wire Services: An Update," *Journal of Communication* 33 (Spring 1983): 132-148.

69. Haque, "Is U.S. Coverage of News in Third World Imbalanced?" pp. 523-524. Some confusion in dividing stories by country of origin has arisen from the fact that many Third World stories are transmitted through communications centers, such as London or New York. For example, most news from Latin America is relayed via New York. See Leonard R. Sussman, "Information Control as an International Issue," in *The Communications Revolution in Politics,* ed. Gerald Benjamin (New York: The Academy of Political Science, 1982), p. 183.

70. Boyd-Barrett, "Media Imperialism," p. 130.

71. Elihu Katz, "Cultural Continuity and Change: The Role of Mass Media," in *Communications Policy for National Development,* ed. Majid Teheranian, Farhad Hakemzadeh, and Marcello L. Vidale (London: Routledge & Kegan Paul, 1977), p. 133.

72. Kelly, "Access Denied," p. 255.

73. David M. Abshire, "A New Dimension of Western Diplomacy, in *International News,* ed. Fascell, p. 40.

Readings

Adams, William C. *Television Coverage of International Affairs.* Norwood, N.J.: Ablex, 1982.

——. *Television Coverage of the Middle East.* Norwood, N.J.: Ablex, 1981.

Pollock, John Crothers. *The Politics of Crisis Reporting: Learning to Be a Foreign Correspondent.* New York: Praeger, 1981.

Rice, Michael, with Jonathan Carr, Henri Pierre, Jan Reifenberg, and Pierre Salinger. *Reporting U.S.-European Relations: Four Nations, Four Newspapers.* New York: Pergamon Press, 1982.

Richstad, Jim, and Michael H. Anderson, eds. *Crisis in International News: Policies and Prospects.* New York: Columbia University Press, 1981.

Robinson, Gertrude Joch. *News Agencies and World News.* Fribourg, Switzerland: University Press, 1981.

Said, Edward W. *Covering Islam: How the Media and the Experts Determine How We See the Rest of the World.* New York: Pantheon, 1981.

Trends in Media Policy

In Shakespeare's *Julius Caesar* Brutus urges his fellow conspirators to act while the time is ripe:

> There is a tide in the affairs of men
> Which, taken at the flood, leads on to fortune;
> Omitted all the voyage of their life
> Is bound in shallows and in miseries.
> On such a full sea are we now afloat;
> And we must take the current when it serves
> Or lose our ventures.[1]

Communications policy stands on just such a threshhold in the waning years of the twentieth century. New technologies have solved old problems and made new policy directions possible, but old policy concepts linger. Unless there is a bold attempt to take control of the tides of change, the chances for new information ventures and for retaining a genuinely free press may vanish.

In this chapter we shall trace the forces for changing communications policies and the obstacles that lie in the way. We shall outline some of the areas of disenchantment with mass media performance that have fueled the quest for new directions and the steps taken by dissatisfied communicators and audiences to improve and supplement the existing information supply. Major new technologies and the advances that they make possible, as well as the potential impact of these developments on politics and policy alternatives, will be examined. Finally, we shall peer into the murky crystal ball to try to discern the general shape of future communications policies that will set the stage for the continuing interaction between the mass media and the American political system.

Current Dissatisfactions with the Media

The 1960s and 1970s were an era of political disenchantment in the United States. Many people became dissatisfied with major political institu-

341

tions and blamed them for the ills of society. True enough, vocal protesters always have been in the minority. They are vastly outnumbered by the "silent majorities" whose silence is interpreted as approval of the political system or resignation to its unavoidable shortcomings. But even the silent have often felt that the times were out of joint, if only because of the increase in publicly voiced dissent.

The media, particularly television, are among the targets of public protest. The Washington Broadcast Bureau of the Federal Communications Commission (FCC) receives more than 100,000 complaints annually from viewers dissatisfied with television fare.[2] Most complaints concern the display of obscenity, excessive crime and violence, infringement of equal time and fairness provisions, undue or objectionable attention to racial and religious matters, and excessive or offensive advertising.

In addition to the formal complaints lodged with the FCC, a host of less formal criticisms have been made as well.[3] Media critics call television a vast intellectual wasteland. They chide the networks for slavish submission to the dictates of rating systems, blaming shallow programming and cheap appeals to human emotions on the desire to capture huge audiences. They complain about the small amount of social and political criticism and the large amount of support for the status quo. These attacks are often extended to the print media as well.

Media orientations toward politics have been criticized as both too liberal and too conservative. Sniping from the left about the media's subservience to the establishment and insensitivity to the concerns of the politically powerless and economically deprived has been balanced by criticism from the middle and the right. Conservatives accuse the media of demeaning the status of American business and labor and of respected professions such as medicine and law. The media, they argue, are unduly romantic about the woes and virtues of the poor, the disadvantaged, and the racially different.[4] In the process, the media allegedly undermine national security and hurt the nation's prestige at home and abroad. The media also have been accused by liberals and conservatives alike of invading the privacy of the individual and impairing the fairness of the judicial process.

The merits of these charges do not concern us right now. Their gist is that the media do not serve "the public interest." That elusive concept is always measured by political yardsticks of disputed accuracy and validity. What is important to an understanding of media policymaking is the response to perceived media deficiencies. How do dissatisfied Americans cope with shortcomings in their information supply? Coping strategies can be grouped into three types: (1) various forms of informal criticism, expressed regularly or sporadically, (2) establishment and use of formal criticism mechanisms, and (3) use of alternative media.

Informal Criticism

Informal criticism has come from within the journalism profession as well as from the general public. Specialized journals that frequently review media performance, such as the *Columbia Journalism Review,* publish criticism by media professionals. Many review journals have been short-lived because they could not maintain enough subscribers to pay their expenses. The *Chicago Journalism Review,* despite its widely acknowledged excellence, died an untimely death in the mid-1970s, only a few years after its birth. The *Washington Journalism Review* has long been teetering on the brink of financial disaster. The degree of influence wielded by such journals is a matter of opinion. Within narrow circles, professional reputations may be affected. But the circulation of these reviews is so limited, and the pocketbook effects of adverse criticism are so negligible, that their pressure on the industry to alter journalistic practices is likely to be small.

A more robust and probably more influential vehicle of criticism has been critical commentary by media commentators attached to high-circulation newspapers and news magazines and to television networks. Columnists such as Les Brown, reporters such as Jonathan Friendly, and TV hosts such as Ted Koppel have become familiar gadflies of the news business and the journalism profession. Their work supplements the efforts of many academic experts who have written critical appraisals of the mass media in recent years. Names such as David Altheide, John Hohenberg, Eric Barnouw, Edwin Diamond, Ben Stein, and Herbert Schiller belong in this group.[5] The media also have been scanned critically, if informally, at professional conventions of journalists and at the counterconventions that they have occasionally provoked.[6] Special workshops, such as the annual Aspen Conference on Communications and Society, have focused more narrowly on specific problems and have publicized reform proposals.

Informal criticism has also come from various public interest groups. In many cases these have been institutions organized for other purposes, such as the national Parent and Teacher Association or the American Medical Association. Others are special media action groups. The National Citizens Committee for Broadcasting and the Children's Television Workshop, discussed more fully in Chapter 2, are examples. Criticism by public interest and media action groups, like most other forms of informal criticism, have had only moderate impact on media policies.

Formal Criticism

Formal criticism comprises protests about media performance lodged with the appropriate government agency that has corrective powers. Earlier we mentioned the FCC's Broadcast Bureau in Washington as a formal center for citizen complaints. We have also mentioned FCC hearings prior to granting broadcast licenses or when license renewals have been challenged. In such hearings, interested parties have a chance to present their perspectives on media policy, in hopes of countering media industry pressures and the pro-industry biases that public regulatory bodies usually develop.

Despite widespread recognition that it is desirable to provide the public with such formal avenues for criticism and policy suggestions, there are a number of unsolved problems. Most fundamental and least solvable is the problem of making sure that the complaints and suggestions thus aired are representative of community beliefs. The laudable desire to listen to the voices of dissent may lead to inadequate concern about the merits of dissenters' claims and the damage to more general public interests.

A few examples of questionable protests will illustrate the problem. Some of these protests were ignored; others were heeded. The 1978 mini-series "Holocaust," which dramatized Nazi atrocities, was loudly opposed by a variety of groups claiming that it generated anti-German feelings and hatred between Jews and gentiles. Yet it was widely acclaimed by many critics and attracted between 38 and 48 million viewers nightly. Similarly, in 1977, between 30 and 40 million people watched each episode of the "Godfather" I and II series, which dealt with Mafia ventures. Most of these viewers considered the program worthwhile. Yet thousands of Italian-Americans denounced the show and complained through various public channels that it slandered Italians. Stories about abortion, drug addiction, the activities of religious cults, or the exploits of discredited politicians have often been suppressed or toned down because of the flood of protests they might invite.

Lack of money can be a major barrier to using formal protest channels to challenge industry representatives effectively in an FCC hearing or before a court of law. In the past, protest groups have had to rely on their own limited resources, except when the broadcast industry has voluntarily shouldered their legal fees. Because payments in such cases were restricted to legal costs, protest groups have been encouraged to undertake litigation rather than to negotiate settlements. It has been suggested that the FCC should pay the expenses of protest groups. But, unless Congress allocates special funds for this purpose, the resources of the commission are far too slim to do so.

In general, lawsuits involving claims about harmful television programming have failed. A widely publicized example is the trial of Ronny Zamora, a teen-ager who was convicted by a Florida court for murdering an 83-year-old woman. His parents sued the three networks for negligent programming, claiming that television shows had incited and taught their son how to murder. The suit was dismissed by a federal judge who ruled that the media had not been negligent.[7] In 1978 a California court likewise dismissed a negligence suit against NBC brought by the parents of a young rape victim. The rape had mimicked a scene from the movie "Born Innocent," which had been shown on television four days earlier.[8]

To enhance public influence on communications policy, there have been proposals to place ombudsmen—formal spokesmen for the public's interests—in various bodies that deal with communications policy. Alternatively, a central ombudsman office has been proposed to assist public interest groups and individuals in preparing and presenting their complaints and suggestions. Thus far, these proposals have not been implemented. However, nearly two dozen newspapers have set up ombudsman facilities to permit readers to challenge news policies.[9] Readers' concerns and ombudsmen's activities are regularly reported by the papers.

Media Councils

Another avenue for channeling criticism to bring about changes in media performance is the "media council." Media councils are elected or appointed bodies that hear and investigate complaints about mass media output. They then publicize their findings, using the power of publicity to diminish undesirable media practices. Generally, media councils lack power to enforce their recommendations. Media councils have been used in Great Britain and in some American states, including Minnesota, and in some cities, including Seattle.

Controversy over the merits of media councils came to a head in the United States in 1973 when a private research organization, the Twentieth Century Fund, created a task force to look into the establishment of an independent, private National News Council to monitor the major national news sources: wire services, the weekly news magazines, and the national newspaper syndicates. The council, as proposed by the task force, was "to receive, to examine, and to report on complaints concerning the accuracy and fairness of news reporting in the United States, as well as to initiate studies and report on issues involving the freedom of the press." [10] With members drawn from the public and the journalism profession, the council was intended as a forum for independent appraisals of the fairness and representativeness of media performance. Its findings were to be released to the public in reports and press releases. But, aside from the power of publicity, there would be no means to enforce the council's recommendations.

Although media councils have earned substantial respect and approval in Britain and although they have worked well in the United States, the press has strongly opposed them.[11] Major U.S. media rejected two to one the Twentieth Century Fund proposals for a National News Council. The council, they feared, would impair editorial independence by publicizing its appraisals of the merits of ongoing news policies. Newspeople claimed that such a watchdog organization was unnecessary because they were serving the public well. Despite media opposition, however, the National News Council was set up in 1973. Several news organizations gave space to its activities and reports, but it never became a major force in arbitrating questions of media ethics. It finally was dissolved in 1984.[12]

Alternative Media

Information needs that have been neglected or poorly served by the regular media have been met by hundreds of specialized media. These include a spate of publications concentrating in whole or in part on political commentary. The *New Republic, Mother Jones,* the *National Review* and, at times, the *New Yorker* are examples. More recently, new technologies have made it feasible for interest groups to make and distribute audio and video tapes on controversial political issues. Antinuclear and environmental groups, for example, have created and distributed tapes either for individual use or for broadcast.[13]

Alternative media also include professional and trade journals devoted to a multitude of human interests such as religion, sports, fine and popular arts, automobiles, stamp collecting, and bird watching. If audiences numbering into thousands and even millions of people constitute a "mass," these are, by definition, mass media.[14] Modern means of information distribution bridge the distances that physically separate people so that they can be brought together as a mass audience for specialized publications. The demand for targeted information has increased in recent years; witness the mushrooming of specialized magazines such as the popular *People Magazine, Psychology Today,* or *Sports Illustrated,* or the even more focused *Ski, Photography,* or *Car and Driver.* Their popularity changed advertising strategies and led to the demise of broadly oriented magazines such as *Look, Life,* and the *Saturday Evening Post.*

Alternative media also have developed in the newspaper field. A large foreign language press in the United States serves various ethnic and nationality groups. *Editor and Publisher* has chronicled the existence, in an average year, of some 250 foreign language newspapers published in 40 different languages. Another 250 papers, on an average, cater to the needs of black audiences.[15] Local community newspapers, published daily, every other day, or once a week, present community news.[16] The metropolitan press does not have space for such news, which would be of little interest to most of its readers. Instead, it often targets special news supplements to specific neighborhoods within cities.

Radio stations in many American cities serve specialized groups, and a few cities have specialized television outlets. An average of 400 radio stations serve, almost exclusively, the needs of ethnic groups, especially blacks and Hispanics. Other stations, including a number of television stations, provide periodic special programming for ethnic groups and other specialized audiences. The lush growth of specialized media serves as a partial antidote to the concentration of ownership in the more general mass media that we described in Chapter 2. The potential role of cable television, yet another means for serving special community interests, will be discussed more fully later in this chapter.

For many people, the term "alternative media" conjures up visions of the politically radical, iconoclastic, counterculture newspapers that were plentiful in the late 1960s and early 1970s, a time when dissatisfaction over the Vietnam War was at a peak and large numbers of people, particularly youth and minorities, opposed the positions taken on the war and other issues by the regular media. Dissenters therefore created the "underground" press. The name was applied because these media carried on the flagrant opposition to government policy that is often forbidden in other countries, driving such media into locations hidden from the police. "Underground" actually was a misnomer for the American media of protest because they were allowed to operate quite openly. But it gave them an aura of fighting the establishment at great personal risk.

The mushrooming of protest media in the 1960s and 1970s—at one time there were nearly 1,000 underground newspapers and 400 counterculture radio stations—testifies to the vitality and flexibility of the mass media system.[17] The abrupt decline of underground media with the end of the Vietnam War—there are only a handful left, and most of them either have turned middle-class or have become predominantly pornographic—also shows that when the demand ends, the system is able to prune its unneeded branches.[18]

Underground media, such as the *Seed,* the *East Village Other,* the *Berkeley Barb,* the *Rat,* or *The Great Speckled Bird,* went beyond rejecting the current political establishment. They also rejected the values and culture of American mainstream society. In this they differed from social-responsibility journalism that supports basic American values and attacks only their violations. Politically, the underground media were generally left-wing in orientation: Communist, Socialist, or Anarchist. They used a style that attracted attention by being totally subjective and visually and verbally shocking. Profanity, explicit sexual pictures, and arousing cartoons and drawings abounded because the staffs of these media felt that their attacks on American society must be shocking and exciting to succeed.

The rise of the underground press shows that mass media can still be started and operated with modest means. The media of the sixties were financed mostly through advertising for such things as counterculture records, music productions, X-rated movies, and classified advertisements for sex partners, nude models, drugs, and similar attractions. Staffs were paid meager salaries or no salaries at all.[19] The papers concentrated on features rather than regular news stories, assigning their limited personnel only to stories that they planned to use rather than covering a full series of regular beats. For daily news and some features, they relied on cooperative news services such as the Underground Press Service (UPS) and Liberation News Service (LNS).

To beat the high cost of printing, the underground media used offset processes that permitted them to duplicate their pages at a fraction of the cost of regular printing. As soon as they were ready, most of the papers were peddled on street corners near university campuses. There were no set numbers of issues per year, no regular publication schedules, no business staffs or circulation departments. At the height of the underground press, readership was estimated at 10 million, with most issues used by several people.

Underground media in the sixties were not limited to the comparatively unregulated print realm. They also flourished in the regulated broadcast field. Underground radio stations featured mostly rock music and disc jockeys who commented on society, sexual matters, the drug culture, and other counterculture interests. The FCC rarely interfered with their unconventional activities, except when they flouted the law too brazenly. For instance, when a Texas rock station tipped off the local drug community about a drug raid planned by police, there was an investigation into the sources from which the station had received the advance information.

The tolerance of the government for such broadcasts demonstrates that governmental control over media content, however offensive, has a light touch. Few countries equal and none exceeds the freedom to express radical viewpoints presently enjoyed by American media. In fact, some of the causes pressed by underground news sources ultimately became part of the mainstream of politics. In the end, loss of public support rather than official censorship led to the steep decline in this genre of journalism. Neither technical nor legal barriers stand in the way of a revival, should social conditions provide the necessary incentives.

The Impact of New Technologies

Insufficient diversity in mass media offerings is one of the main complaints about the mass media. But now technology has opened up virtually unlimited channels for electronic transmission of news and entertainment.[20] Already media outlets available in small communities have multiplied, sharply reducing the dangers of local monopoly control over information. Cable television can further increase the number of television channels available virtually anywhere. Systems now in operation, or in the planning stage, project that they will supply from 20 to 100 separate channels.

Satellites can beam an almost limitless number of radio and television programs to all parts of the world, which can be received through over-the-air and cable channels. During the late 1970s, a single RCA communications satellite, Satcom I, stationed in a fixed orbit some 22,300 miles above the equator, carried enough programs in its leased channels to fill the needs of even the largest multiple-channel cable systems many times over. Since then, even larger satellites have been added, and commercial television stations now can receive satellite programs directly. This frees them from dependence on current network programming because satellites carry an extensive array of new programs in addition to network offerings. Programming options have thus been vastly expanded.

In 1980, the FCC granted permission for up to 25 new satellites to be launched by 1986. Space for various types of electronic transmissions, including television, is available for rent from the satellites' owners. Once programs have been placed on the satellite, they can be transmitted anyplace when an appropriate receiver dish is available.[21] Video tapes and video discs store electronic fare, allowing people to watch what they want when they want it. Pay cable and pay over-the-air television give access to channels carrying special entertainment or special interest programs at moderate costs. Warner Cable has developed QUBE, an interactive cable system that permits limited access to individual programs. People pay solely for those programs they choose to watch. For instance, students can enroll in television courses viewable only by people formally enrolled in the course. They can interact electronically with their instructor. Newspapers can now be printed and transmitted electronically as well. Laser beam and optical fiber technology have been added to the arsenal of communication tools.

Although a number of technical puzzles still require solution and although costs for some technologies need to be brought down, we have truly moved from the age of channel scarcity to the age of plenty. The opportunity to talk back to our electronic servants through two-way communication has also moved from the realm of science fiction to the realm of reality. Two-way channels on cable television have become commonplace, permitting viewers to be seen and heard and to interact with others watching the same programs. Older two-way communication technologies, such as two-way radio and the telephone, have also been perfected and are used to integrate outlying areas with the social service systems available in more populated centers. In Alaska and northern Canada, for example, these technologies deliver educational and health services and give people a greater voice in government policies.[22]

Barriers to Development

Usually a look at technology tells us what is possible rather than what is likely to happen, particularly in the short run. A number of political barriers block wider use of new mass communication technologies. Above all, the usual bureaucratic barriers must be surmounted. Many new developments never get off the ground because bureaucracies impose too many regulations to guard against possible abuses. Unrealistically high standards are frequently prescribed, raising costs beyond economically feasible levels. State and local rules, piled on top of federal regulations, complicate the picture even further. Not only do they add more requirements, but rules issued by various jurisdictions often conflict. Every major technological revolution—and the information transmission revolution is major—has brought about economic and political dislocations. Such massive changes are fought by those whose knowledge and equipment will be made obsolete by them. Communications technologies involve large investments so that their sudden obsolescence becomes a major financial blow.

Early entrants in a field also develop a squatter's mentality about rights they have acquired, such as the right to use certain broadcast frequencies or particular technologies. To justify retaining what they already have, they point to the market needs that they are filling. Newcomers, on the other hand, want to reallocate facilities afresh on an equal basis. Newcomers also want to mandate the use of more advanced technologies, even before they have established a market for these technologies and services or can guarantee that such a market will develop. This raises the specter of wiping out proven interests in favor of new claimants whose prospects for success are uncertain.

Obstacles have also arisen because competing new technologies benefit various groups unevenly. Each group fights to win acceptance for whatever technology and regulations seem most beneficial to the interests it favors. Battles may be prolonged and final decisions delayed. Because bureaucratic inertia sets in once the initial decisions have been reached, power struggles are fiercest before the status quo is determined. While these power struggles are going on, technology continues to advance, raising new problems requiring solution. This further delays the green light for implementing new systems.

Many programs made possible by new technologies threaten the jobs of current providers of similar services in other sectors of the economy. For instance, round-the-clock cable educational programs, structured like regular classrooms, are operating successfully in several localities. Medical programs teach people better medical self-care methods. Such programs, especially if expanded, may be unwelcome competition for the teaching and health professions. Televised programs, set up at high cost and featuring outstanding practitioners and facilities, may establish standards for professional performance that average institutions cannot meet. They also may feature sensational aspects of professional activities, generating dangerously false perceptions. All of these considerations lead to resistance from professionals whose support may be essential.

The Emergence of Cable Television

A brief account of the rocky history of cable television development in the United States will illustrate the problems posed by technical innovations. It will also illustrate the many political decisions that must be made to fit a new information technology into the existing legislative and administrative structure. Moreover, it will remind us that technological progress marches on relentlessly. The costly cable technology may already be outmoded before it reaches maturity. Cheaper technologies, involving direct broadcasting satellites to receiver dishes on earth, may be the wave of the future.

When community antenna television (CATV)—commonly known as cable television, the transmission of television signals through a coaxial cable—first became available in 1949, it was viewed by established broadcasters as a serious threat. They feared that the availability of numerous television channels capable of transmitting original and relayed programs would lead to a large menu of programs similar to the variety then offered by radio shows. This would splinter television audiences. Smaller audiences would mean smaller advertising revenues and smaller profits for existing stations. In turn, this might mean poorer programming because reduced revenue would necessitate curtailment of expenditures. Television networks were also concerned that cable operators would be able to pirate, rather than buy, their signals and broadcast the programs they had produced at high cost. Ultimately, cable television, coupled with satellite technology, might destroy the networks entirely if superstations could pick up programs directly from satellites and broadcast them nationwide.[23]

The initial response of the FCC to cable technology was typical of regulatory agencies. The commission protected the status quo with regulations that prevented the newcomers from infringing upon established interests. These regulations sharply limited the types of programs that cable television stations could broadcast when they competed with established network services. Consequently, the growth of the cable industry was stunted.

Interest group pressures ultimately persuaded public officials that cable technology was in the public interest because it could reach people in locations inaccessible to regular television signals. The idea of breaking the near monopoly enjoyed by the networks over broadcasting also became attractive. So did the possibility of opening up many new channels for broadcasting to groups hitherto shut out by a limited spectrum. By 1972, these pressures were sufficiently strong to produce an easing of FCC regulations on the types of programs that cable television could broadcast. The cable system had a new lease on life. However, in what is also a typical move when new technologies arise, the FCC imposed a number of very costly regulations to force cable television to serve public needs that had never been met in the past. These included the requirement for a minimum of 20 channels, including channels for broadcasting by the general public, educational institutions, and local governments. There were also requirements for establishing two-way capabilities and for carrying signals of local broadcasters.

When these rules turned out to be still too burdensome to allow rapid development of CATV, they were eased again in 1976. Service requirements imposed on the new industry were loosened further after court rulings questioned whether cable television was sufficiently scarce to justify regulation and after successful legal challenges by cable operators.[24] Then, in 1979, the FCC issued a lengthy research report on the economic impact of cable broadcasting. It concluded that cable was only a minor economic threat to the established industry and did not endanger the industry's "ability to perform in the public interest." In the wake of these findings, the federal shackles were removed from the industry, one by one.[25]

Meanwhile, the resistance of the established industries to this new competition, marked by opposing stances in FCC proceedings and unwillingness to work cooperatively, had gradually softened. In fact, a number of them, heeding the old adage, "If you can't lick 'em, join 'em," invested heavily in cable facilities. These investments came after the FCC eased controls regarding crossownership and admission of the networks to the cable market. The graphic on the next page illustrates the rapid explosion of the cable industry in the 1970s and early 1980s.

Today the old-line media enterprises see cable largely as a new delivery system for the news and entertainment programs that they already produce. Table 11-1 shows how heavily the established media industry has invested in the new technology. In fact, if present trends continue, including the escalation of costs for entering the cable business and surviving the initial

Table 11-1   Media Penetration of Cable Systems, 1981

Category of Owner	Numbers of Systems	Percent of Systems
Broadcasters	1,776	38%
TV program producers/distributors	967	21
Newspapers	729	16
Publishers	545	12
Telephone companies	149	3
Theater owners	144	3
Miscellaneous	134	3
TV manufacturers	97	2
Community or subscriber control	96	1

NOTE: Owners who do business in more than one category are counted in each. Ownership can be full or partial.

SOURCE: Adapted from Benjamin M. Compaine, Christopher H. Sterling, Thomas Guback, J. Kendrick Noble, Jr., *Who Owns the Media? Concentration of Ownership in the Mass Communications Industry,* 2d ed. (White Plains, N.Y.: Knowledge Industry Publications, 1982), p. 386. Reprinted by permission.

Figure 11-1 The Cable TV Explosion

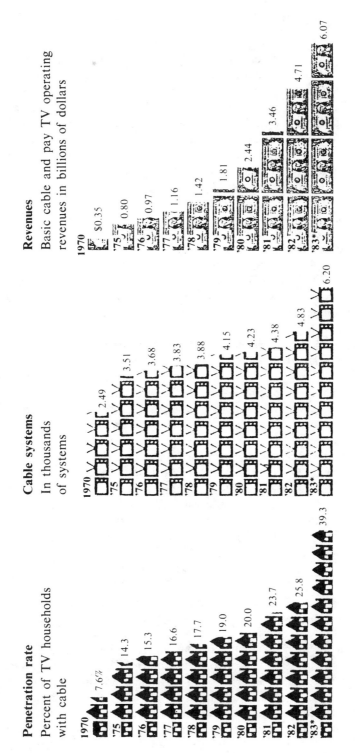

Penetration rate
Percent of TV households
with cable

1970

'70 7.6%
'75 14.3
'76 15.3
'77 16.6
'78 17.7
'79 19.0
'80 20.0
'81 23.7
'82 25.8
'83* 39.3

Cable systems
In thousands
of systems

1970

'70
'75 2.49
'76 3.51
'77 3.68
'78 3.83
'79 3.88
'80 4.15
'81 4.23
'82 4.38
'83* 4.83
6.20

Revenues
Basic cable and pay TV operating
revenues in billions of dollars

1970

'70 $0.35
'75 0.80
'76 0.97
'77 1.16
'78 1.42
'79 1.81
'80 2.44
'81 3.46
'82 4.71
'83* 6.07

*Estimates

SOURCE: Paul Kagan Associates and Television Digest's Television Factbook. Chicago Tribune Graphic. *Chicago Tribune*, October 30, 1983, p. 12. Reprinted by permission. Tribune Media Services, Inc.

years, oligopoly may become the dominant cable pattern. The chances that this will occur are increased by the prevailing climate of hostility to government interference with market forces.

The FCC's willingness to let old-line media buy cable systems is in sharp contrast with its nearly total prohibition of telephone company activity in the cable field. Telephone companies are allowed to serve only remote areas that cable cannot profitably reach. Should the telephone companies receive permission to freely enter the cable business, the estimates for growth of the cable audience will rise sharply because existing telephone wiring could then be adapted. Fears that the giant AT&T telephone enterprise might monopolize the cable scene led to its exclusion from the cable market.[26]

FCC rules and the opposition of the established industries are not the only hurdles faced by the cable industry. There are numerous local political hurdles as well. Laying of cables requires permission from local authorities. To avoid undue duplication of facilities, franchises must be granted. The franchising process has been highly political, in terms of both the selection of particular companies and the determination of the conditions of the franchise. Unable to pay the costs of bidding for a contract, to grease the wheels of politics, or to finance initial red-ink years, small enterprises have been squeezed out. In the policy area, options are wide-ranging in the absence of congressional agreement on nationally mandated rules.[27] Franchisors and franchisees must agree on the time to be allowed for constructing the system and the life of the franchise (usually 15 years). Agreement also must be reached about requirements regarding public service and open-access channels and service for outlying areas where costs will exceed profits temporarily or permanently.

Service to rural areas may pose insurmountable economic problems, particularly in the western plains and the Rocky Mountain states. Alternatives to cable, such as microwave relays or satellite broadcasts, or transmission over telephone wires, may have to be considered. Difficult decisions have to be made in choosing appropriate governmental agencies to supervise the execution of cable contracts and to ensure that programming serves the public interest. Finally, major controversies need to be settled regarding the nature of the fee structure and the manner in which government ought to exact its tribute.

Regulatory Options

Governments have several policy options for dealing with cable systems. First, they can play a hands-off, *laissez-faire* role, allowing the system to develop as its private owners please.[28] This is the policy advocated in various proposals to revise the Communications Act of 1934. The precedent for this policy is the traditional stance of government toward the print media. If we believe that government should regulate information supply only when transmission channels are scarce, as happened with early radio and television, then it makes sense to leave cable television unregulated. When electronic broadcast outlets are as plentiful as they are now, market forces presumably come into play. Necessary services then will be supplied in a far more flexible and responsive way than is possible when government regulations intervene.

The only restraints that may be needed are safeguards to protect national security and maintain social norms. Hence only the usual controls applied to print media—limits on publication of security information, limits on obscenity, some protection of the interests of children—should be applied to cable television. Regulations to ensure that the availability of two-way circuitry does not pose a hazard to privacy also may be necessary. People must be protected from unauthorized prying into their viewing habits and disclosure of their identity when two-way circuitry is used for public opinion polls or voting.

A second policy option involves treating cable television as a *common carrier,* like the telephone or rail and bus lines. This would make transmission facilities available to everyone on a first-come-first-served basis. The owners of cable facilities would not broadcast their own programs. Instead they would lease their channels to various broadcasters for fees that would be subject to government regulation. Such open access would obviate current complaints that cable operators selectively exclude certain program services, thereby dooming them to failure. The rationale for designating CATV as a common carrier would be similar to that used for the telephone. It is a widely needed vital resource for the transmission of information that should be available to everyone wishing to send messages.

The FCC and various local governments like the common carrier concept. It has been adopted for dealing with communications satellites. But the Supreme Court held in a 1979 decision that cable could not be considered a common carrier. An Arkansas operator, Midwest Video Company, therefore could not be required by *federal* regulations to provide public access channels.[29] The ruling pleased the cable industry because it preserved its control over policymaking. However, the ruling does not bar state and local authorities from imposing common carrier status on the industry. Congress, too, has renewed its attempts to introduce at least some common carrier features into cable operations. A bill, introduced in 1983 by Rep. Timothy E. Wirth of Colorado, chairman of the House Energy and Commerce Subcommittee on Telecommunications, is an example. The bill would require operators of large cable systems to lease channels to programming services that could not otherwise gain access.

The third policy option is to confer *public trustee* status on the cable industry. This status is akin to that of the television and radio industry at the present time. Owners of cable facilities would have full responsibility for programming, but would be required to meet certain public service obligations. These might include adherence to the fair and equal time provisions, the right of rebuttal, and limitations on materials unsuitable for children or offensive to community morality standards. They might also encompass rules about access to cable to ensure availability of public and government access channels, including facilities to broadcast public education, public safety, and medical and social service information.

The rationale for conferring trustee status on broadcasters has been twofold. In the past the scarcity argument has been powerful, but it obviously makes no sense for cable television today, which can provide virtually unlimited channel capacity. The other argument for trustee status is that television is a highly influential medium that should be regulated to make sure valuable programs are broadcast and harmful ones avoided. Regulations are necessary to guarantee that certain canons of fairness are observed. This is a powerful argument with strong support in much of the world. It is the argument that Third World nations have made so persuasively, as discussed in the last chapter. But it is not the argument on which the American system was built, and it is incompatible with the First Amendment.

Paying the Piper

Whether cable television is treated like any private enterprise, like a common carrier, or like a trustee, its costs have to be paid. There are three possibilities for financing, each with different policy consequences: advertiser support, audience payments, and government subsidies.

Like television at present, CATV can be sustained by its advertisers. This means that programming must have mass appeal. Hence it is bound to share the strengths and weaknesses of current programming. Sponsor influence may increase in the cable age because competition for sponsors becomes keener when channels multiply. Many stations, particularly those with small audiences, may even find it difficult to attract enough sponsors to pay for their operations.

Because of the drawbacks of advertising-supported programming and the difficulty of securing enough advertising, cable television has relied fairly heavily on audience payments. These have generally taken the form of a monthly service charge for the facilities, to which an installation charge has often been added. Special additional programming may be available for a flat rate of $7 to $10 monthly or on a per program basis. This method of financing has been quite popular in many foreign countries; in the United States, however, it has met with some resistance. Americans do not like to pay for services in locations where good services already exist free of charge. Aside from mountainous areas, free service is readily available in all parts of the United States.

By the mid-1980s, much of the initial resistance had been overcome. Forty percent of America's households had been cabled, and many were paying for special programs in addition to their standard monthly fees. Although a number of programming services had succumbed to competition and some new cable ventures were in financial difficulties, the industry as a whole was thriving. Moreover, the worst fears of old-line broadcasting entrepreneurs had not materialized. Viewership had dropped only moderately, and financial returns remained sound. As had been true with past innovations, the new media had not mortally wounded their predecessors.

A major social drawback of service charges for cable television is that poor families that most need many of cable's specialized programs are least able to pay. Middle-income families who already enjoy many social advantages benefit most. Education and information resources made available to them through cable programs enhance their status, leaving lower class people farther behind.[30] This problem could be reduced through government subsidies paid to the cable industry on a basis similar to financing public television, or through government subsidies paid to the poor. The latter system seems preferable to avoid making cable financially dependent on government, thereby endangering cablecasters' freedom of action.

The Shape of the Future

Regulation versus Deregulation

New technologies in the communications industry require a complete rethinking of the scope and purposes of federal regulation of broadcast media. The 1934 Communications Act was premised on the notion of scarcity of transmission facilities. This made it essential to parcel them out equitably and to make certain that the limited number of franchises served broad public interests. Fifty years later the basic regulatory mechanism remains intact although its raison d'être has largely vanished. Despite mushrooming broadcast outlets, total deregulation and reliance on traditional First Amendment values are still distant goals. Dissatisfaction with the services supplied by private entrepreneurs has fueled opposition to deregulation. The major umbrella organization against deregulation is the Telecommunications Research and Action Council (TRAC), which includes 120 organizations representing labor, civil rights, church, and consumer groups.[31]

At the international level, pressures also are mounting for increasing government control and responsibility for media performance. This is happening at a time in history when the lines between free print and regulated electronic media are blurring. The price of progress in electronic transmission may be the loss of freedom from government regulation. To prevent this, Sen. Bob Packwood of Oregon has introduced a constitutional amendment to explicitly extend First Amendment rights to the electronic media.

A major challenge faces broadcast policymakers today. They can yield to domestic and international pressures and make government the arbiter of what is good and safe news and entertainment for the public, or they can leave that role in private hands, at the mercy of nonelected media tycoons. Given these alternatives, this author casts her vote for the latter option, believing with Thomas Jefferson that "error of opinion may be tolerated where reason is left free to combat it." [32]

Two-way Communication and Televotes

Another important area of public concern about the impact of the communications revolution relates to two-way communication, which has been hailed as the gateway to genuine direct democracy. In the future the public business presumably can be conducted in front of the television set. Citizens can watch the proceedings of legislative bodies and cast votes of approval or disapproval.

Pilot projects already have been conducted in the United States and abroad.[33] In San José, California, for example, school board meetings were televised. All sides of controversial school issues were aired, and the televised discussion was supplemented by newspaper articles. The public was then given a chance to vote on policy suggestions through two-way cable or through ballots printed in the local newspapers. Unfortunately, participation was uneven. In San José, as in most of the other "televote" projects, the bulk of votes came from middle-class people. Most lower class people did not participate as had been hoped.

Another problem has been the reluctance of public officials to implement the policies supported by televotes. There are several reasons. On the national level, the possibility for electronic voting raises important constitutional issues. The United States now is a representative democracy with elections at regular intervals. Between elections, officials make decisions they consider to be in the public interest. The Constitution did not provide for direct democracy governed by a series of plebiscites. Quite aside from the constitutional and legal questions, the merits of direct democracy at various governmental levels in the United States remain highly controversial. Widespread adoption of electronic plebiscites, with or without extensive prior information campaigns, is therefore unlikely in the foreseeable future.

The possibility of using the two-way circuitry for educational programs of various types, particularly those that would improve the status of disadvantaged groups, is less controversial. The major obstacle here, beyond funding and making the technology available, is motivating people to use it.

Both successes and failures have been recorded in initial experimental programs.

Spartanburg, South Carolina, experimented with cablecasts of high school subjects to permit adults to earn high school diplomas without leaving home. Sixty-two percent of the adults in the area lacked a high school diploma. The 15-week program made use of interactive technology; students used an eight-button terminal to answer the teacher's questions and ask for help with problems. For people who took the course, results were as good as those obtained from actual classroom attendance. But the program had to be discontinued because too few people were enrolled to keep the per-pupil cost within reasonable limits.[34]

By contrast, a program geared to senior citizens in Reading, Pennsylvania, became very popular. This program linked three senior citizen centers and connected them to various public places such as the public schools and the city council. Whenever the centers were hooked up with a public facility, such as a city council session, questions asked by city council members, and their answers, could be heard and viewed in all the centers. Participants in the three centers could also interact with each other. All programs were produced and conducted by senior citizens. Potentially shut-in and shut-out adults were thus reintegrated into the community. They became more aware of their mutual problems and problems of the community at large. The community benefited from hearing senior citizens' views about public policies.[35]

Two-way cable has offered a variety of programs to general audiences, but they have been less popular than expected. Warner Amex Cable Communication's QUBE system, which serves 350,000 viewers in Columbus (Ohio), Cincinnati, Pittsburgh, Dallas, Houston, and St. Louis suburbs, rarely attained more than 2 percent participation for its interactive programs. These included talent contests, astrology shows, exercise classes, interactive games, football games, town meetings, and public hearings involving federal agencies. In the course of a month, cumulatively about one-quarter of QUBE subscribers chose to participate in some form of two-way programming. Game shows with a chance to win prizes and public policy questions attained the highest response rates. In 1984, QUBE two-way services were sharply curtailed. The disappointing results of the program, which had run for six years, were attributed partly to audience reluctance to participate and partly to unattractive program formats and technical difficulties in responding when several viewers were watching one televison set.[36]

Fragmentation of the Broadcast Audience

A major concern brought into focus by the availability of large numbers of channels on cable television is the question of national consensus. Fears have been expressed that specialized television fare in news and entertainment will not only diminish attention to politics but also fragment the national consensus that is now supported by national media. As we discussed in Chapter 5, nationwide dissemination of similar news has been a powerful source of shared political socialization. As news becomes fragmented, people are likely to be socialized in disparate ways. If political programming becomes available on scheduled channels only, will people choose to watch it? A music fan, tuned in to an all-music station, may watch music programs only; a black or Hispanic person may tune in only to stations concerned with black and Hispanic affairs. Minorities thus may miss out on happenings in the broader culture.

The multiplicity of cable television channels may splinter the nation into hundreds of audience groups. Consequently, messages from national officials may reach vastly diminished audiences unless a large number of broadcasters agree to have their programs preempted at some particular time. Specialization of media may make it much more difficult for the government to reach all publics with government messages. Several versions of public messages, each tailored to different audiences, may then be required. This may lead to more political manipulation. On the positive side of the ledger, narrow casting raises the possibility of a better fit between audience needs and public messages. Government programs may operate more successfully, given ampler opportunities for one- and two-way communication with selected audiences. The electoral chances of minority candidates and parties may grow with increased ability to target their messages to selected audiences. The possibilities for change are staggering, but too ill-defined as yet to hazard predictions.

Fears that fragmentation of the broadcast audience will lead to political fragmentation are not shared by everyone, of course. Many people point out that the national consensus was not ruptured when alternative media were used in the past. They argue that fragmented interests create the demand for fragmented media rather than the reverse. If there is political and social consensus, people will seek out information pertaining to the larger community. Even if the new media system will lead to increased fragmentation, many people do not find this objectionable, believing that pluralism is preferable to the melting-pot ideals of prior generations.

A media-induced push toward pluralism may herald a push toward more local control over information programs. We have already mentioned the common locally imposed requirement that cable systems must reserve channels for local government affairs. This gives local governments a better chance than ever before to air their concerns before local audiences. Channels reserved for local school systems or for police and fire departments likewise serve to publicize local institutions. If publicity means power, the new communications media may enhance the power of local institutions, possibly at the expense of national ones. The two-way capacity, which often makes programming attractive to local audiences even if it lacks the polish of national shows, may allow local organizations to reach much larger constituencies than was hitherto possible.

While the possibilities for strengthening local communities through increased publicity are good, CATV, when combined with satellite technology, also has the ability to deflect interest away from the local scene and produce global villages of like-minded people. The birth of national cable television networks, such as the Cable News Network owned by Atlanta-based Turner Communications, or Westinghouse's Group W Cable, are examples of movement in this direction.[37] Programs can also be created for specialized audiences and disseminated to these audiences all across the nation. For instance, medical information can be relayed through cable to doctors throughout the country; so can programs on crime fighting for police personnel or opera performances for opera buffs. This is akin to the services presently rendered by specialized journals and magazines with national circulations.

Public Television

Yet another issue brought to the fore by the coming age of broadcast plenty is the fate of public television. As we discussed in Chapter 2, public television was organized to provide an alternative to the typical programming available on the commercial networks. It also was intended to be an outlet for programs geared to minorities. These are the very services that cable television presumably will perform on a commercial basis. Since public television has always depended on public subsidies and since, aside from its children's programs, its audiences have been quite limited, pressures to abandon it will be strong.

The Consequences of Change

The concerns we have outlined thus far are undoubtedly not the only ones ahead. Many others will require decisions that go far beyond solving technical issues. The direction of communications policy is at stake, and with it the tone and possibly the direction of American politics generally. John M. Eger, a former director of the White House Office of Telecommunications Policy, has remarked that this is indeed a time of decision. "For as we are moving into a future rich in innovation and in social change, we are also moving into a storm center of new world problems." The new technologies are "a force for change throughout the world that simply will not be stopped, no matter how it is resisted." And then he asks, "Are we ready for the consequences of this change? Are we prepared to consider the profound social, legal, economic, and political effects of technology around the world?" [38]

Currently, the answer is "no." In the communications field, the structure for policymaking at all governmental levels is fragmented and ill-suited to deal. with the existing problems, to say nothing of those that must be anticipated.[39] Policies are improvised when pressures become strong, yielding in a crazy-quilt pattern to various industry concerns, to public interest groups, to domestic or foreign policy considerations, to the pleas of engineers and lawyers, and to the suggestions of political scientists and economists. Narrow issues are addressed, but the full scope of the situation is ignored.[40] Neither Congress nor the executive branch is willing to enter this thicket of controversy at a time when so many other battles must be fought. It is not likely that policy leadership will emerge. "Muddling through" was the watchword for the 1970s and muddling through is likely to be the watchword for the 1980s as well.

Summary

Many people are dissatisfied with the performance of the mass media, especially television. In this chapter we described media councils and other channels for airing this dissatisfaction and noted the limited effects that criticism usually has had in changing media content. We also surveyed briefly the many alternative media created to fill the gaps left by the major mass media. These media are organized either to serve demographically distinct population groups or to cater to particular substantive concerns or political orientations.

Among alternative media, the underground press is especially interesting. During the 1960s it demonstrated that government will tolerate a journalism that attacks major domestic and foreign policies, even in wartime. The mushrooming of underground print and broadcast media during the Vietnam War era also showed that, in a business dominated by giants, it is still possible for small enterprises to operate successfully on a shoestring. The limited demand by the general public for published radical dissent, however, makes it difficult to finance such publications over long periods of time.

In this chapter we also explored the social and political consequences of technological advances in mass media. We briefly described some of the new electronic tools and sketched their capabilities in bringing about the age of broadcast plenty and the age of two-way mass communication. Their impact on life and politics in the United States could be enormous, but it is impossible to predict at this early stage of development. Two-way circuitry has been hailed as the gateway to genuine direct democracy and as a great educational tool. However, fragmentation of the broadcast audience has also raised fears of political fragmentation, and electronic plebiscites are as yet too controversial to be adopted widely.

We also examined various aspects of regulatory policy that will be required to integrate the new media technologies into the existing mass media regulatory structure. Most importantly, we pointed to major political changes that could arrive, almost unannounced, if the political impact of new technologies is not considered and guided carefully. Use of electronic transmission facilities could subject the print media to the same government regulations as electronic media. A bastion of freedom might fall. The forces pushing in the direction of greater government control of media content are strong at a time when most types of media use some form of electronic transmission. Whether the mass media are regulated more tightly or given freer rein, deliberate choice, rather than draft, should be the basis for the decisions.

Notes

1. *Julius Caesar,* act 4, scene 3, line 218.
2. David Gergen, "The Message to the Media," *Public Opinion* 7 (April/May 1984): 5-8.
3. Joseph R. Dominick and Millard C. Pearce, "Trends in Network Prime-Time Programming, 1953-74," *Journal of Communication* 26 (Winter 1976): 70-80; Eric Barnouw, *The Sponsor: Notes on a Modern Potentate* (New York: Oxford University Press, 1978); Bernard Rubin, *Media, Politics, and Democracy* (New York: Oxford University Press, 1977); and Edward Jay Epstein, *Between Fact and Fiction: The Problem of Journalism* (New York: Vintage, 1975).
4. John Hohenberg, *A Crisis for the American Press* (New York: Columbia University Press, 1978) and Lee B. Becker, Robin E. Cobbey, and Idowu A. Sobowale, "Public Support for the Press," *Journalism Quarterly* 55 (Autumn 1978): 421-430.
5. David Altheide, *Creating Reality: How TV News Distorts Events* (Beverly Hills, Calif.: Sage, 1976); Barnouw, *The Sponsor*; Edwin Diamond, *The Tin Kazoo: Television, Politics, and the News* (Boston: MIT Press, 1975); Herbert Schiller, *Mass Communication and American Empire* (New York: Augustus M. Kelly, 1969); and Ben Stein, *The View from Sunset Boulevard* (New York: Basic Books, 1979).
6. "The A. J. Liebling Counter-Convention," *Chicago Journalism Review* (May 1972): 16-24.
7. *Zamora v. State,* 361 So. 2d 776 (Fla. 1978).
8. *Olivia N. (a minor) v. National Broadcasting Company,* 74 Cal. App. 3d 383 (Cal. 1978).
9. Donald T. Mogavero, "The American Press Ombudsman," *Journalism Quarterly* 59 (Winter 1982): 548-553, 580.
10. *Chicago Journalism Review* (April 1973): 20.
11. John E. Polich, "Newspaper Support of Press Councils," *Journalism Quarterly* 51 (Summer 1974): 199-206 and Robert Schafer, "News Media and Complainant Attitudes Toward the Minnesota Press Council," *Journalism Quarterly* 56 (Winter 1979): 744-752.
12. Jonathan Friendly, "National News Council Will Dissolve," *New York Times,* March 23, 1984.

13. Erik Barnouw, "Historical Survey of Communications Breakthroughs," in *The Communications Revolution in Politics,* ed. Gerald Benjamin (New York: The Academy of Political Science, 1982), p. 20.
14. W. Phillips Davison, "Functions of Mass Communication for the Collectivity," in *Mass Communications Research: Major Issues and Future Directions,* ed. W. Phillips Davison and Frederick T. C. Yu (New York: Praeger, 1974), pp. 66-82.
15. Leo W. Jeffres and K. Kyoon Hur, "The Forgotten Media Consumer: The American Ethnic," *Journalism Quarterly* 57 (Spring 1980): 10-17; Roland E. Worseley, *The Black Press, U.S.A.* (Ames, Iowa: Iowa State University Press, 1971); and Henry La Brie III, ed., *Perspectives of the Black Press: 1974* (Kennebunkport, Maine: Mercer House Press, 1974).
16. Morris Janowitz, *The Community Press in an Urban Setting: The Social Elements of Urbanism,* 3d ed. (Chicago: University of Chicago Press, 1980).
17. They are described more fully in John W. Johnstone, Edward J. Slawski, and William W. Bowman, *The Newspeople* (Urbana, Ill.: University of Illinois Press, 1976), pp. 157-181; Laurence Leamer, *The Paper Revolutionaries: The Rise of the Underground Press* (Simon & Schuster, 1972); and Jack A. Nelson, "The Underground Press," in *Readings in Mass Communication,* ed. Michael C. Emery and Ted Curtis Smythe (Dubuque, Iowa: W. C. Brown Co., 1972), pp. 212-226.
18. "Up From the Underground," *New York Times Magazine,* February 15, 1976.
19. Johnstone, Slawski, and Bowman, *The Newspeople,* pp. 157-179.
20. Ithiel de Sola Pool, *Technologies of Freedom* (Cambridge, Mass.: Harvard University Press, 1983), pp. 152-156.
21. Benjamin M. Compaine, Christopher H. Sterling, Thomas Guback, and J. Kendrick Noble, Jr., *Who Owns the Media? Concentration and Ownership in the Mass Communications Industry,* 2d ed. (White Plains, N.Y.: Knowledge Industry Publications, 1982), pp. 414-418.
22. Heather E. Hudson, "Implications for Development Communications," *Journal of Communication* 29 (Winter 1979): 179-186.
23. Superstations: WTG in Atlanta, WGN-TV in Chicago, and KTVU in San Francisco.
24. *Home Box Office, Inc. v. FCC,* 567 F.2d 9, D.C. Circuit, 1977; certiorari denied, 434 U.S. 829, 1977; *FCC v. Midwest Video Corp.,* 440 U.S., 689, 1979.
25. Compaine, *Who Owns the Media?* p. 381. Pay television had been freed from federal controls in 1977. Remaining federal controls were dropped by 1979. Ibid., p. 407.
26. Ibid., pp. 390-393.
27. However, FCC regulations prevail over conflicting state regulations. *Capital Cities Cable v. Crisp,* No. 82-1795, June 18, 1984.
28. Benno C. Schmidt, Jr., "Pluralistic Programming and Regulation of Mass Communication Media," in *Communication for Tomorrow: Policy Perspectives for the 1980s,* ed. Glen O. Robinson (New York: Praeger, 1978), p. 214.
29. *FCC v. Midwest Video Corp.,* 440 U.S., 689, 1979.
30. George A. Donohue, Phillip J. Tichenor, and Clarice N. Olien, "Mass Media and the Knowledge Gap: A Hypothesis Reconsidered," *Communication Research* 2 (1975): 3-23.
31. *Congressional Quarterly Weekly Report,* January 21, 1984, p. 94.
32. First inaugural address.
33. Ted Becker, "Teledemocracy: Bringing Power Back to People," *The Futurist* (December 1981): 6-9.
34. William A. Lucas, "Telecommunications Technologies and Services," in *Communication for Tomorrow,* ed. Robinson, p. 248.

35. In *Journal of Communication* 28 (Spring 1978): 148-167, see Red Burns and Lynne Elton, "Reading, Pa.: Programming for the Future"; Eileen Connell, "Reading, Pa.: Training Local People"; and Mitchell L. Moss, "Reading, Pa.: Research on Community Uses."
36. Sally Bedell Smith, "Two-Way Cable TV Falters," *New York Times,* March 28, 1984.
37. The relationship of cable television use to other media use patterns is discussed in Gerald L. Grotta and Doug Newsom, "How Does Cable Television in the Home Relate to Other Media Use Patterns?" *Journalism Quarterly* 59 (Winter 1982): 588-591, 609.
38. John M. Eger, "A Time of Decision," *Journal of Communication* 29 (Winter 1979): 204-207.
39. Lucas, "Telecommunications Technologies and Services," p. 248.
40. Ithiel de Sola Pool, "The Problems of WARC," *Journal of Communication* 29 (Winter 1979): 187-196.

Readings

Atschull, J. Herbert. *Agents of Power: The News Media in Human Affairs.* New York: Longman, 1984.

Benjamin, Gerald, ed. *The Communications Revolution in Politics.* New York: The Academy of Political Science, 1982.

Bennett, W. Lance. *News: The Politics of Illusion.* New York: Longman, 1983.

Kessler, Lauren. *The Dissident Press: Alternative Journalism in American History.* Beverly Hills, Calif.: Sage, 1984.

Pool, Ithiel de Sola. *Technologies of Freedom.* Cambridge, Mass.: Harvard University Press, 1983.

Robinson, Glen O., ed. *Communication for Tomorrow: Policy Perspectives for the 1980s.* New York: Praeger, 1978.

Weaver, David H. *Videotex Journalism: Teletext, Viewdata, and the News.* Hillsdale, N.J.: Erlbaum, 1983.

Index

367